The Breast Cancer Wars

The Breast Cancer Wars

Hope, Fear, and the Pursuit of a Cure
in Twentieth-Century America

Barron H. Lerner, M.D.

OXFORD
UNIVERSITY PRESS

2001

OXFORD
UNIVERSITY PRESS

Oxford New York
Athens Auckland Bangkok Bogotá
Buenos Aires Calcutta Cape Town Chennai Dar es Salaam
Delhi Florence Hong Kong Istanbul Karachi
Kuala Lumpur Madrid Melbourne
Mexico City Mumbai Nairobi Paris São Paulo Shanghai
Singapore Taipei Tokyo Toronto Warsaw

and associated companies in
Berlin Ibadan

Published by Oxford University Press, Inc.
198 Madison Avenue, New York, New York 10016

Oxford is a registered trademark of Oxford University Press

Library of Congress Cataloging-in-Publication Data
Lerner, Barron H.
The breast cancer wars : hope, fear, and the pursuit of a cure
in twentieth-century America / Barron Lerner.
p. cm.
Includes bibliographical references and index.
ISBN 0-19-514261-6
1. Breast—Cancer—United States—History—20th Century. I. Title.
[DNLM: 1. Breast Neoplasms—history—United States.
2. Breast Neoplasms—surgery—United States.
3. History of Medicine, 20th Cent.—United States.
4. Mastectomy—history—United States. WP 11 AA1 L616b 2001]
RC280.B8 L375   2001
616.99'449'00973—dc21   00-06391

3 5 7 9 8 6 4 2

Printed in the United States of America
on acid-free paper

To Cathy

"War is a science, with rules to be applied, which good soldiers appreciate, recall and recapitulate, before they go to decimate the other side."

—From the Broadway musical *Pippin*

Contents

Preface   xi

Abbreviations   2

1   Introduction   3

2   Establishing a Tradition   15
    William Halsted and the Radical Mastectomy

3   Inventing a Curable Disease   41
    Breast Cancer Control after World War II

4   The Scalpel Triumphant   69
    Radical Surgery in the 1950s

5   A Heretical Interlude   92
    Biology as Fate

6   Reality Check   115
    Breast Cancer Treatment and Randomized
    Controlled Trials

7   "I Alone Am in Charge of My Body"   141
    Breast Cancer Patients in Revolt

8   No Shrinking Violet   170
    Rose Kushner and the Maturation
    of Breast Cancer Activism

9   Seek and Ye Shall Find   196
       Mammography Praised and Scorned

10   "The World Has Passed Us By"   223
       Science, Activism, and the Fall of the
       Radical Mastectomy

11   The Past as Prologue   241
       What Can the History of Breast Cancer
       Teach Us?

12   Risky Business   276
       Breast Cancer and Genetics

13   Epilogue   291

       Glossary of Breast Cancer Operations   297

       Sources   298

       Notes   301

       Index   371

Preface

n 1977, my mother, Ronnie Lerner, was diagnosed with breast cancer. I was sixteen years old. A series of fragmented memories about her cancer remain with me. I remember being told that the lump she had discovered would almost surely prove to be benign. I remember hugging her in the driveway of our home when she returned from her doctor's office, having learned that the tumor was, in fact, cancerous. I remember finding out that after her mastectomy, she would receive chemotherapy, which was a relatively new way to treat the disease.

Part of the reason that these memories are so fragmented is that in subsequent years, we never discussed cancer very much. A private person, my mother preferred to keep most of her thoughts to herself as she gradually recovered. Not ones to readily discuss uncomfortable topics, my father, sister, and I were quite content with this arrangement. This experience led me to believe that this quiet, stoic approach was characteristic of women who had breast cancer.

Over the years, other assumptions took hold. For example, I came to believe that my mother had lived because she had dutifully discovered her cancer at an early stage and because of the aggressive treatment she had received. I also assumed that the happiness of surviving cancer was necessarily tempered by the negative consequences of having had the disease. After all, my mother had never resumed several of the activities and friendships that she had enjoyed before becoming ill.

As a medical student and resident in the 1980s, I learned how my family's collective memories about my mother's illness drew on both reality and myth. My research for this book further demonstrated this point. In

contrast to what we had come to believe, chemotherapy and other therapeutic interventions actually "cured" only a fraction of those who received them. Other women would have recovered even without such
treatment. Similarly, tumor biology—not just how promptly a woman
discovered her cancer—played a major role in determining how long
she would survive.

Most strikingly, my research revealed how other women with breast
cancer often responded in a dramatically different fashion than had my
mother. For example, Rose Kushner, a Baltimore journalist diagnosed in
1974, had made her breast cancer into a public crusade to inform women
about the disease and their treatment options. In direct contrast to our
dinner table, Kushner's was dominated by endless discussions of breast
lumps, stubborn surgeons, and anxious patients. In 1976, the NBC correspondent Betty Rollin had published *First, You Cry*, a vivid account of her
experiences with breast cancer.

Finally, it hardly required extensive research to realize how women diagnosed with breast cancer in the 1990s seemed to make friends rather
than lose them. As of this writing, breast cancer in the United States has
become a national phenomenon, perpetually discussed in magazines and
on television and the Internet. Survivors meet each other at races, support groups, and corporate-sponsored galas. Yet other women still prefer
to deal with their breast cancers more quietly, either by themselves or
with their families.

As I worked on this book, I also learned the difficulties of conducting
historical research on a subject that was the cause of active, often acrimo-
nious debates. Some individuals reading my published or unpublished
work criticized me for supposedly taking sides on a given controversy.
While I would be the first to admit that no history is "objective," such
persons seemed unwilling or unable to acknowledge my efforts to present my arguments in an even-handed matter. Indeed, a few persons I
had interviewed stopped returning my calls. In this manner, the polariza-
tion that I document during breast cancer control in the twentieth century manifested itself in my attempts to tell the story of such efforts.

Despite these incidents, the number of people who have enabled me
to complete this book is legion. Several research assistants, including
Mary Anna Denman, Jennifer Nelson, Cindy Chen, and Martin Rivlin,

rounded up and summarized countless articles and books. Special thanks go to Jennifer Roemer, who not only amassed large amounts of material but also forced me to organize it in a coherent manner. Sheila King, Lily Hernandez, and Shameem Ali of the Columbia Health Sciences Library dutifully signed out books for me and found missing volumes with great aplomb.

My colleagues at the Columbia University College of Physicians and Surgeons have also provided great assistance. Fellow members of the Center for the Study of Society and Medicine, which is run by David Rothman, have provided crucial feedback on my work. Susan Lauer Pena and Jason Hamrick helped in preparation of the manuscript and countless other tasks. My fellow physicians in the Division of General Medicine, which is run by Steven Shea, graciously covered my patient panel for six months, which enabled me to complete a first draft of the book. Donald Kornfeld, head of the Institutional Review Board, calmly handled a series of revised proposals. Others at Columbia, including Myron Weisfeldt, Herbert Pardes, Allan Rosenfield, and David Rosner, codirector of the new program in the History of Public Health and Medicine, have also been very supportive of my research. Finally, I gained valuable insight by attending the weekly breast cancer conferences organized by the Department of Surgery.

This project could not have been completed without considerable funding support, most notably from the Robert Wood Johnson Foundation. The foundation's generosity has enabled me to complete two books on the history of medicine in the twentieth century. While representing a small percentage of its overall largesse, the foundation's grants have made an enormous difference in my career. Other funding support for this project has come from the Burroughs Wellcome Fund, through its grant program to support research in the history of medicine. In addition, financial support from the Arnold P. Gold Foundation and the Vidda Foundation has enabled me to merge my research in the history of medicine and medical ethics with my teaching efforts at Columbia. Special thanks for securing this funding go to Arnold and Sandra Gold, Russ and Angelica Berrie, and Jay Meltzer.

Archivists and librarians across the country have given me access to remarkable collections of primary sources. I thank them all, but wish to single out Carol Tomer and Fred Lotzenheiser of the Cleveland Clinic Archives; Nancy McCall and Gerard Shorb of the Alan Mason Chesney Archives of Johns Hopkins University; Richard Wolfe, formerly of the Countway Library at Harvard Medical School; Elizabeth Fee of the National Library of Medicine; Elaine Challacombe of the University of Minnesota Archives; Micaela Sullivan-Fowler of the University of Wisconsin; Martin Hackett of the University of Pennsylvania Archives; and Steve Novak at the Columbia Health Sciences Library. Staff members at the Schlesinger Library of Radcliffe College, the Gerald Ford Presidential Museum, the State Historical Society of Wisconsin, and the University of California at San Diego were generous with their time and interest. Jack Termine sent me helpful files from the archives of the Health Sciences Center at Brooklyn. Judy Norsigian and Norma Swenson gave me access to the files of the Boston Women's Health Book Collective. Special thanks go to the American Cancer Society for generously sharing its records. Joanne Schellenbach and Robert Smith, among others, facilitated my research at the ACS. Many of these archives also supplied me with illustrations. Pedro Martinez was extremely helpful in reproducing them for the book.

The personal papers of physicians, patients, and others involved in breast cancer control during the twentieth century provided important data. Among those who kindly permitted access to such records are John Bailar, Alice Haagensen, Carol Bodian, Helen Pack, Beatrice Black, George Black, Nancy Orr, Betty Rollin, Hiram Cody, Xenia Urban, Ann Ormrod, Maryel Locke, James Stone, Gene Stone, George Moore, Herman Zuckerman, and the late Philip Strax. Additional material was also obtained through a Freedom of Information Act request from the National Cancer Institute. Gordon Schwartz and Xenia Urban allowed me to borrow videotapes.

Either formally or informally, I interviewed dozens of persons during the course of this project. I thank them all for sharing their time and insights. Special thanks go to Harvey Kushner, George Moore, Helen Pack, Sherwin Nuland, John Bailar, Barbara Seaman, Ruth Spear, Maryann Napoli, Kathy Conway, Henry Leis, and Nathaniel Berlin. The interviews were capably transcribed by Dixie Kuehnel of Mercury Manuscripts.

Many other people have read all or parts of this book. In doing so, they have improved it immensely. These individuals include David Rothman, Regina Morantz-Sanchez, Ruth Cowan, Hiram Cody, Anne Kasper, Susan Ferguson, Jonathan Sadowsky, Tom Garrett, Donna Russo, and Mark Frankel. David Rothman helped with the epilogue at an especially trying moment. Others who have provided advice or comments include Sharon Batt, Susan Lederer, Joel Howell, Chris Lawrence, Cornelia Baines, Gil Welch, Chris Feudtner, Leslie Reagan, Kirsten Gardner, Lisa Belkin, Victor Grann, Ruby Senie, Karolyn Siegel, Freya Schnabel, Jay Meltzer, Paul Edelson, Sherri Brandt-Rauf, and Gwen Darien at *Mamm* magazine. Extremely helpful feedback also came from my editor at Oxford, Peter Ginna, and my agent, Michele Rubin. Both Peter and Michele have helped to shape this book in countless ways. Thanks also to Jeffrey House at Oxford, who was involved in the initial stages of evaluation.

I received helpful comments on my work during meetings of the Robert Wood Johnson Generalist Faculty Physicians Scholars Program, the American Association for the History of Medicine, and the American Public Health Association and in response to talks given at the bioethics centers of the University of Pennsylvania and Case Western Reserve University and the history of medicine departments of the University of Michigan and the University of Wisconsin-Madison. Valuable feedback was also obtained by attending conferences organized by Georgina Feldberg at York University, Keith Wailoo at the University of North Carolina, and Wolfgang Eckart at the University of Heidelberg.

Portions of this work were previously published in the *Annals of Internal Medicine*; the *American Journal of Public Health*; and *Breast Cancer: Society Shapes an Epidemic*, published by St. Martin's Press, LLC. I thank the publishers for permission to use the earlier material as part of this book. The quotation from *Pippin* is used courtesy of Warner Brothers Productions.

My greatest thanks go to my family. The basement of our house, where I wrote much of this book, is known as the "bad zone," and with good reason. Completing such a project takes away precious time that could be spent with my wife, Cathy Seibel, and my children, Ben and Nina. Their love and understanding are immensely appreciated. I must confess, however, to having experienced perverse joy when Ben's first-grade teacher informed us that he spends much of his free time at school working on his "books." I lovingly dedicate this book to Cathy, who is not only my greatest fan, but also my best editor.

Besides Cathy, Ben, and Nina, I owe a great debt to other family members. My mother-in-law, Ellen Seibel, has provided child care in times of both emergency and calm. So has Margaret Sefa Frempong, Ben and Nina's longtime nanny, who has become family. As they always have, my parents, Phillip and Ronnie Lerner, and my sister, Dana Lerner, have provided emotional support and good advice as this book was conceived and then materialized.

My mother's quiet perseverance in the face of a terrifying disease has been an inspiration to our entire family. Although each woman responds to her breast cancer differently, all of these survivors have much to teach us.

The Breast Cancer Wars

Abbreviations

AAUW	American Association of University Women
ACS	American Cancer Society
AMA	American Medical Association
ASA	American Surgical Association
ASCC	American Society for the Control of Cancer
BCDDP	Breast Cancer Detection Demonstration Project
BRCA1/BRCA2	Genes involved in regulating the growth of breast cells
BSE	Breast self-examination
DCIS	Ductal carcinoma in situ
FOIA	Freedom of Information Act
HIP	Health Insurance Plan of Greater New York
LCIS	Lobular carcinoma in situ
MGH	Massachusetts General Hospital
NABCO	National Alliance of Breast Cancer Organizations
NBCC	National Breast Cancer Coalition
NCI	National Cancer Institute
NIH	National Institutes of Health
NSABP	National Surgical Adjuvant Breast and Bowel Project
NSABP B-04/B-06	Trials of breast cancer treatment conducted by the NSABP
NSABP P-01	Trial of tamoxifen to prevent breast cancer conducted by the NSABP
RCT	Randomized controlled trial
WFA	Women's Field Army (of the ASCC)

Introduction

n a medical school amphitheater in 1963, the assembled physicians and students were watching two people: a woman whose breast cancer had been treated with a radical mastectomy fifteen years previously, and her surgeon, who had just summarized her case. A hand went up in the audience: "What was the psychological effect of the surgery?" asked the questioner. "Did the patient have feelings about losing her breast?"[1]

As one of the medical students in attendance, William Bennett, later recalled, this question was answered not by the patient but by the surgeon. The operation, he explained, had given the patient her only chance for a longer, cancer-free life. And the missing breast, the surgeon stated as he elevated the fully exposed, remaining one, had "no cosmetic value." The audience never actually heard from the woman with breast cancer. Rather, Bennett reported, she "sat utterly immobile throughout the presentation."[2]

From the vantage point of the twenty-first century, Bennett's recollections make us acutely uncomfortable. Why was the patient seemingly invisible to the surgeon? Why did the surgeon consider her breasts expendable? Why did the patient remain silent? What was she thinking as her doctor casually lifted her remaining breast in front of a roomful of strangers?

A logical starting point for answers to these questions is turn-of-the-century Baltimore, Maryland. There, William Halsted, a reserved and often acerbic professor of surgery at the Johns Hopkins School of Medicine, was popularizing a dramatic operation for breast cancer: the radical mastectomy. Halsted believed that his operation, if performed early enough in the course of the disease, could substantially prolong the survival of patients. Developed at one of America's premier medical schools and disseminated across the country and around the world by Halsted's trainees, the radical mastectomy came to symbolize the possibilities of "scientific" surgery. As the surgeon displayed the cured breast cancer patient to his assembled colleagues in 1963, he was participating in a medical success story. As late as 1968, nearly 70 percent of American women with breast cancer still received Halsted's original operation.

Yet the story of the radical mastectomy was much more complicated. Throughout the twentieth century, many physicians and patients remained uncomfortable with the procedure. First, the radical mastectomy was highly disfiguring, entailing removal of the cancerous breast, nearby lymph nodes, and the two chest wall muscles on the affected side. Second, despite the apparent cures produced by the operation, mortality from breast cancer in the United States did not change significantly after its introduction. Third, surgeons in numerous other countries, such as Canada and England, had gradually abandoned the radical mastectomy in favor of less extensive procedures that they believed provided equivalent survival. By the early 1970s, women across the United States were vocally challenging the hegemony of both the radical mastectomy and the medical profession itself. Radical mastectomy, performed mostly by male surgeons on female patients, had become a touchstone for dissatisfaction with a patriarchal and authoritarian medical system. Far from remaining quiet, women with breast cancer carried tape recorders into doctors' offices and wrote books and articles about their experiences.

In 1993, thirty years after the patient sat silently in the medical school amphitheater, the mastectomy scar of another woman with breast cancer was exposed. But this woman was Matuschka, a model, and she had chosen to proudly display her chest on the cover of the *New York Times Magazine*.[3] No one had to ask Matuschka how she was responding to her disease.

This book is a history of breast cancer diagnosis and treatment in twentieth-century America.[4] Although it covers the entire century, it focuses on the years from 1945 to 1980. During this period, efforts to achieve a cure for breast cancer, which had become the leading cancer killer among women, accelerated dramatically. Yet at the same time, critics began to question what the aggressive diagnostic and treatment efforts were accomplishing. Much of the book focuses on the combination of early detection and radical surgery. Why did the early discovery of breast cancers become the focus of control efforts? Why did the radical mastectomy achieve such prominence and then remain so popular? Why did the operation finally go into decline after 1975? But the book also explores other topics in the world of breast cancer, such as the introduction of chemotherapy and laboratory testing for a genetic predisposition to the disease.

The Breast Cancer Wars begins with the premise that disease cannot be understood outside its social and cultural context. For many years, such a statement would have been highly contested. Until the 1960s, most historians of science and medicine characterized the history of their fields as a progressive search for truth, with heroic scientists and physicians gradually unlocking the mysteries behind diseases such as breast cancer and using these insights to help patients.

By the 1970s, however, historians were challenging this concept from several angles. Social historians rejected so-called "great man" histories and studied how ordinary people shaped historical eras and topics.[5] Feminists argued that the roles of women—both famous and unknown—needed attention, and that men had often achieved successes by subjugating women.[6] Finally, historians of medicine and science focused on the patient's experience of illness, crafting a critique of the medical profession as overbearing and even coercive. Later work was even more provocative, arguing that diseases such as breast cancer were "socially constructed"—that is, that social and cultural factors influenced how the actual biology of diseases was understood and represented. A disease does not exist, the noted medical historian Charles Rosenberg has written, "until society decides that it does—by perceiving, naming and responding to it."[7]

The history of breast cancer since 1900 provides an excellent opportunity to revisit and build on this rich historiographic tradition. To be sure, a series of "great men" played major roles in this story by advancing knowledge about the disease. None was more renowned than Halsted, whose pioneering accomplishments led one historian to call him the "greatest surgical scholar" the United States has ever produced.[8] Halsted's radical mastectomy was based on the premise that an extensive local operation, carried out early enough, could remove all existing cancer cells. Yet he knew that such a supposition alone was inadequate; he needed to prove the value of the operation. When, in 1898, Halsted reported that radical mastectomy patients lived longer on average than women who had received less extensive operations, his strategy of early and definitive surgical intervention became the reigning paradigm for breast cancer management for three-quarters of a century.

Other historical figures greatly influenced breast cancer diagnosis and treatment in the twentieth century. In the 1950s, for example, Jerome Urban, a young and technically gifted breast surgeon at New York's prestigious Memorial Sloan-Kettering Cancer Hospital, argued that Halsted's radical mastectomy was inadequate therapy for many cancers. Urban devised the extended radical mastectomy, which necessitated the removal of women's ribs in search of elusive cancer cells. At the same time, George Crile, Jr., a surgeon at the Cleveland Clinic, argued the opposite: neither radical mastectomy nor Urban's more extensive operation was ever indicated. In 1955, Crile, a provocateur who loved to challenge surgical dogma, abruptly stopped performing radical mastectomies in favor of smaller surgical procedures. "It is time," he wrote, "to . . . abandon those operations which consistently fail to palliate or cure."[9]

During the 1970s and 1980s, Bernard Fisher, a surgeon and researcher at the University of Pittsburgh, attempted to resolve this dispute by introducing more sophisticated statistical methodologies into the evaluation of breast cancer therapy. With dogged persistence, Fisher was able to convince skeptical physicians and breast cancer patients to participate in a series of randomized clinical trials that compared various treatment options. Ultimately, Fisher would show that removal of only the tumor or the breast, with or without radiation therapy, resulted in survival comparable to that achieved with Halsted's much more dramatic operation. Fisher argued that his findings not only spelled the death of the radical mastectomy, but also proved a theory long seen as heretical: most breast cancers, by the time they were detected, had already spread throughout the body. Accordingly, chemotherapy, which treated this "systemic" or "metastatic" disease, was more important than local surgery or radiation therapy for achieving a cure.

"Great women" also contributed to advances in breast cancer. For example, Vera Peters, a Canadian radiotherapist, published data in the 1960s indicating the effectiveness of limited surgery and radiation in the treatment of early breast cancer. An outsider in many ways—a woman, a radiotherapist, and a Canadian—Peters was at times excoriated by her surgical colleagues at medical meetings. Other famous women were breast cancer patients, such as Shirley Temple Black, Betty Ford, and Happy Rockefeller. When these women revealed their diagnoses in the 1970s, the media and breast cancer patients credited them with bringing the disease into the open and saving lives. "I thank God and you," wrote one woman to Ford in 1974, "that I found it in time."[10]

Yet what social historians have emphasized is the importance of placing these personal accomplishments in their proper historical context. As Goethe once wrote, "the most beautiful discoveries are made not so much by men as by the period."[11] Thus, in order to understand why the radical mastectomy triumphed, one must look beyond Halsted to the larger social system in which the procedure was introduced and understood. To what extent did Americans' growing faith in scientific medicine in the early twentieth century influence the spread of the radical mastectomy? To what degree did the professionalization of surgery—for which Halsted was largely responsible—reinforce the notion of a "surgical solution" to a dreaded disease such as breast cancer? This latter question was no less relevant in 1963 when Urban's extended radical mastectomy was featured in a *Time* magazine cover story on a series of daring new surgical procedures. "If they can operate," read the tag line, "you're lucky."[12]

The zeal to find a cure for breast cancer was most vividly embodied by the work of the American Cancer Society (ACS), which had been founded in 1913 as the American Society for the Control of Cancer. Dominated by surgeons, the cancer society eagerly adopted Halsted's paradigm of early diagnosis and radical surgery as a way to lower mortality from cancer, which had become the second leading killer in the United States by the 1930s. The ACS placed particular emphasis on breast cancer, the most feared of women's cancers. Emphasizing that less extensive breast cancers had better outcomes, cancer society educational materials entreated women to show breast lumps to doctors immediately. Later, the

ACS would strongly encourage healthy women to examine their own breasts and have regular mammography. These screening programs sought to find even smaller, presumably more curable, cancers.

Yet for much of the first half of the twentieth century, the ACS, the American College of Surgeons, and other anticancer organizations faced a persistent dilemma. Even as they optimistically characterized breast cancer as a curable disease if discovered early, the death rate from the disease among American women—roughly 25 per 100,000 women—had not budged for decades. Undaunted, physicians, public health officials, and laypersons in the 1950s sought to accelerate America's efforts to win its "war" against breast cancer.

This use of military terminology to describe breast cancer control was not limited to the 1950s but occurred throughout the twentieth century. Given that metaphors provide "insight into society's shared values,"[13] an examination of such language can provide an explanatory framework for the evolution of breast cancer diagnosis and treatment. Why did American society feel the need to do battle against breast cancer? What impact, if any, did World War II and the Cold War have on anticancer efforts? Was the fight against breast cancer different from those waged against other cancers or other diseases, such as tuberculosis? Was the war on breast cancer distinctively American? How did breast cancer control in the United States compare with similar programs in Canada, Great Britain, France, and other countries?

The Breast Cancer Wars will also examine the relationship of metaphorical language to the scientific knowledge generated regarding breast cancer. Can data ever be neutral during a war? In 1978, when confronting her own breast cancer, Susan Sontag answered "no" to this question, and urged society to abandon disease metaphors.[14] To what extent was Sontag correct? Has the desire to fight breast cancer led surgeons to operate more, radiotherapists to radiate more, and oncologists to administer more chemotherapy? And, if so, have such decisions necessarily been wrong? Are military metaphors and related messages of hope useful—indeed, necessary—for patients experiencing potentially fatal illnesses?

To begin to understand these issues, it is necessary, as social historians have argued, to hear the patient's voice. Although breast cancer does affect a tiny subset of men, this book focuses exclusively on the experiences of female cancer patients. Not only has breast cancer been a major cause of death and debility for women, but the disease affects an organ that the feminist scholar Marilyn Yalom has described as the "most obvious sign of femaleness."[15] Given the association of the breast, and therefore mastectomy, with sexuality, intimacy, and motherhood, a focus on women is essential to this story.

Feminists and other authors writing about breast cancer—in particular, radical mastectomy—have consistently emphasized gender concerns. Many of these works grew out of the women's health movement that began in the early 1970s. Seeking "equality and individual self-determination in every aspect of life," this loosely based network of activists found most male doctors to be "condescending, paternalistic, judgmental, and noninformative."[16] Building on these sentiments, many women authors explained the persistence of unnecessarily radical breast surgery in the United States on the basis of sexism in a patriarchal society and a paternalistic medical profession. As the journalist Ellen Frankfort wrote in 1972, "pair of shoes, pair of scissors, pair of breasts—it's all the same to doctors who behave toward women as if they're constructed of detached parts for them to probe, palpate and poke."[17] "The question arises," wrote another feminist critic, "should amputation, mutilation, and maiming and crippling of a woman's body be considered a cure?"[18]

Yet more recent work in feminist history has warned of the perils of analyses that portray both women and women patients solely as passive victims. As the historians Rima Apple and Regina Morantz-Sanchez have argued, women encountering disease have been both actors and reactors.[19] Women have played vital roles in both defining the experience of illness and in responding to the recommendations and demands of medical professionals.

The approach of Apple and Morantz-Sanchez provides a rich and nuanced strategy for exploring the history of breast cancer. To what extent did women patients passively accept the advice of enthusiastic screening campaigns and authoritarian male surgeons? Were women successfully able to influence how their breast cancers were diagnosed and treated? Did women who received radical mastectomies or other aggressive treatments see themselves as victims or as fortunate? How did class and race influence how women experienced breast cancer? Finally, how did these responses change after 1970 as women patients became more vocal and growing numbers of women entered the medical profession?

One source for answers to these questions is the illness narratives written by women with breast cancer. Although a few of these had appeared earlier in the century, by the 1970s dozens of women each year recounted their experiences in books or articles in women's magazines. Many of these works explicitly urged women to refuse radical surgery or at least demand to learn about all possible therapeutic options. Others, such as Betty Rollin's First, You Cry, focused more directly on how the diagnosis and treatment of breast cancer had interrupted and then influenced their lives.[20] By the end of the decade, narratives had also begun to address another controversial issue, breast reconstruction after mastectomy. Implicit in this discussion was a question both personal and political: Could life after breast cancer ever return to "normal"?

The growing decision-making power of women with breast cancer in the 1970s was perhaps the most conspicuous example of the wider challenge to the traditional authoritarian physician-patient relationship in the United States. Indeed, beginning in 1979, states passed "informed consent" laws mandating that women with breast cancer receive information regarding all possible treatment options. How did physicians respond to these newly empowered woman patients, seeking second opinions and bearing tape recorders? How did practitioners, accustomed to debating medical controversies behind closed doors, respond when their colleagues, such as George Crile and Boston surgeon Oliver Cope, "went public," offering their opinions in women's magazines such as Ms. and the Ladies' Home Journal?

Some physicians addressed these upheavals in breast cancer treatment by relying on increasingly sophisticated statistical techniques. The years after World War II witnessed a dramatic change in how doctors both gained and applied knowledge. Epidemiologists and other proponents of new statistical methods, such as population-based studies and randomized controlled trials, rejected the earlier pattern of medical decision-making in which experienced clinicians made choices for individual patients. The debates over breast cancer detection and treatment in the postwar decades provide an excellent example of how these competing models of evaluating medical options came into conflict. As biostatisticians sought to improve the "science" of medicine, was the "art" of clinical experience vulnerable? Moreover, how were physicians supposed to decide which types of information were truly "scientific" and thus medically relevant?

These questions about how clinicians and patients obtain and use knowledge are at the heart of the last historiographic trend mentioned above, the social construction of disease. The history of breast cancer in the twentieth century is replete with examples of seemingly objective terminology, the actual meanings of which reflected the cultural context into which they were introduced. For example, physicians for decades have used terms such as "five-year cure" and "ten-year cure" to measure the outcomes of breast cancer treatment. Although "cure" in the public mind refers to a permanent disappearance of the disease, these phrases actually signify only that there is no clinical evidence that the cancer has returned. How did this curious use of the term "cure" come into acceptance and why has it persisted?[21] How does this word affect patients' treatment decisions and their expectations about recovery? Even the term "cancer" became controversial when scientists in the 1930s discovered abnormal cells that looked cancerous but had not invaded the breast tissue. Should such cells be called cancer? More provocatively, does calling such cells cancer make them cancer?

One other term that physicians have used to guide screening and treatment decisions is "risk." For example, surgeons comparing radical mastectomy with other therapies generated data indicating the various risks associated with each of the options. Because they were based on statistics, physicians tended to characterize these risk assessments as objective. But to what extent did doctors' own opinions influence how they interpreted these data and then discussed them with their patients? Similarly, how did women with breast cancer incorporate their personal beliefs about blame, responsibility, and uncertainty when arriving at treatment decisions supposedly based on a scientific risk-benefit calculus?

The layout of this book is roughly chronological. It begins with William Halsted, asking how one surgeon and his operation came to have such a profound effect on the history of breast cancer treatment. Halsted's radical mastectomy probably reached its peak in popularity after World War II, as the American Cancer Society accelerated its push for early detection and wide surgical removal of breast cancers. Yet this era also saw a rejection of Halsted's operation as insufficiently radical. Surgeons such as Jerome Urban who treated breast and other cancers designed a series of "superradical" operations that removed ribs, limbs, or multiple internal organs to try and ferret out every last cancer cell.

As the strategy of early and aggressive treatment for breast cancer reached its apex in the 1950s, opposing voices began to challenge the "can do" ethos that propelled America's war on cancer. Loosely united under the banner of "biological predeterminism,"[22] a small group of renegade physicians and biometricians used the new statistical approaches to challenge the optimistic claims that breast cancer was being defeated. These critics suggested that the inherent biology of individual breast cancers—as opposed to early intervention—most influenced whether patients lived or died.

This emphasis on the biological variability of breast cancers, now a well-accepted notion, called into question the logic of performing the same operation on all women with the disease. Physicians such as Bernard Fisher thus called for randomized controlled trials comparing radical mastectomy with smaller operations, including simple mastectomy (which removed only the breast), and lumpectomy (which removed only the tumor). Yet surgeons declined to participate in such studies until the early 1970s, when the controversy over radical mastectomy erupted out of its medical confines. Writing as feminists, patients, consumers, or some combination thereof, women authors filled the pages of magazines and newspapers with a fierce challenge to the Halsted radical mastectomy and, by extension, to medicine's status quo. The most prominent of these critics was Rose Kushner, a Baltimore journalist diagnosed with breast cancer in 1974, who published numerous articles and books detailing her experiences with the disease.[23]

It was also in 1974 that Betty Ford and Happy Rockefeller, wives of the President and Vice-President-designate, respectively, announced that they had been diagnosed with breast cancer. These disclosures were a shot in the arm for the growing efforts to improve early detection of breast cancer. Yet within a year, a project established by the American Cancer Society and the National Cancer Institute to promote the use of mammography was embroiled in controversy. Although clearly of value for women aged fifty and older, mammograms raised complicated issues, such as the detection of noninvasive "precancers." What was the biological significance of such lesions? How was one supposed to "treat" what was essentially a predisposition to disease?

By the late 1970s, radical mastectomy in the United States was finally on its way to obsolescence. But what had finally caused physicians to abandon their reliance on Halsted's procedure? Was it Fisher's carefully executed randomized trials, the rebellion of women patients, or a combination of the two? What made a minority of surgeons continue to recommend the Halsted radical into the 1980s? And why did certain women still willingly accept the operation?

The "breast cancer wars" described in this book—in particular, the debates over aggressive treatment, early detection, and statistical uncertainty—are not merely of historical interest. Breast cancer remains the most common non-skin cancer in American women, causing 175,000 cases annually. Roughly 40,000 women die of the disease each year. Ongoing efforts to reduce these numbers raise the same types of challenging questions that have characterized past breast cancer control efforts. Should women under age fifty undergo routine screening mammography? Does finding a small number of cancers in such women justify the negative ramifications, such as unnecessary biopsies, for others who are tested? Who should pay for such testing? In the case of treatment, is more necessarily better? Should women with tiny cancers that appear localized to the breast undergo what amounts to preventive chemotherapy? When should women choose high-dose as opposed to standard chemotherapy? Should stem cell transplants for metastatic breast cancer still be performed, even though studies to date suggest that they are no more effective than chemotherapy?

More generally, who should make these decisions, women or their doctors? How can patients hope to evaluate all the information that is now available, in magazines, on the Internet, or from the expanding network of advocacy organizations? Finally, as some activists have charged, is all of this attention to breast cancer screening and treatment distracting American society from pursuing a more productive goal—primary prevention of the disease by eliminating environmental and other toxins?

These questions have become even more pressing since the recent discovery that women possessing certain hereditary genetic mutations may have as high as a 50 to 85 percent likelihood of developing breast cancer during their lifetimes. The prevalence of these mutations may be as common as one in forty among groups such as Ashkenazi Jews.[24] Obtaining information about one's genetic status has proven highly appealing for some women, given the potential that such knowledge may enable them to reduce their risk for breast cancer. Yet this technology has raised many concerns. Not all women who possess these genetic mutations will develop breast cancer, especially if they have no strong family history of the disease. And in any event, no proven mechanism yet exists for "treating" these women, who, after all, are not diseased but only at risk of disease. Despite these uncertainties, media coverage of genetic testing has often characterized these mutations as inevitably dangerous, terming them "time bombs" on a "genetic battlefield."[25]

The persistence of these familiar military metaphors—in both genetic testing and, indeed, all aspects of modern breast cancer control—poses compelling questions for the historian. What can we learn from earlier "wars" against the disease? Can awareness of history prevent the future overuse of unnecessary and even harmful procedures such as radical mastectomy? Yet cautionary tales that point out past mistakes should not overshadow a more important historical lesson: the evaluation of diagnostic and therapeutic interventions for diseases such as breast cancer has always depended on time and place.[26] History can remind us how modern improvements in technology and statistical analysis do not eliminate the influence of social and cultural factors on the interpretation of scientific data.

In March 1999, the New York Times reported that Matuschka, the model who had displayed her scarred chest for the newspaper's magazine in 1993, had won a malpractice decision against her surgeon. Matuschka claimed that her surgeon had misled her into choosing a mastectomy when, in retrospect, a lesser procedure would have been adequate.[27] Given Matuschka's unabashed display of her anatomy, her apparent regret over losing her breast may have come as a surprise to many. But it should not have. Outside the picture frame, Matuschka was much like any other breast cancer survivor, trying to resume a life that had been forever changed. Ultimately, it is this struggle with mortality and hope that this book attempts to illuminate.

Establishing a Tradition

William Halsted and the Radical Mastectomy

"I do not despair of carcinoma [cancer] being cured somewhere in the future, but this blessed achievement will, I believe, never be wrought by the knife of the surgeon."[1] So wrote University of Pennsylvania surgeon D. Hayes Agnew in 1883. Yet despite the skepticism of Agnew and others, physicians have performed mastectomies on women with breast cancer for thousands of years. At the same time that Agnew was preaching the limits of surgery, William Halsted was developing an extensive operation that he believed to be advantageous and potentially curative. Halsted relied heavily on studies of anatomy and physiology in explaining how breast cancer spread and how it might best be treated. But his radical mastectomy also achieved great popularity because it was congruent with a series of changes in medicine and American society at the turn of the twentieth century. By the time of Halsted's death in 1922, breast cancer had become a "surgical disease" and his radical mastectomy was almost universally employed by his devoted disciples. Yet critics would continually challenge Halsted's theories and results, including the notion that his celebrated procedure was actually "curing" the women who underwent it.

Early History of Breast Cancer

The earliest descriptions of what was likely breast cancer can be found in the Edwin Smith Surgical Papyrus, which dates from ancient Egypt (3000–2500 B.C.). Hippocrates, the Greek physician credited with placing medicine on a rational basis, also wrote of "hard tumors within the breast" in the fifth century B.C.[2] It was Galen, a second-century A.D. Greek physician living in Rome, who first situated breast cancer within a broader explanatory framework of disease. Galen ascribed to the humoral theory, which explained diseases as resulting from an imbalance of the body's four humors: blood, phlegm, black bile, and yellow bile. Breast cancer, he claimed, was caused by an excess of black bile, which could best be treated by bleeding, purgation, and a special diet. Thus, Galen was among the first to conceptualize breast cancer as a localized manifestation of a systemic disease that affected the whole body. However, even Galen argued that the breast should be cut off "when the tumour is situated on the surface of the body."[3]

Citing such evidence, historians have characterized the history of breast cancer as an ongoing debate as to whether the disease was a systemic phenomenon or a localized process amenable to surgery. Yet before the introduction of anesthesia (which prevented pain) and antiseptic or aseptic technique (which prevented infection after the operation) in the mid-nineteenth century, even those who ascribed to the latter theory acknowledged the limitations of surgery. The French writer Frances Burney's devastating account of her mastectomy in 1811 vividly demonstrates the excruciating nature of surgery in this era:

Yet—when the dreadful steel was plunged into the breast—cutting through veins—arteries—flesh—nerves, I needed no injunctions not to restrain my cries. I began a scream that lasted unremittingly during the whole time of the incision—& I almost marvel that it rings not in my ears still! so excruciating was the agony. . . . Oh no! presently the terrible cutting was renewed—& worse than ever, to separate the bottom, the foundation of this dreadful gland from the parts to which it adhered—Again all description would be baffled—yet again all was not over,—Dr. Larrey rested but his own hand, &—Oh Heaven!—I then felt the Knife [rack]ling against the breast bone—scraping it![4]

Burney, incidentally, lived for twenty-nine years after the operation, leading some to speculate that she did not, in fact, have cancer.

The pain that patients perforce experienced did not stop many surgeons from removing breasts, either by cutting away the tissue with a scalpel or burning it away with a cautery. "Yet if there is any barbarity here," wrote the eighteenth-century French surgeon Nicolas Le Cat, "it is born from pity and from humanity itself, and is very salutary."[5] Indeed, such operations often removed large masses that involved much of the breast, had ulcerated, and were malodorous. As a result, patients often forced the surgeon's hand, demanding a mastectomy to "moderate the symptoms, prolong life, and perhaps work a cure in combination with other means."[6]

By the late nineteenth century, growing evidence suggested that the origins of breast cancer were local, thereby further justifying a surgical approach. In studying pathological specimens (tissues removed from the body), the German scientist Rudolf Virchow had demonstrated that cancers arose from isolated collections of cells that had become diseased. At least initially, Virchow argued, such tumors spread locally through the lymph nodes as opposed to the blood stream. The lymph nodes acted as filters, temporarily slowing the spread of the cancer. Building on these theories, German surgeons, such as Richard von Volkmann and Lothar Heidenhain, began to recommend removal not only of the cancerous breast but also the surrounding skin and fat, the axillary (underarm) lymph nodes, and the so-called fascial tissue that covered the pectoralis muscles of the chest wall.[7]

Non-German physicians had also begun to treat breast cancer with such extensive surgery. For example, in 1867 English surgeon Charles Moore presented a paper, titled "On the Influence of Inadequate Operations on the Theory of Cancer," that recommended such extensive tissue removal that the tumor itself would not even be seen during the operation.[8] But it was in Germany that the union of pathology and surgery had taken hold most strongly in the diagnosis and treatment of breast cancer. So in 1878, the young physician William Halsted set out for Germany in order to supplement his medical training.

William Stewart Halsted

The son of a wealthy merchant, William Stewart Halsted was born in New York City in 1852. After attending Andover and Yale, Halsted graduated from New York's College of Physicians and Surgeons in 1877. He in-

terned at Bellevue Hospital before setting off to Europe, as was then customary for top graduates of American medical schools. Many aspects of
European medicine profoundly influenced Halsted. For one thing, he became impressed with antiseptic surgery, which had been introduced by
University of Glasgow surgeon Joseph Lister in the 1860s and had spread
to the continent. Lister, born in England in 1827 and educated at London's University College, had become an early advocate of the "germ
theory" of disease, which posited that infections were caused by tiny microorganisms visible only under the microscope. Having concluded that
these organisms were causing postoperative infections, Lister began to
treat surgical wounds with carbolic acid, a process he termed the "antiseptic principle."[9] Lister's rates of infection plummeted.

When Halsted returned to New York in 1880 and was appointed visit-
ing surgeon at Bellevue and Roosevelt Hospitals, he became one of the
first American proponents of antisepsis. Halsted himself devised another
innovation—the use of rubber gloves—that also reduced the spread of
infection after surgery. In 1889 Halsted had realized that Caroline Hampton, an operating room nurse, was experiencing skin inflammation from
the mercuric chloride solution being used during surgery. Halsted asked
the Goodyear Rubber Company to fashion gloves that could prevent such
a reaction. Halsted's interest in Hampton's hands was more than professional. The next year, the Johns Hopkins surgeon would marry her.
Meanwhile, rubber gloves went on to become standard protocol in the
operating room, not for their antiallergic properties but because they
prevented surgeons and nurses from introducing microorganisms into
the operative field (see figure).[10]

Halsted drew his most lasting impressions during his travels in Germany.
Remarkable advances were occurring in German medicine, largely due to
the growing application of laboratory research to clinical practice. German
scientists studying fields such as pathology, physiology, and chemistry argued that better knowledge of the body and its abnormal function could
help surgeons and other physicians treat disease. Halsted was also impressed with the work of Theodor Kocher, a Swiss surgeon. When performing dissections, Kocher carefully cut apart and separated tissues,
meticulously controlled bleeding, and used the finest silk sutures. To
Kocher, surgery needed to be both conservative and preservative, enabling

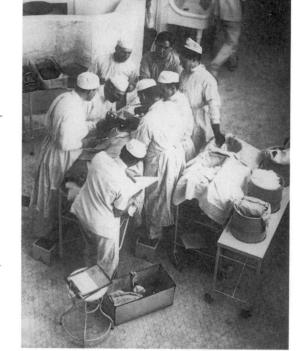

William S. Halsted, performing the "All Star Operation," at the opening of a new surgical amphitheater at the Johns Hopkins School of Medicine in 1904. Among the others present are Joseph Colt Bloodgood and Harvey Cushing. Note the use of surgical gloves.

Courtesy of the Alan Mason Chesney Archives of the Johns Hopkins Medical Institutions.

the remaining tissues to contribute to the healing process. Halsted, already careful when operating, readily embraced Kocher's technique.[11]

Halsted's gentle surgical approach fit well with other aspects of his perfectionist nature. Once he moved to Baltimore in 1888 to join the staff of the Johns Hopkins Hospital, Halsted ordered his linens, dress shirts, and suits from European cities such as London and Paris, where he then had them laundered each summer. As his former surgical resident Emile Holman later recalled, "the Professor" personally selected the food and wine for dinner gatherings "and supervised the laying of the tablecloth, which was ironed after being accurately placed on the table."[12]

Although Halsted's name would become forever linked with heroic surgery and the war on breast cancer, he himself was hardly a vocal crusader. Not one to conspicuously espouse his views, Halsted convinced others of his medical theories largely by demonstrating his brilliance in the laboratory and operating room. Indeed, for a full-time professor at a medical school, Halsted spent much time by himself: "He was diffident, distant, and almost inaccessible under ordinary daily circumstances."[13] One of Halsted's residents, the future neurosurgeon Harvey Cushing, even claimed that his mentor "spent his medical life avoiding patients— even students when this was possible."[14] Halsted was also possessed of a "biting, withering sarcasm" that bordered on scorn.[15] The surgeon's longtime Hopkins colleague William Osler provided a somewhat more sympathetic assessment, writing that Halsted and his wife were both "a little odd. They cared nothing for society, but were devoted to their dogs and horses."[16]

It was perhaps this detachment that enabled Halsted to champion the use of highly disfiguring operations for diseases such as breast cancer. While in Europe he had attended the lectures and operations of Volkmann and the Vienna surgeon Theodor Billroth, who argued that breast surgeons should remove more tissue than they had before. Prior to recommending such procedures himself, however, Halsted conducted a series of laboratory experiments that investigated tissue healing, suturing technique, and skin grafting. Once convinced that extensive but meticulous operations offered better outcomes for thyroid goiters, abdominal hernias, and breast cancers, he developed new procedures for these conditions.

In the case of breast cancer, Halsted in 1882 began to perform the radical mastectomy, which resembled the procedures of Moore and Volkmann but also removed the larger of the two chest wall muscles, the pectoralis major. Halsted's explanation for this addition was straightforward: he believed the muscle contained cancer at the time of most operations.[17] Later, drawing on the work of New York surgeon Willy Meyer, Halsted would also excise the second chest wall muscle, known as the pectoralis minor. Although Meyer developed his version of the radical mastectomy roughly contemporaneously with Halsted, it was Halsted's name that would ultimately remain affixed to the operation—for better and for worse.

Halsted's radical mastectomy drew directly on his understanding of the physiology of breast cancer. Building on Virchow's work, Halsted believed that breast and other cancers began as small foci that then enlarged in a slow, orderly, centrifugal manner before spreading to local lymph nodes.[18] Extensive operations, if done early enough, could thus potentially prevent so-called local recurrence: return of the cancer in the field of operation, including the underarm and the chest wall. Essential to Halsted's radical mastectomy was not only the amount of tissue removed but the need to extract it all in one piece, a method known as *en bloc*. Halsted believed that an *en bloc* dissection avoided the two possible causes of local recurrence: (1) cutting through cancerous tissue and thereby liberating cancer cells, and (2) introducing cancer into the operative site with a knife contaminated by cancer cells. Finally, Halsted used a skin graft from the thigh to replace the extensive area of skin removed by the wide dissection.[19]

By 1900, the medical historian Gert Brieger has written, the term "operating theater" was giving way to "operating room," connoting an increased concern with the outcome of surgery as opposed to its performance. Even as Halsted stressed the importance of meticulous surgical technique, he embodied this new trend. Recalling a presentation given by a German surgeon who had followed his patients for twenty years, Halsted wrote, "His methods of observation were new to me; his knowledge was inspiring."[20] Halsted would use this method of retrospective case review as he began to publish data on his radical mastectomy.

Halsted published his first article on this subject in 1895, reporting on fifty cases of breast cancer treated by what he called the "complete method." By this time, Halsted had become professor of surgery at Johns Hopkins and was one of the preeminent surgeons in the United States. In his paper, Halsted carefully explained how his procedure built on the teachings of Virchow, Volkmann, and other Germans. The more extensive operations of these surgeons had been laudable, Halsted believed, but were simply not enough. In making this claim, Halsted listed the high rates of local recurrence of breast cancer reported by the Germans, which ranged from 51 to 85 percent. In contrast, Halsted reported local recurrence among only three of his fifty patients, constituting what he termed a "remarkably good" rate of six percent.[21]

Whereas Halsted's paper dealt extensively with local recurrence, its title — "The Results of Operations for the Cure of Cancer of the Breast" — suggested a different goal: the "cure" of cancer of the breast. To what extent were Halsted's patients cured? A closer look at the data suggests that his radical mastectomy was less impressive than advertised. For example, another eight of the fifty patients had experienced "regionary" recurrences located in the skin surrounding the operative site. Of the patients without local recurrence, most had been followed for less than two years, and in some cases for as little as two months. At least nineteen of the fifty patients had already died.[22] Although the vast majority of these had not had a local recurrence, terming them "cured" was quite a different matter. Halsted's use of the term "cure" would actually turn out to be quite ambiguous.

By the time the American Surgical Association met in New Orleans in 1898, Halsted had accumulated seventy-six patients whose operations had occurred at least three years earlier. Once again, his results surpassed those of other surgeons but also demonstrated the limitations of his procedure. Of the seventy-six patients, only forty (52%) had lived three years without a local or regionary recurrence. Thirty-five of the women (46%) had died.[23] Nine years later Halsted again argued his case before colleagues at the American Surgical Association. Of 210 patients followed three years beyond their operation, Halsted labeled eighty-nine (42%) as three-year cures, although fourteen of these patients had subsequently died of breast cancer. Overall, 135 of the 210 women (64%) had died of breast cancer despite their surgery.[24]

This 1907 presentation was notable because Halsted had also compared the outcomes of patients whose axillary lymph nodes contained cancer with those whose nodes were negative. He reported that while two out of every three of the latter were cured, only 25 percent of those with positive lymph nodes lived three years. Strongly believing that the prognosis of early cases of breast cancer was favorable, Halsted had expected nothing less. "[W]e no longer need the proof which our figures so unmistakably give," he wrote, "that the slightest delay is dangerous."[25]

It is hard to overestimate the impact of Halsted's findings. "How few, indeed," gushed Maine physician Frederic H. Gerrish after Halsted's 1898 presentation, "can show such a record of work—clinical, operative, pathologic—as has just been displayed."[26] The next speaker, Rudolph Matas, New Orleans surgeon and one of the few people able to develop a close personal relationship with Halsted, wrote that "we are under lasting obligations to Dr. Halsted for the suggestion and demonstration of an operation which synthesizes in itself all the resources that modern surgery can bring to bear against this most formidable disease."[27] Countering the fatalistic belief that an aggressive operation "only accelerates [breast cancer's] progress and fatal termination,"[28] Halsted had injected hope and optimism. Halsted, Gerrish concluded, "has our grateful acknowledgments for the brilliant light which he has thrown upon these dark places of surgery."[29]

Patients who had undergone radical mastectomy generally responded positively to Halsted and his operation. "I still recall with pleasure my brief acquaintance with you and others, and my stay at the Hospital," a Tennessee woman wrote to Halsted.[30] "Again I wish to thank you for your wonderful attention and interest," wrote a Maryland secretary, "and to assure you that the recollection of these favors will never be effaced from my memory."[31] Halsted responded in a formal but courteous fashion to his patients. He often solicited news about their physical recovery from surgery, using this information to revise his operative technique and develop better arm exercises for his patients. Halsted was thus likely gratified with the news he received from a New York schoolteacher in 1916. "You will be interested to know that I have been able to paint with a great deal of ease this summer," she wrote. "I owe it all to your skill and am grateful to you every day."[32]

Radical Mastectomy in Context

But it was not solely Halsted's data that caused radical mastectomy to become the treatment of choice for breast cancer. Rather, the operation fit with a series of historical developments that fostered its acceptance among both physicians and the public. For one thing, "spectacular innovation" was occurring at the Johns Hopkins Medical School.[33] The school, founded in 1893, had come to embody a series of educational reforms—taking place in Germany and at a few American medical schools—that sought to put medicine on a more "scientific" footing. Educators at Hopkins revamped the standard medical school curriculum, adding new courses, laboratory studies, and hospital-based clinical clerkships to didactic lectures. Hopkins required entering students to have graduated from an accredited college and hired eminent faculty members who emphasized their role as teachers. Among these were William Osler, the outgoing and learned Canadian-born physician who was the "greatest clinical teacher of his day."[34] Another was William Welch, a pathologist who had befriended Halsted in New York and invited him to join the Hopkins faculty. Together with the gynecologist Howard Kelly, Halsted, Osler, and Welch would comprise the "great four" doctors of the early Johns Hopkins.

The reaction to the innovations at Hopkins was highly positive, and other American medical schools attempted to implement similar curricular reforms. This process was facilitated in 1910 by the publication of a report entitled *Medical Education in the United States and Canada*. Commissioned by the Carnegie Foundation and written by a nonmedical educator, Abraham Flexner, who visited all 155 medical schools in the two countries, the so-called "Flexner report" fervently recommended the Hopkins model as the prototype for future medical education.[35]

These changes in the training of physicians helped to validate Halsted's radical mastectomy. Halsted's operation was respected simply because he was at Johns Hopkins Medical School, which had come to symbolize Flexnerian medicine at its best. Moreover, his operation was thoroughly "scientific," based on physiological understandings of disease, developed through laboratory experiments, and tested in the clinic. Finally, the places where radical mastectomies were performed—modern, technologically sophisticated hospitals such as Johns Hopkins Hospital—proved central to the operation's success. Growing public confidence in surgery in the early twentieth century helped to attract patients to large urban institutions.[36] Hospital trustees and administrators liked the fact that many of these patients paid for their surgery, and rewarded their surgical staffs with privileges and authority.

Beyond Halsted's association with hospital-based, progressive medical education and more scientific surgery, he himself had become an icon. Halsted was a relentless innovator, challenging traditional surgical dogma and devising new techniques and operations. His legendary status is demonstrated by the dozens of articles and books published in the twentieth century that memorialize both the man and his achievements. Author after author describes how Halsted performed emergency gallbladder

Halsted, as he appeared in a 1932 painting, William Stewart Halsted, *by Thomas C. Corner.*

Courtesy of the Alan Mason Chesney Archives.

surgery on his mother, saved his sister from postpartum hemorrhage by transfusing her with his own blood, commissioned his own pavilion to perform antiseptic surgery at Bellevue, singlehandedly introduced gentle surgical technique to America, and developed a suture technique that permitted intestinal tract surgery. The accuracy of such stories is less important than their constant retelling, which ensured that Halsted personally received credit "for the magnificent surgical heritage of our country."[37] In 1952, the pediatrician Edwards Park would even compare him to Descartes and Einstein.[38]

Another chapter of the Halsted saga, his cocaine addiction, only further burnished his image, at least after his death. After discovering in 1885 that cocaine could serve as an excellent local anesthetic for minor surgical procedures, he had become addicted to the drug. Between 1886 and 1888, Halsted had two long admissions to the Butler Hospital, a psychiatric facility in Providence, where he attempted to break his dependence. Halsted improved enough at Butler to accept the position at Johns Hopkins in 1888, although he likely replaced his addiction to cocaine

with one to morphine. Osler later attributed some of Halsted's reclusive-
ness and eccentricities, which included abruptly leaving the operating
room during surgery, to his drug problems. When the extent of Halsted's
addictions became known after his death, the "daily battle through
which this brave fellow lived for years" made his achievements seem
even greater to his students and biographers.[39]

One of Halsted's innovations that indubitably fostered the acceptance
of the radical mastectomy was his development of America's first program to train young surgeons. Prior to Halsted, surgeons generally
learned their craft through informal apprenticeships. Admiring the prestige enjoyed by German surgeons, who underwent many years of formal
training, Halsted instituted a system at Hopkins in which surgeons became academic "clinician-scientists," trained in surgery, pathology, bacte-
riology, and physiology. The Hopkins training program relied heavily on
chief residents, who were taught by Halsted and then supervised other
residents on the surgical service.[40]

Physicians trained by Halsted, including Joseph Bloodgood, Harvey
Cushing, Samuel Crowe, and Walter Dandy, went on to become preeminent surgeons at Johns Hopkins and other medical schools across the
country. Eleven of Halsted's residents established their own surgical residency programs. In this manner, they continued Halsted's legacy by pass-
ing on operations such as the radical mastectomy to succeeding
generations of surgeons. None of Halsted's accomplishments was
greater, wrote his friend Rudolph Matas, "than in the selection of the
group of young men who he chose to carry on his apostolate and to
transmit his teachings."[41] One Halsted disciple, Donald J. Ferguson, a surgeon at the University of Chicago, said he wished he could have tattooed
Halsted's phrase—"the suspected tissues should be removed in one
piece"—on the foreheads of his residents.[42]

Besides connecting surgeons of succeeding generations, Halsted's residency training program had the additional effect of helping to profes-
sionalize American surgery. In the years before the introduction of
anesthesia (1846) and antiseptic technique (1867), surgery was accompanied by high death rates. Taking advantage of these breakthroughs, surgeons in the United States formed the American Surgical Association
(ASA) in 1880. Between 1880 and 1890, more than a hundred new opera-

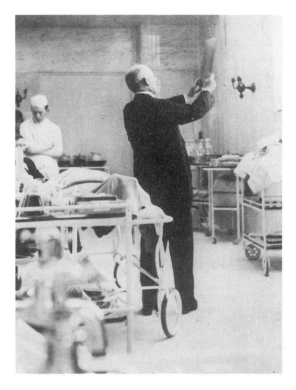

Halsted making a teaching point on the same day as the All Star Operation, 1904.

Courtesy of the Alan Mason Chesney Archives.

tions were introduced either in America or abroad.[43] Patients became less likely to die during or after surgery. Members of the ASA and the American College of Surgeons, founded in 1913, consciously attempted to distinguish themselves from general practitioners and gynecologists, who also performed breast and other general surgical procedures at this time. The most effective mechanism for producing this "higher type of surgeon"[44] was Halsted's strategy of training residents in the basic sciences and surgical research. Graduates of surgical training programs would not only learn about "scientific" operations such as the radical mastectomy, but would also come to believe that they were the most appropriate persons for carrying out such procedures. As Boston surgeon Edward Reynolds remarked in 1920, " '[w]here you find a new growth get it out,' is almost in itself the dictum of surgical authority today."[45]

Surgical authority in the treatment of cancer also came from a somewhat unlikely place: the pathology laboratory. Until the late nineteenth century, pathologists generally examined either corpses or body parts that surgeons had excised. Yet surgeons increasingly saw themselves not merely as technicians who removed diseased organs, but as diagnosticians whose operations could provide insights into the causes, mechanisms, and consequences of disease.[46]

Thus, there arose a need to examine pieces of tissue in a way that could actually help guide the management of the patient. After 1895, physicians began to advocate the use of so-called "frozen sections." In these procedures, surgeons biopsied (removed) a small piece of tissue, which was then studied under the microscope as the operation proceeded. The results of frozen sections, by either confirming or disproving suspected diagnoses, would determine what operation the surgeon would pursue. In the case of breast cancer, growing reliance on frozen sections meant that women diagnosed as having the disease underwent "one-step" procedures, in which both the diagnostic biopsy and mastectomy occurred during the same operation. Although some pathologists showed interest in performing frozen sections, others did not. As a result, surgeons themselves filled the gap, forming a subspeciality known as surgical pathology. By 1922, the American Society of Clinical Pathologists had been founded.[47]

Once again, this expansion of surgical domain could be traced back to Halsted, whom his longtime chief resident Joseph Colt Bloodgood called a "pathologist of first rank."[48] Halsted, William Welch, and other American physicians who had studied in Germany had imparted this more activist model of pathology to their junior colleagues. Halsted insisted that his residents generate "voluminous notes" that described both the gross and microscopic pathology of excised tissues.[49] By the 1920s, surgeons paid increasing attention to the study of pathological specimens and the training of surgical residents in this skill. In so doing, these men helped to centralize more authority in the person of the surgeon. It was hard to argue with the recommendation of radical mastectomy when the surgeon himself had both found a breast abnormality in his office and then definitively diagnosed it as cancer in the laboratory. The colorful nicknames of these early surgical pathologists, such as "Bloody" (Bloodgood of Hopkins) and "Wild Bill" (William C. Clarke of Columbia-Presbyterian) well exemplified the centrality of bold operations to the professional identity of surgeons in this era.[50]

The stature of the radical mastectomy was also amplified by the growing concern with the problem of cancer in North America and Europe. For much of the nineteenth century, infectious diseases had caused enormous mortality. The early sanitarians reponded to this situation by organizing public health campaigns to clean up garbage and purify the water supply. Of special concern was tuberculosis, which was the leading cause of death in many American and European cities in the 1880s and 1890s. Robert Koch's 1882 discovery of the bacterium that caused tuberculosis led health officials to design programs to prevent the spread of the disease from person to person. In the United States, these efforts received considerable support from the National Association for the Study and Prevention of Tuberculosis, a voluntary organization formed in 1904 to educate the public about the control of tuberculosis.[51]

Whether or not these public health efforts were responsible, rates of tuberculosis and other infectious diseases had declined considerably by the 1910s and 1920s. Physicians and laypersons began to turn their attention to the control of noncommunicable diseases, such as heart disease and cancer, which would become the two leading causes of death in the United States and Europe by 1930. Yet in the case of cancer, raising public awareness of the disease was no easy task. The grave prognosis of those struck by cancer, historian James T. Patterson has written, led Americans to view it as "the dread disease." As Patterson notes, public use of the word "cancer" remained relatively rare during the first half of the twentieth century.[52] As late as 1955, half of Americans stated that they had never had a close acquaintance who had cancer, suggesting that people with the disease were concealing their diagnoses. When Americans did speak of cancer, it was as a "sinister" disease that "tore at the flesh, often ravaging one's private organs."[53]

Part of this fear of cancer, later termed "cancerphobia," resulted from Americans' ignorance about it. Lacking a clear infectious cause such as the tuberculosis bacterium, cancer was mysterious. Misinformation, such as the notion that injuries to the body or tight clothes could cause breast or other cancers, was rampant. Meanwhile, quacks and other unorthodox healers preyed on the public, promising that nostrums such as "California Water of Life" and "Mild Combination Treatment" would produce miraculous cures.[54]

It was the dread of cancer, as well as the accompanying fatalistic attitude toward the disease, that educational campaigns attempted to combat.

Among the earliest efforts was a book, *The Control of a Scourge*, written by English physician Charles P. Childe in 1907. Childe sought to convince the public that cancer, despite its aura of despair and pessimism, was actually quite curable. He attributed much of the "dogma of the incurability, of the hopelessness of cancer" to the fact that "[t]his deadly monster is allowed to stalk unchallenged through the land."[55] The key to control of breast and other cancers, Childe argued, was to catch them early enough: "[A] period exists in every cancer . . . when it is local, when it is operable, when it is curable."[56] In a chapter entitled "Danger Signals," Childe urged women to immediately show any breast lumps, no matter how small, to their physicians.

Despite its attempts to open discourse, Childe's book was itself a victim of the continued reticence regarding the disease. His publisher, remarkably, had requested that he omit the word "cancer" from the title.[57] Not surprisingly, Childe's book did not find a wide audience in America. But his crusade was soon taken up by a new organization, the American Society for the Control of Cancer (ASCC). The ASCC was founded in New York in 1913 by a group of ten physicians and five laypeople. Five of the ten physicians were surgeons; three others were gynecologists, who also performed cancer surgery.[58] The ASCC drew on the strategies of the antituberculosis movement and anticancer efforts that had begun in Germany. The group's founding coincided with the publication of an article entitled "What Can We Do About Cancer?" by the well-known journalist Samuel Hopkins Adams. In the piece, published in the *Ladies' Home Journal*, Adams sought to dispel the many myths associated with cancer. Most important, he reiterated Childe's theme that early cancer was curable.[59]

By 1919, the ASCC had established three axioms that would guide anticancer efforts in America for the rest of the century:

1. Cancer is at first a local disease.
2. With early recognition and prompt treatment, the patient's life can often be saved.
3. Through ignorance and delay, thousands of lives are needlessly sacrificed.[60]

As had Childe, the ASCC stressed "danger signals," such as irregular bleeding or discharge, a sore that did not heal, persistent indigestion and weight loss, and, in the case of the breast, "any lump."

Cancer society officials were careful to balance this rather ominous language with what Patterson has termed a "Message of Hope." "Cancer is curable if treated early," read one representative ASCC poster in 1919. Treatment, of course, meant radical surgery, especially given the preponderance of surgeons and gynecologists among the founders and officials of the cancer society. As a result, the organization readily incorporated Halsted's theories into its publicity, which, in turn, appeared to confirm their validity. "Cancer begins as a local disease," ASCC literature definitively stated. "If recognized in time it can often be completely removed and the patient cured."[61] Other organizations promoting anticancer efforts made similar claims. By blurring actual medical findings with the understandable desire to present breast cancer control in a positive light, such language enhanced the prestige of the radical mastectomy and of those who performed cancer surgery. Other options, as portrayed, simply made no sense.

By 1915, the Halsted radical mastectomy had become recognized as the "established and standardized operation for cancer of the breast in all stages, early or late."[62] In their 1917 textbook on breast diseases, John B. Deaver and Joseph McFarland claimed that there was only one surgeon left in the United States who still believed that routine removal of the pectoral muscles was unnecessary. Such a claim, they continued, was "a voice from the grave of the imperfect, incomplete surgery of carcinoma."[63] The hegemony of the radical mastectomy—not only in the United States but throughout the world—was further strengthened by the publication in 1924 of a review of 20,000 cases of breast cancer by Janet Lane-Claypon, an English statistician. Over the succeeding decades, physicians often approvingly cited Lane-Claypon's report, which reported that 43.2 percent of women survived three years after a radical mastectomy, as opposed to only 29.2 percent of women receiving less extensive operations.[64]

Calls for Less Surgery

Even as the radical mastectomy became the treatment of choice for breast cancer, some physicians questioned what it actually accomplished. For example, while Rudolph Matas praised Halsted at the 1898 American Surgical Association meeting, he also carefully spelled out what he believed to be the limitations of the procedure. The words used to describe the operation, such as "radical" and "complete," he wrote, are "anatomical misnomers."[65] Even if the radical mastectomy appeared to encompass all the cancerous tissue at the time of surgery, it was actually impossible "to root out the evil with any degree of certainty."[66] Although breast cancer tended to spread to the axillary nodes first, there was no way to tell whether it had already moved to other lymph nodes beyond the scope of the operation.

In New Orleans, Halsted himself had acknowledged the inadequacy of the radical mastectomy, reporting that he had begun to perform an even more extensive operation in order to remove additional cancer cells.[67] He announced that "almost invariably" the supraclavicular region, the tissue above the clavicle [collar bone], was "cleaned out."[68] In addition, Halsted stated that one of his residents, Harvey Cushing, had in three cases extended the dissection into the anterior mediastinum, the column of tissue that contains the heart and its blood vessels. As of 1921, in some cases, Halsted was still excising the supraclavicular glands.[69]

Yet, as Matas had implied, the ability to perform the more extensive dissection did not prove its value. Indeed, Matas feared that involvement of the supraclavicular glands indicated "that a zone of infection [cancer] has spread beyond them, and that the key to the general lymphatic system has been hopelessly surrendered to the enemy."[70] In such a circumstance, most surgeons agreed, pursuing an extensive local dissection made little sense.

Perhaps in response to these concerns, surgeons continuing the Halsted tradition after his death from gallbladder disease in 1922 performed only the standard radical mastectomy. Yet even this procedure was seen as too extreme by a small but growing number of opponents in the 1920s and 1930s. One such critic was English surgeon Lord Berkeley Moynihan, who surprised a New York City audience in 1929 by claiming not to have operated on a case of breast cancer for over a year. The surgical attack on breast cancer, Moynihan stated, had reached its limit.[71]

Why had the Halsted operation suddenly lost popularity among some surgeons? For one thing, the operation was disfiguring, leaving women with a deformed chest wall, hollow areas beneath the clavicle and the underarm, and, at times, persistent pain at the operative site and arm swelling known as lymphedema. Surgeons learned about these consequences of radical mastectomy from patients and their families. "I have been in bed helpless every [day] since July 21, 1913," a Maryland woman told Halsted. "My arm is so swollen now that I can't help myself."[72] One of the most telling sets of correspondence between Halsted and a family member was with the husband of a Virginia woman who underwent a radical mastectomy in 1914. While appreciative, the man nevertheless termed Halsted's operation "dreadful," noting the "bodily mutilation and the consequent humiliation growing out of it."[73] For her part, the patient was most concerned with the issue of recurrence, frequently informing Halsted of various symptoms, such as headaches and neck swelling, that she feared were due to the breast cancer.[74]

The most vocal critic of radical mastectomy to emerge in the 1930s was the English physician Geoffrey Keynes. An assistant surgeon at London's St. Bartholomew's Hospital, Keynes was a Renaissance man, who would also achieve considerable renown as a poet. His brother was John Maynard Keynes, the famed English economist, whom Geoffrey liked to call "my clever brother Maynard."[75] Taking on the teachings of Halsted at the 1937 meeting of the American Surgical Association, Keynes provocatively stated that "radical surgery entails, in addition to an appreciative [sic] operative mortality, a really hideous mutilation."[76] Keynes also questioned Halsted's basic assumption that breast cancer spread slowly through local lymph nodes, hypothesizing that the disease in fact entered the bloodstream and spread throughout the body early in its course. Other critics of radical mastectomy, presaging a debate that would erupt in the 1950s, suggested that the ultimate fate of breast cancer patients had less to do with the surgery performed than the innate aggressiveness of individual cancers. "Cures," wrote New York surgeon Frank S. Mathews in 1932, "depend . . . on a mystical something that pathologists are now exploring and which is spoken of as the biology of the tumor."[77]

What alternative treatment did these physicians propose? By the late 1920s, a few had begun to argue that radiation, either by itself or accompanied by surgical removal of the tumor or breast alone, was as or more effective than radical mastectomy. In 1895 Wilhelm von Roentgen, a German physicist experimenting with cathode-ray tubes, inadvertently discovered a new type of ray that could penetrate solid substances, including flesh. When used with photographic plates, these new rays, termed "x-rays" by Roentgen, could generate images of the inside of the human body. Within months of the discovery, physicians began to speculate about the ability of x-rays to kill cancer cells, thereby shrinking or eliminating tumors. At least two American women with carcinoma of the breast, one a thirty-six-year-old Boston woman who had already endured several operations, received x-ray treatment in 1896.[78]

But numerous problems arose during the first decades of radiotherapy. Physicians had to learn how to use radiation equipment and what dosage was most appropriate for various cancers. The strength of early x-rays was less than 150 kilovolts, meaning they could not reach cancers located in the deep tissues of the body. Still, American physicians readily employed radiotherapy to palliate (ease the symptoms from) inoperable cancers. After World War I, they also began to administer x-rays as a supplement to radical mastectomy, hoping that radiating the scar and surrounding tissue would further improve outcomes.[79] A major change in philosophy occurred in the 1920s when advocates first argued that radiation alone could be used as first-line therapy for potentially curable cases of breast cancer. That is, rather than using Halsted's radical mastectomy, a woman would receive only radiotherapy. Physicians administered one of two types of radiation: (1) external orthovoltage radiotherapy aimed at the breast, axilla, and supraclavicular area, or (2) tubes or needles of radium that were implanted directly into the cancerous tumor.[80]

The growing interest in radiation was not only a reaction against surgery. Just as Halsted had promoted "scientific surgery" as the best modality for treating breast and other cancers, other physicians—including some surgeons—saw radiotherapy as a way to advance their careers while bringing therapeutic advances to patients. One Iowa physician, for example, wrote that proper postoperative radiotherapy required "skill and courage."[81] Invisible, yet powerful, x-rays also held a fascination among the public. Also promoting the adoption of radiation therapy was the gradual improvement of equipment, which had initially delivered only low voltages and caused destruction of the skin, lungs, and other nearby tissues and organs. An important technological advance occurred in the 1930s with the introduction of supervoltage radiotherapy, which could direct much higher voltage x-ray beams onto the cancer while avoiding damage to healthy tissue. However, linear accelerators that could provide supervoltage did not become widely available for decades.[82]

Physicians in European countries embraced the possibilities of radiation even more enthusiastically than their American counterparts. In France, for example, the legacy of Pierre and Marie Curie encouraged physicians to implant radium, which the scientists had discovered in 1898. Support for irradiation proved especially strong in England, where the British Radium Commission was studying the use of multiple forms of radiotherapy in the treatment of breast and other cancers. English surgeons such as Keynes, Duncan C. L. Fitzwilliams, and Philip H. Mitchiner published articles suggesting that these alternatives to radical mastectomy were as effective while "less mutilating and soul destroying."[83] For example, Keynes in 1937 reported 83.5 percent three-year survival for patients with cancer confined to the breast who had been treated with radium implants; in contrast, 79.2 percent of radical mastectomy patients with comparable cancers at a neighboring hospital had survived this long.[84]

Among the strongest American supporters of irradiation was the eminent pathologist James Ewing, who became chief physician of New York's Memorial Hospital in 1913. Having become disenchanted with what surgery could accomplish, Ewing encouraged Memorial breast surgeons to compare radical mastectomy with radiotherapy. One Memorial physician, Burton J. Lee, appeared to confirm Ewing's hunch. In 1928, Lee told readers of the *Annals of Surgery* that there was "no apparent advantage in favor of surgery, combined with irradiation, over treatment by irradiation alone."[85] Similar results were obtained by physicians who combined radiation treatment with a less extensive operation than radical mastectomy. For example, Brooklyn surgeon Edwin J. Grace reported 53 percent three-year cures among patients who had simple mastectomy (breast removal only) and radiation treatment; this figure was comparable to or better than cure rates among radical mastectomy patients.[86]

To be sure, the problematic nature of such data was well appreciated. In their comprehensive 1940 textbook, *Treatment of Cancer and Allied Diseases*, New York City surgeons George T. Pack and Edward M. Livingston noted how such case series potentially generated biased information. Most notably, Pack and Livingston argued, physicians used radiation on only a percentage of their breast cancer patients, who possibly represented those with the best prognosis. In addition, patients receiving radiation also underwent variable amounts of surgery, ranging from no operation to removal of only the cancer to removal of only the breast. As a result, it was unclear whether the three-year cures were attributable to radiation or to this "incidental" surgery. Finally, Pack and Livingston noted, cases receiving radiation alone relied only on the clinician's judgment as proof that cancer had existed. Lacking "histologic proof of diagnosis," it was possible that lesions supposedly cured by radiation were not even cancer in the first place.[87]

Advocates of radiotherapy did not necessarily reject Pack and Livingston's arguments. For one thing, Pack, who would become one of America's most prominent cancer experts, had training in radiation therapy as well as surgery and pathology. Rather, critics of radical mastectomy hoped to introduce some skepticism into those who reflexively supported Halstedian dogma. "[W]e do at least aspire," wrote Mitchiner and his colleagues in 1938, "to give our surgical colleagues food for reflection before they so lightly and unheedingly advocate radical removal in all cases of carcinoma of the breast."[88] Similarly, Keynes wrote that he did not wish "to make any dogmatic claim on behalf of radium."[89]

Perhaps because so many of the physicians experimenting with radiotherapy were surgeons, relatively little animosity existed between the advocates and foes of radical mastectomy in the 1930s. Noting that radiation treatment was challenging the dominant position of surgery in the treatment of cancer of the breast, Kentucky surgeon Walter O. Bullock even speculated that in the near future, "the last word in the chapter on surgical technique in this field will have been written."[90]

The notion of the Halsted radical mastectomy as an imperfect but acceptable operation may have best been exemplified by a 1932 piece written by Dean Lewis and William F. Rienhoff, Jr., two of Halsted's surgical heirs at Johns Hopkins. Lewis and Rienhoff reviewed 950 patients with breast cancer treated at Johns Hopkins between 1889 to 1931, 798 of whom (84%) had received a radical mastectomy. The authors began their paper with a rather remarkable admission: Halsted's original fifty patients had had a local recurrence rate not of 6 percent, as reported by Halsted in 1898, but of over 30 percent. Moreover, of the 420 Hopkins patients known to be dead, less than one-third had survived as long as three years.[91] By pointing out that Halsted's meticulous dissection did not reliably prevent local return of breast cancer and that women were dying shortly after their extensive operations, such data were hardly a ringing endorsement of the Halsted radical mastectomy. Nevertheless, Lewis and Rienhoff remained unwilling to reject their mentor's teachings. They ultimately favored continued use of Halsted's complete mastectomy rather than "a less radical operation supplemented by the very questionable effect of radiation."[92]

Exploring the Meaning of "Cure"

Part of the confusion over Halsted's operation stemmed from the fact that the utility of the procedure could be measured in different ways. Was the goal of extensive tissue removal only to prevent a recurrence of the cancer in the region of the breast, or was it to lengthen the patient's life? Both Halsted and other authors assigned the term "cure" to each of these goals, thereby complicating attempts to assess the value of the radical operation.

In his 1895 paper, Halsted had seemed to emphasize the importance of preventing local return of the cancer. Most surgeons, he wrote, considered breast cancer as "radically" or "permanently" cured if three years had passed without evidence of a recurrence in the operative site.[93] Indeed, it was this concept that led to the adoption of the term "three-year cure." Lewis and Rienhoff reiterated Halsted's point of view in their 1932 review article, noting that "the main standard by which the operative treatment of carcinoma of the breast may be judged is the cure of the disease locally." "If the disease has been cured locally," they continued, "the operator has fulfilled his responsibility."[94] This achievement, which has also been termed a "surgical cure," underscores the degree to which surgical accomplishment almost came to assume more importance than patient survival during the early twentieth century.[95]

Yet Halsted also used the term "cure" in a quite different manner. "The efficiency of an operation," he wrote in his 1895 paper, "is measured truer in terms of local recurrence than of ultimate cure."[96] While this statement again stressed the importance of preventing local recurrence, it concurrently suggested that cure represented something beyond this goal. Others, such as Charles Childe, also used the word "cure" to connote "lasting relief" in which cancer patients eventually "succumb to some other complaint, without ever having experienced any sign or symptom whatsoever of a return of the disease."[97] For Childe, therefore, recurrence of breast cancer either locally or somewhere else in the body—even after several years—meant that the surgery had not been curative. Many authors struggled with the contradictory ways in which "cure" was used and urged their colleagues to be more rigorous in their choice of terminology. Some put the word "cure" in quotation marks and noted, as did New York surgeon B. Farquhar Curtis in 1894, "that the expression . . . can hardly be employed in a strict sense."[98] Others proposed alternate terms to describe how long patients lived after their breast cancer operation; Lewis and Rienhoff favored "longevity"; Iowa surgeon C. A. Kunath argued for "survival."[99] Nevertheless, in many instances, physicians remained inexact, using "cure" to connote either no local recurrence or the permanent absence of breast cancer from anywhere in the body.

Although these imprecise usages of terms such as cure and recurrence may frustrate modern attempts to understand how Halsted-era physicians chose among breast cancer treatments,[100] they are less surprising in historical context. When Halsted and Willy Meyer began to promote radical mastectomy in the 1890s, they were treating cancers that often took up as much as one-quarter of the breast. Simple breast removal, the standard treatment of the day, might remove the offending mass, but surgeons knew that cancer would shortly reappear on the chest wall or in the axilla. These rapid recurrences caused understandable distress for patients and doctors. By dramatically lowering the local recurrence rate (although not as significantly as first advertised), Halsted's and Meyer's revolutionary surgical innovations were "curing" the visible manifestations of the cancer. It was natural to think of such patients as cured even if there was quite possibly silent cancer in the lungs, liver, bones, or brain. In this sense, physicians in the early twentieth century accepted an inherently ambiguous term such as three-year cure. It was what it was, no more or less.

Yet by the 1920s and 1930s, the medical and, to some extent, popular representations of breast cancer were changing. Women, responding to growing coverage of cancer by newspapers and lay magazines, came to doctors more promptly.[101] Because their breast cancers were on average smaller, much less local recurrence would take place after radical mastectomy. Thus, once the operation was over, breast cancer became an invisible disease. The issue was less whether it would recur locally than whether it would return elsewhere in the body. Whereas Curtis in 1894 had reported only occasional cases in which patients had succumbed to breast cancer five to ten years after their operation, by 1932 Mathews could write: "Most striking to me has been the observation that patients go to their grave with distant metastases [areas of cancer], often living a considerable period with them, yet, at the moment of death showing no evidence of recurrence in the scar or immediately underlying tissue."[102]

As breast cancer evolved from a disease that recurred visibly and rapidly into one that returned invisibly and more slowly, the designation of three-year cure had less relevance. Indeed, physicians had begun to speak of five-year cures by the 1920s. Yet the tendency to describe the Halsted radical mastectomy as curative persisted, even though what it originally "cured"—local recurrences—had increasingly little relevance in an era of earlier detection. Thus, the more extensive operation became the treatment of choice for less advanced breast cancers as well. "Whether or not small tumors needed radical mastectomies," the journalist Ellen Leopold has written, "radical mastectomies needed smaller tumors."[103]

The historical assessments of William Halsted and his radical mastectomy have often said as much about the era in which they were made as about the man and his operation. Books published in the 1940s and 1950s, such as The New Science of Surgery (1946) and The Century of the Surgeon (1956), depicted Halsted as a hero.[104] After 1970, women challenging the radical mastectomy derided him and his followers for their ignorance and arrogance.[105] Others criticized Halsted for different reasons. In his 1984 book, The Secret World of Doctor and Patient, psychiatrist and law professor Jay Katz upbraided him for generating definitive theories from uncertain data. In a similar vein, the journalist Cornelia Shaw Bland has asked, "[W]hat induced this serious clinical scientist to claim favorable results from such a small number of dead, dying and doomed women[?]"[106]

As Bland herself notes, the answer lies in understanding the historical context in which Halsted performed research and cared for patients. The radical mastectomy was not just a treatment but part of Halsted's larger effort to bring science to the practice of surgery. Having used anatomic and laboratory studies to demonstrate that cancer was amenable to radical surgery, Halsted then passed down this gospel to successive generations of surgeons. In this manner, the radical mastectomy both drew on and helped promulgate the growing promise of scientific surgery. The prestige of the operation was only further enhanced by the fact that surgeons themselves had developed the criteria by which the curative potential of the procedure was evaluated. For their part, Halsted's patients, or at least those who corresponded with him, appeared to willingly place their trust in the man, his operation, and the surgical profession.

Inventing a Curable Disease

Breast Cancer Control after World War II

Although there were disagreements over the value of Halsted's radical mastectomy, there was nearly total unanimity on another of the Johns Hopkins surgeon's tenets: the earlier treatment for breast cancer began, the better. In the years after World War II, the American Cancer Society (ACS), building on its experiences in publicizing the Pap smear for cervical cancer, spearheaded a major campaign to discover breast cancers earlier. The centerpiece of this effort was to teach women to examine their own breasts in the hopes of discovering smaller, presumably more curable cancers.

To motivate American women to participate, the ACS and other anticancer organizations used combat metaphors that linked the "war" on breast cancer with the recent American military triumph. They also promoted their efforts by using the rhetoric of fear, a not uncommon tactic in what had become America's latest political conflict—the Cold War. Beyond their connection to military language, breast self-examination and routine breast examination by physicians raised important issues regarding women's privacy and sexuality. To what degree would women scrutinize their breasts, or let male doctors do so, especially when the "reward" for finding a cancer was a radical mastectomy?

Fatalism Persists

"I was met by a powerful odor as we opened the doors to the institution," wrote the surgeon Claude Welch, recalling his first visit to

Pondville Hospital in 1929. "Decaying, infected cancers on living patients have distinctive, sickly sweet, nauseating odors that make it easy to diagnose cancer of the cervix on that basis only."[1] Pondville, which was located just outside of Boston, Massachusetts, was one of several recently established institutions in the United States devoted exclusively to the care of cancer patients. Other facilities included New York City's Memorial Hospital, Buffalo's Roswell Park Institute, and Boston's Collis P. Huntington Hospital.

Although the founding of these hospitals demonstrated the growing concern with cancer as a pressing public health problem, the institutions, as originally conceived, predominantly served the terminally ill. Such facilities thus revealed a fault line among those involved in cancer control. Some regarded cancer as a disease that could be conquered, but well into the twentieth century, many physicians continued to classify cancer as a "degenerative disease" that "results from a wearing out of the organism's natural barriers to unregulated growth."[2] Contributing to this perception was the image, conveyed by Welch, that cancer inexorably progressed until it "rots the flesh."[3] "Such conditions," noted Boston cancer specialist Robert B. Greenough, "amply justify the pessimism of the general practitioner in regard to the cure of cancer."[4]

Despite the efforts of Halsted and his followers, this fatalism often applied in the case of breast cancer. One surgeon remarked to New Jersey physician Edward J. Ill in 1924 that all eighty-eight patients on whom he had operated had subsequently died of the disease. It was still commonplace for patients to wait months or even years before showing a breast lump to a physician. Indeed, delay was so expected that the "mammary carcinoma summary sheets" in use at New York's Presbyterian Hospital contained a space for doctors to check off the patient's duration of symptoms. Printed choices ranged as high as thirty-six months or over. Because these delays led to very large tumors, many surgeons remained reluctant to attempt curative surgery. Thus, breast cancer patients often did not qualify for a radical mastectomy.[5]

This passivity toward breast and other cancers was precisely what frustrated medical and lay groups issuing anticancer statements. In 1932, for example, the American College of Surgeons sponsored a conference simply entitled, "Cancer Is Curable." "All this cheer," wrote Time magazine quite candidly, "was for morale, to cheer up the public."[6] Physicians at Pondville and the other cancer hospitals began admitting larger numbers of patients with earlier cancers that had better prognoses. In addition, in 1932, Pondville opened a "Cured Cancer Clinic." Although designed in part to follow cancer patients after discharge, the clinic functioned also as a public demonstration that persons with the disease could indeed be cured. From its inception, clinic staff invited as visitors any local practitioners who "did not feel very hopeful regarding the prognosis of those with cancer."[7]

Another group that sought to dispel the pessimism regarding cancer was the United States Congress. In 1937 it authorized the establishment of a National Cancer Institute in Bethesda, Maryland, that would fund research regarding the causes and treatment of cancer. Acting soon after the successful development of sulfonamide antibiotics to treat bacterial infections, legislators believed that federal support of cancer research could generate similar accomplishments.[8]

At the same time, the American Society for the Control of Cancer (ASCC), which had inaugurated such strategies in the 1910s, accelerated its efforts to "fight cancer with publicity." Like most voluntary health organizations of the era, the ASCC relied on the largesse of wealthy benefactors and smaller donations from ordinary citizens. Many of the latter were persons with cancer or the relatives of those who had died. Although the cancer society's board was composed of both laypersons and physicians, doctors dominated the organization in the interwar years. The resultant medical focus made the ASCC less successful than the National Tuberculosis Association in generating effective publicity campaigns.[9]

Contributing to the ASCC's problems was the continued silence and stigma that surrounded the diagnosis of breast and other cancers. In an attempt to raise public awareness about cancer and its curability, the cancer society in 1936 formed the "Women's Field Army" (WFA), whose goal was to promote "trench warfare with a vengeance against a ruthless killer."[10] Women could join the army by contributing one dollar annually. The WFA took its military motif seriously. Army literature routinely included a diagram of the "Sword of Hope," which the ASCC had adopted as its emblem in 1927 (see figure). The sword's hilt was formed from a twin serpent caduceus, the traditional symbol of the medical profession.

Cover of pamphlet issued by the Women's Field
Army of the American Society for the Control of
Cancer, 1939.

Reprinted by permission of the American Cancer
Society, Inc.

The WFA was organized vertically, complete with an officer corps and
foot volunteers. Members wore brown uniforms with insignia of rank.
By 1943, the army numbered between 350,000 and 700,000 members.[11]

The cancer society's use of a war metaphor was hardly accidental. As
evidenced by the war on poverty and the war on drugs, Americans often
characterize efforts to combat important social problems in terms of battle. Such language has also characterized public health campaigns, such
as the war on tuberculosis in the early twentieth century and later wars
on polio and AIDS. Cancer, in a sense, was the perfect enemy. Derived
from the Latin word for crab, cancer was associated with the powerful
image of a crab growing out of control and eating away at the body's organs. In addition, according to a 1939 survey, 76 percent of Americans
cited cancer as the disease they most feared.[12]

ASCC officials explicitly recognized the potential for war imagery to
generate interest in its cause. "The name 'Army' was chosen," director
Clarence Cook Little later recalled, "because the whole emphasis of the

Society from the outset had been militant—the 'sword' symbol, the slogan 'Fight Cancer With Knowledge,' [and] posters of St. George and the Dragon."[13] These military allusions became even more commonplace with the stirrings of war in the late 1930s. Military language not only energized public opinion against cancer but also provided cancer patients and their families with the inspiration they wanted and needed. In this sense, war metaphors fit well with the cancer society's goal of maintaining "optimism in the face of danger and threat."[14]

Other Western countries, including Canada, England, France, and Germany, had established cancer control agencies by the 1930s. However, the emphasis on mobilizing the public against the cancer nemesis was most pronounced in the United States, with its rich historical legacy of citizens forming interest groups in order to promote social reform. "Europeans," Little stated, "have toward the cancer problem a much more patient, long-time attitude than we do in America."[15] The English physician William Sampson-Handley agreed, noting that his people often shut their minds to "unpalatable" information and thus were not inclined to "worry about the risks of life."[16] Anticancer organizations outside the United States, such as England's Imperial Cancer Research Institute, the French Association for the Study of Cancer, and the National Swiss League Against Cancer, tended to focus more on collecting vital statistics and promoting research than waging a war of propaganda against the disease. One exception to this rule was the anticancer campaign mounted in Nazi Germany in the 1930s, but as the historian Robert N. Proctor has argued, this effort focused more on prevention than cure.[17]

The ASCC's simultaneous emphasis on fear and hope was also self-serving. Cancer society officials carefully tailored their message to maximize donations from the public. "The attitudes towards cancer which seem to be most closely associated with the tendency to give to the campaign," reported one official, "are the beliefs that today cancer is one of the most terrible diseases in the country but that we are making definite progress in getting it under control."[18] Thus, aggressive, optimistic military terminology not only provided an effective way of disseminating the ASCC's worthy message, but also helped to ensure that the organization would itself survive to lead the charge against cancer. Moreover, battle language also performed "ideological work" within the cancer society and the medical profession, encouraging a hopeful mindset in the face of often uncertain and ambiguous accomplishments.[19]

Why did the ASCC decide to declare war on women's cancers? For one thing, cancer had historically been seen as a "female disease." During the nineteenth century, women supposedly accounted for three-fifths of all cancer cases. Concerns about the high mortality from cancer of the uterine cervix had helped to spark formation of the ASCC in 1913. Moreover, in the years before physicians routinely explored the interiors of bodies by x-rays and surgery, women's cancers were among the most amenable to public education efforts. Breast cancers occurred in an organ located on the outside of the body, while uterine cancers often revealed themselves by irregular vaginal bleeding.[20]

By the 1930s, this focus on women's cancers seemed more appropriate than ever. "[W]omen suffer more from cancer than do men," explained WFA literature. "This disease killed more women in 1935 between the ages of forty and sixty-five than any of the other horsemen of death."[21] Uterine and breast cancers were the top two causes of cancer deaths among American women, causing 16,300 and 14,000 deaths, respectively, in 1938.[22] Moreover, the WFA argued, cancers of these organs were curable in 70 to 80 percent of cases if found and treated in time.

But the decision to designate women as the "volunteer soldiers who carry the burden of the work"[23] did not merely stem from the high prevalance of women's cancers. Rather, the enlistment of women drew on longstanding gender roles that designated wives and mothers as responsible for the health and well-being of themselves, their families, and communities. Because women were relegated to the "private sphere" of the home, their citizenship was tied into the production of other healthy citizens. "It is a women's war," noted a WFA pamphlet, "because they have the patience, devotion, and the courage needed."[24] As the historian Leslie Reagan has written, "Women have long been taught that cancer is their special concern and that, indeed, to worry about cancer is their duty."[25]

To be sure, those women who joined or supported the WFA eagerly embraced the task of convincing fellow women to heed cancer's warning signs. "The organized women of America," stated Congresswoman Edith Nourse Rogers in 1937, "can do much to drive the scourge from the land."[26] Many women in the WFA, such as its first national commander,

Marjorie G. Illig, were involved in women's clubs and saw the cancer work as a natural extension of these activities. Indeed, in the early 1930s, the American Association of University Women (AAUW) had begun its own cervical cancer awareness campaign, aspects of which would later inform WFA efforts. Articles in women's magazines also emphasized the WFA's message of prompt attention. "[B]ecause she acted without delay," read one article on breast cancer in the *Ladies' Home Journal*, "Mary Roberts Rinehart helped herself to beat her biggest opponent."[27]

Although these educational efforts did not exclude poor and minority women, neither did they make special overtures to such groups. For one thing, women in the WFA and AAUW tended to be white and middle-class. In addition, in contrast to diseases such as tuberculosis, which predominated among the poor, cancer was seen as a disease that affected all women. Indeed, in the case of breast cancer, the limited data indicating that morbidity and mortality from the disease were higher among the wealthy may have discouraged targeted publicity efforts in poor and minority neighborhoods.[28]

Yet as early as the 1940s, there were also data demonstrating that poorer women had more advanced breast cancer by the time they saw a doctor and were thus less likely to receive a potentially curative radical mastectomy. This finding suggested that messages about early diagnosis were not reaching all populations equally, something confirmed by the cancer society's own research. For example, awareness of ASCC propaganda was lower among persons who had not completed high school and who earned less than $2000 annually. Whereas only 10 percent of whites had never heard of the cancer society, this figure reached 33 percent among African Americans.[29] The ASCC and later the ACS worked with local African American organizations to disseminate anticancer messages. Among the most active groups was the Colored Division of the Georgia Division of the ACS, which joined forces with the Atlanta Metropolitan Council of Negro Women.[30]

Even though hundreds of thousands of American women joined the WFA in the 1930s and 1940s, it remained difficult to prove that they had changed their behavior as a result. Articles in the medical literature continued to bemoan the fact that cancer patients did not come to the doctor promptly. "Delay kills!" warned one cancer society poster from the early

1940s, claiming that more people died every two weeks from a delayed cancer diagnosis than had died at Pearl Harbor. "[D]elay in early diagnosis and treatment," one group of authors would write as late as 1954, "continues to be the greatest single hurdle to be overcome in the fight to cure cancer."[31]

Clinical research appeared to support the ASCC's claims regarding delay. For example, one 1938 article found that a woman with breast cancer was one-third more likely to qualify for a potentially curative operation if she came to the doctor within three months of discovering a lump.[32] Yet few involved in anticancer efforts truly believed that earnest entreaties about danger signals alone would truly achieve the ultimate goal of making cancer into a curable disease. It is little wonder, therefore, that news of George Papanicolaou's new test of cervical cytology caused such excitement among the cancer society leadership.

The Pap Smear

Not unlike Halsted, George N. Papanicolaou was a somewhat reluctant hero. The son of a physician, Papanicolaou was born in Greece in 1883. After graduating from medical school at the University of Athens, he studied biology in both Germany and France. Papanicolaou returned home to serve in the Balkan War during 1912 and 1913, but he and his wife Mary emigrated to New York after the war. Having been hired as a laboratory assistant at Cornell University Medical College to research sex determination, the Greek scientist began to make smears from vaginal fluid. First, Papanicolaou performed microscopic examinations on the normal cells that he discovered, a procedure known as cytology. Next, however, in "one of the most thrilling experiences of my scientific career,"[33] he began to find cytologic evidence of gynecological malignancies in the fluid specimens. Specifically, in January 1928, Papanicolaou reported that he had detected cells that were characteristic of cervical cancer. Because these cells came from the outside portion of the cervix, they had not clearly invaded the cervical tissue, normally a criterion for diagnosing cancer. Papanicolaou believed that such cells were precancerous and thus made possible the earlier diagnosis of cervical cancer. The

New York World agreed, touting his discovery as a "new cancer detection method,"[34] but many of Papanicolaou's colleagues proved much less interested. Accordingly, he put aside his cytology work and turned to different areas of research for more than a decade.

In the early 1940s, Papanicolaou's colleagues at Cornell urged him to revisit his earlier work. He began a study at New York Hospital that took routine vaginal smears of all women admitted to the gynecological service. Ultimately, in a 1943 publication entitled "Diagnosis of Uterine Cancer by the Vaginal Smear," Papanicolaou reported the discovery of 179 unsuspected cases of uterine cancer, 127 of which were cancers of the cervix. "This experience would seem to indicate," wrote Papanicolaou in characteristically understated fashion, "that the vaginal smear method . . . forms a reliable accessory method for the study of carcinoma of the cervix of the uterus."[35]

Once again, many physicians downplayed the importance of Papanicolaou's study. Some argued that a cervix could not be called cancerous unless an examiner could see and feel the lesion. Others, prefiguring future controversies in the diagnosis of breast cancer, questioned whether these cancer-like cells were necessarily harbingers of cancer and whether a hysterectomy was thus justified as "treatment." Finally, others emphasized the logistical impossibility of pathologists "looking at a thousand or ten thousand slides to find one positive and all the rest negative."[36]

Having pushed the message of early cancer diagnosis and treatment for thirty years, the ASCC quickly discounted such arguments. Indeed, thanks largely to the efforts of Mary Lasker, the cancer society in the 1940s was experiencing both a rejuvenation and refocusing of its efforts. Lasker was the dynamic and energetic wife of New York City advertising executive Albert Lasker, who had developed the successful campaign urging women to reach for a Lucky Strike cigarette instead of a sweet. In 1943, having recently established the Albert and Mary Lasker Research Foundation for medical research, the Laskers were surprised to learn that medicine had little to offer their housekeeper, who had developed cancer of the uterus. Mary Lasker quickly learned that the ASCC provided no support for cancer research and raised only a few hundred thousand dollars each year—a figure, she noted, "that wouldn't even be a suitable sum for an advertising campaign for a toothpaste."[37] Lasker was also perturbed at the lack of progress that the cancer society had made in making cancer a household word. As Clarence Little had informed her, the word "cancer" could not even be mentioned on the radio.[38]

Mary Lasker acted quickly. Using business and social connections, she convinced the ASCC leadership to revamp its board of directors, filling it with influential and prominent business leaders. Lasker's goal was to convert the cancer society from a small organization controlled by physicians into a professional fund-raising agency that used the latest techniques in advertising and marketing. It did not take long. In 1945, the ASCC, having jettisoned its rather awkward name in favor of the more streamlined "American Cancer Society" (ACS), raised more than $4 million. (In the 1950s, Lasker would have even more success lobbying Congress for dramatic increases in the annual research budget of the National Cancer Institute [NCI]). The ACS enrolled celebrities, ranging from the comedian Milton Berle to Dwight D. Eisenhower, to promote fund-raising.[39]

As Lasker had wished, the new ACS money was earmarked to rejuvenate educational efforts and to support innovative research into the diagnosis and treatment of cancer. Papanicolaou's vaginal sampling method, now known as the Pap smear, ideally suited Lasker's agenda. It had been developed in the laboratory as a result of scientific research. And it was a technique that lent itself to a widescale publicity effort.

The man who ultimately engineered this campaign for the ACS was Charles S. Cameron. Cameron was a dynamic, articulate man who had graduated from the Hahnemann Medical College in Philadelphia in 1935. Between 1938 and 1942, Cameron trained as a surgeon at New York's Memorial Hospital. Memorial was itself undergoing a series of changes at the time. In 1945, it received a donation of $4 million from two General Motors executives to establish the Sloan-Kettering Institute for cancer research.[40] Over time, the institution became known as the Memorial Sloan-Kettering Cancer Center. During the middle and late 1940s, the newly reorganized ACS maintained a close working association with the physicians—particularly the surgeons—at Memorial Sloan-Kettering. The president of the ACS from 1944 to 1947 was Frank Adair, chief of the breast service at Memorial. Tall, handsome, and graying, Adair, who was known to patients and staff as the "Great White Father," may have performed as many breast operations as any surgeon ever had. In 1946, at Adair's suggestion, the ACS named Cameron as its medical director.

By this time, Cameron had become familiar with the research of Papanicolaou, who worked across the street at Cornell. In contrast to other physicians who downplayed the significance of the Pap smear, Cameron "got the idea that this was a great opportunity to save lives." Ensconced in his new position, Cameron "pushed the Cancer Society for backing this full tilt."[41] Among other things, Cameron urged the ACS to sponsor the First National Cytology Conference in Boston in 1948 as well as additional research into the prognostic significance of the lesions that the Pap smear discovered.

At Papanicolaou's urging, the ACS initially avoided an all-out campaign to promote Pap testing until enough individuals across the country had received adequate training in reading cytology specimens. Yet once this infrastructure was in place, it became difficult for Cameron and the cancer society to hold back. "Can we justify delaying any longer a vigorous campaign to press the use of the smear?" Cameron asked his colleagues at the 1951 annual ACS meeting. "My conscience and the opinion of those with the widest experience in its use say no."[42]

By the early 1950s, Cameron was traveling across the United States, extolling the virtues of the Pap smear to crowds in churches, gymnasiums, and school auditoriums. Although Cameron presented Papanicolaou's early statistics in his presentations, definitive data that the Pap smear saved lives hardly existed at this time. In urging "for women sere [over 40], a vaginal smear, twice a year,"[43] what Cameron was really selling was the test itself, an intervention that seemed to hold the promise of saving lives. As the sociologists Adele E. Clarke and Monica J. Casper have argued, the ACS and NCI "enrolled" the Pap smear because it fit their goal of developing simple, interventionist technologies for detecting early cancer.[44]

Replete with both war metaphors and calls for individual responsibility for one's health, Cameron's messages were also characteristically American. Having emerged from the Depression, defeated the Germans and Japanese in World War II, undergone an economic boom, and invested in scientific research, the United States suddenly seemed within reach of making cervical cancer a curable disease. A lesson of "incalculable importance" learned during the war needed to be replicated in prosperous, postwar America: "with unlimited money to spend we can buy the answer to almost any scientific problem."[45] The Pap smear, Cameron stated, was a "precision weapon"; Papanicolaou himself was an "Ameri-

A 1954 cartoon exemplify-
ing the American Cancer
Society's increasing emphasis on medical science and
research in conducting its
"war" on cancer.

Reprinted by permission
of the American Cancer
Society, Inc.

can success story" and a "giver of life."[46] "[T]he American character,"
Cameron wrote in the *Journal of the American Medical Association* in 1951, was
not "panicked by cancer or by any other enemy" but "continues to look
reality straight in the face, to fear what deserves to be feared, and then do
something about it."[47]

This effort to get Americans to fear cancer and then vanquish it fit well
with a Cold War climate that "left few doubts about the appropriateness
of fear or the dangerousness of the world."[48] Red-baiting politicians of
the early 1950s, such as Wisconsin Senator Joseph McCarthy, used fear-
mongering to call attention to the dangers that Communists in the State
Department supposedly posed to the United States. While the ACS in no
way emulated McCarthy's manipulative tactics, the organization successfully played into the fears of the era. Cancer of the cervix or the breast—
just like the metaphorical "cancer of Communism"—needed to be
rooted out from its source. The survival of Americans was at stake.[49]

In the case of the Pap smear, according to the ACS, women needed to
show initiative. As Arthur I. Holleb, Cameron's successor as medical direc-

tor of the cancer society, later recalled, "You were supposed to tell your doctor you hadn't had a complete physical exam—underlining complete—if you hadn't had a Pap smear."[50] This message resonated with the audiences Cameron addressed, who often rewarded the surgeon-turned-preacher with standing ovations.

Searching for Early Breast Cancers

The story of Charles Cameron and the Pap smear provides essential background for understanding the ACS's fierce advocacy of breast self-examination (BSE) after 1950 (see figure). Sensing great impending success in lowering mortality from cervical cancer, ACS officials sincerely and fer-

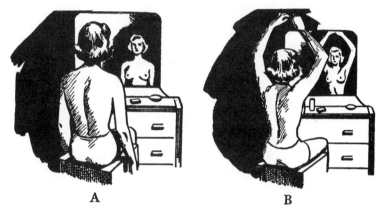

Diagram teaching women how to perform breast self-examination.

vently believed that BSE offered the same prospects for the "arch-killer" of women, breast cancer. The idea of checking one's breasts for lumps was not new. During the first decades of the twentieth century, physicians had periodically urged women to "feel for a lump." Waiting for a lump to appear, wrote New York surgeon Hugh Auchincloss in 1929, was "late" advice.[51] Nazi public health propaganda urged BSE as early as 1936.[52] This notion of finding smaller, more curable cancers was entirely consistent with Halsted's paradigm of early intervention for breast cancer.

However, neither BSE nor routine examinations of breasts by physicians received much attention in the United States until the 1950s. As historians of medical technology have argued, merely developing a new innovation does not itself ensure its dissemination. Rather, the new tool must await a hospitable cultural setting. As of 1950, the time was ripe to promote breast examinations as a new "weapon."[53]

By this time, the ACS was shifting its earlier emphasis on all women's cancers to breast cancer in particular. Even prior to the introduction of the Pap smear, which ultimately did lower mortality from cervical cancer, rates of that disease were falling. As a result, by 1947, breast cancer had overtaken uterine cancers (including those in the cervix and the body of the uterus) as the most common cancer and the leading cause of cancer death among American women.[54] Approximately 25 women per 100,000 population died from breast cancer annually.

Breast cancer also raised concerns for women of all ages. Like most cancers, the incidence of the disease dramatically increased as women got older. Studies from New York and Connecticut, for example, revealed that the number of new cases of the disease, which was less than 100 per 100,000 women at age forty-five, increased to over 200 per 100,000 women after age seventy-five. Yet despite the lower rates of breast cancer among young women, disease in this population warranted special concern. Most clinicians strongly believed that "carcinoma of the breast is more malignant when it occurs in the young than in the aged."[55]

Finally, breast cancer spoke directly to women's sexuality and privacy. Once again, World War II had played a role, as pin-ups of large-breasted starlets such as Betty Grable and Rita Hayworth came to symbolize the women of the homefront. "Men fighting overseas," Marilyn Yalom wrote in *A History of the Breast*, "looked to the female bosom as a reminder of the values that war destroys: love, intimacy, nurturance."[56] In the postwar years, the growing popularity of "torpedo brassieres" and sweater girls, such as Jane Russell and Marilyn Monroe, highlighted the degree to which the breast represented female allure and attractiveness.[57]

If the female breast had become an American national treasure, the persistently high rates of breast cancer threatened its status. It was thus a propitious time to try to popularize breast examinations. Although an unfortunate consequence might be a mastectomy, diligent breast examination also focused attention on the need to care for one's healthy breasts.[58] In 1950, the ACS and the National Cancer Institute released a film entitled "Breast Self-Examination," which, along with a series of educational leaflets on BSE, served as the backbone of a major push to increase the early detection of breast cancer. The campaign met with a good public response. In 1955, *Good Housekeeping* reported that over five million women had attended screenings of the film; moreover, as many as 92 percent of Iowa women who had seen it had subsequently performed BSE. By 1967, over 13 million women had seen the film.[59]

Many women strongly approved of breast self-examination, seeing as empowering the idea of taking action in an uncertain situation. "My life was saved," announced one Philadephia woman in 1955, "because I practiced breast self-examination."[60] In the same year, another woman told Cleveland cancer specialist George Crile, Jr., that "[p]eople gain some satisfaction from the belief that they have free will and some control over their lives. The individual standing alone in a capitalistic society says 'If I am vigilant it can't happen here.'"[61] Among the strongest advocates for breast cancer screening were women physicians, such as Elise S. L'Esperance of New York's Strang Prevention Clinic, who helped to establish over 250 "cancer detection centers" across the United States.

The ACS, NCI, and the medical profession were aware of the potential pitfalls of promoting routine breast examination. Columbia-Presbyterian Medical Center breast surgeon Cushman D. Haagensen, who appeared in "Breast Self-Examination," instructed women to examine their breasts only once every two months "to prevent the development of an abnormal fear of cancer." Haagensen also urged physicians to examine breasts in a gentle, precise, and orderly manner. Noting that he had seen breasts bruised by rough examinations, he warned that "palpation must never be so heavy-handed that it distresses the patient."[62] A small number of physicians also discussed the psychological repercussions of the search for breast cancer. "The breast . . . is the emotional symbol of the women's pride in her sexuality and motherliness," wrote Richard Renneker and Max Cutler, a Chicago psychoanalyst and surgeon, respectively. "To threaten the breast is to shake the very core of her feminine orientation."[63]

Despite these examples of concern from physicians, women often remained hesitant to join the search for small breast cancers. Many women instructed in BSE, Philadephia physician Catherine Macfarlane reported in 1949, stated, "I should be afraid to do that."[64] Such reluctance likely stemmed from both fear of finding cancer as well as the possible sexual connotations of touching the breast. Yet the ACS and other anticancer organizations chose to disregard this latter issue, never mentioning it during BSE publicity campaigns.

Physicians' examinations of the breasts generated similar problems. Although some of the earlier reluctance of women to expose their private parts to the examining eyes and hands of the male physician had abated, reticence persisted well into the twentieth century. As late as 1966, 19 percent of women surveyed by the ACS admitted feeling embarrassed by a cancer examination and 10 percent said they "dislike[d] a doctor touching [them]."[65] This discomfort likely stemmed in part from the potential implications of viewing and touching the breast. For decades, x-rays and other images of women's bodies, while purportedly obtained for medical purposes, had provided visual and even sexual pleasure to observers.

Breast examinations raised the same concerns about the "male voyeuristic gaze."[66] In order for women and physicians to be taught to perform breast examinations, the ACS and other educational groups needed to generate images of breasts and the proper examination technique. Yet in contrast to medical textbooks, which generally depicted diseased breasts, these new images by definition displayed healthy breasts without obvious deformities. The images varied widely. Some consisted of diagrammatic sketches of women performing or receiving breast examination. Others were photographs of actual women, often cropped to conceal the face of the subject. In many instances, however, the medical images veered into pornography.[67] Women depicted in such images

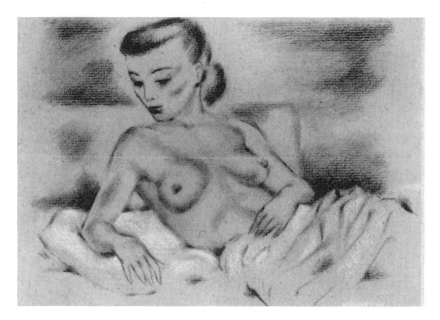

Courtesy of the University of Pennsylvania Archives, I. S. Ravdin Collection.

tended to be young and thin with firm breasts. For example, in a 1951 color pamphlet entitled "Self-Examination of the Female Breast," distributed by the Philadephia branch of the ACS, several very attractive women sit partially undressed in their bedrooms (see figure). Most egregious may have been a 1958 diagram of "Molly the model," a thin and buxom young woman undergoing a breast examination by a male physician. Molly's pose, sitting in panties in a chair with one arm behind her head, was much more suited for a men's magazine than for a doctor's office.[68]

"Don't paw the breast," Haagensen entreated the surgical residents at Columbia. "Caress it."[69] Haagensen's language—like the images of women and breasts contained in educational literature—underscored the sexual and political tensions that characterized the new push to make breast cancer a curable disease. Using data demonstrating the lower mortality rate of early breast cancers, the ACS attempted to characterize routine breast examination in as clinical a manner as possible. But the strategy raised understandable fears and anxieties among both women and their doctors.

C. A. CONSHUS, M.D., Says–

If Molly the model had knowed
That that wee little lump was
a node
She would not have neglected
To have it inspected
Till into a cancer it growed.

C. A. Conshus will tell you
it's best
Not to pass up a lump in your
breast.
Though it may be benign,
It's a clear warning sign,
Get your doctor to give it a test.

POINT — Breast

DANGER SIGNAL — Any thickening in the breast or elsewhere.

Reprinted with the permission of the Pennsylvania Medical Society from the February 1958 issue of the *Pennsylvania Medical Journal*.

And even those women willing to participate in breast examination sometimes balked when they learned what would result from the "successful" detection of a small breast cancer: radical mastectomy. Writing to Crile regarding her sister's unwillingness to see a physician for a breast lump, a Nebraska woman explained: "She has a terrible fear of Cancer, and seems to know that they will remove both breasts if they operate. For that reason I can understand why she would just as soon go along believing that everything is alright just being left alone."[70] In his many writings on breast cancer, Haagensen continually emphasized how fear kept women from examining their breasts and showing lumps to doctors. "She is afraid first that she will be mutilated and second that she will lose her life," Haagensen wrote in 1957. In offering a solution, however, he could address only the second problem: "We need some method of convincing these women they can be cured."[71] Whereas Haagensen was able to acknowledge the disfigurement that a Halsted radical mastectomy entailed, he could not promise patients with breast cancer anything less extensive. To survive, "you basically had to pay a price if you were a woman."[72]

As the campaign to promote breast examinations in the United States accelerated, it was increasingly described in terms of personal responsibility. As with the Pap smear and other anticancer efforts, the language of responsibility drew on three factors: (1) the growth after 1920 of the "new public health," in which an informed public was expected to adopt healthier behavior; (2) American individualism, which prized initiative and action in the face of uncertainty; and (3) the familiar gender roles, in which men assigned women accountability for maintaining health and preventing disease.[73]

Echoing the Women's Field Army propaganda of the 1930s, the breast cancer literature after World War II was replete with admonitions to women to do their duty or suffer the consequences. "Prompt action is the prerequisite to survival," wrote Raymond F. Kaiser of the NCI in 1950. "The key to control of breast cancer lies in the hands of women themselves."[74] A *Look* magazine article on the film "Breast Self-Examination" stated that "American women, properly informed, can virtually conquer the fatal aspects of this dreaded disease by their own initiative."[75] A particularly common approach was to tell the story of a woman whose recent or impending death had resulted from her unwillingness to participate in breast cancer detection strategies.

Characterizing an aspect of medicine in terms of a military campaign ensures that "someone or something must bear the burden of blame for defeat."[76] Thus, it is hardly surprising that the line between responsibility and blame proved quite thin during the war on breast and other cancers. At times the ACS and cancer specialists criticized general

Educational message as it appeared in "Rex Morgan, M.D.," 1952.

practitioners and surgeons who did not actively pursue the diagnosis and treatment of cancer. Male patients received their share of blame if they disregarded any of the danger signals of cancer. But given the long-standing assumption that women needed to maintain their health in order to preserve the family unit, breast cancer patients who had not examined their breasts or reported their lumps promptly were especially "guilty" of "negligence."[77]

In 1945, for example, the popular health magazine *Hygeia* reported that a woman who did not detect and act upon a breast cancer in its "early, most curable stage" had "no one to blame for the consequences but herself."[78] The woman who permitted a breast lump to grow, wrote the surgeon Frank G. Slaughter in 1946, "has committed suicide almost as certainly as if she had blown out her brains with a pistol."[79] Even the comic strip figure Rex Morgan, M.D., criticized women who had not attended a talk he gave on the early detection of breast cancer (see figure). "People," he observed in a 1952 strip, "seem to want something spectacular or dramatic to make them take time out from their usual pursuits."[80]

Another way that physicians assigned blame was to criticize women for their "false modesty"—an unwillingness to display their breasts despite the threat of cancer. Yet, such depictions belittled female anxieties about the dangerous and sexualized meanings of such a display. The persistence of this mindset was evident in a 1981 book on women's health, which continued to cite "late detection"—as opposed to breast cancer itself—as the reason so many women required mastectomies.[81]

Questioning Tradition: George Crile, Jr.

The debates over BSE and breast examinations by physicians were only part of a larger dispute about the "selling" of early cancer detection in the United States. Since its inception, the ACS had been cognizant that its health messages often used alarmist language and the fear of cancer to induce behavioral change. By the 1950s, as the ACS accelerated its efforts to promote Pap smears and routine breast examinations, its publicity practices garnered more scrutiny, both inside and outside the organization. "You must be baptized in the faith that there is a job to be done for cancer," Cameron often told his colleagues.[82] Yet was it ever justifiable to exaggerate the value of early detection if one truly believed that lives could be saved as a result?

One physician who resoundingly answered "no" to this question was George Crile, Jr., who was known as Barney. Barney Crile was the son of George Washington Crile, a highly prominent American surgeon at the turn of the twentieth century. The senior Crile had become a surgeon in the late 1880s, just as radical surgery was coming into vogue. He achieved his greatest fame by describing how many patients receiving radical operations went into shock: their blood pressure fell and their organs received inadequate blood flow. While not rejecting aggressive procedures, the elder Crile, as had Halsted, argued for a "physiological" approach that anticipated and sought to mitigate the disturbances that accompanied surgery. In so doing, his biographer Peter English has argued, George Washington Crile "ushered in a therapeutic revolution."[83]

Crile Sr.'s caveats regarding radical surgery initially generated considerable criticism from both surgeons and physiologists. But as his career progressed, he grew increasingly comfortable with his role as reformer. A prolific writer on both medical topics and their relation to society, Crile was highly driven and supremely confident. At the Cleveland Clinic, which he helped to found in 1924 at the age of sixty, he was simply known as "The Chief." Toward the end of his career, however, Crile's innovative work was challenged by a new group of investigators who studied shock in soldiers during World War I. By sticking to his old ideas, English wrote, "research on shock had clearly passed him by."[84]

George Washington Crile's wife, Grace, gave birth to their third child, Barney, in 1907. Barney Crile grew up in an affluent and often formal household. At dinner, his father wore a tuxedo and his mother an evening gown. Weekends were spent in the country where the family would ride horses. Barney Crile later characterized his father, who had served in the cavalry during the Spanish-American War, as a "dangerous" rider. But despite taking several bad falls, the senior Crile continued to ride.[85]

Barney Crile worshiped his father and planned to become a surgeon from an early age. But he was only an average student, first at University School in Cleveland and then at Hotchkiss. At Yale University, Crile's major interest was in sports; he played football and ran track. Yet during his time at Yale, Crile found one course, entitled "The Science of Society," to be especially compelling. In later years, Crile would claim that this class, taught by a "skeptic and disbeliever named Keller, who accepted no one's word for anything," had "implanted in me the seeds of disbelief."[86] If so, Keller's course ultimately had a profound effect on the history of medicine in the United States. Crile would eventually become the most outspoken heretic in the world of breast cancer surgery or, as one admirer later stated, the person who "brought the can opener to the picnic."[87]

Arriving at Harvard Medical School in 1928, Crile realized that he had been right to follow in his father's footsteps. The language of science, he later wrote, "was almost part of my nature, I had been born to it."[88] Crile performed in a stellar manner at Harvard, graduating first in his class in 1932. Unimpressed with the surgeons he had watched during medical school, he chose an internship at Barnes Hospital in St. Louis. There, Crile studied with Evarts Graham, a renowned surgeon who had recently performed the first successful removal of an entire lung in a patient with cancer.

Crile returned for his general surgery residency to the Cleveland Clinic, where he frequently had professional disagreements with his father. "But when," Crile later asked, "did a son ever heed what his father told him?"[89] Specifically, Crile had "fallen under the spell" of Tom Jones, a highly skilled Clinic surgeon. Jones was a strong advocate of radical cancer surgery, and Barney Crile, eager to learn, began to perform aggressive operations throughout the body. "I was young and stubborn," he later recalled, "and thought bigger must be better."[90] Among the radical operations Crile performed was the resection of a cancer of the pancreas. His patient was only the seventh such person to survive this procedure.

Another development greatly influenced Barney Crile when he returned to Cleveland to train with his father. Despite having lost considerable eyesight due to glaucoma and cataracts, the seventy-year-old senior Crile was still operating everywhere in the body. In the 1930s, few general surgeons subspecialized; many operated not only on the breast and abdomen but also performed gynecologic surgery and neurosurgery. Among the younger Crile's unfortunate duties was being called in to stop the extensive hemorrhaging of blood that resulted from his father's operations on the thyroid and adrenal glands.[91] But the old man remained defiant and continued operating. Barney Crile was left with deeply ambivalent feelings toward his father. On the one hand, he respected how he had challenged surgical tradition. At the same time, however, he identified in his father the same intransigence that the elder Crile had found in others.

Barney Crile entered the military in 1942 and was stationed at naval hospitals in New Zealand and San Diego. In later years, Crile liked to cite this period as the beginning of his apostasy. "My wartime service with the Navy," he wrote in a memoir, "taught me that universal acceptance of a procedure does not necessarily make it right."[92] Specifically, Crile came to question the standard treatment of both appendicitis and pilonidal sinuses. In the case of appendicitis, he questioned the "almost . . . religious principle" that emergent surgical intervention was absolutely necessary, especially on poorly equipped naval vessels.[93] Crile conducted a study demonstrating that patients could safely be stabilized with penicillin until they could be evacuated to better hospital facilities. Similarly, when Crile grew dissatisfied with wide surgical excision of pilonidal sinuses, small cavities in the lower back, he devised an alternative approach that involved shaving the surrounding hair and draining the sinuses with a catheter.

Upon returning to the Cleveland Clinic after the war, Crile had become his father's son, a self-professed skeptic, who "consistently stood against many of the things that most surgeons believed."[94] Crile's major crusade over the next forty years would be to question the "bigger is better" approach to surgery that he had previously embraced. Returning to his father's earlier view of cancer surgery, Crile would argue that smaller operations could often achieve as much as larger procedures, while causing many fewer physical and psychological side effects.

Concurrent with Crile's criticisms of radical cancer surgery, discussed below in Chapter 5, was his revolt against the publicity tactics of the ACS. In the early 1950s, both at medical meetings and in medical journals, Crile expressed doubts about the cancer society's relentless advocacy of early detection followed by aggressive treatment. By 1955, however, he had concluded that his efforts were having little effect because patients never were able to hear and evaluate his arguments. "[A]t every meeting in which I present this [contrary] point of view," he wrote, "the surgeons tell me that in their community the public is so indoctrinated by the concept of early diagnosis and radical treatment that it would be impossible for them to deviate from this much-advertised pattern."[95]

Crile felt there was no other way to "stir up the processes of thought" than to "appeal to the physicians through the public."[96] On October 31, 1955, he published an article, "A Plea Against Blind Fear of Cancer," in *Life* magazine; the next week, Viking Press published his book, *Cancer and Common Sense*. Crile's decision to "go public" with his doubts about early and aggressive surgery was by far the most heretical of his deeds. Codes of medical ethics, such as that issued by the American Medical Association (AMA), equated such behavior with advertising or quackery and thus condemned it. A 1958 AMA document, for example, criticized physicians who "appear in the press as doing extraordinary things above their fellows."[97] Indeed, correspondence regarding the article and book that agreed with Crile's basic arguments nevertheless took him to task for violating the physician-physician covenant. "I think it is too early for the public to be brought in on this," remarked Cleveland surgeon Norman Thiessen. "There are a lot of controversial things in medicine and they should be kept in medicine until we are reasonably sure of our ground."[98]

Messages of Fear

What was the crux of Crile's argument against the cancer society? Writing a year after the Army-McCarthy hearings, which led to the censure of

Joseph McCarthy, Crile charged the organization with demagoguery. "Those responsible for telling the public about cancer," he wrote in *Life*, "have chosen to use the weapon of fear, believing that only through fear can the public be educated." Although Crile did not cite the ACS by name, his target was obvious.

The message of fear, Crile believed, was exacerbated by the media, which exploited the public's interest in the "melodramatic and frightening."[99] In one case, he reported, a seventy-five-year-old woman had suffered an irreversible stroke that had left her paralyzed and near comatose. The family, however, appeared most concerned about whether the patient had cancer, replying "Thank God!" when they were told there was no cancer present. Cancer activists, Crile charged, had created "a new disease, cancer phobia," that "causes more suffering than cancer itself."[100]

In making this claim, Crile was not only referring to the emotional repercussions of ACS propaganda that announced, "No one is safe from cancer" and "Cancer is the greatest and cruelest killer of American women between the ages of 35 and 55."[101] He also was explicitly taking on the dogma of early detection, which he believed to be of clear value for cervical cancer but not necessarily as useful for breast and other cancers. By overemphasizing their point, Crile believed, advocates of early diagnosis led both physicians and patients to favor operations that were either too extensive or entirely unecessary. "I repeat," Crile wrote to a critic of the *Life* article, "cancer phobia is causing death, death resulting from unnecessary operations accepted in cancer's name."[102]

Crile's critique, like most of those he would register over the next decades, was scattershot and arguably as exaggerated as the propaganda he was condemning. One reviewer criticized his "speculative hypotheses, which are products of the imagination."[103] Nevertheless, it was clear that Crile's message struck an important chord with the medical profession and the public. Crile reported that of the roughly 200 letters he received in response to the *Life* article, only seven were unfavorable. A typical response was that of Honolulu physician J. E. Strode, who told Crile that "[m]uch of what you have to say, in my opinion, has been long overdue, and I congratulate you on your courage to speak up in such a forceful manner."[104]

If anything, members of the public were even more vehement in their praise for Crile and their dissatisfaction with the ACS. In criticizing televi-

sion and newspaper coverage of cancer, an Alabama woman who had undergone two operations for benign breast tumors wrote that the "agoniz-
ing, crippling fear of cancer has tried to hold me in bondage."[105] A Texas
woman praised Crile's "sincere truthfulness" as having "lightened the
burdened hearts of many frightened people."[106] One Los Angeles man
who had recently undergone surgery for stomach cancer leveled an especially vitriolic attack on the ACS, claiming that it was "over-emphasizing
[and] over-dramatizing the disease" and thus frightening away patients.
He was most upset about the cancer society's use of military language
and imagery, terming the Sword of Hope "that bloody sword." "I am not
aware that I am making any fight either for or against cancer," he wrote.
"Precisely what can I do about it? What choice do I have?"[107]

Most of the objections to Crile's article and book came from within the
medical profession. Due to both Crile's message and the concerns that he
had violated the ethical standards of medical practice, news of the upcom-
ing Life article had caused a major panic at organizations such as the ACS
and American College of Surgeons. In the days leading up to the article,
University of Pennsylvania surgeon Isidor S. Ravdin, who was active in
both of these groups, participated in a flurry of phone calls and telegrams
aimed at planning a formal response to Crile's charges. Ultimately, Life ran
two responses along with the article: (1) a series of short letters from influential surgeons; and (2) "A Statement Disagreeing with Dr. Crile,"
jointly authored by leaders of the ACS, NCI, and the AMA. Earlier diagnosis of cancer, wrote Charles Cameron and the authors of the joint statement, was still "the brightest hope" for curing the disease. "Dr. Crile,"
they warned, "offers a dangerous, fatalistic philosophy of cancer."[108]

As debate between Crile and his critics raged, some commentators
asked more provocative questions about the role of hyperbole in conducting a public health campaign. "How can we wave a red flag grace-
fully?" queried one physician, Peter J. Steincrohn, in the Washington Evening
Star. "I see no way except to be thankful for any warnings we receive."[109]
Remarking that Crile may have unfairly targeted the ACS, an editorialist in
the Des Moines Tribune wrote, "People did not have to be told that cancer is a
dread disease."[110]

Among the most incisive comments on cancerphobia came from
Cameron himself. These ruminations, however, largely took place behind

closed doors, often at annual meetings of the cancer society between 1949 and 1955. First, Cameron readily acknowledged that the ACS took quite seriously the charges that it caused cancerphobia. In 1949, the society mailed a questionnaire to a sample of members of the American Board of Psychiatry and Neurology "to examine the validity of the charge that cancer propaganda is harmful to the general public by producing an unwarranted increase in the level of fears and anxiety."[111] Having found that only 11 percent of respondents "clearly disapproved" of the program, Cameron interpreted the survey "as offering no reason for us to reduce our pressure."[112]

Yet, in language that nearly echoed that of Crile, Cameron acknowledged the limitations of early detection. "We advertise that early cancer can be cured," he stated, "yet that precept does not apply equally to all types of cancer."[113] In 1952, he went so far as to propose a five-year study of whether early detection worked: "If the precision weapons designed to detect early cancer of the skin, mouth, breast, lung, uterus and rectum . . . cannot produce measurable results in a five year period, we shall have reason to reconsider the validity of all cancer control."[114] Cameron added that he believed the results of such a study would validate the ACS's claims.

Ultimately, however, there was little room for ambiguity during a war. For example, Cameron's best-selling 1956 book, The Truth About Cancer, expressed no doubts about the cancer society's mission. The ACS and other groups did tone down certain aspects of their publicity, such as removing foreboding images of tombstones and avoiding definitive statements such as, "Early cancer can be cured." But for the most part, these organizations continued to emphasize the dual message of fear and hope that the founders of the ASCC had initially promoted. The lay public, wrote an Iowa public health official, "must be imbued with a reasonable optimism as to the curability of [localized] cancer."[115] In this setting, hyperbolic statements were justified as a "principle of health education" if they motivated Americans to save their lives.[116]

In the years after World War II, the American Cancer Society sought to dispel any lingering notions that cancer was a uniformly incurable disease. The organization's rejuvenated campaign to defeat cancer fit well in a country that had just won World War II and found itself engaged in a new global struggle. Yet as the ACS pushed for earlier detection of breast and other cancers, a seemingly paradoxical situation was taking place. Rather than designing less extensive operations to remove smaller cancers, surgeons in the 1950s would develop a series of superradical operations that made Halsted appear conservative. In pursuit of elusive cancer cells, they would remove internal organs, ribs, arms, and legs. Why did a surgical solution to the problem of cancer become even more compelling after 1945?

The Scalpel Triumphant

Radical Surgery in the 1950s

"Today, it should be said, I believe," announced University of Minnesota surgeon Owen H. Wangensteen at the 1950 meeting of the American Surgical Association in Colorado Springs, Colorado, "the Halsted operation for cancer of the breast is outmoded; it is not radical enough; it is an incomplete operation for cancer of the breast in patients exhibiting axillary metastases."[1] Believing that breast cancers reaching the underarm lymph nodes had also already spread to tissues not removed by the standard radical mastectomy, Wangensteen devised the so-called superradical mastectomy, which entailed the splitting of a patient's clavicle, ribs, and sternum (breast bone) in pursuit of cancer cells.

The years after World War II thus witnessed efforts to outdo even Halsted in the attack on breast cancer in the United States. What factors can explain why this occurred? Once again, an examination of military metaphors helps to provide an answer. Just as the language of war revealed the cultural and professional forces that promoted early detection of cancer, so, too, such metaphors spoke to the surgical profession's ability to establish the criteria by which the successful treatment of cancer would be evaluated. As on the battlefield, courage and valor in the operating room would almost become ends unto themselves.

The postwar era also permits a closer examination of the influence of gender on breast cancer therapy. Throughout the 1950s, surgeons carried out superradical operations for numerous types of cancers, removing any organs and limbs believed to contain cancer. One surgeon even accused a colleague of having performed a "humanectomy."[2] Does the existence of these extensive operations for other cancers refute the feminist critique about the sexist and misogynistic underpinnings of breast cancer surgery? Or did gender still play a major role?

Lessons of War

There has long been a popular association between surgeon and soldier. Writing in 1862 about the growth of surgery during the early nineteenth century, New York physician Austin Flint noted that "the daring surgeon enjoyed somewhat of the eclat which belongs to the hero of the battle-field."[3] In 1923, surgeons John Deaver and Stanley Riemann described the modern surgeon as a "general armed . . . for the battle against insidious disease."[4] More concretely, advances made during emergency wartime operations have provided skills for the returning surgeon. In World War I, for example, surgeons gained experience using blood transfusions to treat shock.[5]

During World War II, hundreds of prominent and soon-to-be-prominent American surgeons, such as Edward D. Churchill, Dwight E. Harken, and Claude E. Welch, served in the armed forces. Future leaders in breast surgery—George Crile, Jr., of the Cleveland Clinic, Edward F. Lewison of Johns Hopkins University, and Donald J. Ferguson of the University of Chicago, to name but a few—served as well. These surgeons rarely performed cancer operations during the war, but they gained experience treating conditions ranging from appendicitis to amputations to the removal of bullets and shell fragments. "I felt at home in any part of the body," Ferguson later recalled, "after fishing shrapnel out of people from head to toe."[6]

Technological advances promoted the surgical cause. Whereas Barney Crile was using penicillin and the other new antibiotics to forestall surgery, many surgeons were using these so-called "God's powders"[7] to attempt previously unthinkable operations, such as open-heart surgery. These antibiotics, surgeons believed, prevented the postoperative infections that often caused death in patients who had done well during the operation. Indeed, the Surgeon General had reported a remarkable 96 percent survival rate among injured World War II military personnel.[8]

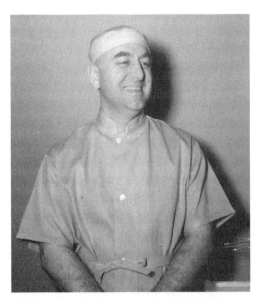

George T. Pack, circa 1940.

Courtesy of Helen Pack.

Returning surgeons, and those who had remained in the United States, drew an explicit connection between wartime developments and the future of cancer surgery. The answer to cancer treatment, wrote the physician Frank Slaughter in *The New Science of Surgery*, "lies in the same principles that have saved thousands of lives during World War II—early surgery and adequate surgery."[9]

As a result, cancer researcher Michael Shimkin later noted, "surgeons went radical and then superradical" during the decade following World War II.[10] Foremost among these surgeons was George T. Pack of Memorial Sloan-Kettering Hospital in New York. Born in Antrim, Ohio, in 1898, Pack had an early experience with heroic surgery. When he developed appendicitis as a high school student, his family doctor had performed a lifesaving appendectomy on the family's kitchen table. Pack went on to study pathology at Ohio State University before enrolling at the Yale University School of Medicine. By all accounts, Pack was a brilliant student. Upon graduating from Yale in 1922, he was named Professor of Pathology at the University of Alabama School of Medicine. Because he preferred taking care of patients, Pack subsequently completed a surgical residency at Memorial Hospital between 1928 and 1931. He also spent considerable time at the Curie Foundation Institute of Radium in Paris, receiving training in radiotherapy.[11]

Upon completing his surgical training, Pack leapfrogged up the chain of command, being named Chief of the Gastric Service at Memorial in 1931. Once in his new position, Pack "boldly attacked the problem of cancer of the gastric cardia [body of the stomach]."[12] For decades, surgeons had operated on cancers located only at the lower end of the stomach, known as the pylorus. Rejecting the commonly accepted notion that other stomach cancers were inoperable, Pack devised a series of procedures permitting the removal of the complete stomach. These operations, known as total gastrectomies, required the surgeon to reconnect the esophagus to the intestines. An even more aggressive procedure used for far-advanced stomach cancer was the extended total gastrectomy, which also removed the spleen and pancreas in an en bloc dissection. In 1958, Pack and colleagues reported that 25 percent of patients undergoing potentially curative operations for gastric cancer had lived for five or more years.[13]

Emboldened by wartime improvements in anesthesia and blood transfusion, as well as the availability of antibiotics, Pack began to apply radical surgical techniques to other types of cancers. Although a growing number of surgeons had begun to subspecialize, operating, for example, only on the head and neck, general surgeons such as Pack remained comfortable operating almost anywhere in the body. As of 1966, organs he removed for cancer included the esophagus, pancreas, spleen, and colon (large intestine). He also removed up to 80 percent of the liver for cancers involving that organ. By this time, Pack had performed over 200 interscapulothoracic ("fore-quarter") amputations, which entailed separation of the clavicle (collarbone), scapula (shoulder blade), and an arm when these portions of the body contained breast or other cancers. He had also completed over 200 hemipelvectomies, which required removal of the "hind-quarter": a leg and an adjacent bone from the pelvis.[14]

Fellow surgeons admired Pack's dexterity in the operating room. "To see his skillful use of the scalpel," the New York surgeon Roald N. Grant remarked, "was an unforgettable experience for thousands of surgeons."[15] Pack, in contrast to many of the Halstedian surgeons of the era, was also fast. On certain days, he traveled to New York, New Jersey, and Connecticut, operating at hospitals in all three states. Pack also performed surgery in many foreign countries, operating on, among others, Argentina's Eva Peron, when she was diagnosed with cervical cancer in 1951.[16] "George Pack," concluded fellow surgeon Max Chamberlain, "has accomplished more than eleven surgeons would in their combined lifetimes."[17] Pack's surgical colleagues praised his legendary status at a 1963 Christmas Party by composing a rhyme to the tune of the popular song "Mack the Knife":

> In the morning
> In the O.R.
> Comes a surgeon
> Big as life.
> And they tell me
> He needs no urgin
> For they call him
> Pack the knife.[18]

Pack was hardly the only surgeon performing superradical operations after 1945. His colleague at Memorial, Alexander Brunschwig, had designed an operation, known as pelvic exenteration, for the treatment of end-stage gynecological cancers. Brunschwig recommended this operation for women whose cervical, uterine, or ovarian cancers involved multiple pelvic organs and were otherwise untreatable. The most radical version of exenteration involved removal not only of the women's gynecological organs, but also the bladder and rectum. A patient's ureters were inserted into her colon, which in turn was connected to the outside by a colostomy. It was through this opening in the abdomen that patients would permanently pass both their stool and urine.[19]

The use of superradical procedures in the 1950s was not limited to the United States. Surgeons such as Erling Dahl-Iversen in Denmark, M. Margottini in Italy, S. A. Kholdin in Russia, and Eduardo Caceres of Peru (who trained at Memorial Sloan-Kettering) mastered such operations and pioneered others. However, radical surgery achieved its greatest popularity in America, mostly at large medical centers that had the staff and facilities to carry out such extensive procedures.[20]

Surgeons learned these superradical techniques by observing colleagues either at institutions such as Sloan-Kettering or the University of
Minnesota, where Owen Wangensteen had built a remarkably innovative
surgical department. Born to hardworking Norwegian parents on a farm
in Park Lake, Minnesota, in 1898, Wangensteen had had as meteoric a career as Pack, having become chief of surgery at his alma mater in 1930 at
the age of thirty-one. Wangensteen placed special emphasis on experimental laboratory research and devised multiple new operations based
on this work. In addition to the superradical mastectomy, these included
the so-called second look operation for colon and other cancers, in
which Wangensteen prophylactically explored the abdomens of patients
who had no clinical evidence of recurrent disease.[21]

Superradical surgery received favorable coverage in American popular
magazines. A 1956 *Reader's Digest* article, for example, reported on a woman
from Oklahoma who had had 80 percent of her cancerous liver removed
(presumably by Pack) at Sloan-Kettering. "[H]er name," wrote the author,
"can be chalked up in the winning column in the ceaseless battle against
cancer."[22] In a 1958 piece entitled "Victims Turned Victors," *Life* reported
that 800,000 living Americans had been cured of cancer, many by aggressive operations.[23] *Time* magazine conveyed this hopeful message in 1963
when it announced to its readers that "if they can operate, you're lucky."[24]

In developing these operations, Pack, Brunschwig, and their contem-
poraries drew on existing understandings of cancer physiology, namely,
that "the cure of cancer implies that the cancer should be eliminated
completely from the body."[25] "Everyone really believed," retired Cleveland surgeon Robert Hermann recently recalled, "that the secret to cancer
surgery was to take more—bigger operations, wider fields, chase down
the lymph nodes."[26] The radical surgeons often cited the wartime improvements in intraoperative and postoperative care as having enabled
them to perform procedures that would formerly have been too dangerous. Yet, it is wrong to interpret such statements as proving that new
technologies, such as blood transfusion and antibiotics, were themselves
the primary causes of advances in cancer surgery after 1945. Rather, as
with the rise of the Halsted radical mastectomy earlier in the century, social factors led to the acceptance of superradical surgery as a medically
indicated procedure. Specifically, such operations gained popularity be-

cause they fit with a cultural climate that saw increasingly aggressive invasion of the body as an appropriate way to counteract disease.[27]

The relationship of military metaphors to surgical practice after World War II helps to demonstrate this point. Factors such as masculinity, self-esteem, hope, and individualism have always promoted "wars" against disease.[28] With the successful defeat of Nazi Germany and Japan, the apparent value of such concepts had become much less abstract. American soldiers, who were mostly men, had, through a combination of optimism, determination, courage, and perseverance, successfully vanquished their enemies.

It was these exact traits that surgeons sought to bring to America's postwar battle against cancer. Indeed, it might be argued that the fight had become less metaphor than simile. The surgeon, like the soldier, literally needed to conduct all-out war, just as the United States had done in places such as Normandy and Hiroshima. Terming breast cancer a "formidable enemy," Columbia-Presbyterian surgeon Cushman Haagensen wrote in 1946 that performance of insufficiently radical surgery "is nothing less than surgical cowardice."[29] "Disease still stands relentlessly barring our way," Pack wrote in 1953. "We shall have to wrestle with it often and fiercely before the final conquest. For today, the victory must lie in the struggle itself."[30]

The degree to which medical interventions had almost come to have a military justification was perhaps best exemplified by the so-called "commando operation," a radical surgical procedure for head and neck cancer that became popular after the war. The term "commando" actually had nothing at all to do with its medical basis, but rather commemorated the fact that the cancer operation had been developed at New York's Memorial Hospital just as the Allies were launching their commando raids on Dieppe, France.[31] Success on the battlefield, it seemed, portended success in the operating room.

Surgeons were only too happy to become the soldiers of the postwar era. Although the status of the surgical profession had risen throughout the first decades of the twentieth century, surgeons had returned from the war with an even greater "confidence and bravado" that led one surgeon to claim that all surgeons were "cancer specialists."[32] The growing authority of surgeons after World War II was exemplified by their growing use of mechanistic, reductionistic language to describe their efforts. "One may justifiably and ruthlessly remove multiple organs if the patient thereby is given a reasonable prospect of a cure or a shorter life worth living," Pack wrote in 1951.[33] "The purpose of the surgeon to divorce the patient from his cancer appears to be limited solely by the ability of the human remnant to survive." Although such stark language generates discomfort today, Pack was merely conveying in dramatic form the great promise that radical surgery seemed to offer for cancer in the 1950s.

America's affinity for aggressive surgery was hardly surprising. Just as the American Cancer Society invoked personal responsibility when encouraging breast self-examination among women, so, too, did superradical operations appear to demonstrate American initiative. "[I]ndividualism, fighting spirit and the power of thought to shape one's life course," the sociologist Deborah Lupton has written, "are particularly evident in American society."[34] Anthropologist Howard F. Stein has agreed, noting how Americans' search for "rapid, instant and disposable" solutions has caused "greater directedness" on the part of clinicians.[35] In such a setting, the radical, activist surgeon had become a "kind of culture hero."[36]

Many American surgeons themselves either explicitly or implicitly acknowledged how cultural factors influenced their work. University of Pennsylvania surgeon Isidor S. Ravdin, himself a former two-star general who had been chief of medical operations in the China-India-Burma theater during World War II, patriotically termed radical surgery done early in the course of disease an "All-American operation."[37] "We surgeons and all who profess to be enlisted in the service of our fellowman," Wangensteen stated, "are on our own individual pilgrimages."[38] Brunschwig liked to remark that he was uninterested in surgeons who had done 1000 of the same operations. "Tell me about the guy who did the first one," he would state.[39] "[T]o create a better America and eventually a better world," Pack wrote, "it is necessary for the individual citizen to acquire a consciousness of his own responsibility and destiny in the nation." Each individual, he continued, needed to utilize "his talents in full," becoming, "by his conduct, his work, his thought and his relationships with his fellowmen . . . a positive force for good." In Pack's case, his goal was clear: "to cure more cancers than anyone else in the world."[40]

As Pack's statement suggested, this drive to be the "biggest or best" was not limited to the operating room. Sloan-Kettering's Jerome Urban was perhaps at his most competitive when fighting a strong wind during yacht races in St. Croix. Partially paralyzed after a 1987 stroke, Urban continued to race his yacht and make frequent presentations on breast cancer surgery at meetings throughout the world. At Urban's funeral in 1991, former American Cancer Society Medical Director Arthur I. Holleb explicitly equated Urban's "remarkable zeal for his surgical studies" with any outdoor activity that was "competitive and somewhat risky." Urban's behavior, Holleb stressed, symbolized his "passionate hatred of breast cancer."[41] Pack, despite his busy operating schedule, somehow also managed to find the time to raise Guernsey cows that consistently won blue ribbons at the National Dairy Congress. Even after four episodes of congestive heart failure in his sixties, Pack continued to operate.

"A Chance to Cut Is a Chance to Cure"

Although the aggressive cancer surgery performed after World War II played into admired American cultural traits, it would not have achieved such acceptance and praise unless physicians and patients thought that it worked. Surgeons did generate data that they believed indicated the efficacy of superradical cancer surgery. But the nature of these statistics and the manner in which they were presented earned them a legitimacy that went beyond the numbers reported in medical journals.

Postwar cancer surgeons did acknowledge the limitations of their craft. "For anyone to imply," stated Ravdin, "that the surgical profession refuses to realize the present inadequacies of surgical therapy is a gross exaggeration of the truth."[42] Radical surgeons took pains not to minimize the often dramatic consequences of their operations. Brunschwig readily termed his pelvic exenteration a "brutal and cruel procedure."[43] Other surgeons, such as Pack and Wangensteen, cautioned that much of what radical procedures often accomplished was palliation as opposed to cure.

Despite these caveats, surgeons enthusiastically recommended radical operations to many patients. For one thing, palliation itself was often a reasonable goal, particularly for patients whose cancers caused them ongoing pain and suffering. Surgeons were well aware that many cancers had advanced to the point where only a portion of the tumor could be removed. "Those one, two, three and four years of comfort that have been given by the application of surgical methods," Pack wrote in 1952, "must not be discarded as failures."[44] Although other surgeons clearly would have disagreed, Mississippi surgeon Dawson B. Conerly even termed radical mastectomy in a patient with positive axillary lymph nodes a "palliative procedure in the management of cancer of the breast."[45]

Yet at the same time, the lines between "cure" and "palliation" and between "surgical cure" and "permanent cure" remained blurred despite periodic efforts to clarify them. After all, it was hard to imagine a cancer patient awakening from surgery and not wanting to know if the surgeon had "gotten it all." As an old surgical adage went, "a chance to cut is a chance to cure." This powerful image of a surgeon heroically removing all the cancer, which persists among patients and families today, obscured the fact that many cancer operations did not actually have such a goal.

Surgeons themselves often conflated the actual medical rationale for radical cancer surgery with the presumed value of performing such challenging operations. In other words, surgeons became proponents of specific radical procedures because they had been trained in an environment that saw surgical bravado as desirable.[46] Thus, articles in the medical literature praised not only radical surgery but the surgeons who performed these procedures. In advocating the "widest radical surgery untrammeled by ancillary radiation," British surgeon Gordon Gordon-Taylor cited his "sharp knife," "stout heart," and "unquenchable optimism."[47] A surgeon, wrote Pack, "must have a vicarious form of courage to suffer these patients' illnesses, consider them objectively and do the operations if it is actually possible for it to be done."[48]

It was not simply the act of cutting that portended a favorable outcome but also the skill of the experienced surgeons who operated. "Cut well, tie well, get well," was a saying popularized by the noted Baylor University heart surgeon Denton Cooley. The most telling surgical aphorism may have been, "Lesser surgery is done by lesser surgeons," a favorite of Memorial Sloan-Kettering's Jerry Urban. In this phrase, Urban pithily conveyed the sentiments of a generation of surgeons who equated more surgery with both better skills and better outcomes. Given such beliefs, the ability to do heroic cancer surgery came quite close to being an end unto itself. As his University of Minnesota colleague Harold S. Diehl wrote in a somewhat circular tribute to Owen Wangensteen in 1962, "[h]is brilliant and daring pioneer work in the extension of gastrointestinal and breast surgery has given the medical profession a more profound sense of what 'radical' surgery can mean."[49]

Despite their faith in the inherent value of skillful cancer operations, surgeons nevertheless required some type of evidence that radical and superradical procedures worked. One powerful type of "proof" used was the case study. Pack, for example, was not only a master surgeon but a master salesman for what he could accomplish. Physicians at Memorial Sloan-Kettering had often heard the story of how Pack had performed his first total gastrectomy for stomach cancer in the 1930s: he had defied the orders of a senior surgeon who had said the operation was not indicated and that the patient was terminal. The man subsequently lived for over twenty years. On another occasion, Pack invited a prominent New York surgeon to give grand rounds on stomach cancer at Memorial, knowing full well that this physician believed that patients with the disease were incurable. At the end of the conference, Pack introduced about twenty patients with stomach cancer who had survived at least five years. As Pack's colleague Guy Robbins recalled, "this quieted down the guest speaker."[50]

Even though such cases were anecdotal, these narratives of cure inspired both surgeons and patients. One woman, having read the 1956 *Reader's Digest* article on radical surgery, wrote Barney Crile asking why her sister with liver cancer was not a candidate for radical liver removal.[51] A patient treated for melanoma took a similar stance. "At any time during the two years [of therapy]," he stated, "if I or my doctor had accepted the fatalism of melanoma, I wouldn't be here today."[52] At times the data were more visual in nature. An article by Brunschwig published in *Cancer* in 1948 contained a photograph of a smiling, healthy-appearing woman who had undergone pelvic exenteration four and a half months earlier with few residual difficulties.[53] Even though Brunschwig did not make such a claim for his palliative operation, the picture strongly suggested that she had, indeed, been cured. In a review article on pelvic exenteration published in *Cancer* in 1948, Brunschwig noted that no prospective patient had refused the operation that he himself had called "brutal and cruel."[54]

Breast Surgery: What Medicine Did Best

Given the growing emphasis on increasingly radical surgery, it was hardly surprising that surgeons such as Owen Wangensteen and Jerry Urban decided to devise breast cancer operations that were more extensive than the Halsted procedure. Based on the existing medical knowledge regarding cancer, there was logic to these efforts. As Halsted himself had realized, the decision to limit the dissection to breast, axillary nodes, and pectoral muscles was arbitrary. A certain percentage of breast cancers, by definition, had moved beyond these areas and could thus not be cured by the standard operation. A 1949 paper by two English physicians, surgeon Richard S. Handley and pathologist A. C. Thackray, made this point vividly. In fifty patients with breast cancer, Handley and Thackray biopsied the internal mammary lymph nodes (located under the rib cage) adjacent to the cancerous breast. The authors found that nineteen (38%) of the women had positive nodes; moreover, this figure increased to 52 percent if the women had positive axillary nodes and to 70 percent if the cancer was located in the medial (inner) half of the breast.[55]

Wangensteen saw these data as a call to action. A surgeon, he stated, was like a hunting dog whose pursuit of a pheasant had been blocked by a fence. But, Wangensteen reminded his colleagues, "the surgeon has the alternative of taking the fence down."[56] Missouri's Everett D. Sugarbaker agreed, warning his colleagues against "surgical hopelessness."[57] Wangensteen's superradical mastectomy entailed the dissection of four more sets of lymph nodes than the Halsted radical, including the supraclavicular nodes (which Halsted had attempted) and the internal mammary nodes. Urban's extended radical mastectomy, which would later earn him the appellation "the most radical of the radical surgeons,"[58] was similar to Wangensteen's operation. To remove the internal mammary nodes, Urban removed several ribs and split the sternum with a chisel. Patients received a large skin graft at the operative site. In contrast to Wangensteen, however, Urban omitted dissection of the supraclavicular nodes.

Women diagnosed with metastatic breast cancer in the 1950s became candidates for other interventions, such as the surgical removal or irradiation of the estrogen-producing ovaries. By eliminating a woman's ability to produce estrogen, physicians could slow down or reverse the growth of some advanced breast cancers. Surgeons also attempted much more dramatic procedures to alter hormonal status, such as the removal of both adrenal glands or the pituitary gland located near the brain.[59]

Not Wangensteen, Urban, nor the other surgeons who emulated them discounted the gravity of these operations. Of the first 64 breast cancer patients who received a superradical mastectomy from Wangensteen or his colleagues, eight (12.5%) died during or shortly after the procedure. One of these may have been an obese, diabetic woman with palpable axillary nodes, on whom Wangensteen's colleague George E. Moore performed his first and only superradical breast operation. The patient died shortly after the operation. "I shouldn't have done it," Moore recently stated.[60] Superradical breast surgery was also highly disfiguring. In addition to the extensive tissue loss that accompanied a standard radical mastectomy, women undergoing the procedure were left with a permanent defect in the rib cage that created a marked concavity in the center of their chests. If the surgery was performed on the left side, only a thin layer of skin stood between the patient's heart and the outside of her body. In some cases, despite the grafting of skin and subcutaneous tissue from other parts of the body, the normal landmarks of the remaining breast and nipple were lost altogether.[61]

Surgeons had performed equally dramatic operations for breast cancer before, such as Pack's arm removals and the operations to suppress hormonal function. But these procedures had been palliative, buying time for patients with metastatic breast cancer who had no other options. The new radical breast surgery, in contrast, was designed for potentially curable breast cancers—usually those located beneath the nipple or in the medial portion of the breast. In treating such patients, surgeons were by definition offering procedures to some women with breast cancers that had not spread beyond the area covered by the standard radical operation. For example, out of the first 175 patients who received Urban's extended radical mastectomy between 1951 and 1955, only 63 (36%) had positive internal mammary nodes.[62] In retrospect, therefore, the other 112 patients had lost portions of their ribs unnecessarily. Yet the performance of needlessly radical surgery on the majority of patients did not deter Urban or his colleagues. By 1978, surgeons at Memorial Sloan-Kettering had performed over 900 extended radical mastectomies.[63] As would increasingly become the case over the next several decades, many breast cancer patients were treated aggressively to potentially cure the few.

Despite Urban's continued advocacy, the extended radical mastectomy won only a limited number of converts. First, in order to complete the operation without complications, a surgeon needed to have the considerable skills of Urban. Second, the statistical evidence in favor of the operation was far from conclusive. Although Urban estimated that extended radical mastectomy in selected patients improved five-year survival by roughly 10 percent over a radical mastectomy, others found no difference between the Halsted operation and more radical variants.[64] As a result, neither the extended nor superradical breast operations gained significant followings.

Left without a reliable operation of the ultraradical variety, surgeons after World War II embraced the standard radical mastectomy with new fervor. By the mid-1940s, the previous decade's debates over the use of surgery versus radiotherapy had been settled in favor of the Halsted procedure. Pack and Livingston, in their influential 1940 textbook, The Treatment of Cancer and Allied Diseases, had called for an end to "radiological experimentation," claiming that radical mastectomy consistently produced better survival rates.[65] Similarly, Haagensen reported that five-year survival after radical mastectomy at Columbia-Presbyterian had gradually increased from 26.6 percent in 1915–19 to 52.5 percent in 1940–42, attributing this improvement to both earlier detection of breast cancers and more meticulous surgery. "Every single carcinoma cell must be removed if cure is to be achieved," he wrote, "and a thoroughly radical operation offers the best chance of accomplishing this."[66]

In 1943, Memorial Hospital's Frank E. Adair published an extremely influential paper on radical mastectomy in the Journal of the American Medical Association. Reviewing 1,383 cases of breast cancer treated at Memorial between 1920 and 1936, Adair found that the five-year survival rate of those who had received a radical mastectomy was 62.8 percent as compared with only 24.2 percent of those receiving only radiotherapy. On this basis, he rejected the use of radiation as the primary treatment for breast cancer. Yet Adair and other breast surgeons did advocate the use of postoperative radiation to the underarm area, particularly when the axillary lymph nodes removed during a radical mastectomy revealed cancer.[67]

Cushman D. Haagensen, circa 1945.
Courtesy of Alice Haagensen.

To some degree, the growing support for radical mastectomy stemmed from the encouraging statistics that Haagensen and Adair were generating. In addition, the postwar climate favoring extensive surgical intervention also promoted the operation, once more radical versions had been rejected. But other cultural factors particular to breast cancer focused attention on the Halsted radical mastectomy as the paradigmatic operation for cancer surgery. Most notably, these included a revival of the meticulous approach to surgery epitomized by Halsted's original breast operation and the beliefs of the male surgical profession about the aging breast.

The rebirth in interest in Halstedian surgery can be traced to the efforts of Columbia's Haagensen. Like Wangensteen, Haagensen was of Norwegian ancestry. Born in North Dakota in 1900 to a country doctor and his wife, Haagensen went to the University of North Dakota and then Harvard Medical School, graduating in 1923. After completing an internship at Boston City Hospital, however, his plans were interrupted: he developed pulmonary tuberculosis and took the rest cure for three years.

When Haagensen returned to medicine in 1929, his early interest in general surgery had shifted to the study of cancer. To learn more about this topic, he undertook laboratory research, first at Memorial Hospital and then at Columbia-Presbyterian Medical Center, where he moved in 1932. Once Haagensen arrived at Columbia, the renowned surgical pathologist Arthur Purdy Stout became his mentor. Interestingly, although Haagensen had been hired by the department of surgery, he had never actually completed formal training in the field. As a result, perhaps, Haagensen ultimately chose to limit the surgery he performed to the radical mastectomy.

One of the major influences on Haagensen during his Harvard years had been Harvey Cushing. Cushing, the preeminent neurosurgeon in the United States in the first half of the twentieth century, had trained under Halsted at Johns Hopkins. Haagensen rapidly became enamored of the meticulous surgical technique that Cushing had learned from Halsted and passed down to his residents. Once in New York in the early 1930s, Haagensen had spent considerable time observing the operations of another Halstedian surgeon, George Semken, at the city's Knickerbocker Hospital.[68]

Despite all of the attention paid to breast cancer, few physicians in the 1930s and 1940s showed an inclination to become specialists in the field. For one thing, the diagnosis and treatment of breast cancer was fairly straightforward; many general practitioners even performed mastectomies themselves. Most general surgeons performed breast operations, but viewed other procedures—such as gastrointestinal surgery—as more challenging. Indeed, excluding gifted surgeons such as Jerry Urban, it was often said that surgeons who focused on the breast were not able to perform more complicated operations.

Haagensen, with his reverence for Halsted, viewed this situation as paradoxical. Given that the legendary surgeon had used breast cancer to highlight his surgical technique and his theory of the centrifugal spread of cancer, it seemed to Haagensen that the diagnosis and treatment of breast cancer deserved special emphasis. During the 1940s and early 1950s, Haagensen gradually became America's "first breast specialist,"[69] culminating with the publication of his comprehensive textbook, Diseases of the Breast, in 1956.

Haagensen's writings on breast cancer reflected both his deep interest in the disease and his allegiance to Halsted's principles. "I have too much respect for breast cancer not to give it my best shot," he often remarked.[70] An enormous amount of the 1956 book was devoted to the pathology of breast cancer, an area in which Haagensen, like Halsted before him, had become an expert. Haagensen, his longtime colleague Raffaele Lattes wrote, was "an excellent surgical pathologist who did not need any help in interpreting the histological findings on his own patients."[71] Haagensen's office at Columbia was located in the Department of Surgical Pathology.

Foremost in Haagensen's teaching to residents was the need to perform surgery with the bloodless Halsted technique. "We believe sincerely," he stated, "that it is a fundamental principle of cancer surgery that it must be meticulous, gentle [and] precise."[72] Along these lines, Haagensen, unlike most surgeons, refused to burn away tissue with an electric cautery when performing a radical mastectomy. The cautery, he believed, caused cancer cells to enter the bloodstream. Instead, Haagensen dissected with a scalpel and smooth forceps only, tying off each individual blood vessel with small mosquito clamps and the finest silk sutures. As had Halsted, Haagensen believed that such a careful dissection, performed en bloc, with a skin graft from the thigh, and encompassing breast, skin, axilla, and pectoral muscles, was the only way to ensure that all possible cancer cells had been safely removed. The Haagensen version of the Halsted operation also stressed the importance of closing the surgical wound with thin skin flaps. That is, the surgeon needed to painstakingly remove any potentially cancerous breast tissue that remained adherent to the skin. The skin had to be so thin, Haagensen often remarked, that one could read a newspaper through it. As generations of impatient surgical residents learned, he viewed the axillary dissection as incomplete unless thirty to forty lymph nodes were removed. Given the delicate nature of Haagensen's radical mastectomy, the operation generally took five to six hours to complete. "Weary not in well doing," Haagensen often stated, quoting the gospel of St. James.[73]

Both Haagensen and his surgical philosophy generated criticism. Many found the tall, intense surgeon to be either aloof or authoritarian, too unwilling to listen to other points of view.[74] Some surgeons ridiculed the long operations performed by Haagensen and other Halsted devotees, arguing that there was no proof that slower surgery was superior. To them, Haagensen's claims that adequate radical mastectomies had to last at least five hours and invariably required a skin graft made little sense. Tales that circulated about radical mastectomy demonstrated this skepticism. One such story, often told by Barney Crile, concerned a surgeon at Boston's Peter Bent Brigham Hospital in the 1930s who was a devotee of the traditional Halsted procedure. Upon noting one afternoon that this surgeon had been operating on the same patient since early morning, a colleague had apparently chided him: "Hurry up . . . or it will metastasize."[75] In another instance, when a particularly methodical surgeon asked the anesthesiologist, "How is the patient, doctor?" his colleague had supposedly replied, "Much older, doctor."[76]

Despite such criticism, Haagensen's focus on breast diseases and his invocation of Halsted proved immensely popular among many surgeons. The year 1952 was the 100th anniversary of Halsted's birth, and his disciples formed a Halsted Centennial Committee to honor him. At the celebration, held in Baltimore on February 6–9, 1952, speaker after speaker cited the Hopkins surgeon's continued influence. University of Cincinnati surgeon B. Noland Carter even went so far as to construct a genealogy that connected Halsted and his residents to the then-current surgical leadership in the United States. The fact that the innovations of a man born 100 years earlier still dominated surgical practice was celebrated, not questioned. "I was very proud of that pedigree," New Haven surgeon Sherwin B. Nuland recently recalled.[77] Also in 1952, the *Reader's Digest* featured Halsted in its column, "The Most Unforgettable Character I've Met." A Halsted-like cult began to form around Haagensen, with trainees remarking that "everything I know about breast surgery I learned from Dr. Haagensen" and thanking Haagensen for having "guided our lives" in "this troubled world."[78]

Surgeons also relished the technical aspects of the surgery carried out by Haagensen and other Halsted devotees. As Haagensen liked to state, the radical mastectomy was "elegant" and "satisfying." By definition, each operation was identical: the surgeon identified the familiar landmarks and performed as meticulous a dissection possible. While performing a radical mastectomy, Haagensen would urge those in attendance to study the well-dissected axilla, which was "like an open book" before the surgeon.[79] "There was something beautiful about skeletalizing the axillary vein," Nuland stated. "Part of the aesthetic was these complicated beautiful dissections we used to do."[80] In this manner, radical breast surgery in the 1950s achieved both a ceremonial and a ritual status, representing the pinnacle of the surgeon's art.[81]

Many surgeons also found appealing the image of the "gentleman surgeon" embodied by Halsted and Haagensen. When Beall Rodgers visited Presbyterian Hospital in 1947 as a prospective resident, the surgical staff reminded him of the surgeons depicted in the famous Thomas Eakins painting, *The Agnew Clinic*. "I looked around at that young group of residents and the attendings in their starched white coats, all of them wearing neckties, all of them with hair cuts. . . . I said I want to join them. This is where I want to be."[82] Rodgers was well aware that some of these surgeons were arrogant prima donnas, even with violent streaks. Yet just as Halsted's mastectomy gained prominence due to its curious mix of radical but gentle dissection, so, too, were breast surgeons a combination of soldier and gentleman.

For their part, many women patients responded positively to the image of the all-powerful doctor. Upon learning from her physician husband that she would need a radical mastectomy if her breast lump turned out to be cancerous, Marion W. Flexner "tried hard not to disappoint him."[83] When starting a possible radical mastectomy in 1959, George Pack discovered the following note attached to his patient's surgical gown:

I hope in your probings that you will find
These bothersome lumps to be pure and benign.
If God has chosen the other way
Don't spare me doctor, tell me this day.
Bodily pain is easier to take
The other an adjustment I must make.
Whatever the story, courage I don't lack
I trust and love you, dear Doctor Pack.[84]

Haagensen received countless letters from grateful patients, thanking him "not only for a successful operation, but for [his] kindness and great understanding."[85] One radical mastectomy patient relished having "found a doctor who cares enough to take the time to do it right."[86]

It is important to examine such statements critically. With patient autonomy and informed consent still twenty years away, American physicians in the 1950s possessed enormous power. The occasional breast cancer patient who made her own decisions notwithstanding, doctors in this era had almost unlimited discretion in determining what treatment a breast cancer patient would receive. Indeed, articles in both medical and lay publications reported that many physicians also chose whether or not to inform cancer patients of their diagnoses. "I am convinced," New York surgeon Henry W. Cave wrote in 1955, "that not to know the truth will cause the least mental anguish to many patients and that a surgeon may have to carry out deception, no matter how distasteful this may be to him."[87] Of course, many patients, especially those with cancer of an external organ, such as the breast, eventually were told or figured out their diagnoses.

Having received a recommendation of radical mastectomy from a benevolent, paternalistic physician, most women simply accepted this advice. Perhaps they might not have done so had they learned that doctors were actively discussing other treatment options amongst themselves and that small numbers of women were seeking out alternative therapies. Nevertheless, for both physicians and women in the 1950s, radical mastectomy, with its direct connection to the pioneer Halsted and the rise of modern "scientific" surgery, came to embody the best of what medicine had to offer all cancer patients.[88]

"One of the Most Dispensable Parts of the Body"

To what degree did gender account for the continued devotion of male surgeons to the Halsted radical mastectomy? As we have seen, surgeons in the 1950s readily performed aggressive surgery on both male and female patients with cancers of the stomach, colon, or extremities, removing these body parts with extensive dissections that produced crippling debilities even as they potentially extended life. Surgeons also attacked prostate cancer with considerable gusto in this era, treating men with the radical prostatectomy, which removed the prostate gland, seminal vesicles, and a portion of the bladder. As with breast cancer, this operation was used even for tiny cancers incidentally discovered when an enlarged prostate was removed to relieve urinary obstruction. More often than not, men receiving a radical prostatectomy wound up incontinent of urine and impotent.[89]

Yet the ways in which male physicians conceptualized the cancerous female breast further promoted its radical removal. General surgeons, who were overwhelmingly male, dutifully noted the breast's central role in providing sexual pleasure to women and men and nurturance to newborn babies. The breast, Pack and Livingston had stated, had important "sexual, esthetic and psychological significance."[90] At the same time, however, many male physicians saw these functions as having only temporary importance. That is, when a woman had finished having her family and had (presumably) experienced a decline in sexual appetite, the importance of keeping one or both breasts declined considerably. This was especially true, moreover, in the presence of life-threatening cancer.

Multiple articles on breast cancer in the medical literature thus characterized the aging female breast as expendable. The breast, as described by one surgeon, was a "nonvital and functionless gland."[91] New York's Roald Grant termed the breast "one of the most dispensable parts of the body."[92] This type of language was not limited to American surgeons. Canadian physician T. A. Watson termed the breast "a superficial easily disposable utilitarian appendage."[93]

Such statements were grounded in the sexist assumptions of male-dominated society. Just as David Reuben, in his 1969 bestseller, *Everything You Always Wanted to Know About Sex*, would argue that menopausal women were not functional women and lived "in the world of intersex,"[94] male physicians discounted the importance of breast loss in women who were menopausal or had finished nursing their children. "We can say [her breasts] have served their purpose and she is now ready to accept their retirement," wrote the Chicago physicians Richard Renneker and Max Cutler in 1952.[95] Since doctors readily recommended radical mastectomies for younger women with cancer, male opinion of breast utility was hardly the only relevant factor in determining which women received surgery or what operation they received. Yet, medicalized characterizations of normal aging breasts as "ptotic" (drooping) or "atrophic" (wasting away) could not but help promote the notion that they were somehow defective and thus especially expendable if cancer was present.[96]

The perception of the female breast as expendable likely encouraged a small number of physicians to propose prophylactic mastectomy of the remaining breast in women diagnosed with breast cancer.[97] Once again, this proposal was based in part on medical data: such women were at higher than average risk of developing cancer in the remaining breast. "The breasts are paired organs and should be considered as an anatomic system," argued breast surgeon Henry P. Leis, Jr.[98] Yet the concept that the second breast should be "sacrificed," with its connotations of male rescue and female renunciation, also spoke to existing gender stereotypes.

Perhaps the most striking example of the enormous power of the surgical profession in the years after World War II was the behavior of certain of its members. When confronted with a frustrating situation in the operating room, they screamed at residents and nurses and flung instruments against the walls. One junior surgeon recalled how he was accosted after failing to describe a patient's anatomy to an attending surgeon's satisfaction:

> He never said a word until one day I met him in the elevator and he grabbed the front of my shirt and pushed me up against the wall. And he said, "Have you had second thoughts? Have you really learned now how to do the anatomy? Give it to me."[99]

Although some of these outbursts led to suspensions, such bullying was, for the most part, tolerated. Surgeons, despite their flaws, represented the best—indeed, only—hope in the fight against breast cancer. Yet this authority rested less on the proven value of the radical mastectomy than what it had come to represent: an intervention that combined growing scientific knowledge and surgical precision with American ingenuity and heroism. The experiences of World War II easily lent themselves to the metaphorical postwar battle against breast cancer.

Male surgeons advocating radical and superradical mastectomies were not simply sexists or sadists "biased toward surgical solutions and overly willing to perform unnecessary operations" on women.[100] The expansion of radical surgery for breast cancer—like other cancers—resulted most directly from the authority of the surgical profession to establish how cancer would be defined, explained, and then treated. Yet the role played by gender should not be ignored. Because male-dominated society devalued the breasts of aging women, cancer surgeons viewed these organs as particularly expendable. When women rebelled against the radical mastectomy in the 1970s, they would challenge this notion that physicians had the right to decide what their patients valued. But a more immediate threat to surgical authority was on the horizon. Just as radical surgery was reaching its apogee, a group of critics began to question the basic assumptions that underlay Halsted's theories about breast cancer.

A Heretical Interlude

Biology as Fate

"*[T]*he doctrine of synonomy of 'early' treatment and curability should be recognized for the shibboleth which it is."[1] With these words, published in 1951, Los Angeles cancer surgeon Ian MacDonald committed no less than apostasy. As his colleagues were pushing the frontiers of surgical intervention to new limits, MacDonald was challenging the very foundation on which such operations were based: Halsted's belief that early, aggressive intervention cured more cancers. Rather, MacDonald argued, the behavior of breast and other cancers was "biologically predetermined"—there was often little that the medical profession could do to alter the fate of cancer patients.

MacDonald was hardly the first physician to challenge Halsted, but his words fell on fertile ground. As breast cancer surgery grew more radical in the 1950s, a small but growing number of surgeons were becoming uncomfortable. A percentage of women diagnosed with breast cancer also objected to radical operations and at times insisted upon lesser procedures.

What made the debates over early intervention in the 1950s so powerful, however, was the growing role played by biometricians, statisticians who studied biologic data. These critics, many of whom lived outside the United States, conducted sophisticated statistical analyses that challenged the standard assumptions that early detection of breast cancer was indeed "early" and that radical surgery actually "cured" breast cancer patients. While preliminary and themselves controversial, the new studies nevertheless were the first to make the claim that the biology of individual breast cancers played a major role in prognosis. And the research was also a harbinger of the growing role that biostatistics and epidemiology would subsequently play in debates over managing breast cancer at the bedside. The assumption that individual surgeons could and should determine the best treatment for individual patients could no longer be taken for granted.

Early Voices of Caution

When Geoffrey Keynes had first argued against routine radical mastectomy in the 1930s, his reception at surgical meetings in the United States had been far from positive. "None of us have been burnt at the stake," he wrote in 1954, "but feelings have run pretty high."[2] Even in his native England, an admirer remarked, he was regarded as an "eccentric."[3]

Yet even as Keynes was being vilified, several novel research studies were calling into question what radical breast surgery was said to accomplish. For example, in both England and the United States, researchers had charted the outcomes of breast cancer patients who had received no treatment at all. One such study was published by Boston surgeon Ernest P. Daland in 1927. Daland reviewed 100 cases of untreated Boston women with breast cancer, including those whose cancers were too far advanced to warrant surgery, those whose medical problems made surgery too dangerous, and those who had simply declined an operation. Women in this latter category were hardly limited to Boston. One was the writer Charlotte Perkins Gilman, who refused a mastectomy at the time of her diagnosis and ultimately committed suicide three years later when the disease progressed.[4]

Daland discovered that the 100 women had lived an average of 40.5 months, or over three years, after being diagnosed with breast cancer. Their overall five-year survival was 22 percent.[5] Whereas this figure did not match that of a comparison group of 66 treated women, 42 percent of whom had lived five years, Daland nevertheless believed that his results were "extraordinary."[6] Treatment of operable patients had not even doubled five-year survival.

Daland's own conclusion was understated, noting that future evaluation of breast cancer therapies needed to take into account "that many of the patients would have lived many years without such treatment."[7] As debates over breast cancer treatment grew increasingly heated over subsequent decades, however, Daland's work would often be cited as having demonstrated that radical surgery was of little or no value. Once, Daland recalled regretfully in 1961, a colleague introduced him as "Dr. Daland, who believes in no treatment."[8]

A contemporaneous line of research, initiated by another Boston surgeon, Robert B. Greenough, challenged physicians to view breast cancer as more than just one disease. Drawing on earlier work by the German pathologist D. P. von Hansemann and his own training in surgical pathology, Greenough claimed that microscopic examination of breast cancer specimens revealed three classes of disease: cancers of low malignancy (class I), which were usually cured; those of high malignancy (class III), which were usually lethal; and those of medium malignancy (class II). In a study of 73 patients published in 1925, Greenough found that 13 (68%) of 19 patients with class I cancers were alive after five years, compared with 11 (33%) of 33 patients with class II cancers and zero out of 21 patients with class III cancers.[9] Although Greenough remained a strong advocate of the Halsted radical mastectomy throughout his career, this research suggested to some physicians that the treatment of all breast cancers by a uniformly radical method was illogical.

Related to Greenough's work was the concept of "clinical staging," in which surgeons estimated the spread of breast cancer before they performed operations. In 1905, a German physician named Steinthal had divided his cases of breast cancer into three stages: stage I, small tumors apparently localized to the breast; stage II, larger tumors that involved the axillary lymph nodes; and stage III, tumors that had invaded the tissues surrounding the breast. Having concluded that he could not cure his stage III patients by surgery, Steinthal stopped operating on them.[10]

Although staging became quite popular in Germany and Scandinavia, it did not become commonplace in the United States until the 1950s, with the work of Cushman D. Haagensen and Arthur Purdy Stout at Francis Delafield Hospital in New York. Delafield, opened as a public hospital by New York City in 1950, was affiliated with Haagensen and Stout's home institution, Columbia-Presbyterian Medical Center. As surgical pathologists, both men agreed with Greenough's notion that cancer cells could reveal degrees of malignancy. They also grew interested in staging, noting that "the first step toward [the proper use of surgery] is careful selection of patients for whom it can be used with benefit."[11] In 1949, Haagensen and Stout reviewed 495 radical mastectomies performed at Presbyterian Hospital between 1935 and 1942, finding that more than half of the women had either died or had recurrent breast cancer.[12]

By the early 1950s, Haagensen and Stout had developed the Columbia Clinical Classification System, which staged breast cancers from A to D, of which only A and B were considered operable. The letters A to C roughly corresponded with Steinthal's stages I to III. Stage D, later known as stage IV, referred to breast cancer that had metastasized throughout the body. The development of staging systems for breast and other cancers, which led to patients being deemed operable or inoperable (and, by extension, curable or incurable), further enhanced the authority of surgeons to dictate the management of cancer.[13]

But Haagensen and Stout's system, like others based on preoperative clinical assessment, had one major limitation. Once surgery had been performed and pathologists had examined the mastectomy specimen, inaccuracies in the original staging could be discovered. For example, it was well known that roughly 30 percent of patients with a negative axilla on physical examination would ultimately be found to have breast cancer in these lymph nodes. Clinically stage I, such patients actually had stage II disease. Because staging thus generated confusing information, Haagensen and Stout in the early 1950s developed a technique designed to increase the accuracy of preoperative assessment: the triple biopsy.

As had his role model Halsted, Haagensen emphasized the importance of following breast cancer patients over time. Haagensen's staff at Columbia thus devoted considerable resources and time to maintaining contact with all of the surgeon's patients. Indeed, as an emeritus professor in 1984, Haagensen would publish data regarding 1,036 patients, some of whom he had followed for forty-seven years.[14] Haagensen was convinced that his follow-up system enabled him to identify pathological findings that reliably indicated inoperability. These included evidence of disseminated cancer at the time of operation, such as spread to the liver or bones, or evidence of extensive disease in the region of the affected breast.[15]

Haagensen used this information in devising his triple biopsy, in which he examined tissue from the original breast mass, the internal mammary lymph nodes, and the nodes at the apex (top) of the axilla. Haagensen declined to perform radical surgery on women found to have cancer in the breast and in either of the other two areas. Believing that such patients were incurable, he sent them for palliative radiation therapy.

As Haagensen expected, the use of the triple biopsy substantially lowered the operability rate. In reviewing the cases of 156 women who received a triple biopsy between 1952 and 1955, Haagensen reported that only 79 (51%) had received a radical mastectomy. Use of the triple biopsy had prevented thirty-seven more "futile" radical mastectomies than his usual stringent clinical staging criteria would have. The roughly 50 percent operability rate was in marked contrast to the "indiscriminate use of the operation" at other institutions in New York State, which Haagensen claimed was as high as 93 percent.[16]

Although Haagensen was quite certain that the triple biopsy prevented unnecessary surgery, the technique irked surgeons at institutions such as Memorial Sloan-Kettering, who favored giving as many women as possible the chance of a surgical cure. While not doubting Haagensen's intentions, these surgeons believed he was being far too stringent in so limiting his use of radical mastectomy. Indeed, it is worth remembering that Haagensen, who would be excoriated by women activists in the 1980s as one of the last supporters of the traditional radical mastectomy, was for years more commonly criticized as being too conservative in his application of the Halsted procedure. Haagensen was almost a "non-Halstedian," his future rival Bernard Fisher would later admit, in his suggestion that "one more lymph node dissection will not cure more cancers."[17]

As Haagensen sought to restrict the use of radical mastectomy to patients with only stage A or B disease, a radiotherapist was arguing that a different treatment could cure even more of these cases. Reviving a strategy that had attracted some adherents in the 1930s, Robert McWhirter of Edinburgh's Royal Infirmary began to treat all of his operable breast cancer patients with a combination of simple mastectomy and radiotherapy to the axillary, supraclavicular, and internal mammary node areas. It is not surprising that this latest challenge to Halsted emanated from the British Isles, whose physicians were not indebted to the Johns Hopkins surgeon and were the most experienced radiotherapists in the world.[18]

McWhirter's efforts stemmed in part from his belief that case selection by Haagensen and others was exaggerating the utility of the radical mastectomy. Because surgeons published the results only of cases they had treated, the overall value of the procedure as a therapy for all cases of breast cancer in a community was not being assessed.[19] In presenting the five-year results of his own technique in 1948, therefore, McWhirter was careful to include all cases of breast cancer that had been referred to the Royal Infirmary in 1941 and 1942. McWhirter reported that 197 of 459 women (43%) had survived five years; in contrast, between 1935 and 1940, when radical mastectomy had been the main treatment at the Infirmary, only 32 percent of patients had lived five years. He also reported that five-year survival among his patients who had qualified for simple mastectomy and radiotherapy was 62 percent, a figure that even topped Haagensen's statistics.[20] McWhirter hypothesized that his results were superior to radical mastectomy because surgeons, despite their *en bloc* technique, spread cancer cells throughout the body when performing axillary dissections. Another advantage of his strategy, McWhirter stated, was that postoperative swelling of the arm was "almost unknown."[21]

Even though they supported McWhirter's plea for standardized data reporting, surgeons challenged his findings. Some emphasized the side effects of radiotherapy, which had lessened, but still persisted. Others, such as California surgeons David H. Sprong, Jr., and William F. Pollock, objected to the seemingly irrational omission of lymph node dissection, stating that the thought of deliberately leaving cancer—albeit irradiated cancer—in the axilla "is not an attractive one."[22] Yet most of McWhirter's critics, in a pattern that would become numbingly familiar at medical meetings over the next quarter-century, simply presented their own case series, which had supposedly attained better five-year survival rates. To break this impasse, McWhirter allowed an eminent pathologist, Lauren V. Ackerman of Washington University in St. Louis, to review his data. Concluding in 1955 that there was "nothing magical" about McWhirter's work, Ackerman remained unconvinced of the superiority of less extensive surgery. For one thing, Ackerman noted, forty-seven women receiving simple mastectomy and radiotherapy had suffered "extensive irradiation damage," such as lung fibrosis and rib fractures.[23]

As had been the case with Keynes, criticism of McWhirter's data often approached the personal, in both England and the United States. Upon hearing a presentation by McWhirter in 1948, English surgeon Reginald Murley later recalled, the surgical section of the Royal Society of Medicine responded with "studied disbelief, indeed, rudeness."[24] When being coached for his examinations in surgery, English surgeon Harold Ellis was warned, "Harold, don't mention McWhirter when you go up for your examinations [or] they'll kill you."[25] After a presentation at the University of Cincinnati, where Halsted disciple Mont Reid had long advocated radical mastectomy, surgeons there made "ashes and blood" out of McWhirter.[26] The threat posed by McWhirter's technique was so great that few noticed when Memorial Sloan-Kettering's Frank E. Adair, himself an ardent advocate of radical mastectomy, commented at a breast cancer symposium attended by McWhirter that "[t]he interesting fact in comparing these papers is not their great differences but in the striking similarity of therapeutic results."[27]

Although McWhirter's name would most commonly be associated with the "heresy" of the 1950s and 1960s, when the hegemony of the radical mastectomy received its strongest challenge to date, McWhirter was a Halstedian. That is, he accepted Halsted's theory that breast cancer spread in a centrifugal manner and that treatment needed to emphasize thorough local and regional control of the disease. McWhirter simply believed that his technique of simple mastectomy and radiotherapy achieved Halsted's goal better than did Halsted's operation. As such, the true rebels of this period were Ian MacDonald and his fellow biological predeterminists, who provided early evidence that the claims being made about the lifesaving potential of prompt breast cancer detection and radical surgery were exaggerated.

Biological Predeterminism

MacDonald's decision to take on the cancer establishment emanated from his growing dissatisfaction with the claims made for "early diagnosis" and "prompt treatment." Decrying the notion that cancers discovered earlier were necessarily smaller and more curable, he wrote that "[a]ny experienced clinician realizes that such an oversimplification is sheer absurdity."[28] Also stimulating MacDonald was a rather wide streak of iconoclasm. The son of a Baptist minister and a 1928 graduate of the McGill University Faculty of Medicine in Montreal, MacDonald had received training in pathology, radiotherapy, and surgery over the next decade. Some of this training had taken place at New York's Memorial Hospital, where staff members were actively debating the merits of surgery versus radiotherapy in the treatment of cancer. Eventually, MacDonald settled in Los Angeles, where he worked at both Los Angeles County Hospital and St. Vincent's Hospital. Like Barney Crile, MacDonald reveled in taking opposing viewpoints and challenging dogma. This contrariness was most evident in MacDonald's persistent unwillingness to acknowledge the link between cigarette smoking and lung cancer, vilifying the "Volsteadian intent" of anticigarette campaigns well into the 1960s.[29] Ironically, MacDonald would die in 1968 after inadvertently setting himself on fire while smoking.

In the case of breast cancer, MacDonald had fewer blinders. In a 1951 article in *Surgery, Gynecology and Obstetrics*, entitled "Biological Predeterminism in Human Cancer," MacDonald presented retrospective data suggesting that both promptness of presentation and the size of a breast cancer had considerably less influence on outcome than was generally accepted. Thus, of 53 patients who had come to the doctor within one month of finding a lump, 31 (59%) already had cancer in the lymph nodes, and thus had a worse prognosis than those with negative nodes. At the same time, 10 (56%) out of 18 breast cancers that were one centimeter or less in diameter had already spread beyond the breast. MacDonald presented similar data showing that women who had delayed for long periods of time or had large tumors (over five centimeters in diameter) at times had negative axillary nodes.[30]

Suffering from the same selection biases that McWhirter had criticized, MacDonald's findings were hardly representative of all breast cancer patients. Nevertheless, he believed that his data demonstrated that early intervention for breast and other cancers was being oversold. In other words, so-called early cancers were not necessarily early in their course nor more localized when discovered. What determined the outcome of breast and other cancers, MacDonald posited, was less the promptness of treatment than their "biologic potential." As a result, physicians were administering futile radical treatment for many cancers that were predestined to be lethal. "Rigid ideas of prognosis in terms of duration and dimension," MacDonald concluded, "should be abandoned in favor of an attempt to evaluate the biological potential of a neoplasm in an individual host."[31] MacDonald acknowledged that little was known about such biologic factors but suspected that they were related to the inherent aggressiveness of the cancer cells and the patient's bodily defenses.

Surgery, Gynecology and Obstetrics printed another article in 1951 that made claims similar to those of MacDonald. In reviewing the published literature on breast cancer, W. Wallace Park and James C. Lees agreed with MacDonald that breast cancer propaganda routinely confused "early in the sense of less extensive and early in the sense of shorter duration."[32] Moreover, Park and Lees argued, the term "five-year cure" was being used in an inexact manner. Not only did such a phrase conflate cure and survival, as others had pointed out, but it wrongly implied that the chosen intervention had effected the cure. That is, just because women diagnosed promptly and treated with a radical mastectomy survived five years did not necessarily mean that either the early diagnosis or the radical nature of the surgery was responsible. Yet these apparent cures served as a powerful validation for the surgical enterprise. In actuality, Park and Lees estimated, radical treatment actually improved survival from breast cancer in only 5 to 10 percent of cases. Once again, biology was key.[33]

Although they were also clinicians, Park and Lees had not come to most of their conclusions based on clinical work. Park, who was Scottish, and Lees, who was English, were biometricians. Their article was replete with complicated statistics and graphs that were almost entirely unknown in journals such as Surgery, Gynecology and Obstetrics. To be sure, the application of statistics to medical practice had a long history, dating back at least as far as the "numerical method" developed by France's Pierre Louis in the early nineteenth century. By using data from aggregate numbers of patients, Louis had argued that the common medical practice of bloodletting was of dubious value. But as the medical historian Harry M. Marks has argued, Louis's teachings had relatively little influence over the next century. Prior to 1950, investigators continued to rely on clinical experience as opposed to statistics in assessing treatment efficacy. Park and Lees's paper would actually presage what Marks has termed the "triumph of statistics" in medicine, in which physicians finally acknowledged the importance of statistical findings among populations of patients.[34] Indeed, Park and Lees issued a clear warning to clinicians about the role that the biometrician would henceforth play in the evaluation of medical interventions. In the world of biometrics, they wrote, the patient had become a "unit":

> We do not treat a woman with a lump in the breast as an individual cancerous patient on whom skill and craftsmanship suited to the individual problem should be applied. We treat her as a unit in the class of cancer of the breast with the assumption that all units of the class are equally subject to three or four rules of probable behavior which have been found empirically to hold for the class regarded as an aggregate of equal units.[35]

Another biometrician who began to study breast cancer after World War II was a Canadian of Scottish ancestry, Neil E. McKinnon. McKinnon had graduated from the University of Toronto Medical School in 1921 and had completed additional training in both medicine and pathology. However, he subsequently joined the university's School of Hygiene, giving up clinical practice for a career of teaching public health and running a laboratory involved in vaccine and serum production.

Writing in 1993, a former student, David Stinson, recalled that McKinnon's lectures "were even more eccentric than he. Students stayed away from them by the hundreds."[36] But Stinson also admiringly remembered McKinnon's startling pronouncements on breast cancer beginning in 1947. Mortality from the disease in Ontario, McKinnon had discovered, had not changed appreciably from 1909 to 1947 despite widespread educational efforts by lay cancer societies in Canada. A later study performed by McKinnon had confirmed that death rates in England, Wales, Denmark, and five states in America had also remained stable during this period. These data convinced McKinnon that the "insistent propaganda and publicity" regarding breast cancer control in Canada and elsewhere had achieved little.[37]

Consistent with the theory of biological predeterminism, McKinnon provided two related explanations as to why early detection and radical surgery had not lowered the death rate from breast cancer. First, he posited that cancers discovered when confined to the breast were usually slow-growing, indolent lesions that had "little if any tendency to give rise to metastases."[38] Because women would not have died from these cancers in the first place, removing them did not actually prevent a breast cancer death. "Curing non-lethal lesions," McKinnon opined in a 1955 article, "does not reduce mortality."[39] At the same time, he argued radical surgery had no impact on breast cancers that would ultimately kill women because such tumors had spread—via the bloodstream—prior to the surgery. Thus, McKinnon concluded, radical mastectomy was too much in the case of stage I cancers and too little for those that had reached stage II or beyond. McKinnon was well aware that his claims, if correct, entirely invalidated Halsted's theory that cancer spread gradually and locally. Yet he warned that dogmatic authority was both "an effectual obstacle to truth and a ready means of self-deception."[40]

Meanwhile, an energetic and highly committed physician in New York, Maurice M. Black, was reaching nearly identical conclusions, but through the study of pathological specimens. A man of diverse interests, Black also wrote poetry about breast cancer for his patients and colleagues. A 1943 graduate of New York Medical College, he joined the school's faculty in 1949. Under the tutelage of his mentor, Francis D. Speer, Black became an expert pathologist, with a particular interest in breast cancer. Black both reviewed tissue specimens and saw patients, which was common for pathologists in the 1950s. What struck Black from his earliest inquiries was the heterogeneous nature of the disease—that is, all breast cancers did not appear similar under the microscope. Building on Greenough's work, Black concluded that pathological specimens revealed important information about both the biology of a patient's tumor and how well her body was fighting it. For example, Black argued that the so-called nuclear grade, which reflected the configuration of cell nuclei seen under the microscope, helped him determine the aggressiveness of individual patients' breast cancers. Cancers of high nuclear grade had a good prognosis and thus did not require drastic treatment. Agreeing with McKinnon and Park and Lees, Black also concluded that radical mastectomy did not appreciably alter outcomes, even in unfavorable cases. Patients with aggressive cancers died anyway.

When Black and Speer published their early findings in a 1953 article in the New York State Journal of Medicine, they made five points:

1. The five-year survival is invalid as criterion of cure.
2. Five-year survivals are not appreciably influenced by delays of weeks or months before surgical intervention.
3. The majority of so-called operative cases of breast cancer have already undergone occult dissemination [i.e., silent metastasis] at the time of surgery.
4. The curative effect of radical mastectomy does not exceed 10 per cent.
5. The use of ultraradical surgical attempts to cure breast cancer is not consistent with the biology of the disease.[41]

The authors believed that their work both supported MacDonald's theory of predeterminism and began to explain the biological factors that were at play.

These critics of traditional beliefs and practices proved to be thorns in the side of the cancer establishment, constantly challenging physicians at medical meetings to justify their continued advocacy of early, radical breast surgery. Black, for example, continually railed about the "power of ritual, vested interests and wishful thinking over reason."[42] But Barney Crile was losing patience with these efforts to create change within the system. In addition to taking on the publicity tactics of the American Cancer Society in his 1955 *Life* magazine article and *Cancer and Common Sense*, Crile had also approvingly cited MacDonald's theory of biological predeterminism. What good is earlier diagnosis, he asked, "if there is no good reason to believe that people would live longer as a result of earlier treatment?"[43] Concurrently, Crile strongly criticized the use of superradical cancer operations. Such surgery, he wrote in *Life*, was too often a "cruel waste" that "causes great expense, untold suffering and usually shortens the span of life."[44]

This critique of aggressive cancer surgery was not limited to iconoclasts such as Crile and MacDonald. Johns Hopkins University surgeon Harvey B. Stone analogized such operations to "burning down the barn to get rid of the rats."[45] Superradical procedures led to "shocking disfigurement" as well as an inability, depending on the operation, to speak, walk, work, eat, or digest food. Taking aim at his colleagues, Stone stated that "the surgeon who has great manual dexterity and great courage, not combined with good judgment and a sense of responsibility, is a dangerous

George Crile, Jr., with surgical residents, circa 1958.
Courtesy of the Cleveland Clinic Foundation Archives

person."[46] "[I]t seems to me," commented an unnamed professor of surgery in a 1954 article, "that a good deal of misery has been perpetrated upon patients on grounds that they have an incurable disease anyway."[47] Superradical surgery, according to another critic, was "cutting an inch wider and deeper each year, until we are sometimes through into the mattress."[48]

Crile's most controversial position was not his critique of superradical surgery but rather his growing opposition to standard radical cancer operations. For example, in 1950 he discontinued radical neck dissections on patients with papillary cancer of the thyroid, which he believed was slow-growing and responsive to treatment with oral thyroid extract. In 1955, Crile also completely stopped performing the classic Halsted radical mastectomy, likely becoming the only surgeon in the United States to have done so. Crile had become friendly with Reginald Murley, who had recently reviewed Geoffrey Keynes's data on the treatment of breast cancer at St. Bartholomew's Hospital from 1930 to 1939. Murley and his colleagues had essentially confirmed Keynes's results, finding a "remarkable similarity in survival rates" among patients receiving radical mastectomy or one of several other treatment strategies, which included simple mastectomy or tumor excision, often with supplemental radiation. Murley's results convinced Crile that any treatment that excised the primary cancer and either removed or irradiated the axillary lymph nodes provided as effective local control of breast cancer as did a radical mastectomy.[49]

Crile was also influenced by a patient who, several years earlier, had "stubbornly refused" anything but excision of her breast cancer and had survived for over fifteen years.[50] Just as the miracle cures of super-radical operations encouraged surgeons to offer such procedures to other patients, Crile's case indicated to him the merits of limited surgery. Beginning in 1955, he offered either a simple mastectomy (breast removal only) or a lumpectomy (which he termed "partial mastectomy") to selected patients, although most received a modified radical mastectomy, a Halsted-like procedure except that it left one or both of the chest wall muscles in place. Intimately related to Crile's rejection of radical surgery was the participation of the patient in the decision-making process. "I have always believed," he wrote to a patient, the famed environmentalist Rachel Carson, in 1960, "that intelligent people in responsible positions . . . are entitled to know everything that is known about such ailments."[51]

The publication of Crile's arguments in the lay press elicited powerful testimony critical of the traditional approach to cancer. Discussing her sister, one woman wrote to Crile that "[s]he needed your book, not the five major operations which failed to prolong her life and made what was left of it a torture."[52] Several friends, wrote a Pennsylvania man, "had radical operations for cancer and lived only a short time."[53] Health professionals also wrote to Crile. "Many of our surgeons," wrote a Brooklyn physician, "seem to have forgotten that the human being has a soul and with their radical procedures have certainly not improved the status of the patients they had hoped to assist."[54] Among the most powerful statements came from a New York City nurse. Radical surgery, she wrote, had caused "untold suffering and human degradation . . . . I see patients brutally tortured everyday—though the torture is inflicted with the most humane intentions."[55]

Radical breast surgery raised additional concerns, as women struggled with the loss of a body part associated with femininity and motherhood. For example, a Texas woman, whose breast and chest wall muscles had mistakenly been removed although there was no cancer present, told Crile, "I was defeminized, nothing would ever be the same."[56] Other physicians reported similar testimony from breast cancer patients. In the 1940s, Oliver Cope, a Boston surgeon who would later become an ardent opponent of radical breast surgery, saw several patients whose mastectomies had caused them anguish. "I feel abnormal, having lost my breast," one of the women told him.[57] Another revealed to Cope "how disrupting, how depressing it had been to have to accept the disfigurement."[58] This type of reaction strengthened the resolve of Crile and Cope to challenge the dogma of radical breast surgery.

To be sure, patients of Jerry Urban or George Pack who had undergone radical or superradical breast surgery would likely have found such accounts puzzling. After all, didn't the more complete operation offer the best chance of survival? But women with breast cancer chose different strategies for dealing with their disease and then responded differently to the treatments they received. Unfortunately, physicians in the 1950s proved as unable to address this variability in women's responses to breast cancer as they were unable to acknowledge the biological variability of the disease. As a result, the concept of biological predeterminism became a lightning rod for increasingly contentious debates over what aggressive breast cancer screening and treatment could accomplish.

"To Rely on Biologic Character Atrophies Thought"

The American cancer establishment proved quite willing to air the views of its opponents. For example, many of the articles that questioned the value of early breast cancer intervention appeared in American surgical journals, most notably *Surgery, Gynecology and Obstetrics*. Both Lees and McKinnon were invited to participate in a roundtable discussion at the Second National Cancer Conference, held in Cincinnati, Ohio, in May 1952, and cosponsored by the American Cancer Society, the National Cancer Institute, and the American Association for Cancer Research. Massachusetts General Hospital surgeon Grantley W. Taylor, in welcoming Lees to Cincinnati, thanked him for challenging "some of our basic assumptions in regard to cures and curability of cancer."[59] Despite these overtures, however, any sincere attempts to evaluate the statistical arguments of the predeterminists would continually be hindered by concerns about nationalism, professional authority, and the proper role of determinism in medicine.

For their part, the biological predeterminists often viewed members of the Halsted school with contempt. In Cincinnati, surrounded by breast cancer experts who viewed early detection and immediate, radical surgery as gospel, Lees remarked that such a model was "great nonsense and contradicted by all practical experience."[60] "[E]very clinician knows from his own experience," McKinnon stated in Cincinnati, "that neither a small lesion nor a short duration in typical cancer provides a reliable basis for a good prognosis."[61]

Following their presentations, Taylor responded to both McKinnon and Lees in Cincinnati in a humorous manner. For example, after McKinnon's talk he remarked that "the devil can quote scripture to his purpose."[62] Yet the presence of such comments at a scientific meeting also bespoke the intense frustration and even anger that the predeterminists' papers had engendered. That both McKinnon and Lees were foreigners did not go unnoticed. "I wish we could let you run on and hear the rest of your thoughts," Taylor remarked to Lees, "but we have mustered a considerable number of people who are eager to, not rend you limb from limb, but at least show evidence of surviving critical capacity among your American readers."[63]

Another major source of tension stemmed from the claim that the population-based statistics of McKinnon and other biometricians had become appropriate guides for clinical practice. For decades, the American Medical Association and other physician organizations had emphasized the role of the educated and beneficent doctor in reaching proper clinical decisions. Although medical practice very much relied on scientific inquiry, the art of medicine required physicians to craft individualized treatments based on knowledge of their patients.

During his presentation in Cincinnati, McKinnon had offered his standard statistical argument that radical mastectomy was almost always unnecessary, either entailing too much or too little surgery. In responding, Taylor clearly indicated his dissatisfaction with use of aggregate data to guide patient care. "A great many of our patients," he stated, "would rather be live women with one breast than appear on [a] mortality table with Dr. McKinnon."[64] A similar disdain for McKinnon's work was conveyed in an article by a fellow Ontario physician, Ivan H. Smith, who wrote that "optimism and service are not usually willing to wait because of a statistical interpretation."[65] The implication was clear: statisticians needed to stay off of physicians' turf. "I have a congenital distrust of straining statistical methods in evaluation of the surgical approach to any disease," admitted Seattle surgeon Charles E. MacMahon.[66] Even Ian MacDonald was uncomfortable with some of the conclusions made by Park and Lees, at one point terming them "those dour wizards of biometry."[67]

Because Crile and MacDonald were American surgeons, and thus part of the "club," the response to them was somewhat more tongue in cheek. Crile, for example, was chided by Harvard Medical School Professor of Surgery Francis D. Moore for having "taken the McWhirter bait, hook, line and sinker." Moore asked Crile, "How does it taste?"[68] Yet Crile was hardly immune from obloquy, not infrequently being chastised and even ridiculed by certain colleagues at surgical meetings. At the 1955 meeting of the American College of Surgeons, for instance, one physician "castigated" Crile and the publishing of his *Life* article during the breast cancer session.[69]

Beyond issues of nationalism and professional identity, what most disturbed American critics of biological predeterminism was its seeming fatalism. Ongoing public health campaigns against tuberculosis, polio, and other infections firmly rejected the inevitability of disease, instead emphasizing salubrious measures that individuals and communities could undertake.[70] Control efforts for breast cancer had followed the same pattern, with the optimistic propaganda of the American Cancer Society consciously underscoring the curability of promptly treated cases.

Thus, the seemingly nihilistic message offered by the predeterminists caused particular concern. Saying that each cancer had an inherent "biological character," argued Memorial Sloan-Kettering pathologist Fred W.

Stewart, was "merely another way of saying that a cancer is cured because there is something about it that is curable." Reliance on such teleological reasoning, he concluded, "atrophies thought."[71] "[T]herapeutic defeatism is the fashion," rued one set of authors in 1957.[72] The view that all breast cancer treatment is futile, Mayo Clinic physicians reported in the *Lancet* in the following year, was reaching young physicians beginning their careers and the general public. The effect, they wrote, was "confusing and demoralising."[73] As expected, a major foe of a biological explanation of breast cancer was indefatigable Memorial Sloan-Kettering surgeon Jerome Urban, who criticized the "unwarranted fatalistic enigmatical attitudes" of the predeterminists.[74] Given the military overtones of breast cancer control, it is hardly surprising that one physician even looked forward to the day when "the therapeutic nihilist can be annihilated!"[75]

In retrospect, MacDonald's choice of the term "biological predeterminism" may have been unfortunate. What he and his followers were actually describing was the biological variability of breast cancer, a concept that was quite widely accepted. Indeed, a closer reading of the medical literature indicates how many of the predeterminists themselves strove to emphasize that early intervention was of some value. "We do not wish to suggest," Black and Speer had written in their 1953 article, "that a fatalistic attitude should replace public awareness and carefully performed periodic examinations aimed at the detection and treatment of breast carcinoma at the earliest possible instance."[76] MacDonald continued to perform radical mastectomies long after Crile had abandoned them, believing that they were the treatment of choice for stage II disease. MacDonald also estimated that early treatment was beneficial in perhaps one-quarter of cases.[77]

The degree to which there was actually common ground between the Halsted and predeterminist models is demonstrated by an unpublished document on breast cancer prepared by the Committee on Cancer of the American College of Surgeons in 1962. The committee, composed of eight surgeons not identified with the predeterminist school, acknowledged that "we must emphasize that in dealing with breast carcinoma certain predetermined factors influence prognosis."[78] In only 25 percent of cases, the committee ultimately concluded, "does prognosis depend upon duration of the disease before treatment."[79] The percentage estimated by this cross-section of academic surgeons was thus identical with that proposed by MacDonald, who was often denounced by such individuals as a "prophet of doom."[80]

A few brave souls tried to steer a middle course between the opposing camps. The surgeon David P. Boyd, for example, claimed that MacDonald's arguments about the importance of biology had been "elaborately" misunderstood.[81] Isidor S. Ravdin informed his fellow surgeons that they were no longer technicians but needed "broad concepts of the total biological needs of the patient."[82] While noting his allegiance to Halsted, Edward F. Lewison, chief of breast surgery at Johns Hopkins, pointed out the apparent limitations of the radical mastectomy.[83] Other physicians, hearkening back to Greenough's work earlier in the century, again proposed a model of breast cancer as having three grades: slow-growing, fast-growing, and intermediate. It was only for these intermediate tumors, wrote one such doctor, "where the question of earliness in diagnosis is of paramount importance."[84] Despite these efforts, however, debate about biological predeterminism remained polarized. It was hard enough fighting a war on the leading cancer killer among women without also admitting that the best weapons available were insufficient.

Modified Radical Mastectomy

One other strategy that was proposed as a type of compromise between the two extremes was a revision of the standard Halsted radical mastectomy. Regardless of whether survival had improved as a result, by the 1950s it was clear that women were coming to their physicians with considerably smaller breast cancers than the egg-sized lesions so common in the Halsted era. In 1959, for example, Guy F. Robbins and his colleagues at Memorial Sloan-Kettering reported that breast cancers diagnosed between 1950 and 1955 were 40 percent more likely to be smaller than two centimeters in diameter than had been the case between 1940 and 1943. Robbins attributed this improvement to the cancer education programs of the American Cancer Society and other groups.[85]

By the 1960s, using soft tissue x-rays known as mammograms, physicians would be able to detect breast cancers as small as one centimeter in diameter. These tumors were called "nonpalpable," because they could not be felt during a physical examination of the breast. Interestingly, physicians had experimented with mammograms as early as 1913, but breast x-rays had never become a routine component of diagnosis. Throughout the 1940s and 1950s, Jacob Gershon-Cohen, a soft-spoken, violin-playing Philadelphia radiologist with a knack for invention, had persistently argued that mammography was a powerful diagnostic tool. But it was Robert L. Egan, a radiologist at Houston's M. D. Anderson Hospital and Tumor Institute, who in the early 1960s most convincingly demonstated how his technologically improved mammograms could help to identify small breast cancers that often could not be detected by physical examination.[86] Although widespread dissemination of mammography as a screening tool did not occur in the United States until the 1970s, its early use also contributed to the discovery of smaller breast cancers.

It was true that these smaller tumors found on breast examination or with mammograms had possibly spread either locally or systemically. But the likelihood of finding invasive cancer in or near the pectoralis major or pectoralis minor, which had originally convinced Halsted to routinely remove these muscles, had clearly diminished. Because loss of so much tissue produced great chest wall deformity, the notion of leaving one or both muscles in place was appealing. Preservation of the musculature also helped to improve a woman's postoperative arm strength.

The first surgeons to report on what became known as the modified radical mastectomy were David H. Patey and W. H. Dyson of London's Middlesex Hospital. In a 1948 retrospective study published in the *British Journal of Cancer*, they reported equivalent five-year survival rates between the Halsted radical mastectomy and their operation, which removed the pectoralis minor but left the pectoralis major in place. Nor had Patey and Dyson found evidence of postoperative local recurrence in the pectoralis major, which was a theoretical objection to the less radical procedure.[87] Early American advocates of the modified radical mastectomy included New York's John L. Madden and Henry P. Leis, Jr. Leis stated that he was motivated to adopt the new procedure due to the drastic "cosmetic and functional results women were routinely suffering in an attempt to save their lives."[88] In the Halsted era, Leis later recalled, women "were faced with the double fear of possible death due to the cancer and the mutila-

tion of their breast."[89] The modified procedure, he believed, at least lessened this second problem.

In contrast to the biological predeterminists, advocates of the modified radical operation did not question Halstedian tenets about how cancer spread. They were simply updating Halsted's operation in an era of
smaller breast cancers. Thus, Patey, Dyson, and the American surgeons
who began to perform modified radicals on small, apparently localized
cancers in the 1950s continued to perform a complete axillary dissection
in order to remove any potentially cancerous lymph nodes.

Another early convert to the modified radical mastectomy was Hugh
Auchincloss, a general surgeon on the staff at Columbia-Presbyterian Medical Center. Born into a prominent New York City family, Auchincloss was a
1942 graduate of Columbia's College of Physicians and Surgeons. Auchincloss's father, also named Hugh Auchincloss, had also been a surgeon at Columbia, and in 1929 had written one of the earliest articles extolling breast
self-examination. Having been trained in the radical mastectomy, the
younger Auchincloss began to study whether an association existed between the number of cancerous axillary nodes found by the pathologist
and the survival of patients undergoing the operation. In a 1963 paper published in the *Annals of Surgery*, Auchincloss reported on 31 patients with positive axillary nodes treated between 1951 and 1953 who had lived for eight
or more years. He found that 27 of the 31 women had had four or fewer
positive nodes; moreover, these positive nodes were overwhelmingly located in the lower two thirds of the axilla nearest the breast.[90]

Auchincloss concluded from these data that "the operation of radical
mastectomy is unnecessarily radical."[91] For patients who had four or
fewer nodes and were thus likely to survive, removal of the breast and a
partial axillary node dissection would eliminate all of the local cancer
with a much better cosmetic result for the woman. Meanwhile, women
with larger numbers of axillary nodes who were likely to die would also
be spared the disfiguring Halsted procedure.[92] Auchincloss's study was far
from perfect. It was retrospective and did not examine the lymph node
status of the 71 patients who had died during the period of the study.
Moreover, Auchincloss straddled the fence about the four cases with
nodes high up in the axillary in which the radical mastectomy might
have been curative. Nevertheless, this study encouraged him to make

modified radical mastectomy—with preservation of both pectoralis muscles—his procedure of choice for operable breast cancer.

Auchincloss knew that his paper would be nothing less than incendiary at Presbyterian Hospital. Not only was Haagensen the chief of the breast service, but Auchincloss had included some of Haagensen's meticulously performed radical mastectomies in his study. "Thus it is with considerable trepidation and much hesitance," Auchincloss gingerly stated at the end of his 1963 paper, "that a more conservative operation is suggested."[93] Haagensen, however, was not mollified by his colleague's gesture of caution. To challenge the radical mastectomy was to challenge surgical authority. Haagensen subsequently prevented Auchincloss from operating with surgical residents at Presbyterian or Delafield Hospitals. Although Auchincloss retained his Columbia affiliation, he subequently performed surgery only at Valley Hospital in Ridgewood, New Jersey.[94]

Haagensen's action, while seemingly vindictive, grew out of his fierce devotion to the Halsted radical and what he believed it accomplished. As a surgical resident at Presbyterian in the late 1960s, David W. Kinne made rounds on a patient whose surgeon (not Auchincloss) had used a modified procedure to treat her breast cancer. "I can remember very vividly," Kinne recalled, "when we came by this patient with the modified radical, showing the wound, no skin graft, [pectoralis] muscle in place." Haagensen and several of the other prominent surgeons on rounds, according to Kinne, simply shook their heads in disbelief. "It was though we had just killed this woman."[95] This horror over the adoption of the modified radical was not limited to Columbia. After Leis made a presentation at a surgical congress, a senior physician stated, "If I had a young surgeon on my staff who did not have brains enough to do a radical mastectomy for a woman with breast cancer, I would dismiss him from my staff."[96]

At the 1952 Cincinnati conference, James Lees noted how any statistical analysis was to some degree dependent on how one chose to define "cancer." "Do we mean by cancer a disease which kills within five years?" he asked. "Do we mean by cancer a disease which kills eventually, which metastasizes, which infiltrates?"[97] When William Halsted devised his model of breast cancer, he could use terms such as "cancer," "cure," and "early diagnosis" inexactly. But with the formal entrance of biometricians into the field of breast cancer, it became clear how such words and phrases could be constructed to have various meanings.

Yet the battle over statistics had barely begun. By the late 1950s, researchers and clinicians had begun to argue that the only way to accurately evaluate the efficacy of breast cancer therapies was through formal randomized controlled trials. In such trials, large numbers of patients were enrolled prior to their treatment and then randomly assigned to various therapies. Randomization posed a direct challenge to clinicians such as Haagensen and Jerry Urban, whose authority as breast surgeons rested on their ability to make individualized treatment decisions for their patients. As debates about radical mastectomy and more conservative operations grew increasingly heated during the 1960s, the construction of another word—"scientific"—would become important. What did it mean to term certain data "scientific" and who had a right to do so?

Reality Check

Breast Cancer Treatment and Randomized
Controlled Trials

O ne physician who strongly cautioned against the growing reliance on biostatistics was Roald N. Grant, a surgeon on the staff
of the American Cancer Society and editor of its medical journal, Ca. Proposed randomized controlled trials (RCTs) comparing radical
and simple mastectomy, Grant wrote in a 1963 editorial, were nothing
short of "scientific Russian roulette." Physicians whose reliance on statistical studies compromised their humanitarianism, he warned, "are likely
to be toppled into the same ugly morass in which the Nazi physicians
found themselves as result of their ventures with human experimentation during World War II."[1]

Grant's invocation of Nazi atrocities demonstrates how debates over
breast cancer treatment after 1960 remained inflammatory. At the same
time, his other choices of language reveal some of the newer issues that
had entered these debates. The words "experimentation" and "scientific," for example, referred to the emerging controversies over the
proper methods for evaluating breast cancer therapies. Advocates of randomized trials believed that these formal experiments were the only legitimate method for generating truly scientific knowledge. The term
"Russian roulette" raised the issues of risk and uncertainty. Even though
the new RCTs were supposed to generate more accurate information,
physicians such as Grant preferred to rely on clinical expertise to decide
which interventions were risky or safe. As the 1960s progressed, it became increasingly difficult to ascertain which data about breast cancer
treatment—if any—represented the "truth."

Amassing Uncontrolled Evidence

Those who came to support randomized controlled trials believed that such studies eliminated the multiple problems associated with retrospective research. Information obtained after patients had already undergone treatment, according to this argument, was invariably biased. Yet even if such data were inferior, the trend that these retrospective studies revealed by the early 1960s was striking: smaller operations, usually accompanied by orthovoltage radiotherapy, appeared to provide equivalent results to radical mastectomy for stage I and II breast cancers. Much of this work, such as that of McWhirter and Murley, emanated from Great Britain, but other European physicians were also conducting similar research.

In 1954, for example, Finnish radiotherapist Sakari Mustakallio had reported very high survival rates for 127 patients treated with only tumor removal followed by radiation. Some 107 (84%) of these patients lived five years, while 13 (72%) of 18 patients with longer follow-up had lived ten years.[2] In France, François Baclesse of the Curie Foundation had begun to treat selected breast cancer patients with tumor removal and radiotherapy in 1937. In 1960 he reported that 38 (72%) of 53 stage I patients and 26 (55%) of 47 stage II patients had survived five years.[3] The results from both of these studies compared favorably with outcomes from radical mastectomy.

In contrast to Mustakallio and Baclesse, who evaluated tumor removal and radiation, two Danish radiotherapists, Sigvard Kaae and Helge Johansen, used a treatment comparable to that of McWhirter: simple mastectomy and radiotherapy. In a 1962 paper comparing this strategy to extended radical mastectomy, recurrence-free five-year survival was better for women receiving the smaller operation, 55 to 49 percent.[4] What made the Danish study particularly noteworthy for this era was its prospective methodology. Kaae and Johansen had enrolled patients in advance to decrease the likelihood that only favorable cases would be selected.

Meanwhile, in the United States, a few physicians had begun to perform retrospective studies of smaller operations, both with and without radiotherapy. As with the European data, their results generally revealed no advantage to radical mastectomy.[5] One of these American researchers was Barney Crile, who, by the early 1960s, had generated data on 56

Cleveland Clinic patients who had received simple mastectomies between 1953 and 1957. At a presentation to the Southern Surgical Association in Boca Raton, Florida, in December 1960, Crile reported that 45 (80%) of these patients had survived three years. Nineteen of 29 (66%) receiving surgery at least four and a half years earlier had survived for this long. In contrast, 30 (75%) of 40 patients receiving either a radical mastectomy or a modified radical mastectomy during these years had survived three years and 16 (59%) of 27 had survived four and a half years. Not only did the simple procedure appear to give equal (or perhaps superior) results, but it also reduced side effects. Crile reported that none of the women receiving simple mastectomy—including those who had subsequently needed treatment of the cancerous axillary nodes—developed lymphedema of the arm.[6]

Crile's study demonstrates the many problems that arose in the retrospective comparison of treatment options. After Crile's talk in Boca Raton, Warfield M. Firor, emeritus Professor of Surgery at Johns Hopkins University, had raised several of these concerns: the two groups of patients had received differing amounts of radiotherapy, clouding the results; the number of cases studied was insufficient; the patients had not been followed for long enough to draw conclusions; and Crile had not provided separate data for those patients who had received the gold standard operation, the Halsted radical mastectomy.[7]

Crile was well aware of the statistical problems of his paper and dutifully included a discussion of confounding factors. He also called for "a series of carefully planned blind experiments" that could provide more definitive answers about the best treatment for breast cancer. Yet at the same time, Crile remained rather confident about his data, stating that even without randomized controlled trials, "no injustice will be done to patients in clinical Stage I who are treated by simple operations without prophylactic radiation therapy."[8]

An additional criticism that applied to Crile's findings was the familiar one of selection bias. Because Crile had apportioned patients to various treatments based on his clinical judgment, critics could always charge that he chose the least sick patients for simple mastectomy, thereby generating an artifically high survival rate for that procedure. Neither Crile nor his followers disputed this possibility. As Roger S. Foster, Jr., a breast surgeon who married Crile's daughter Joan, recalled, "what Barney had were very good seat-of-the-pants hunches."[9]

This concern about selection bias helps to explain why another study—published by two surgeons from Rockford, Illinois, in the *American Journal of Surgery* in 1959—received considerable attention. Simmons S. Smith and Alfred C. Meyer had begun a study of breast cancer treatment in three community hospitals in Rockford intending to demonstrate the superiority of the radical mastectomy. To their surprise, however, they found that 52 (54%) of 97 patients receiving simple mastectomy between 1924 and 1952 had survived five years compared with 173 (53%) of 324 women who had undergone radical mastectomy during the same period. The survival rates for both groups dropped to roughly 30 percent at ten years.[10]

Smith and Meyer's data were of particular interest because they were based on a "natural experiment" that had taken place during World War II. Many of Rockford's full-time surgeons had served in the war, leaving physicians without formal surgical training to perform operations for breast cancer. Because these physicians had never learned the intricacies of the Halsted radical, they had most often used a simple mastectomy. Indeed, more than half of the simple mastectomies performed in Rockford during the years under study took place between 1942 and 1947. Given that the cases treated during these years, on average, were likely of severity comparable to those treated in peacetime, selection bias may have been minimized.[11] Thus, the Rockford data were especially powerful.

Smith and Meyer's study raised concern among surgeons not only because it questioned radical mastectomy but also because the group they termed "occasional operators" had achieved equivalent results to the "experienced surgeons." "[T]he ultimate fate of the patient," the authors wrote, "was not influenced by the quality of the surgery performed."[12] The authors—surgeons writing in a surgical journal—were careful to stress that inferior operative technique was never acceptable, but the threat to surgical authority was obvious.

The interest in the Rockford study induced Michael B. Shimkin, then a statistician at the National Cancer Institute (NCI), to independently review Smith and Meyer's data. Shimkin, born in Siberia in 1912, came to the United States as a child and earned his medical degree from the University of California at San Francisco in 1937. Having grown interested in cancer research, he began work at the newly created NCI in 1937. Shimkin performed laboratory research but also studied biometry, and eventually became the Chief of the Biometry and Epidemiological Branch of NCI in 1954. A "true scientific generalist," he also wrote extensively on the history and philosophy of cancer and gave highly entertaining lectures to medical and lay audiences.[13]

Writing in the *Journal of the National Cancer Institute* in November 1961, Shimkin and his NCI colleagues basically corroborated the Rockford data, but warned that "identifiable differences occurred in the patients, the physicians, and the criteria for the selection of the type of operation."[14] As a result, Smith and Meyer had not scientifically shown that simple mastectomy gave equivalent results to radical surgery but had strongly demonstrated the need for an "objective, prospective clinical test"[15] that could evaluate this hypothesis.

Such a test, Shimkin believed, needed to be a randomized controlled trial. Researchers needed to enroll subjects in such trials prospectively—prior to therapy—and then randomly assign them to receive either the experimental intervention or the control treatment. In the case of breast cancer surgery, patients receiving radical mastectomy would be the controls, as this procedure was the standard of care. The experimental group would receive either simple mastectomy or another smaller breast operation, likely accompanied by radiotherapy. Randomized trials ideally involved "blinding" both physicians and patients to which therapy was being administered. Obviously, such secrecy was not possible in the case of breast cancer surgery; however, treating physicians would not participate in either the randomization process or the data analysis. The various components of randomized trials, according to their advocates, eliminated the biases of both retrospective research and of those prospective studies that allowed physicians to assign different treatments to specific patients.[16] Indeed, because of the formal nature of experimentation that RCTs entailed, it became more appropriate to view the participants not as doctors and patients but as researchers and subjects.[17]

Most historical accounts of the randomized clinical trial have presented its development as the gradual triumph of value-free, objective statistical assessment. But as the medical historians Harry M. Marks and

Ilana Lowy have argued in recent books, such a construction ignores both the potential flaws in RCT methodology and the professional and political factors that contributed to acceptance of the randomized trial as a gold standard.[18] Regardless of the validity of the randomized trial, its increasing hegemony beginning after World War II ensured that statisticians would increasingly play the "policeman's role" in evaluating the efficacy of therapeutic interventions.[19] That is, the decision-making of physicians regarding individual patients would gradually become subordinated to data generated through the evaluation of large groups of patients at multiple institutions.

Although researchers did not conduct the first randomized trials— which evaluated streptomycin in the treatment of tuberculosis—until the late 1940s, the individual components of RCTs had been used previously. Controls dated back hundreds of years. In 1747, for example, the English physician James Lind had compared several treatments for scurvy among sailors, finding that only those receiving oranges and lemons recovered. The first instance of randomization occurred in 1926 in a trial of a gold-based compound, sanocrysin, in the treatment of tuberculosis. Researchers assigned patients to either gold injection (treatment group) or saline injection (control group) by the flip of a coin. After the streptomycin trials, the practice of double-blinding, in which neither researcher nor subject knew the treatment being administered, became the final component of RCTs.[20]

The earliest randomized trials, such as those evaluating streptomycin, had evaluated the efficacy of antibiotic agents in infectious illnesses. The application of RCT methodology was far more challenging in the case of chronic diseases such as cancer, for which endpoints were less definitive, and for operations, the results of which were believed to be dependent on the intuition and skill of the surgeon. In fact, the first randomized trial of a surgical procedure, surgical excision of duodenal ulcers, did not commence until 1957.[21]

Nevertheless, Philadelphia surgeon Isidor S. Ravdin had raised the possibility of some type of controlled trial of radical mastectomy versus less extensive surgery as early as 1942. Support for prospective randomization had accelerated by 1958, when the United States National Advisory Cancer Council, established in conjunction with the founding of the NCI in

1937, volunteered to "sponsor, initiate and underwrite national, cooperative, biometrically designed clinical investigations on the comparative effects of radical mastectomy and of simple mastectomy supplemented
with radiation for carcinoma of the breast."[22] This offer was accompanied by pleas for randomized trials from prominent surgeons, such as
George E. Moore, director of the Roswell Park Memorial Cancer Institute
in Buffalo, New York. It was time to question the assumption, Moore
wrote in 1960, that surgeons always knew what was best for their patients.[23] Nevertheless, the council's proposed study never took place.

Thus, Shimkin used his 1961 review of the Rockford data to renew calls
for a randomized trial. In an unattributed editorial that he authored in the
Journal of the American Medical Association in December 1961, he argued that "agnosticism" had become the only justifiable stand in the matter of breast
cancer treatment.[24] Given that no one knew which therapy was superior, it
was time for "appropriate speciality organizations" to work together and
develop an RCT. Continuing to treat breast cancer either with radical mastectomy or with simple mastectomy, Shimkin believed, was unethical.

Surgeons who wrote letters to Shimkin after his Rockford article indicated their extreme discomfort at the seemingly heretical notion that surgical dissection of the lymph nodes might make no difference. "I cannot
yet find myself believing," Minnesota surgeon J. Bradley Aust remarked,
"that the removal of lymph node positive axillary metastases can do anything but help the patient." Should a randomized trial prove otherwise,
Aust added, "it would leave one with a rather pessimistic attitude about
surgical treatment of lymph node metastases in breast cancer."[25]

Nevertheless, both Aust and Shimkin's other correspondents generally
favored a randomized trial. Only one letter writer, Shimkin noted, "was
against the basic idea of a systematic trial of radical versus simple mastectomy."[26] A missive sent by Philadelphia surgeon Joseph L. Dennis was
typical. "[I]t is hard to impress new ideas and change methods that have
become entrenched as orthodoxy," Dennis wrote. "I admire your 'guts' in
. . . insisting that an ethical medical test should be instituted to see if radical mastectomy is the best method of procedure."[27] Another Philadelphia
surgeon, John M. Howard, stated that the "cooperative preplanned study
which has been suggested by the National Cancer Advisory Council must
certainly be implemented."[28]

Although those who had chosen to write to Shimkin had praised his conclusions, there was hardly a groundswell for an RCT comparing radical mastectomy and lesser surgery. Indeed, many surgeons agreed with Roald Grant that any study that deprived women of the complete Halsted radical was thoroughly unethical.

Trial and Error?

The controversy over randomized trials became immediately apparent when American Cancer Society officials met in New York shortly after the publication of Shimkin's article. At the meeting, Isidor Ravdin, who had endorsed the notion of a controlled trial almost twenty years before, now appeared unenthusiastic about the proposition. "Until we know more about the nature of cancer," he stated, "we can't be sure of any study."[29] In a subsequent letter to Shimkin, Ravdin warned that "[t]he study from Rockford, Illinois, is not a good comparison, and you must not use this."[30] More telling were comments made by Stanford University surgeon John W. Cline at the ACS meeting. "I don't think anyone would be willing to submit a large number of women to simple mastectomy," he argued. "We don't subject somebody to inferior treatment just to prove it is inferior."[31]

Cline's statement succinctly revealed the dramatic epistemological fault line that had emerged in clinical medicine. In believing that inferior treatment was apparent without sophisticated statistical analysis, Cline adhered to the thinking of an earlier era, in which knowledge gained from "clinical expertise" was seen by physicians and the public as most valuable. By using the pronoun "we," by which Cline likely was referring to the medical profession or surgeons, he sought to distinguish these groups from outsiders such as biometricians, whose emphasis was on "clinical science" and not individual patients.[32] The hegemony of the clinician was under attack and Cline was fighting back.

Roald Grant was doing the same in his 1963 editorial and an earlier piece that noted the physician's responsibility for "each life and death action." In this latter article, Grant attacked, with the religious fervor of one reared on Halsted and his radical mastectomy, Michael Shimkin's admission of agnosticism. "Just as there are no atheists in foxholes," he declared, "agnostics are rarely found in operating rooms where faith is the ticket for admission."[33] Grant concluded his editorial with a plea to his fellow male surgeons that was both chivalrous and a cri de coeur: "How many, and whose of our mothers, daughters and wives will it be necessary to sacrifice as scientific controls to find the fleeting moment of truth about the simple mastectomy for breast cancer?"[34]

That the loudest opposition to Shimkin would emerge from a Memorial Sloan-Kettering surgeon in an ACS journal was not surprising. Ever since the Memorial breast surgeon Frank Adair served as president of the cancer society in the mid-1940s, the organization had been dominated by Memorial-trained surgeons such as Charles Cameron and his successor as director of medical affairs, Arthur I. Holleb. The ACS, one surgeon later commented, was the "Memorial Sloan-Kettering alumni association."[35] Because it was "the policy of Memorial Hospital to perform so-called radical mastectomies,"[36] the cancer society supported this approach as well. As a result, the ACS in the 1960s and 1970s manifested a somewhat paradoxical approach to breast cancer control. On the one hand, the organization was progressive in its persistent advocacy of new screening techniques such as breast self-examination and, later, mammography. But it remained highly conservative in its allegiance to radical breast surgery and its early ambivalence, if not opposition, to randomized controlled trials of various treatments.[37]

Just what was the nature of the clinical expertise that breast surgeons believed they had acquired over the course of their careers? And what was its relationship to the notion of "faith" that Roald Grant and others supposedly brought to the operating room?

To these surgeons, expertise connoted extensive experience with all aspects of breast cancer. Surgeons diagnosed women with the disease, staged the extent of the cancer, performed meticulous radical mastectomies, and then evaluated the patients postoperatively. This "hands on" familiarity with breast cancer had become equated with great judgment regarding the disease. Breast surgeons had "seen it all," and felt prepared for whatever cases they encountered. Knowledge about breast cancer was further enhanced when physicians monitored their patients in the years following the operation. "Personal follow-up is . . . of great educational value to the surgeon," Cushman Haagensen wrote. "It is his best way of learning the natural history of the disease."[38]

To those surgeons who believed in radical mastectomy—and they were in the majority—this accrued expertise only further convinced them of the value of the operation. To be sure, this advocacy of radical mastectomy was based on data. Adair, Haagensen, and other radical surgeons had performed their own retrospective studies that they believed showed it to be the superior procedure. Yet the devotion to radical mastectomy also bespoke the type of faith between doctor and patient that Roald Grant had invoked. The ethics of the medical profession demanded that surgeons not participate in experimentation but give patients the treatment most validated by their years of clinical experience.[39] The "contemporary trend to experiment with the individualization of treatment for operable breast cancer," wrote University of Oregon surgeons Clare G. Peterson and William W. Krippaehne, was "particularly distressing."[40] The pugnacious Memorial surgeon Guy S. Robbins was more blunt. "[M]ost people come here not to be guinea pigs," he wrote, "but to get the best treatment available." If radical mastectomy worked, "we better damn well give it and not experiment on people."[41]

Compounding the opposition of many breast surgeons to randomized trials were their concerns about the quality of the surgery apt to be performed in such trials. As Harry Marks has shown, the growth of RCTs depended not only on the acceptance of their more "scientific" methodology but also on the establishment of a cooperative organizational network.[42] To enroll enough subjects to provide valid results, randomized trials of breast cancer therapy would require the participation of dozens of physicians from multiple institutions across the United States.

Radical surgeons, who placed so much weight on their careful technique, found the anonymity of such trials to be entirely unacceptable. How could one evaluate the results of a radical mastectomy without knowing if a skilled surgeon trained in the Halsted tradition had performed the operation? "Every Tom, Dick and Harry" could conceivably operate, University of Chicago surgeon Donald Ferguson later complained.[43] Similar concerns applied when assessing other aspects of RCTs. "Unless there is documentation of quality control of surgery, radiation therapy and pathology, the reporting of statistical data, regardless of the method, is less than valid," wrote Memorial's Guy Robbins. "Multi-institutional studies are especially suspect as to quality control."[44] Indeed, to Robbins and others, the skills of surgeons who would either organize or participate in such trials were, by definition, suspect.

Controlling Uncertainty and Risk

A final explanation for many surgeons' opposition to randomized trials stems from the ways in which these doctors addressed issues of uncertainty and risk. Numerous authors have described the discomfort of clinicians with uncertainty.[45] Uncertainty can prove especially troubling for surgeons, who have long been characterized as men (and women) of action. As the sociologist Joan Cassell has argued, it is characteristics such as decisiveness and certitude that enable surgeons to perform invasive and dangerous procedures in the first place.[46]

Thus, the basic premise of an RCT for operable cancer of the breast— that the proper treatment of the disease was not known—was inherently incompatible with surgical practice. Even if surgeons grasped the need for randomized trials intellectually, an admission of uncertainty conflicted with the authoritative stance they routinely demonstrated in both examining and operating rooms. One surgeon who struggled with the concept of RCTs for breast cancer surgery in the 1960s was C. Barber Mueller, who had trained with the legendary Washington University surgeon Evarts Grahams and had subsequently become chief of surgery at Syracuse University. Mueller recently recalled his discomfort with the notion of performing surgery on a randomized patient:

> When you take a knife to a patient and begin to cut, you have to know where you are going. You are essentially assaulting another person. You have to be convinced that what you are doing is in the best interests of the patient. . . . You can't be indecisive and be a surgeon. Either you do it or you don't.[47]

If admission of uncertainty was unacceptable for surgeons, they had the alternative option of addressing breast surgery in terms of risk. Defined as "the possibility of suffering harm or loss,"[48] risk in the medical setting represented the odds that a bad outcome, such as the postoperative recurrence of breast cancer, would take place. As scholars such as the anthropologist Mary Douglas have noted, risk has generally been discussed through a "paradigm of individual rational choice." In such a model, according to Douglas, people presented with two or more behavioral options act as "hedonistic calculators calmly seeking to pursue private interests."[49] Tied into this construct is the notion that probability statistics used by individuals to guide their decision-making are objective.

But, Douglas argues, to consider risk assessment independent of culture is worthless. Both the cultural setting and personal experiences frame how individuals approach risky decisions. For example, "[a]nger, hope and fear are part of most risky situations."[50] Moreover, risk estimations used to guide clinical decision-making are themselves "cultural constructions." Although researchers may describe such data as scientific, and thus presumably infallible, the ways in which such statistics are presented are actually "tied to contexts of professional production."[51]

The subjective, culturally influenced nature of risk assessment was readily apparent when American surgeons in the 1950s and 1960s discussed various treatment options. Rejecting the possibility that randomized trials might actually generate more accurate data regarding the value of various breast cancer operations, surgeons imposed a risk-aversive framework favoring more radical procedures. The surgeons' behavior exemplified how Americans tend to approach serious medical decisions: they choose what they perceive to be the least risky option. Whereas most contemporary Western societies encourage their citizens "to live life in a prudent, calculating way, and to be ever-vigilant of risks,"[52] Americans, the historian Allan M. Brandt has written, "share a powerful cultural belief in the ability to identify, regulate, control and eliminate risks."[53] To prevent disease, Brandt concludes, Americans have been expected to "exert fundamental control over their own health through careful and rational avoidance of risks."[54]

Although breast cancer patients also favored the least risky procedure, what is most striking is the degree to which the surgeons themselves unilaterally determined what types of risks were or were not acceptable. When Charlotte George asked her surgeon to remove her cancer but leave her breasts, he told her that such a choice "would involve a great deal of risk," adding that there would also be "the uncertainty in your mind" that some cancer remained. After five days of indecision, George opted for a radical mastectomy.[55] "[I]t seems to me," stated Massachusetts General Hospital surgeon Grantley W. Taylor in 1961, "we are under obligation to offer the benefit of the doubt to those patients who may be salvageable, if we carry out a properly planned, properly executed radical operation."[56] Radical mastectomy offered the best likelihood of removing a breast cancer, University of Pittsburgh surgeon Mark M. Ravitch argued, "at a justifiable cost to the patient in risk, deformity, and disability."[57] As late as 1981, a surgeon would justify continued use of the radical mastectomy because it "protects the patient from our uncertainty about the biology of breast cancer."[58]

When surgeons included numerical figures in their arguments, they reached the same conclusion: radical mastectomy, despite its unfortunate consequences, remained essential because it offered the best chance at extending life. The concept that a given patient might have different priorities was not part of the calculus. "We would prefer to perform 10 radical mastectomies in unfavorable cases," Frank Adair argued in 1953, "than neglect to do the radical in one in which we might be mistaken as to prognosis."[59] Surgeons at Detroit's Henry Ford Hospital estimated that only 8 percent of patients benefited from the extensive dissection performed during a radical mastectomy, but concluded that "the rationale of the operation remains sound."[60] This notion of treating many patients aggressively to try and save a few of them was entirely consistent with a risk-aversive mindset.[61] It also enabled physicians to honestly tell individual breast cancer patients that "everything" was being done, a claim that could not easily be made for patients who were randomized among various treatments in controlled trials.

Beginning in the 1970s, breast cancer patients would decry the premise that physicians had the right to deem certain procedures of acceptable or unacceptable risk. They would argue, for example, that breast preservation, not only the prolongation of life, was an acceptable goal to pursue. But in the early 1960s, when surgical authority remained paramount, such questions were raised only occasionally. Randomized controlled trials of radical mastectomy in the United States would have to

wait until an era in which surgeons and other physicians were forced to
acknowledge the uncertainties inherent in, and the differing notions of
risk arising from, the treatment of diseases such as breast cancer.

Interestingly, one of the reasons that the debate over RCTs in the 1960s
remained confined to medical meetings and medical journals was that
many of the usual critics, such as Barney Crile, were themselves ambivalent on the topic. Although Crile believed his uncontrolled simple mastectomy studies had paved the way for randomized trials of breast cancer
therapy, he had reservations about how such trials would be structured.
Most notably, Crile thought that the control group should consist of
women receiving a modified radical mastectomy, not a Halsted radical.
Having performed his last "deforming" radical mastectomy almost a
decade earlier, Crile was hardly about to resume now.[62]

In this sense, Crile shared an important characteristic with his opponents, the staunch advocates of radical mastectomy: he was a surgeon and
wished to reserve the right to recommend specific operations for specific
patients. When later asked why he had stopped doing radical mastectomies in 1955, Crile replied, "I know my own figures, I know my own results, and I'm dead certain of them."[63] Radical mastectomy, he claimed,
"has been proven already not to be any better than the regular [mastec-
tomy]."[64] When C. Barber Mueller switched from radical to simple mastectomy in the 1960s, he, too, was not willing to randomize. When
operating on a woman with a two-centimeter cancer in the inner portion
of her breast—15 to 20 centimeters from the axilla—he had an epiphany.
"It didn't make any sense to dissect out the axillary nodes and not the internal mammaries," he recently recalled. "I removed the breast only." Two
days later, he received an angry call from the pathologist, who objected
strongly and told Mueller that omitting a radical dissection was inappropriate. But having become convinced that simple mastectomy was the best
operation, Mueller "didn't want someone to tell me what was best."[65]

The decision of Crile and Mueller to rely on clinical judgment, as opposed to waiting for the results of randomized trials, raises a provocative
question. At what point does enough evidence exist to warrant a change
in clinical practice? Is insistence on an RCT ever, as claimed by the famed
polio vaccine researcher Jonas Salk, a "fetish of orthodoxy"?[66] By the
early 1960s, decades of uncontrolled studies indicated that conservative

procedures provided roughly equivalent survival to more radical breast surgery. To be sure, such data were disputed by Haagensen and others, but the general trend appeared unmistakable.[67] Was it ethical for Crile and Mueller to bypass formal randomized trials that they believed would simply provide additional proof of what they already knew? One person who concurred that waiting for RCTs was pointless was Irwin D. Bross, a statistician at Roswell Park. Such a study, Bross would later argue, was a "waste of time" and "just beating a dead horse."[68] Ample evidence already existed, Bross believed, that more breast radical surgery would not improve outcomes.

Between surgeons who believed that radical mastectomy remained the treatment of choice and those who believed it was already obsolete, there was little enthusiasm for Shimkin's proposed RCT. As a result, another decade of fiery controversy was inevitable.

Saving the Lives of Wives

If one asks general surgeons who trained or practiced in the 1960s about the raucous debates over radical mastectomy, they will roll their eyes and launch into a series of anecdotes. These stories follow a similar pattern. On the dais, at a surgical conference or a meeting sponsored by a local medical society or medical school, would be one or more advocates of radical mastectomy and one or more supporters of lesser surgery. The proponents of radical operations might include Cushman Haagensen, imposing and thoroughly serious in his defense of Halsted, or his trainee Sven Kister. Alternatively, the radical viewpoint would be represented by the polished, well-dressed Memorial Sloan-Kettering surgeon Jerry Urban or his scrappier colleague Guy Robbins. More often than not, Barney Crile would be their opponent, although by the end of the decade the Canadian radiotherapist M. Vera Peters and Bernard Fisher might also be included.

The format of these events was predictable. Data, for and against radical mastectomy, would be presented. Crile's figures would elicit murmurs and, in the early years, catcalls. By the time questions were solicited from the audience, scientific discussion often gave way to rhetoric. A radical surgeon, on stage or in the audience, might tell Crile that "it is not wise or humane to condemn a woman to be treated with these methods."[69] The handsome and articulate Crile would resist the temptation to engage in a shouting match. Appearing more bemused than angry, he would criticize his fellow surgeons for continuing to "inflict disability" on their patients.[70] The "arena," rued editorialists in 1972, was filled with "gladiators bearing different weapons."[71] The debates about radical mastectomy had become as ritualistic as some believed the operation was.

What was perhaps most notable about these events was how the male physicians so readily offered their views about what women did or did not want. For example, it was not uncommon for radical mastectomy advocates to downplay the extra dissection that the operation entailed, insisting that "the main deforming quality" of the operation was the removal of the breast.[72] Yet, aside from Peters and Crile, who persistently reminded their colleagues to actually discuss these issues with their patients, most of the physicians present were entirely comfortable with the lack of women's voices.

Indeed, the only women physically present at these meetings were the loved ones of the male physicians in attendance. For decades, physicians choosing among breast cancer treatments asked one another: "What would we do in each individual case if the patient were our own wife, mother or sister?"[73] This question was inherently paradoxical. While it seemed to remind physicians to treat all patients equally, the fact that it was so often invoked suggested that a hierarchy of treatments existed. Although a Halstedian surgeon might be willing to "experiment" with lesser surgery on certain patients, he would most certainly recommend a complete radical mastectomy for his family member. Jerry Urban used to get a laugh from his response to the perennial question of how he would treat his wife. He would ask: Do you mean my current wife or my first wife?[74]

Thus it came as a major surprise to his surgical brethren when Crile's wife, Jane Halle Crile, underwent only a simple mastectomy when she developed a one-centimeter breast cancer in 1959. Jane Halle was the third of four daughters of Sam Halle, who owned Cleveland's largest department store. Barney Crile had known Jane since dancing school but they did not begin dating until he was at Yale and she was at Smith. They were married in 1934 and in time had four children. The Criles were avid divers and wrote two books together about their journeys to islands in the Mediterranean Sea and the Pacific Ocean. Crile had sent his wife to a

Cleveland Clinic colleague, Stanley O. Hoerr, who also favored simple mastectomies for small, outer quadrant lesions such as Jane Crile had discovered. Finding no evidence of nodes on examination, Hoerr performed a simple mastectomy but omitted an axillary dissection. At this time, based on animal experiments, Crile had hypothesized that leaving axillary lymph nodes in place, unless they were clinically enlarged, actually helped the body fight breast cancer. Although he did not dictate the nature of his wife's operation, Crile's choice of Hoerr had determined what operation she would receive. "I knew what he would do," Crile later wrote, "and I felt fully responsible for what was done."[75]

In 1961, Jane Crile was diagnosed with metastatic breast cancer. She had complained of pain when breathing and a chest x-ray had revealed that the breast cancer had spread to her lungs. She received radiation therapy and then surgery to remove the lung nodules. Crile later wrote that his wife had responded to her impending mortality with "no trace of fear. There was sorrow, but no dread."[76] Eventually, Jane Crile developed brain metastases. She died in January 1963.

Besides being deeply saddened, much of the surgical community was mortified at what had happened. If you believed Halsted, and most physicians still did, the decision to remove only the breast and not the axillary nodes had quite possibly cost Jane Crile her life. If a node dissection had found and removed cancer, this argument went, it might have prevented future spread of the disease to the lungs and brain. But Crile disagreed. The eventual appearance of metastases merely indicated that his wife had had an aggressive tumor from the start; silent disease, he believed, had almost certainly been present at the time of the first operation. Because his wife had undergone only a simple mastectomy, Crile concluded, she had experienced a very comfortable three years before her death. The fierce debates about radical breast surgery had come home in a most personal way but remained no easier to solve.

Growing Opposition to Halsted

With Crile's approach remaining firmly in the minority, radical mastectomy remained the treatment of choice in the 1960s. Some 83 percent of New Jersey surgeons, for example, indicated a preference for the Halsted radical. According to a 1968 survey of 8,970 United States physicians who treated breast cancer, 68.3 percent of their patients received radical mastectomies. In contrast, only 11.2 percent of women, including those receiving only palliative surgery, underwent simple mastectomy.[77] (The other 20.5 percent had other therapies, such as radiation alone or ovary removal.) Even more striking, the most common overall treatment strategy used by these physicians was a combination of radical mastectomy plus postoperative radiation, although addition of the latter modality to radical surgery worsened side effects, such as lymphedema, and had never been shown to improve survival.

Yet critics of radical treatment continued to propose alternatives including, increasingly, removal of the tumor alone. This procedure, pioneered by Mustakallio and Baclesse, was called either lumpectomy or partial mastectomy and was usually (but not always) accompanied by radiotherapy. Crile, for example, treated selected patients with this technique.

By the late 1960s, the most vocal advocate for "breast conservation therapy" in North America had become Vera Peters. Peters was born in a farmhouse outside Toronto, Ontario, in 1911. Highly intelligent, she graduated from high school at sixteen and the University of Toronto Medical School at twenty-three. In 1935, Peters's mother developed breast cancer and began treatment with Gordon Richards, an innovative radiotherapist. Impressed with his work, Peters began an apprenticeship of sorts with Richards and in 1945 became certified in radiation therapy. Her first research project was to review Richards's use of aggressive palliative radiotherapy for Hodgkin's disease, finding, as Richards had suspected, that one quarter of the patients were actually being cured.[78]

Peters next turned her attention to breast cancer. Although her mother had died, other women appeared to benefit from irradiation. After Richards's death, Peters began to use radiotherapy not only as a palliative measure but also for early-stage patients seeking a cure. Many of these women had refused mastectomy and had been sent to Peters because she was a woman and willing to adminster this unconventional therapy.[79] Peters treated such women with a lumpectomy followed by radiotherapy to the breast and the internal mammary, supraclavicular, and axillary nodes.

In a retrospective chart review of her patients published in the *Journal of the American Medical Association* in 1967, Peters reported a 74 percent five-year survival for women with stage I and II breast cancer.[80] This figure was identical to that of a comparison group of women who had undergone mastectomy and radiotherapy. Armed with these data, Peters became a familiar figure on the breast cancer "circuit," appearing at meetings and conferences in the United States and Canada. While many surgeons sincerely disbelieved her results, some were so hostile that at times she was driven to tears. Not only was Peters a weak public speaker, but she was Canadian, a radiotherapist, and, most important, "one woman in a houseful of men."[81]

Europe had its share of prominent women researchers in the field of breast cancer, such as Denmark's Helge Johansen and England's Diana Brinkley. But Peters was the only North American woman who emerged as a major figure in the study of the disease. This fact is hardly surprising given that the surgical profession in the United States was over 97 percent male, and that the relatively few women surgeons in the country appear to have used radical mastectomy as often as their male colleagues. Although Peters was not an ardent feminist, she consciously emphasized the "emotional toil of radical surgery on the woman."[82] It was an injustice, she would state at a 1974 meeting, "to always insist on an emotionally offensive procedure which leaves a defect and which might not alter the natural course of her disease or her potential for cure."[83] Peters believed the most satisfied patients were those treated with her combination of local excision and radiation. Such concern for the "morale" of patients was highly unusual at scientific meetings, where physicians typically discussed "salvage rates" and referred to patients as "clinical material." Peters was also an early role model for women physicians, caring for children at home even as she traveled around the world making presentations.[84]

Another, male, physician who began to argue in favor of lumpectomy was Leslie Wise. The Australian-born Wise had trained in surgery at London's St. Helier Hospital under Aubrey York Mason, an early advocate of breast conservation. However, when Wise joined the staff of Washington University in St. Louis in the late 1960s, mastectomy was the treatment of choice. Concerned with this discrepancy, he visited the renowned Washington University pathologist Lauren V. Ackerman, who had summarily rejected McWhirter's data in 1955. Ackerman, Wise later explained, was a "mastectomy man," but proved willing to work with his younger colleague. Retrospectively reviewing the St. Helier data from 1950 to 1964, Wise and Ackerman found identical five- and ten-year survival rates for 96 women who received tumor excision and radiotherapy and 207 women who had undergone radical mastectomy.[85] After this study, Wise stated, Ackerman became a "convert" to breast conservation.

The aspect of Peters's and Wise's work that particularly concerned their critics was the perceived inadequacy of lumpectomy as a surgical procedure. In 1957, pathologists at the University of Cincinnati had reported that as many as 54 percent of breast cancers were multicentric[86]— that is, in addition to the obvious tumor, the breast contained small foci of cancer that were detectable only under the microscope. Radiotherapy was designed to treat these foci, but most physicians remained as uncomfortable with leaving easily removable cancer behind in the breasts of lumpectomy patients as they had in leaving it behind in the axillae of McWhirter's simple mastectomy patients. Among the fiercest foes of lumpectomy was the American Cancer Society, which issued a statement in 1971 stating that "the American public should not be stampeded into accepting less proven methods."[87]

As usual, allegiance to radical mastectomy was less evident in Europe. By 1970, according to one estimate, women in England were half as likely to receive radical mastectomy as those in the United States; Crile reported that very few radical mastectomies were being done in either England or France.[88] As American surgeons and radiotherapists debated retrospective data, researchers in Europe had organized randomized controlled trials. Beginning in 1958 at Addenbrooke's Hospital in Cambridge, radiotherapists Diana Brinkley and J. L. Haybittle enrolled stage II breast cancer patients in a prospective trial of simple versus radical mastectomy. Both sets of women received radiotherapy. Reporting in 1966 and 1971, respectively, five- and ten-year survival was equivalent.

In 1972, Sir Hedley Atkins and his colleagues at Guy's Hospital in London reported equivalent ten-year survival for stage I breast cancer patients who received lumpectomy (which they termed "extended tylectomy") and radiotherapy compared with a group that received radical mastectomy and radiotherapy. Among stage II patients, survival was better in the radical mastectomy group, 72 to 56 percent, although this difference disappeared in subsequent studies.[89] Umberto Veronesi, an

Italian surgeon at the National Cancer Institute of Milan, began an RCT comparing radical mastectomy and removal of the quarter of the breast containing the cancer (quadrentectomy) in 1973. Veronesi had unsuccessfully attempted to convince the World Health Organization to sponsor such an RCT as early as 1969.[90]

But such studies carried relatively little weight among United States surgeons, both due to a continued skepticism regarding randomized trials and because the research was being conducted overseas. It would take a tenacious and dogmatic American surgeon—Bernard Fisher—to finally convince enough surgeons and physicians "to accept the concept of, and participate in, rigidly controlled cooperative trials" of breast cancer surgery.[91]

Randomization at Last

The perpetual debates over breast cancer treatment reached their culmination in Chicago on October 14, 1970, at the 56th annual clinical congress of the American College of Surgeons. At the meeting, Crile once more had thrown down the gauntlet. Sixty-three years old and preparing to stop operating shortly, Crile presented data on simple mastectomies and partial mastectomies (lumpectomies) performed at the Cleveland Clinic, reporting a combined 72 percent survival rate for stage I and II cases. Again, these figures were comparable to most case series of radical mastectomy. Noting how breast surgeons in European countries had largely abandoned radical procedures, he analogized the Halstedian approach in the United States to the "Middle Age view of exorcising witches."[92] Most notably, Crile emphasized the need for women to take an active role in decision-making. "The time has come," he stated, "when the woman and not just her doctor has a say about what kind of treatment she will have."[93]

The performance was vintage Crile. Audience reaction was as vociferous as ever. "Are you kidding?" asked the first questioner, to peals of laughter. "Does any reputable surgical figure in this country besides Dr. Crile," asked another surgeon, "support the concept of a limited mastectomy and irradiation?"[94] Crile gave his usual responses, again winning points for courage and candor. But the star of the show in Chicago was not Crile. It was Bernard Fisher.

Fisher completed both medical school and his surgical residency at the University of Pittsburgh. As a Markle Scholar in Medical Science from 1953 to 1958, he received postgraduate training at the University of Pennsylvania and London's Hammersmith Hospital. When Fisher joined the surgical faculty of the University of Pittsburgh in 1959, he began a series of investigations that culminated in what he would later term an alternative hypothesis to the mechanistic Halsted theory. Fisher's first studies questioned the Halstedian notion that cancer spread along lymph channels in an orderly manner and entered the bloodstream only late in its course.

Fisher was hardly the first physician to challenge traditional beliefs as to how cancer spread. Maurice Black and other biological predeterminists, for example, had hypothesized that most breast cancers became systemic early in their course. In addition, the surgeons Warren H. Cole and George E. Moore had ascertained that cancer cells were released into the blood vessels when surgeons operated on colon cancer.[95] But Fisher, working with his brother Edwin, a pathologist, devised a series of experiments to study the biology of cancer in a rigorous manner. Based on extensive laboratory research, the Fishers had developed a new biological model of breast cancer by 1968. Included in this model were two hypotheses: (1) lymph nodes were not, as Virchow had taught, effective barriers to cancer cells but rather an indicator of how the cancer was behaving in an individual patient; and (2) cancers reached the bloodstream quickly, usually disseminating throughout the body before they were discovered.[96]

The next logical step was to determine how best to treat these cancer cells that had become deposited throughout the body. Two highly promising precedents existed. First, in research that would eventually win him the Nobel Prize in Medicine, Charles B. Huggins of the University of Chicago had reported in 1941 that castration of men with prostate cancer led to the temporary regression of the disease. Huggins's work demonstrated how altering the levels of hormones such as testosterone could influence the growth of cancers. Second, based on the accidental discovery made during World War II that nitrogen mustard gas inhibited cell growth, scientists had developed a series of drugs. They hoped that these agents, eventually termed "chemotherapy," could effectively kill cancer cells while sparing healthy tissues. Chemotherapy generated considerable excitement as it could potentially treat cancer that had already spread beyond the site of origin; surgery and radiation were only local treatments.

Physicians originally gave chemotherapy only to patients with widespread cancer, but, in 1958, the National Cancer Institute began to organize cooperative research involving chemotherapy as an adjunct to surgery in potentially curable patients. Chemotherapy given for such a purpose was known as "adjuvant." The participating researchers, from twenty-three institutions across the United States, called themselves the Surgical Adjuvant Chemotherapy Breast Cancer Group. The group's first protocol, which studied the chemotherapeutic agent Thio-tepa, found that the drug delayed recurrence of breast cancer.[97] In 1969, Bernard Fisher would become chairman of the organization, soon to be known as the National Surgical Adjuvant Breast and Bowel Project (NSABP).[98]

In addition to indicating the importance of so-called adjuvant chemotherapy, Fisher's conclusions about early dissemination suggested that aggressive local cancer operations made little sense. Yet in contrast to Crile or Peters, who had used their clinical judgment to initiate alternative therapies, Fisher sought to prove or disprove the value of radical surgery by employing what he believed was a more scientific approach. Earlier researchers, including Halsted and the Germans he had so admired, had also tried to place surgical practice on a more scientific basis. Such physicians had used the term "scientific" in both a descriptive and a rhetorical manner. Proving that something was scientific thus required the "experimental investigation and theoretical explanation of natural phenomena"[99] as well as the ability to convince the medical profession and the general public of the validity of one's findings.

Fisher used the same dual strategy, proposing more rigorous research and then informing his colleagues why this approach, as opposed to all others, was "scientific." In speeches and articles, he commended Crile, McWhirter, and others for providing "guidelines and clues" to the proper treatment of breast cancer. But, Fisher argued, adequate data still did not exist; the best therapy remained unknown. It was not the job of surgeons, according to Fisher, to reach individual conclusions about the least risky procedure and then sell their views to the patient. Rather, surgeons had an "ethical and moral obligation" to participate in randomized trials.[100] "This is the scientific method for which there is no substitute," he stated in 1970.[101] "One of the most important objectives of 'surgical science,'" Fisher wrote the next year, was to place "all operative procedures on a more scientific basis."[102] The RCT, he later claimed, was a "highly sophisticated methodology" that represented "a major step toward transforming medicine from an art to a science."[103]

Most statisticians strongly agreed with Fisher about the scientific nature of randomized trials and favored his strategy of devising hypotheses and then rigorously testing them. But it is less clear that the retrospective data being accumulated, which Fisher criticized as "unsystematic," "worthless," and "nonscience," were in fact bereft of scientific value.[104] In collecting case studies, analyzing them with statistics, and concluding that the curability of cancer depended largely on the innate virulence of the cancer and the patient's defenses, biological predeterminists such as Crile and Black were also doing science: they were conducting experimental investigations and explaining natural phenomena.[105]

By drawing such a stark distinction between his "scientific" efforts and those of earlier investigators, Fisher deftly used rhetoric to convince others that RCTs generated the truth or, at least, the definitive proof that had been lacking. Thus, the need to enroll patients in his clinical trials and accept the results became paramount for the future of surgical science. Other physicians, such as those appointed to the NCI's Breast Cancer Task Force, saw the advantage of this strategy. At a 1967 meeting, task force members had agreed that an RCT comparing radical and simple mastectomy would likely simply validate what decades of retrospective studies had strongly suggested: there was no "real" difference between radical and conservative surgery for breast cancer. Yet, as the radiotherapist James J. Nickson noted, "a convincing study might change the attitudes of surgeons."[106]

In demanding that surgeons admit their ignorance and enroll patients in randomized trials, Fisher was thoroughly upsetting the apple cart. Crile, despite all of his unconventional theories, was at heart, a surgeon: he recommended to his patients what he thought was best. But Fisher was different. To be sure, he had the stereotypical personality of a surgeon. He was confrontational and self-assured, often to the point of arrogance. But Fisher represented a true threat to business as usual in the world of surgery, which he once termed a "miasma of mediocrity" for not embracing his more academic approach to research.[107] In turn, the surgical establishment belittled Fisher and considered him an apostate. Critics also quietly questioned Fisher's surgical prowess, referring to him as someone who "could not operate his way out of a paper bag." What other explanation could there be for his obsession with statistics and his interest in less extensive—as opposed to more extensive—operations?

Yet by the 1970 American College of Surgeons meeting, a sense of change was in the air. Fisher, long the bane of breast surgeons, was finally convincing his colleagues of the need to organize definitive randomized trials. When he importuned, in his usual sonorous and authoritative tone, that surgeons should no longer make decisions based on what was appealing or logical, the audience responded with applause as opposed to derision. They also clapped loudly at his closing statement. "I believe that all of us," he declared, "must get these clinical trials done as quickly as possible and not sit on our butts and continue year after year to go through this same type of masturbation."[108]

By 1971, Fisher would begin enrolling patients in NSABP-04, the first randomized trial in America to compare radical mastectomy with less extensive surgery—in this case total mastectomy with or without radiotherapy. (Fisher preferred the term "total mastectomy" to simple mastectomy, but they both referred to removal of the breast only.) The use of total mastectomy without radiation, which meant that one third of women would not receive any treatment of the axilla unless there was clinical evidence of cancer there, represented Fisher's direct challenge to Halsted. If women in this arm of the trial did as well as those in the other two groups, it would contradict the almost theological belief among doctors that leaving untreated cancer behind necessarily doomed the patient. Not surprisingly, physicians at very conservative medical institutions—such as Memorial Sloan-Kettering, Columbia-Presbyterian, Massachusetts General Hospital, Johns Hopkins, and the University of Chicago—declined to join the thirty-four institutions in the United States and Canada that Fisher recruited to participate in NSABP-04.[109]

· · ·

At the 1971 meeting of the American College of Surgeons in Atlantic City, New Jersey, Cushman Haagensen once again presented data that he believed demonstrated much better ten-year survival among patients receiving a Halsted radical. Exasperated with his critics, he importuned, "How much evidence do you need to be convinced?"[110] In the end, however, the question was less how much evidence was needed than what kind of evidence. To Michael Shimkin, Bernard Fisher, and other physicians who had embraced the new statistical methodology, only the evidence provided by randomized controlled trials was scientifically valid. Yet even as they crusaded for RCTs, at least some advocates quietly admitted that such trials might only prove what they already strongly suspected was true.

As Haagensen, Fisher, and their compatriots debated the treatment of breast cancer behind closed doors in the 1960s, they had almost no idea of the maelstrom that was brewing. Although breast cancer patients had quietly participated in decision-making to various degrees throughout the twentieth century, physicians had remained in charge. After 1970, however, many women with breast cancer would emerge as vociferous critics of the medical profession, asking why radical mastectomies were still being performed and demanding the right to make decisions about their bodies. The interaction between physician and patient—especially between male surgeon and woman patient—would never be the same.

"I Alone Am in Charge of My Body"

Breast Cancer Patients in Revolt

In February 1972, a New York City journalist named Babette Rosmond published in *McCall's* magazine an account of her experiences as a breast cancer patient. In the piece, entitled "The Right to Choose," Rosmond discussed her decision to have a lumpectomy as opposed to a more extensive operation. The article generated more mail than any other in the history of *McCall's*. Typical was a letter from C.C., a California woman who stressed that she was not a woman's liberationist. "Too many of us just sit back and take it when clergy, doctors, etc. tell us that 'it's not good to know too much,'" she wrote. "Hogwash! We're almost into the 21st century, and certainly most of us are well enough adjusted to handle facts."[1]

C.C.'s dissatisfaction with the medical profession was part of a broader revolt in American society in the 1970s against figures and institutions of authority. That breast cancer patients became central figures in the revolt against standard medical practice was unsurprising. Not only were they patients facing an imperious medical establishment, they were women patients who almost invariably encountered male physicians, many of whom were condescending or paternalistic. Moreover, the way that these doctors "healed" was by administering a drastic and disfiguring surgical procedure.

Yet not all women with breast cancer chose to confront their physicians. Some actively sought out surgeons such as Cushman Haagensen or Jerry Urban, who still favored the radical mastectomy and had little interest in discussing other options. Physicians, too, responded variably to the activist patient. Some grew defensive and angry while others, even if perplexed, gradually accepted the sea change in medical decision-making that women such as Babette Rosmond helped to effect.

A Patient Fights the System

Evidence of longstanding concern with the physical and psychological ramifications of radical mastectomy comes from the stories of twentieth-century women—such as Charlotte Perkins Gilman—who had declined surgery. The fact that these women had learned of the side effects of surgery also suggests that at least some breast cancer patients actively discussed the topic amongst themselves. Nevertheless, for a disease that engendered secrecy in the first place, the details and consequences of radical surgery remained the most hidden aspect of breast cancer. For example, despite the American Cancer Society's extraordinary efforts to publicize early detection and radical surgery after World War II, their literature and films never discussed or depicted women with mastectomy scars.[2] One physician claimed that the Halsted radical left "no important disability or deformity."[3] Others told women to "put an old stocking in their bra" and to get on with their lives.[4] The side effects of radiotherapy also received scant discussion.

But some physicians did address the subject of posttreatment complications. William Halsted, for example, had a sincere interest in the arm swelling and immobility that often followed his radical mastectomy and taught his patients exercises to minimize these discomforts. In 1948, Memorial Sloan-Kettering established an "Amputee's Alliance" to provide encouragement for cancer patients who had undergone amputation of a breast or other body part. By the 1950s, many physicians would give a discharged breast cancer patient a pamphlet on postoperative care and exercises, which was seen as a "good morale booster."[5] Not infrequently, assigned exercises involved the motions employed in using a vacuum cleaner or other household items, thereby reinforcing the idea that resumption of domestic tasks was essential to a woman's recovery from surgery.[6]

Patients discussed issues of rehabilitation almost exclusively with their surgeons. Surgeons provided women with the exercises and, at times, solicited follow-up information about their symptoms during office visits.

Allied health professionals, such as social workers or counselors, were rarely involved. At home, women generally performed their exercises by themselves, either with or without the knowledge of family and friends.

But one woman found this strategy to be entirely inadequate. Terese Lasser was a wealthy and well-connected New York woman married to J. K. Lasser, a tax expert and author of the popular book, Your Income Tax. In 1952, Lasser's physician found a small lump in her breast and admitted her to Memorial Sloan-Kettering for a biopsy. Believing that her breast mass would be benign, Lasser had anticipated a minor operation. But when her surgeon found cancer on a frozen section, he performed a standard Halsted radical mastectomy. Lasser was thoroughly devastated by the operation, awakening "wrapped in bandages from midriff to neck—bound like a mummy in surgical gauze."[7] Accustomed to getting answers, Lasser resented the silence that resulted when she asked quite reasonable questions: How could the pain and swelling in her arm be reduced? When could she resume sexual relations with her husband? What should she tell her children? Finally, where could she obtain a prosthesis?

By 1954, Lasser had founded Reach to Recovery, an organization dedicated to providing hospitalized radical mastectomy patients with the type of information she had sought. The name of the organization referred to the reaching exercises of the arm that were a major part of Lasser's rehabilitation program. Either Lasser or another breast cancer participant visited women, providing them with a free gift box containing a temporary "falsie" and "A Letter to Husbands," which urged men to make their wives feel sexually desirable. Lasser expected her volunteers to be upbeat and to wear attractive, tight clothing that emphasized the bustline. By showing patients that they could not distinguish between her real and her missing breast, Lasser emphasized how Reach to Recovery could help them return to a normal way of life as soon as possible. She stressed familiar themes of personal responsibility, stating that women needed to demonstrate a "will to recover."[8]

Certain surgeons reacted angrily to Lasser's program, seeing Reach volunteers as outsiders who were interfering with the doctor-patient relationship. One derisively referred to it as "sort of an Alcoholics Anonymous" session in which "girls who have had radicals are talking to each other."[9] Lasser did attempt to get permission from patients' doctors prior to her visits but was undeterred by rejections. As a result, longtime American Cancer Society medical director Arthur I. Holleb later recalled, she was "often escorted out the front door of Memorial Hospital."[10] Time vindicated Lasser, however, and by the late 1960s, Reach to Recovery chapters existed in cities throughout the United States and the world. She lectured at numerous medical schools and hospitals. In 1969, the ACS took control of Reach to Recovery. Within five years, it reported that half of all women undergoing mastectomy in the United States had received a visit from a Reach volunteer.

The response of most breast cancer patients to Lasser and her troops was highly favorable. After meeting with a Reach volunteer, wrote one woman, "I felt so much better and knew I could look the same as before."[11] A visitor from Reach to Recovery is "full of life and energy and is attractive and has on a pretty dress," remarked Marvella Bayh, who had been diagnosed with breast cancer in 1971 and was the wife of Indiana Senator Birch Bayh.[12] Many women visited by a Reach volunteer themselves signed up to work for the program. "For some time I've been a Reach to Recovery volunteer," noted one such woman, "and find these visits the most rewarding moments one could ask for."[13] Women publicized the Reach program by writing books and articles about their breast cancer and subsequent recovery.[14] By empowering women to openly discuss both their breast cancer and its effects on their lives, even in the face of physician opposition, Lasser embodied what the journalist Barbara Seaman has termed "militant" feminism.

As Reach to Recovery expanded and became more mainstream, physicians and nurses also turned their attention to the psychological effects of breast cancer. Among the earliest efforts was a research project conducted by two Chicago physicians, Richard Renneker, a psychiatrist, and Max Cutler, a breast surgeon. In observing the emotional reactions of fifty breast cancer patients, Renneker and Cutler found that the combination of a deadly disease and mastectomy led to frequent cases of "postmastectomy depression." Noting that the breast was "the emotional symbol of a woman's pride in her sexuality and her motherhood," they stated that breast cancer threatened the "very core" of a woman's "feminine orientation." Renneker and Cutler were particularly critical of the lack of candor that surrounded breast cancer, which caused women to "suffer in silence."[15] Physicians deserved considerable blame for this situation, both because they often concealed the diagnosis of breast cancer from patients and disregarded these women's feelings.

In identifying the personal issues of breast cancer patients and criticizing members of the medical profession, Renneker and Cutler's study, and other similar research by male physicians, represented a major breakthrough in addressing the psychosocial aspects of the disease. As the *Reader's Digest* noted, physicians at academic institutions were beginning to acknowledge how their emphasis on cure had led them to ignore the very real sequellae of their "curative" operations.[16] These complications included rates of arm lymphedema as high as 50 to 70 percent. By 1970, data existed suggesting that more attention to rehabilitation would produce beneficial outcomes. David Shottenfeld and Guy F. Robbins at Memorial Sloan-Kettering reported that exercises had helped 84 percent of breast cancer patients who had survived five years to resume their preoperative activities.[17]

But despite this long overdue attention to emotional and psychological issues, researchers studying these phenomena often projected their own—or societal—expectations onto their findings.[18] This projection occurred most commonly when investigators evaluated the adjustment of breast cancer patients who did not exhibit normative behaviors. In 1967, for example, Patrick B. Friel, Glen C. Nicolay, and Ludwig M. Frank, two psychiatrists and a psychologist from Connecticut, published case studies of "adverse emotional reactions to disfigurative surgery."[19] One patient, a thirty-one-year-old white female, had felt "very angry" and "cheated" upon awakening from her radical mastectomy. She stated that "[she] had two and they stole one," and refused to speak with her surgeon for three days.[20] Viewing the patient's actions in light of an admittedly difficult upbringing, Friel and colleagues deemed her behavior to be deviant. It was "pathological," they wrote, for a patient to state that "[she] would rather be dead than to have this operation."[21]

Such a conclusion was contingent on both a medical and a psychogical assumption. The medical assumption was that the Halsted model of cancer was accurate. As we have seen, however, evidence already existed by 1967 suggesting that a medical basis for declining radical mastectomy quite possibly existed. The psychological assumption was that there was

only one logical way for a woman with a deadly disease such as breast cancer to respond: to do what the doctor said. Yet with feminist sentiments on
the rise, this supposition was also becoming debatable. Ironically, it may
have been the well-meaning attention of certain male physicians to the cultural significance of the female breast that led them to assume that a desire
to keep the breast in the face of cancer indicated some type of abnormal
sexual or maternal fixation.[22] As more and more women in the 1970s took
a hostile view to an automatic radical mastectomy, however, it would become impossible to label all of them as pathological.

Going Public Again

For American women to exercise their options in doctors' offices, they
needed to know that alternatives were available. Beginning in 1970,
breast cancer and the debates over radical surgery became a frequent subject in women's magazines, in newspapers, and on television. Initially, at
least, women interested in publicizing the issue relied on sympathetic
male physicians. The first such connection occurred in Boston.

In July 1969, Maryel F. Locke was the editor of the *Radcliffe Quarterly*, the
magazine of Radcliffe College. Locke had two connections to breast cancer. First, several of her friends had recently been diagnosed with breast
cancer and had been "pushed into agreeing to have a mastectomy if necessary."[23] Second, Locke herself had recently undergone a biopsy of a breast
lump and, in standard fashion, been asked to consent to a "one-step" procedure, in which the surgeon would immediately perform a radical mastectomy if the intraoperative frozen section revealed cancer. Locke, fearing
a misdiagnosis and the unnecessary loss of her breast, objected and refused to sign the consent form. The surgeon agreed to perform only the
biopsy, which came back as negative. After recovering from her biopsy,
Locke fished out an article that she had read about Oliver Cope, a surgeon
at Massachusetts General Hospital (MGH), who advocated less radical
surgery for breast cancer. She decided to contact him.

Cope was born to Quaker parents in Germantown, Pennsylvania, in
1902. He went to Harvard University and Harvard Medical School, from
which he graduated in 1928. A surgical residency at MGH followed, after

which Cope joined the surgical service as a junior faculty member. He quickly became a star in the department, conducting well-received research on the surgical removal of the parathyroid gland. Cope had also begun research on the surgical care of burn patients when the infamous Cocoanut Grove nightclub fire took place in Boston in 1942. The MGH received hundreds of victims, many of whom, doctors concluded, had died from asphyxiation. This realization led Cope and his colleagues to initiate research on the diagnosis and treatment of burns that affected the lungs.[24]

In 1932, Cope married Alice DeNormandie, a native of Lincoln, Massachusetts. The Copes lived in Cambridge, where their home was a gathering point for Harvard faculty members, medical students, and residents. Oliver Cope was extremely well read and played the classical violin at the level of a concert violinist.

Although he was a surgeon at the strongly conservative MGH, both Cope and his wife had liberal ties. Reflecting his Quaker upbringing, Oliver Cope was a lifelong pacifist and raised objections to America's presence in Vietnam as early as 1966. During the 1960s, Cope also became increasingly interested in the psychosocial aspects of illness and the inadequate training of medical students in this area. He helped organize conferences on this topic, and in 1968 published a book entitled *Man, Mind and Medicine*.[25] Cope's calls for training more humanistic physicians in medical school presaged dozens of books on this theme published in the 1980s and 1990s.

Cope's perspective was especially notable because his training was in surgery, a discipline that had generally eschewed a patient-centered approach. Indeed, Cope leveled many of his harshest criticisms at surgical departments, which he believed turned out authoritarian, intellectually lazy surgeons trained in outdated and unnecessarily radical operations.[26] Cope often cited breast cancer as a prime example. Too few of his colleagues, he argued, took notice when breast cancer patients expressed regret or anger after their radical mastectomies. Nor did surgeons acknowledge that 75 percent of women receiving radical surgery ultimately died of breast cancer anyway.

Thus, in 1956, when Cope had encountered a woman who declined a mastectomy, he was ready to try something different. Adamantly refusing to lose her breast, the woman had asked Cope to find another way of treating her.[27] Having spoken to colleagues in the radiation department, who had experience in using x-rays to treat inoperable breast cancers, Cope removed only the patient's lump and referred her for radiotherapy. He subsequently used this treatment for other patients as well. In 1967, at a meeting of the New England Surgical Society, Cope and his colleagues presented preliminary data about the selective use of lumpectomy and radiotherapy at Massachusetts General Hospital. The paper, which was later rejected by the *New England Journal of Medicine*, evoked hostile comments.

Cope's skepticism regarding cancer surgery had also manifested itself in 1962 when he developed bladder cancer that had invaded his prostate. Unwilling to wear a urine collection bag for the rest of his life, Cope rejected the advice of his urological colleagues to have radical bladder surgery. Instead, he convinced MGH radiotherapists to treat him with high-dose radiotherapy. Cope claimed to be the first bladder cancer patient at the hospital to receive x-ray therapy.

By the time that Locke contacted him in 1969, Cope had become further convinced of the futility of radical breast surgery. After they spoke, Locke proposed that Cope write an article on breast cancer for the *Radcliffe Quarterly*. Cope resisted, citing the traditional ethical tenet that proscribed physicians from writing about medical topics for a lay audience. Cope relented only when Locke pointed out that he had recently retired from active practice and would be writing more for a university than a lay publication. To ensure that her readership understood Cope's arguments, Locke extensively edited the article, which was provocatively titled "Breast Cancer: Has the Time Come for a Less Mutilating Treatment?" In the piece, which appeared in the June 1970 issue, Cope extensively reviewed the existing disagreements about breast cancer treatment. Explicitly attacking the style of his surgical colleagues, he concluded that "[women] don't need to be railroaded into having their breast [sic] removed."[28]

Several women's magazines immediately contacted Locke, seeking to reprint the article. When she excitedly informed Cope that *Vogue* was interested, Cope asked her what "Vogue" was. Despite Cope's ignorance, *Vogue* ultimately reprinted the piece in its November 1970 issue. Meanwhile, other women's magazines featured articles that discussed Cope's position. One such piece, published by *Woman's Day* in October 1970, generated 7000 letters.[29]

Scientific controversies go public when debates about knowledge become debates about values.[30] By demonstrating how surgeons arrived at treatment decisions, Cope argued to his readers that doctors' personal preferences—as opposed to scientific knowledge—appeared to be guiding the management of breast cancer. The next physician to expose the dirty laundry of the medical profession made a similar argument. William A. Nolen was a gregarious man of Irish descent who had trained in surgery at New York's Bellevue Hospital in the 1950s and then begun a practice in rural Litchfield, Minnesota, in 1960. Nolen had already obtained a reputation as a heretic by publishing *The Making of a Surgeon*, a humorous, tell-all account of his days at Bellevue. Among other things, Nolen had poked fun at several senior surgeons and revealed that mistakes were commonplace on the surgical service.[31]

After Barney Crile reported 72 percent five-year survival for less extensive breast surgery at the 1970 meeting of the American College of Surgeons, Nolen reconsidered his standard practice of performing radical mastectomies. In the April 1971 issue of *McCall's*, he revealed his epiphany to women across the United States. Given the obvious uncertainty in the treatment of breast cancer, Nolen wrote, "I thought it was time for women—our patients—to hear what we were arguing about."[32] He concluded that "[i]t's her breast and her life. She has a right to know."[33] Meanwhile, Crile, who planned to stop operating in 1972, had refocused his attention toward educating women about breast cancer. Due to his persistent concern that he would be accused of promoting his own practice,[34] Crile had actually not published anything for the lay public since *Cancer and Common Sense* in 1955. As he worked on a new book, *What Women Should Know About the Breast Cancer Controversy*, which would be published in 1973, Crile became a frequent guest on television programs, including the *Today Show* and *Not for Women Only*, hosted by Barbara Walters.

This challenging of traditional assumptions about breast cancer mirrored other changes occurring in American society at this time. Authority was being questioned by civil rights workers protesting segregation, liberals attempting to eradicate poverty, and antiwar protesters objecting to the Vietnam War. In justifying her decision to print Cope's article, Locke approvingly cited how the civil rights movement had similarly encouraged public airing of a controversial topic.[35]

But the questioning of breast cancer physicians' authority drew most directly from the rising feminist movement. Beginning with the publication of Betty Friedan's The Feminine Mystique in 1963, women were objecting to what they saw as the subjugation of the female by a patriarchal society. In 1966, Friedan was instrumental in founding the National Organization for Women, which promoted equal rights for women. Feminist magazines such as Ms., begun in 1972, rejected the content of standard women's publications, which had emphasized fashion and domestic concerns. Symbolic of women's liberation was a protest that occurred in Atlantic City, New Jersey, at the 1968 Miss America pageant. Members of the Women's Liberation Party publicly disposed of their brassieres, which they believed inappropriately displayed their breasts in a manner that men deemed desirable.[36]

This dissatisfaction with how a patriarchal society viewed women's bodies was tied directly to how male physicians evaluated and treated the medical conditions within those bodies. A subset of women activists directed anger at medical practitioners, whom they described as "aggressive, competitive, technically oriented, unemotional, objective and dominant."[37] Echoing other feminist demands, these critics believed that women deserved "access to complete and accurate health care information and . . . the power to make their own decisions concerning their health."[38] Early attention focused on reproductive issues, such as the birth control pill and abortion, in which women argued that the medical profession consistently excluded them from decision-making. For example, in The Doctors' Case Against the Pill, journalist Barbara Seaman charged that paternalistic physicians were concealing from women an active debate within the medical profession about dangerous side effects of the new birth control agents.[39] By the early 1970s, there was a tangible women's health movement, a loosely based network of activists, women providers, and grassroots organizations. Most notable among the latter was the Boston Women's Health Book Collective, which published the first edition of its highly influential health manual, Our Bodies, Ourselves, in 1970.

The connections between feminism and breast cancer activism were clear from the start. For example, at a 1970 Senate Judiciary Committee hearing on the proposed Equal Rights Amendment, a Maryland pathologist, Frances Norris, testified that the "male-oriented" medical profession performed too many radical mastectomies and hysterectomies.[40] But it was Cope, with his liberal proclivities, who most clearly tied breast cancer to women's rights. Seeking common ground with feminist critics of medical practice and medical education, he appeared on a panel with the sociologist Sheryl Ruzek and physician-activist Mary C. Howell at a 1974 meeting of the American Association for the Advancement of Science. "The masculine bias," Cope stated in his talk, "often results in less than good medicine and sometimes cruel care."[41] He also was featured prominently in the popular 1974 feminist film, *Taking Our Bodies Back*.

Having been exposed to the controversies surrounding breast cancer, more women began to write about the subject. Some of these works were fictional, such as Jacqueline Susann's best-selling 1966 novel, *Valley of the Dolls*. In the book, the character Jennifer commits suicide rather than undergo a radical mastectomy. In 1962, Susann herself had initially refused the operation but had then reluctantly submitted. Yet most of the new authors, many of whom were journalists, told true stories—either of their own illnesses or the experiences of other women with breast cancer. Often these topics blurred. Women grappling with breast cancer often drew on informal "female networks" to learn more about the diagnosis and treatment of the disease. The stories of these other women then became part of their own disease narratives. Although women had long written books or magazine articles about breast cancer and its aftermath, these earlier works had largely portrayed the medical profession as beneficent and well-meaning. In contrast, the new narratives, which revealed not only the personal details of illness but also the uncertainty and controversy that these women encountered, were "acts of daring."[42]

The Invisible Worm

Among the first woman writers to tell her story in this manner was a strongly opinionated fifty-year-old New York writer named Babette Rosmond. Rosmond had always loved to write. At the age of seventeen, she had a short story published in *The New Yorker*. Subsequently, she had authored six novels as well as dozens of articles for magazines. At the time of her diagnosis, Rosmond was an editor at *Seventeen* magazine, married to

Babette Rosmond *as she appeared in* 1964.
Courtesy of Jim Stone.

a prominent New York City lawyer, Henry J. Stone, and mother of two sons. Rosmond ultimately described her encounter with breast cancer in *McCall's* and in a 1972 book, *The Invisible Worm*, the title of which was derived from a William Blake poem. She published both works under the pseudonym Rosamond Campion. Despite the grave subject matter, Rosmond's writing was witty and irreverent, leading one of her sons to characterize her as "a rational woman with a geyser of gaiety spouting advice to the uninformed laity."[43]

When Rosmond discovered an olive-sized lump in her left breast in February 1971, she had recently spoken with two friends who had breast cancer. Both women, Rosmond believed, were exceptionally unhappy. One often cried for no apparent reason many years after her mastectomy. The other regretted having agreed to a one-step procedure. After undergoing both a radical mastectomy and radiotherapy, the latter woman had experienced severe pain. "The nerves in the stump of the pectoral muscle are screaming," she wrote Rosmond. Meanwhile, the area "burned" by the radiation was "terribly hot and itchy," ultimately becoming a "thick, reptilian hide that shed gray flakes for a year."[44] Four years after her treatment, Rosmond's friend still had a painful, immensely swollen right arm.

Thus, Rosmond was prepared when a breast surgeon informed her that he planned to perform a biopsy and, if necessary, a radical mastectomy, during the same operation. Only after considerable pleading did the surgeon agree to perform only the biopsy and then wait several days for the final pathological diagnosis. He told Rosmond that she was his first patient who had refused to sign the permission form for a one-step procedure. Noting that she and she alone was in charge of her body, Rosmond characterized her decision to challenge authority as emblematic of the era. "I think what I did was the highest level of women's liberation," she later noted. "I said 'No' to a group of doctors who told me 'You must sign this paper, you don't have to know what it's all about.' "[45] Macmillan, which published The Invisible Worm, explicitly noted the relationship of Rosmond's actions to the women's movement in its press release for the book.

Rosmond's misgivings about the paternalism of the medical profession were confirmed when the biopsy revealed a tiny eight-millimeter cancer that was presumably stage I. When Rosmond declined immediate radical surgery, the surgeon termed her "a very silly and stubborn woman."[46] When she continued to resist and indicated that she wanted to wait three weeks before she decided, the surgeon used his trump card. "In three weeks," he intoned, "you may be dead."[47]

Believing that such a statement was more histrionic than scientific, Rosmond traveled to Cleveland to see Barney Crile. She had learned about Crile from Nolen's article in McCall's. At Crile's request, she did not mention his name in her book and referred to the Cleveland Clinic as a "famous Midwestern clinic." As Rosmond had anticipated, Crile made sure that Rosmond learned all of her options, thereby enabling her to give "informed consent." Informed consent was a legal term, stemming from a 1957 ruling in a California case known as Salgo v. Leland Stanford Jr. University Board of Trustees. In that case, Martin Salgo, who had developed permanent paralysis due to an invasive imaging procedure called translumbar aortography, sued his physicians for not warning him about this potential complication. In finding for Salgo, the court created the requirement of informed consent, which obligated doctors to disclose "any facts which are necessary to form the basis of an intelligent consent by the patient to proposed treatment."[48]

Despite this ruling and a historical precedent of letting patients decline unwanted medical procedures, many physicians remained unwilling to delineate treatment options that they believed to be worthless or dangerous.[49] For example, Rosmond's surgeon initially informed her that discovery of a breast cancer mandated a radical mastectomy; he did not tell her that other options existed. Rosmond believed that surgeons who made decisions for their patients, even under the guise of beneficence, were in fact "arrogant, prejudiced [and] disinterested in human beings."[50] In contrast, Crile, by spelling out the available therapies, had spared her the "severe trauma" of remaining uninformed.

Because Rosmond had a very small, probably localized cancer in the outer portion of her breast, one of the options offered by Crile was a partial mastectomy, his version of a lumpectomy. Rosmond readily accepted this choice, concurrently declining radiotherapy to the rest of the breast, a decision with which Crile was comfortable. In explaining her reasoning, Rosmond stressed the importance of keeping both her breasts, of which she had always been proud. "To me the breasts yield aesthetic pleasure," she stated. "If [a woman] thinks a breast is something useful or rewarding to her, she should be allowed to keep it, and not treated like an idiot child who is taken to the principal and told, 'Naughty, naughty.'"[51] In making such a statement, Rosmond explicitly rejected the conclusion that an "uncooperative" woman with breast cancer was acting in a pathological manner. Other women argued the same point. In a letter to the American Cancer Society, Massachusetts health educator Marie F. Gately, who had experienced "unbelievable pressure" to have a radical mastectomy, wrote, "I do not feel that a woman should be viewed as psychopathic if she is resistant to the idea of a radical mastectomy." Taking aim at Reach to Recovery, she added that a "supportive parade of so-called well-adjusted fellow sufferers may merely indicate that misery indeed prefers company."[52]

Rosmond frequently reiterated that her decision to undergo lumpectomy was not necessarily correct for all women in her situation. "The choice I made was right for me," Rosmond reflected in 1976. "I did not, do not, cannot recommend it for every woman."[53] The Invisible Worm, Rosmond reiterated, was not about lumpectomy but personal choice.

The earliest articles on the breast cancer treatment controversy had a domino effect. Other women's magazines and newspapers began to print articles recounting the opinions of either Cope, Nolen, Rosmond, or local women who had questioned standard management. "Surgery Only Way?" read one headline in the Seattle Times. A Portland woman warned Oregonian readers that "When You've Seen One Breast Surgeon, You Haven't Seen 'Em All."[54] Reviewing the articles on breast cancer in the Reader's Guide to Periodical Literature between 1949 to 1984, the sociologists Theresa Montini and Sheryl Ruzek found a 500 percent increase beginning in 1974. Beginning in 1970, moreover, one out of every four articles on the disease addressed the radical mastectomy controversy.[55]

Books followed, often using breast cancer to demonstrate why women needed to assume greater control of their bodies. New York City journalist Ellen Frankfort began her 1972 book, Vaginal Politics, by describing a group of California feminists who performed gynecological examinations on one another and learned how to carry out early abortions. Moving on to the topic of breast cancer, Frankfort approvingly cited the work of Robert McWhirter, Barney Crile, and Vera Peters. She also hypothesized that male doctors' disregard for the female began in medical school anatomy class, when the fatty breast tissue was "summarily dismissed."[56] A California feminist writer named Dorothy Shinder provided a more radical perspective regarding breast cancer treatment. In Mayhem Against Women, Shinder, a political activist and longtime critic of taxes, sought to "arouse the public" about the "medieval maltreatment, atrocities and discriminatory acts committed against women."[57]

Shinder's book actually revealed a nascent rift within the women's health movement that complicated how women responded to the breast cancer controversy. Shinder epitomized what Barbara Seaman has termed a "downtown" feminist, one who often belonged to radical or militant groups and questioned the basic competency of the medical profession. Shinder told the unfortunate story of "Sara," an attractive single woman who in 1958 had undergone a radical mastectomy at Stanford University Hospital for a seemingly localized three-quarter-inch cancer. By all accounts, Sara experienced extremely severe consequences, beginning with pain and swelling of her arm and progressing to emotional distress that lasted for over a decade. Sara's surgeon, Shinder concluded, had committed the "outrage of mayhem" by performing a massive and unnecessary resection for a small lump.[58] A New Jersey woman who wrote to Rosmond made a similar claim, ruing that "innocent uninformed women" were being victimized by the "bloody hands" of surgeons.[59]

Frankfort's book, in contrast, typified "uptown" feminism, which challenged male domination of medicine by encouraging physicians to include their patients in decision-making. Frankfort, for example, had challenged the California health activists she described, telling them that their self-help techniques were medically dangerous. Rosmond, too, despite her fighting tone, did not view male physicians as brutal sadists who enjoyed (or at least did not mind) mutilating women's bodies. To Rosmond, exclusion of women from the decision-making process was much more egregious than an operation that removed breast and chest wall muscles.

This "right to choose" theme would repeat itself throughout the 1970s among breast cancer patients who spanned the political and social spectrum. Most striking were articles and books authored by women who had rarely, if ever, challenged authority but now proclaimed their right to do so. For example, although Betty Isaac ultimately dedicated her 1974 book, *A Breast for Life*, to her "compassionate" surgeon and her "paternal" psychiatrist, she had initially resisted mastectomy. "It's my flesh! It's my life!" she told her husband. "I can't have an operation I despise just to accommodate [the surgeon], or even you!"[60] New York City artist Win Ann Winkler, while critical of "clenched fist" feminists who defamed well-meaning breast surgeons, nevertheless argued that women had "the right to full comprehension of catch phrases like *lumpectomy, lesser surgery,* and *freedom of choice.*"[61] A Gallup poll conducted at the behest of the American Cancer Society in 1973 demonstrated how quickly women were embracing this expanded decision-making role. Some 48 percent rejected the one-step procedure, standard only a few years earlier, preferring to review various treatment options if their biopsy turned out to be positive.[62]

Within this overall trend, the loudest critics of radical breast surgery were white, middle-class women who lived in large cities such as New York or Boston. Because rates of breast cancer (and thus radical mastectomy) were somewhat higher among more affluent white populations, and because such women more often participated in early detection programs,[63] it was natural that they had taken a strong interest in the arguments over treatment. Although media publicity about excessive use of radical mastectomy did not exclude working-class and minority women, it did not target such women, either. As a result, awareness about treatment options likely spread more slowly in poorer and rural communities.

Articles on breast cancer that appeared in the 1970s in magazines aimed at African Americans generally did not focus on the surgery controversy. In 1971, for example, Ebony editor Eva Bell Thompson detailed the account of her breast cancer "to help others facing radical mastectomy." Thompson's article featured stories of other black women with breast cancer and a diagram of an African American woman performing breast self-examination. Thompson and the singer Minnie Riperton, who told her story to Ebony in 1976, emphasized the importance of publicizing breast cancer to African American communities, where rates of breast examination remained significantly lower than among whites.[64] The omission of overtly feminist themes in such pieces may in part have reflected the relative absence of African American women from mainstream feminist organizations.

But some black women active in progressive politics took note of the breast cancer controversy. In the January 1973 issue of Black News, a radical African American newspaper published in Brooklyn, thirty-eight-year-old Sis. Cherry decided to "share with the Black community" the story of her recent breast cancer. After finding a breast lump, Cherry had read the articles by Nolen and Rosmond in McCall's and decided that if she were to die, she would "go whole, in one piece." Cherry contacted Rosmond, who provided her with Crile's name. Eventually, one of Crile's colleagues at the Cleveland Clinic performed a lumpectomy on Cherry. "Sisters," Cherry urged any readers who discovered a breast lump, "find a doctor who believes that where it is medically possible, it is time for . . . a woman to have a choice of treatment."[65]

Women's activism regarding breast cancer treatment was not limited to the United States. In England, for example, a twenty-nine-year-old breast cancer patient named Jeanne Campbell had rejected as "scandalous" the notion of a one-step procedure leading to radical mastectomy. Campbell chose to undergo lumpectomy and radiation therapy at Guy's Hospital and, before her death from breast cancer in 1981, actively publicized this option to English women.[66] The story in other countries, such as South Africa, was similar. "[M]ale surgeons," wrote one Capetown woman, "seldom placed options before their patients."[67]

Yet the fights over radical mastectomy were the loudest in the United States. It was in America that Halsted's operation had reached its apogee and thus had the farthest to fall. The image of women insisting on participation also fit well with American individualism. When Ms. magazine ran its first piece urging breast cancer patients to challenge their doctors, it was entitled "A Patient's Bill of Rights."[68]

Responses of Women

Babette Rosmond's article in McCall's generated thousands of letters from women and men across the country, roughly 80 percent of which supported her. By 1975, Rosmond had also received 3000 responses to The Invisible Worm. This outpouring of interest indicated the degree to which the issues she raised engaged American women. While the letters of support often overlapped in content, they fell into four broad categories. The first type, from women actively undergoing medical evaluation, asked for the identity and location of Crile. The second group of writers criticized physicians and emphasized a woman's right to choose. The third set of letters recounted as cautionary tales the horror stories of women who had undergone radical surgery. Finally, the last, and most intense, variety of missive came from women who engaged Rosmond as a sympathetic voice as they confronted breast cancer and their own mortality.

Typical of the letters requesting information was one from a New York woman. "Would you PLEASE send me the name of the Doctor who performed your surgery and the name of the hospital where it was done?" she asked. "As you have probably guessed, I face the same dilemma you did."[69] Rosmond, who, at Crile's request, had withheld his name in her writings, gave it to these women. Soon, physicians at the Cleveland Clinic (mockingly termed the "Lourdes of lumpectomies" by one critic) were evaluating and treating a steady stream of out-of-town women who had been "referred" by Rosmond. One such woman, who had undergone a simple mastectomy by Crile's son-in-law, Caldwell B. Esselstyn, Jr., admitted to having bad days, but stated that "it would have been so much worse" if she had received a more radical procedure.[70] Another, who underwent a lumpectomy by Clinic surgeon Avram M. Cooperman, had stated, "I came with two, I'll go with two."[71]

The importance of women making their own decisions was stressed by a California woman who, in 1969, had declined a radical mastectomy in favor of an unspecified smaller operation. "[M]ay we both live many years," she told Rosmond, "to prove how right it is for women to choose—when feasible."[72] Other women had felt incapable of opposing their physicians and now criticized their paternalism and arrogance. "No matter what my arguments," one Massachusetts woman wrote, "his decision was absolute." Her surgeon, she added, was like a salesman who had to have his daily "quota" of radical operations.[73] An Indiana woman with ovarian cancer agreed, telling Rosmond that doctors "SCARE you to death but don't think it necessary to treat you as a partner in making a decision about your own body."[74]

One writer who emphasized the side effects of radical mastectomy was a Virginia woman who had recently found a lump in her right breast. Her mother, the woman informed Rosmond, had undergone a radical mastectomy for "just a suspicious spot," and was left with "one arm twice the size of the other and a hole in her chest—and endless pain in the arm." Indicating that she herself could not live with this type of mutilation, she had decided not to have radical surgery.[75] Similarly, a Pennsylvania woman believed that her mother, who had undergone a radical mastectomy several years earlier, was "horribly disfigured. I too have resolved not to allow the radical method, now used in the treatment of the disease, if [breast cancer] should claim me as a victim."[76] Other women emphasized the emotional side effects of the surgery, such as a Brooklyn breast cancer patient who wrote that Rosmond's "tale of the young woman who started to cry in the middle of a luncheon rings a true bell for me."[77]

One dying patient who wrote to Rosmond was the Indiana woman with ovarian cancer, who believed that surgery and radiation had caused her agony but would not save her life. "Who," she asked, "would burn all your skin, change the color and worst of all ruin the tissue and change it to a kind of mush?" Urging women to expose the "liars and hypocrites," she hoped that other women would "not die the way I am."[78]

Rosmond also began a correspondence and friendship with a New York City woman, E.P., who had undergone a lumpectomy for an eight-millimeter cancer at the Cleveland Clinic in July 1972. Initially thrilled with the results, E.P. wrote Rosmond that the operation had saved her marriage and her life. Six months later, however, she reported that "my luck is not running well." A biopsy of an axillary lymph node had revealed cancer, and she had begun radiation treatment in New York. In June 1974, she told Rosmond of another recurrence and spreading metastases despite radiation, additional surgery, chemotherapy, and Laetrile, an unapproved Mexican cancer remedy that achieved considerable popularity among patients in the 1970s. By February 1975, E.P. was exploring a Japanese cancer vaccine that had supposedly helped 50 percent of terminal cases. "My own health," she admitted, "is deteriorating at an even faster rate."[79] E.P. died on July 8, 1975, having never expressed regret to Rosmond about her choice of treatment.

It was, however, just this possibility of death following lumpectomy which made some women skeptical of Rosmond's decision, no matter how convincing a case she made. In the mind of both surgeons and the public, radical mastectomy retained its image as a "curative" operation. "Only the radical surgery is the positive cure," Betty Isaac was told before her radical mastectomy.[80] One woman, who had undergone two radical mastectomies only four years previously, proclaimed the operations a "total success" and termed herself "cured of cancer."[81] "Mutilating though [the radical mastectomy] may be," *Look* magazine reported in 1971, "it is a lifesaving operation."[82]

A series of women wrote to Macmillan seeking details about Rosmond's subsequent health. "I would sincerely appreciate knowing," queried a Florida woman in 1975, "if Rosamond Campion is still in good health today."[83] "Have you conquored [sic] the disease?" a Los Angeles woman asked Rosmond in 1976. "Has it returned in other parts of your body? Do you think you made the right decision?"[84] Some of these women had themselves undergone mastectomies. "[I] would hope your surgery was just as successful," wrote a New York woman in 1981.[85]

Yet other women who had received more conventional surgery confronted Rosmond, perhaps in order to validate their own choices. Having watched Rosmond on television, one woman stated she had been "appalled" for one and a half hours. "You are a menace to an unsuspecting public," she concluded.[86] A Florida woman chastised *McCall's* for having done a "grave disservice" to the women of America. Referring to Rosmond, she wrote that "it is my opinion that she is a dying woman."[87]

Rosmond had likely offended many of these women by urging patients to question their physicians. Admiration for the medical profession had by no means disappeared by the early 1970s. "How godlike he is," wrote Geraldine Clinton Little about her breast surgeon in *Good Housekeeping* in 1973. "How completely the patient is in the doctor's hands."[88] Marvella Bayh agreed, stating that she "would never want to tie my physician's hands . . . . He is never going to want to do more than is necessary."[89] Indeed, in the same 1973 Gallup survey in which 48 percent of women had rejected a paternalist model of decision-making, 47 percent of women still had favored the one-step procedure.

Responses of the Medical Profession

Just as women responded in varying ways to the possibility of less extensive operations, so, too, did physicians. Many, of course, had already begun to question the radical mastectomy, albeit more quietly than Nolen, Crile, and Cope. New York surgeon Stanley Edelman, for example, stated that "[a] woman in the prime of life should be given the benefit of a 50-50 chance that she need not lose a breast."[90] "Abrasive lack of compassion is not a hallmark of excellence," wrote Florida surgeon F. Gordon King. "Some of my colleagues seem to believe this."[91] Among those who increasingly questioned radical breast surgery were women physicians, whose numbers had finally begun to rise in the 1970s.

Nevertheless, radical mastectomy remained the procedure of choice for operable breast cancer in the early 1970s. Montini and Ruzek reported that surgeons performed 46,000 radical mastectomies in the United States in 1974, down only slightly from the 51,000 performed in 1965. Surgeons performed simple mastectomies or lumpectomies in well under 10 percent of cases.[92] Why, with numerous alternative procedures available and an increasingly dissatisfied population of women patients, did surgeons so tenaciously hold onto the procedure that Halsted had proposed over seventy years earlier?

Once again, physicians pointed to medical theory and statistics to justify their continued support of radical mastectomy. They argued that lumpectomies left behind areas of cancer because breast tumors arose from multiple foci within the breast; that radiotherapy and chemotherapy, while becoming more potent and widely available, were not yet reliable enough to limit the amount of surgery performed; and that, pending the results of Umberto Veronesi's and Bernard Fisher's clinical trials, no smaller operation had ever given as good or better results than radical mastectomy.

Such physicians were entirely sincere in their belief that more surgery would cure more women. While admitting he did not yet know how many more lives mastectomy saved as compared with lumpectomy, New York oncologist Ezra M. Greenspan favored more surgery. "[T]o the single patient in whom [mastectomy] makes a difference," he stated, "it's a 100 percent difference."[93] For Jerry Urban and other surgeons, it was a question of never giving up. "You save all of these patients," he stated at a breast cancer symposium in New York. "That's the point."[94] "[W]e must not condemn a woman as being incurable," wrote New York surgeon Irving M. Ariel, "on the basis of theoretical logistics."[95] When Los Angeles surgeon William P. Longmire, Jr., finally performed his first lumpectomy in the late 1970s, he experienced profound discomfort. Longmire had a direct connection to Halsted, having learned the radical mastectomy at Johns Hopkins in the 1930s with Halsted's trainee William F. Rienhoff, Jr. After performing the lumpectomy, he later recounted, "I kept feeling the scar. I wasn't sure whether the mass I was feeling was cancer." This indecision went on for six to eight months, until Longmire told the patient that he wanted to do a mastectomy. She agreed. He found no cancer in the specimen.[96]

Perhaps the best evidence of the persistent faith of surgeons in the Halsted paradigm was their response when Barney Crile's second wife, Helga Sandburg Crile, developed breast cancer in 1974. Sandburg was the daughter of the famous biographer and poet Carl Sandburg, and an accomplished author in her own right. Given that Sandburg's cancer was less than one centimeter in diameter without evidence of metastases, both she and Crile favored a lumpectomy. Her stepson-in-law, Caldwell Esselstyn, performed the surgery. But Sandburg noted the same disapprobation from her husband's colleagues that had occurred fifteen years earlier when Crile's first wife, Jane Halle Crile, had received what they believed to be inadequate treatment. When Sandburg attended cocktail parties at medical meetings, physicians would often approach her and tell her that she had made a mistake. For their wives, they would have recommended at least a modified radical mastectomy as the more appropriate intervention. Surgeon Gordon Schwartz recalls having seen Haagensen publicly accuse Crile of trying to kill Sandburg.[97]

But a purely medical explanation for the persistence of radical mastectomy is unsatisfying. Other factors also induced these physicians to dig in their feet and defend an anachronistic procedure. Some of this obstinancy can be traced to the potential legal, economic, and professional ramifications of changing to less extensive operations. From a legal perspective, certain surgeons believed that recurrent cancer following a smaller procedure made them liable—because they had both done an inadequate operation and deviated from standard surgical custom. "We are very leery of malpractice," stated Memorial Sloan-Kettering's Guy Robbins.[98] Some surgeons who performed less radical operations required their patients to sign release forms protecting them in the event of recurrence. In addition, a switch to more conservative surgery would also have represented a tacit admission that decades of radical mastectomies had, in retrospect, been unnecessary. Women who had received these extensive operations, therefore, could theoretically also sue. Economically, smaller operations meant two to three times less reimbursement for surgeons, both because such procedures cost less and because patients remained in the hospital for shorter periods. The degree to which such economic concerns actually influenced treatment decisions is difficult to measure, although Crile consistently claimed they played an important role.[99]

Surgeons willing to risk legal or economic repercussions were reticent to change their surgical approach for another reason: tradition. As Gerald P. Murphy, who succeeded George Moore as head of the Roswell Park Memorial Institute, noted, "You don't practice medicine one way for 30 years and then change with the reading of one article—you need to see it 10-20 times, hear it at conferences and national meetings, hear your respected leaders have a consensus—then you're interested."[100] Having long equated successful operations with both technical expertise and removal of as much tissue as necessary, the notion of purposely doing less was entirely foreign to most breast surgeons. Admitting that he did "a little more surgery than I should on the average patient," Jerry Urban disparaged "all this small crappy stuff."[101]

The hierarchical nature of the surgical profession also promoted conformity. One woman told Rosmond that her Kansas City surgeon would not perform Crile's procedure because "he would be severely criticized by his conferees if he attempted it."[102] California surgeon Max R. Gaspar stopped doing radical mastectomies only when he believed he would not "get lynched."[103] Faculty members also passed down this emphasis on preserving the status quo to the next generation of surgeons, whose training, it was believed, needed to include the traditional radical mastectomy. "Surgeons are basically trained by rote," Avram Cooperman recently noted. "'This is what the disease is, this is how we treat it, this is how I do it.'"[104] "Surgeons are like Marines," Sherwin B. Nuland concurred. Tradition is "drilled into them all the time."[105]

Finally, many surgeons held on tightly to the radical mastectomy because they did not like patients—especially women patients—telling them what to do. Confronted with women who wished to know all of the possible treatment options for breast cancer, these surgeons did not simply indicate why operations other than radical mastectomy were medically inappropriate. Instead, they characterized these patients as foolishly rebellious. "Now the surgeon is faced with a patient," stated Atlanta surgeon John P. Wilson, "who presents herself with a lump in her breast, a copy of an article from *Vogue* magazine, a quotation from the 'Today' show, and a preconceived notion of how she should be treated."[106] "Women," remarked the cancer society's Arthur Holleb in 1975, "are marching on clinics and private offices waving copies of *McCall's*, *Good Housekeeping*, *Ms.*, *Playgirl*, or the supplement of their local newspaper."[107] Other surgeons even spoke of women who were being "killed by such-and-such a magazine."[108]

The degree to which male physicians criticized their more activist patients is further revealed by their reliance on patronizing gender stereotypes. When one New York City woman scheduled for breast surgery at New York's Beth Israel Hospital told her surgeon that she wanted more time to think about the operation, "he just shook his head and told my husband what a foolish idea I seem to have." She signed out of the hospital, "against everyone's wishes."[109] Even William Nolen admitted he was guilty of "protectionism," in which a physician "took a paternal, protective attitude" toward his women patients while at the same time treating his men patients as equals.[110] When women cited their postoperative appearance as a factor weighing against radical mastectomy, male doctors accused them of being vain. Marie Gately, for example, was told she had a "Venus Complex." Avoidance of adequate surgery due to "feminine whims," warned Irving Ariel, might result in a "dead woman with a somewhat more pleasant-appearing chest wall."[111] Physicians also expressed their discomfort with women who sought second and third opinions by terming this activity "shopping around." This invocation of a stereotypical woman's pastime trivialized the attempts of these patients to gain control of their destiny.

Although it may be possible that surgeons criticized women because their advocacy of untested smaller operations seemed so misguided, the reverse is more likely true. That is, these doctors' preconceived notions about gender led them to ridicule what these women were proposing. Having little respect for the messenger, it was impossible to respect the message. In this manner, the persistence of radical mastectomy had less to do with medical indications than with male physicians asserting power in the face of waning authority.

The ways in which issues of authority and gender subsumed the medical debates over radical mastectomy were vividly demonstrated on a series of television programs in the early 1970s, many of which featured Rosmond, Crile, and physicians favoring a more traditional approach to breast cancer. One particularly notable performance occurred on January 21, 1973, on the nationally syndicated David Susskind Show. In addition to Rosmond and Crile, Susskind's guests were Memorial Sloan-Kettering breast surgeon Jerome Urban; the oncologist Ezra Greenspan; Susan Schack, a woman who had undergone a radical mastectomy; and Terese Lasser, founder of Reach to Recovery.[112]

Citing extensive medical data in support of either radical or at least modified radical mastectomy, both Urban and Greenspan warned that the safety of breast conservation remained unknown. The fact that Rosmond had lived for over one year since her operation proved nothing about either her lumpectomy or those that other women might receive. Noting previous instances in which "sensationalist" therapies for cancer had proven worthless, both physicians agreed that "the worst doctor is his own doctor." Schack indicated that she and other breast cancer patients were entirely content with their choice of radical surgery, stating, "They function as women, I function as a woman." Lasser stressed the role of Reach to Recovery in helping breast cancer patients achieve sexual fulfillment in their marriages, noting that women needed the admiration and companionsip of a man. Although she applauded Rosmond and Crile for challenging physicians, Lasser concluded that women ultimately needed to do what their doctors recommended.

But it was the petite Rosmond, sitting next to Susskind and wearing a Cheshire cat–like smile, who dominated the show. She constantly interrupted the doctors and made sarcastic remarks while they were speaking. Rosmond even chastisted Crile, her own surgeon, when he stated that a breast was useless in a woman over sixty-five years of age. When Urban argued that a mastectomy could actually enhance a marriage, Rosmond asked, "Why do you assume everyone is married?" Rosmond also took on Lasser, who had so defiantly challenged the surgeons of Memorial Hospital twenty years earlier, for advocating better breast forms rather than a woman's choice.

Susskind strongly questioned Rosmond's aggressive stance. At one point, to emphasize she was not a physician, he called her "Mrs. Civilian." Later, Susskind attempted to provoke Crile by charging that he had been "overruled" by Rosmond by acceding to her wishes for a lumpectomy. Greenspan also challenged Rosmond, stating that women should not participate in decisions "so professional, so technical, so involved, so biological that they cannot begin to understand the facts."

Although activist women patients caused great consternation in the medical world, even more anger was directed at the physician whistleblowers who had first alerted women to the breast cancer treatment controversy. Even though Crile and Cope had waited until they were semiretired, they, like Nolen, had violated traditional medical ethical precepts by going public. A year after his *McCall's* article, Nolen noted, "plenty of doctors still won't speak to me."[113] Meanwhile, Crile was encountering the most scathing criticism of his career. In his usual fashion, both provocative and somewhat careless, Crile had extended his attack on radical surgery by suggesting that fee-for-service surgeons performed

George Crile, Jr., in semiretirement, circa 1978.

Courtesy of the Cleveland Clinic Foundation Archives.

unnecessary operations to increase their earnings. Ultimately, in 1975, the Cleveland Academy of Medicine reprimanded Crile for airing his views to the public instead of the medical profession.

It was Cope, however, who generated the most enmity among his colleagues. Although radical surgeons disagreed violently with Crile's data, they saw Cope's research in breast cancer as particularly unsophisticated. "Beware of Cope," warned the American Cancer Society's Arthur Holleb. "He is an enthusiast."[114] In addition, in contrast to Crile, who was playful and disarming, Cope was more pedantic and importunate, prone to "deliver himself of a vast plea"[115] that surgeons admit their chauvinism and cut less. Cope also tended to speak even less carefully than Crile, implying at times that mastectomy was never necessary in the treatment of breast cancer.

Cope became especially controversial at his conservative home institutions, Harvard Medical School and Massachusetts General Hospital. Often pointing to his earlier, more traditional research on burns and parathyroid disease, Cope's colleagues disapproved of his approach to breast cancer. Cope had become an "advocate" as opposed to a "scholar," longtime Harvard surgeon Francis D. Moore remarked.[116]

This profound dissatisfaction with both Cope's style and his claims regarding lumpectomy and radiotherapy culminated in a highly irregular episode in 1972 in which Massachusetts General Hospital physicians reviewed Cope's data without informing him. But when MGH surgeon Claude E. Welch mentioned this chart review to Barney Crile at a medical meeting, Crile immediately wrote to Cope and to MGH Chief of Surgery W. Gerald Austen, who knew of the project. Cope was deeply disturbed by what had occurred. Having been shown several letters and a copy of a preliminary report, he wrote, "I can hardly believe my eyes . . . . The secrecy of the investigation and the report has been unethical and unbecoming to members of a surgical staff."[117] Although Austen apologized to Cope and stated that his colleagues had fully planned to discuss the findings with him, the damage had been done.

Another group that responded to Nolen, Crile, and Cope was the American Cancer Society. In 1971, the ACS drafted a policy statement entitled "Conservative or Radical?" which delineated its views on breast cancer treatment. Aspects of the statement were quite moderate. Although the cancer society continued to recommend mastectomy, it did not mandate radical mastectomy, and noted that favorable studies of lumpectomy and radiotherapy did exist. Pleased with these conclusions, even Crile at one point termed the statement "very wise and correct."[118] This spirit of cooperation was also evident in several letters that Rosmond received from individual members of the ACS, one of whom had praised her book as "exquisite, gentle and strong."[119] Nevertheless, the cancer society was still dominated by male radical surgeons, and its statement ended on a confrontational note. Echoing Cope's earlier charge that women were being *railroaded* into mastectomy, it concluded that "the American public should not be *stampeded* into accepting less proven methods" (my emphasis).[120] And in the media, ACS medical director Arthur Holleb continued to characterize lumpectomy as an "almost useless procedure."[121] As with the debates in the 1950s over the early detection of breast cancer, moderate voices, although present on both sides of the treatment controversy, too often went unheard.

•   •   •

A surgeon had no control over when cancer left the breast, former Columbia University breast surgeon Frank E. Gump recently explained. But he certainly had control over how big he made his operation.[122] The wide excision and meticulous dissection afforded by the radical mastectomy enabled surgeons to provide maximum control of a dire and unpredictable disease. The operation served this role not only in the operating room but in the doctor's office, where the recommendation of radical mastectomy represented the surgeon's commitment to perform the best operation he could to save a woman's life. Yet there was a quid pro quo extracted for this effort. As Jerry Urban noted, in exchange for his services, the patient needed to "put her faith in my judgment."[123] When women came to surgeons' offices questioning radical mastectomy, they directly challenged the tremendous professional authority that the medical profession had long taken as a given. It is hardly surprising, therefore, that most surgeons remained "prisoners of their theoretical constructs" and held onto the procedure.[124]

But by the mid-1970s, the battle lines that seemed so clearly demarcated had begun to blur. The images of women as either angry rebels or victims of imperious breast surgeons proved too simplistic. Meanwhile, surgeons, other physicians, women with breast cancer, and organizations such as the American Cancer Society began to examine the complex ways in which the diagnosis and treatment of the disease affected the lives of individual women. The person most responsible for these new developments would be a journalist and self-proclaimed "Yiddish humorist" named Rose Kushner.

No Shrinking Violet

Rose Kushner and the Maturation of
Breast Cancer Activism

he year 1974 has rightly been called the turning point for breast cancer awareness in the United States. In that year, both Betty Ford and Happy Rockefeller were diagnosed with breast cancer and made public their experiences. But it was Rose Kushner, another woman diagnosed in 1974, who had an even greater impact on how Americans understood and responded to breast cancer. Kushner's one-woman crusade against the radical mastectomy and the one-step procedure later developed into a sophisticated strategy for enlightening physicians, women, and governmental officials about breast cancer.

By the late 1970s, Kushner's voice had been joined by those of a growing number of women who wrote about their own experiences with breast cancer. These illness narratives described breast cancer not just in terms of feminism and patients' rights but as an unwelcome visitor that inserted itself into every aspect of a woman's life. In these narratives, women discussed a broad range of subjects—including marriage, work, sex, body image, and emotional adjustment—as well as how these issues influenced their treatment decisions. The degree to which the political had become the personal was best exemplified by debates over breast reconstruction, which became available in the mid-1970s. Was a woman who desired reconstruction succumbing to the norms of a male-dominated society or making an independent statement about her needs and desires?

Famous Patients

The first famous breast cancer patient in the 1970s was neither Ford nor Rockefeller but Shirley Temple Black, the former child movie star and future

United States Ambassador to the United Nations. The forty-four-year-old Black had discovered a lump in her left breast in September 1972. She immediately saw her regular physician in Woodside, California, who examined her, performed a mammogram, and concluded that her mass was most likely a benign cyst. However, he recommended a biopsy and referred Black to a surgeon. Believing there was no urgency, Black scheduled the biopsy for early November, allowing her to work for six weeks in her new position with the President's Council on Environmental Quality.

Having read about Barney Crile, Black was aware of the controversy surrounding breast cancer treatment. In addition, she had at least one friend who had undergone and later regretted the one-step procedure. Black thus decided to undergo only a biopsy and then review her options. "I find intellectually distasteful," she later wrote, "the prospect of waking up and finding that someone else had made a decision and taken an action in which I, lying quite inert on the operating room table, had had no voice."[1] When the biopsy revealed a two-centimeter cancer without evident spread, Black rejected her doctor's recommendation of a modified radical mastectomy in favor of a simple mastectomy and dissection of a small number of axillary nodes. These nodes tested negative for cancer.

After discussions with her family, Black decided to reveal the details of her illness to the public in the February 1973 issue of McCall's. In a later McCall's article that discussed the 50,000 pieces of mail she had received, Black was praised as courageous for having "rip[ped] away the veil of secrecy and shame associated in our society with breast cancer."[2] Interestingly, the United Nations, where she would serve as a United States representative, was one of many employers that refused to hire cancer patients unless they had survived five years.[3]

Black's explanation of her role as a patient activist was telling. In contrast to women like Rosmond and later Kushner, who encouraged women to confront their physicians, Black was more conciliatory. Even as she vigorously defended "my right to do with my body exactly what I wish to do," she apologized to the medical profession "for trying to be knowledgeable about the details of this most complicated question."[4] Nor did Black subsequently become a vocal advocate for lesser surgery. The sole area of controversy that received emphasis was Black's decision to delay her biopsy, for which she was gently upbraided by American

Cancer Society representatives. Black later urged women with a breast lump to "go to a doctor immediately and get it diagnosed."[5]

Although Black's breast cancer generated considerable interest, it was dwarfed by what occurred when Betty Ford developed the disease in 1974. Ford was the wife of Gerald R. Ford, who had become the 38th president of the United States when Richard M. Nixon resigned on August 9, 1974. Gerald Ford and Elizabeth (Betty) Bloomer had married in Michigan twenty-five years earlier. As her new husband achieved increasing prominence in the United States House of Representatives, eventually becoming House Minority Leader, Betty Ford shouldered much of the role of raising their four children. Yet as wife of the vice-president and then as First Lady, Ford had developed a reputation as an outspoken feminist. Although readily admitting she was no bra-burner, she spoke approvingly of women's liberation, abortion rights, and passage of the Equal Rights Amendment.

Thus, when Ford was diagnosed with breast cancer, the media closely scrutinized how she made decisions regarding her treatment. Ford, who was fifty-six years old, had not discovered the right breast lump herself. Rather, it was detected during a routine physical examination on September 26, 1974. The presidential physician, William Lukash, immediately arranged for a consultation with two surgeons, Captain William Fouty, chairman of surgery at the Bethesda Naval Hospital, and J. Richard Thistlethwaite, civilian consultant to the hospital. Both surgeons agreed that an operation was urgently needed. Plans were made to admit Ford on Saturday, September 28.

Ironically, across the street from the hospital, the National Cancer Institute had scheduled a seminar for Monday, September 30, that would reveal the preliminary data from Bernard Fisher's NSABP-04 trial. Fisher planned to announce that the study, which began in 1971 and had enrolled 1700 patients, had thus far found no difference in outcomes for women receiving either a radical mastectomy or a total (simple) mastectomy with or without radiotherapy. Fouty, who performed Ford's surgery and obtained consent from her, knew of this impending announcement. Yet like most surgeons of the era, he continued to believe that a Halsted radical mastectomy was the least risky procedure because the axillary lymph nodes potentially contained cancer. Fouty recommended this operation to Betty and Gerald Ford, although he did mention that some physicians had begun to advocate the use of less extensive surgery. "Mrs. Ford asked intelligent questions," Thistlethwaite later reported, "and accepted all our advice."[6] This advice included the use of a one-step procedure, in which Ford would not be awakened in the event of a positive biopsy. Ford later stated that she "listened to [Fouty], believed him and did not really consider any alternative."[7]

During the surgery, Fouty found a two-centimeter tumor, a frozen biopsy of which revealed cancer. Fouty thus proceeded to perform a radical mastectomy, removing Ford's right breast, axillary lymph nodes and pectoral muscles. When the final pathology report revealed three positive lymph nodes, doctors prescribed a course of a new chemotherapeutic agent, L-phenylalanine mustard (L-PAM). In another study, Fisher had recently shown that this agent led to longer disease-free intervals in breast cancer patients with axillary disease.[8]

There was an enormous outpouring of support for the popular First Lady, who had insisted that the American public be fully informed about her condition. As with Shirley Temple Black, Ford received over 50,000 pieces of mail, most of which praised her candor and wished her luck. Roughly 10 percent of the correspondence came from women with a history of breast cancer. "You have made us love you in this short while," wrote one Illinois woman. "[M]ay God give you strength and return you to us in good health."[9] Perhaps most emblematic was a cartoon from an Ocala, Florida, newspaper showing a sketch of the United States that simply read: "Mrs. Betty Ford. Get well soon. The Nation."[10]

Women also responded to Ford's diagnosis by flocking to physicians and radiologists to have breast examination and mammography. Two years earlier, the ACS and the National Cancer Institute had begun the Breast Cancer Detection Demonstration Project (BCDDP), which sought to enroll 270,000 women nationwide in a program of early breast cancer detection. Ford's breast cancer was a huge boon to the BCDDP as well as to the philosophy of early detection. "I was one of the many thousands of women," one New York woman recalled in 1978, "who tore, and I mean literally, over to [the] Guttman Institute to commence a yearly mammogram and thermogram program."[11] The Guttman Institute and other BCDDP sites soon reported waiting lists of several months. Barbara

Walters surprised viewers of the *Today Show* by demonstrating breast self-examination while fully clothed.[12]

Another woman who grew concerned about breast cancer in the wake of Betty Ford's operation was Margaretta (Happy) Rockefeller, wife of the vice-president-designate, Nelson Rockefeller. The daughter of a wealthy Philadelphia family, Happy Rockefeller married the prominent New York politician and grandson of financier John D. Rockefeller in 1963. When performing self-examination shortly after Ford's announcement, Rockefeller was surprised to find a hardened area in her left breast that was the size of a fingertip. When mammography confirmed the presence of a suspicious mass, she entered Memorial Sloan-Kettering Cancer Center for a biopsy and, if necessary, mastectomy.[13] The operation was performed on October 17, 1974, less than three weeks after Betty Ford's surgery.

Rockefeller's surgeon was Jerry Urban. By the 1970s, Urban, now the acting chief of the breast service at Memorial, had reached the pinnacle of his career. Rockefeller was only one of hundreds of prominent women who eagerly pursued his services. As had Ford, Rockefeller consented to a one-step procedure, which was to be followed by a modified radical mastectomy in the event of a positive frozen section. Unbeknownst to Rockefeller, Urban also performed a "mirror image" biopsy of the corresponding portion of her right breast, which had indicated no evidence of cancer preoperatively. Urban recommended this procedure because his research had suggested that 15 to 20 percent of women with breast cancer had either silent cancer or a possible precancer, known as carcinoma in situ, in their other breast.[14]

When the frozen section of the left breast biopsy revealed cancer, Urban performed the planned modified radical procedure. Several days later, pathologists informed Urban that the mirror-image biopsy contained lobular carcinoma in situ (LCIS), cancer-like cells that were generally believed to represent future cancers. The area of LCIS was roughly the size of two pinheads. Urban told Nelson Rockefeller of the results, for which Urban recommended a preventive mastectomy of the right breast, but the two men decided not to inform Happy Rockefeller until she was well enough to undergo the second operation. Upon learning the results of the mirror-image biopsy, she consented to a simple mastectomy of the right breast, which Urban performed in early December 1974. As had Ford, Rockefeller also publicized her bout with breast cancer, writing an article in *Reader's Digest* entitled "If It Should Happen to You."[15]

Although women universally welcomed the increased attention to breast cancer, some criticized the decision of both Ford and Rockefeller to undergo a one-step procedure, in which they seemed to surrender decision-making to their physicians and husbands. The reporters at the press conference questioned Ford's choice of a radical mastectomy, mentioning the option of less extensive surgery four separate times.[16] Noting Ford's "support of women's rights and the E.R.A.," one group of Buffalo health feminists felt especially betrayed. In a letter to Ford, they stated that thousands of women annually underwent radical breast surgery that was mutilating, crippling, and medically unsound. "We question," the women concluded, "the rapidity of the medical diagnosis in your case, and the absence of any time for you to . . . consider alternatives to radical mastectomy."[17]

But none of these women had called the White House to try and prevent Betty Ford's mastectomy. Rose Kushner had.

Rose Kushner

Kushner, who was born Rose Rehert in Baltimore in 1929, had several connections to medicine. As a pre-medical student in the late 1940s, she had served as a psychiatry research assistant to Horsely Gantt, who used Pavlovian theory to study behavior modification. In 1951, she married Harvey Kushner, then an engineering student; the couple had three children. Upon returning to college in the 1960s, Rose Kushner studied experimental psychology. But when she graduated from the University of Maryland in 1972, her degree was in journalism.

As a freelance writer in the early 1970s, Kushner often focused on medical topics, such as depression and Tay-Sachs disease. Having once dated Johns Hopkins medical students and helped them with their homework, she often remarked that she was "left with no awe of the medical profession and its 'mystique.'"[18] Kushner also wrote regularly about the Vietnam War and was proud of having "told off" General William Westmoreland.[19]

Rose Kushner, circa 1986.
Courtesy of Harvey Kushner.

When Kushner found a "tiny elevation" in her left breast in June 1974, she promptly went to the public library, where she discovered Barney Crile's *What Women Should Know About the Breast Cancer Controversy* but little other information. Next she proceeded to the nearby National Library of Medicine and the library of the National Institutes of Health. By the time Kushner had completed her review of the breast cancer literature, she had reached two conclusions: (1) the Halsted radical mastectomy, with its mandatory removal of the pectoralis muscles, was an outdated operation; and (2) the one-step procedure was both unnecessary and inadvisable. In making this latter conclusion, Kushner drew on an old joke that Johns Hopkins medical students liked to tell. In the joke, a freshman medical student undergoes amputation of his penis after the intraoperative frozen section reveals cancer. But the good news, the student is told after the operation, is that the permanent section was benign. "[H]orror stories about inaccurate frozen-section diagnoses were part of every student's conversation," Kushner later recalled, and "I made up my mind that nothing would ever be done to me on the basis of a frozen-section diagnosis."[20]

Kushner was able to convince her family surgeon to perform only a biopsy. He had anticipated a negative result. Kushner later recounted the surgeon's anger at having biopsied a breast cancer without performing an immediate mastectomy. Rattling the bars of her bed in the hospital recovery room, he snapped, "I never should have let you get away with it."[21] Kushner's problems with physicians were only beginning. When she sought out a surgeon who would be willing to perform a modified radical mastectomy, she got eighteen straight rejections. Finally, Thomas L. Dao, chief of breast cancer at Buffalo's Roswell Park Memorial Institute, agreed to perform the operation. The pathology report revealed a cancer that was one centimeter in diameter. All of the axillary lymph nodes were negative.[22]

Kushner had stumbled into the story of her journalistic career and she knew it. "Vietnam will have to wait," she announced in August 1974, "while I finish a crusade to tell American women—and through them American doctors—what I have learned."[23] No one who knew Kushner doubted her commitment to this task or her ability to succeed. By her own admission, she had "a streak of stubbornness and a loud voice."[24] Kushner also cultivated the persona of an overbearing but concerned Jewish mother with "what others might call chutzpah."[25] Yet even those who found her to be confrontational emphasized her honesty and her intense devotion to publicizing breast cancer. Kushner never hesitated to let others know if she disagreed with them.

As Kushner recuperated from her operation, she began to write about both her personal experiences and what she had learned about breast cancer. On October 6, 1974, she published an article, "Breast Cancer Surgery," in the *Washington Post*. In characteristically self-deprecating fashion, she later joked that she would have gotten breast cancer sooner if she had known it would get her into the *Post*. Kushner then started writing a book. In preparation, she traveled to England, Scotland, Scandinavia, and Russia, discovering, as she expected, much less devotion to the Halsted radical mastectomy than in the United States. Having returned to her home in Kensington, Maryland, she dictated the book in seven weeks, "as if a fire were in me."[26] Harcourt Brace Jovanovich published *Breast Cancer: A Personal History and Investigative Report* in 1975. The book jacket contained a quote from Thomas Dao, stating, "Every woman in the United States should read this book."[27]

Dao's excitement was not unwarranted. For the 22,000 persons who ultimately purchased the book, *Breast Cancer* contained a voluminous amount of previously unpublished information about the cause, diagnosis, and treatment of breast cancer as well as advice and contacts for women who either had or possibly had the disease. But Kushner focused most of her attention on the two controversial topics—radical mastectomy and the one-step procedure—that she had identified in her earliest research. "Why are most surgeons in the United States still doing the disfiguring and disabling Halsted radical," she asked, "when the modified radical is just as good?"[28] Like Crile, Kushner believed that women with breast lumps delayed seeing their physicians because they feared such dramatic surgery. Unless the one-step was changed, she wrote in 1975, "it's impossible for any woman to have a finger in her own destiny, because she's unconscious."[29]

This language reveals the degree to which Kushner tied her crusade into the issue of women's rights. It came as little wonder, she noted, that the one-step was used for a cancer that overwhelmingly affected women. "No man is going to make another man impotent while he's asleep without his permission," she wrote. "But there's no hesitation if it's a woman's breast."[30] In 1975, Kushner and a friend, Dorothy Johnston, established and "womanned" a hotline, known as the Breast Cancer Advisory Center, that thousands of women would eventually call to discuss their lumps, their mastectomies, and their emotional problems. In addition to fielding phone calls at all hours, Kushner answered thousands of letters from women seeking information about breast cancer, some of which were simply addressed to "Mrs. Breast Cancer, Kensington, Md."[31]

Kushner's feminist perspective came through most clearly when she attempted to intervene the night before Betty Ford's possible one-step radical mastectomy. Kushner used several personal connections in Washington to try and inform President Ford that both a radical mastectomy and a one-step procedure were not indicated. She also called the White House directly. Finally, Kushner reached the economist Milton Friedman, one of Ford's speechwriters, who listened to her pleas and told her to wait. When Friedman returned to the phone, Kushner later wrote, he told her, "I am sorry. The President has made his decision." Infuriated by this "male-chavinist-piggery," she wrote, "That line has got to be engraved somewhere as the all-time sexist declaration of no-woman rights."[32]

Although Kushner later wrote that Betty Ford had been "butchered unnecessarily,"[33] what most irritated her was the First Lady's apparent exclusion from the decision-making process. In all of her writings, Kushner distanced herself from women who simplistically characterized the continued use of radical mastectomy as a male conspiracy against women. She often noted, for example, that the treatment of prostate cancer in men—normally a radical prostatectomy leading to incontinence and impotence—was as archaic as the treatment of breast cancer. "As for the accusation that mastectomies are male-chauvinist inventions created to butcher women," she wrote, "militant Women's Libbers should drop the charge."[34] Kushner preferred to see herself as a civil libertarian rather than an advocate of women's liberation. She often approvingly cited the "Bill of Rights for Patients," issued by the American Hospital Association, that codified the ability of patients to direct their medical care. Indeed, by the mid-1970s, growing numbers of consumer advocates had turned their attention to breast cancer, disseminating medical information to the public through organizations such as New York's Center for Medical Consumers and *Consumer Reports*.

Kushner's major target, therefore, was not men but rather the medical profession and how it went about its business. In researching her book, Kushner had administered a "psychological questionnaire" to 130 women who had contacted her after her *Washington Post* article or subsequent television appearances. Acknowledging that she had an "unrandom, unscientific, biassed [sic] sample," Kushner nevertheless concluded that these women felt "duped" because they had not been offered options prior to surgery. "[T]hey were bitter and resentful about this omission," she wrote.[35] The problem, Kushner believed, was that ignorant physicians, relying on outdated theories, were forcing women into one-step radical mastectomies. "It's the arrogance of the profession I want to attack," she stated. "Gen. William C. Westmoreland and the Pentagon are no match for the average corner-surgeon and the American Medical Association when it comes to hiding important information from the public."[36] Not just she but other women, Kushner emphasized, were entitled to treatment by breast cancer specialists like Dao.

What most set Kushner apart from other critics of physicians was her inclination and ability to debate actual medical topics. Using techniques that AIDS activists would employ in succeeding decades, she learned the literature and then aggressively challenged the knowledge of medical professionals. For example, arguing that multiple studies since 1962 had shown it to be of no value, she told one physician, "I do wish you would reconsider your use of 'prophylactic' irradiation of the axilla after radical mastectomy as a routine procedure."[37] Renowned physicians, such as Bernard Fisher, grew accustomed to having their presentations interrupted as Kushner rose and challenged their data and conclusions. Perhaps most remarkably, by the late 1970s Kushner was on the payroll of the National Cancer Institute, reviewing grant applications and revising literature written by cancer specialists. The NCI even distributed Kushner's booklet, "If You've Thought About Breast Cancer," as part of its educational outreach efforts.[38]

Many physicians were completely astounded by Kushner's behavior and responded angrily when she criticized them in public. She often came home in tears after such events.[39] Members of both the American College of Surgeons and the American Cancer Society were highly critical of her book; one surgeon termed it "a piece of garbage."[40] The ACS was especially upset at Kushner's criticisms of its Reach to Recovery program. Kushner was appalled at the fact that women "in a free and democratic society" still needed their surgeon's permission to be visited by a Reach volunteer. She also believed that Reach's emphasis on postoperative rehabilitation deflected attention from the more important issue of preoperative counseling on treatment alternatives. The ACS, she added for good measure, moved "with the speed of a senile snail."[41]

Yet despite her willingness to criticize, Kushner loved to network, and actively sought to build bridges to all of her opponents. Likely stemming from a combination of political savvy and a genuine desire to convince others of her beliefs, she maintained a steady stream of communication with almost anyone who would call or write back. For example, Kushner assured Terese Lasser of Reach to Recovery, "I certainly did not and do not want to deprecate [your] work."[42] After several physicians had taken her to task at a November 1975 breast cancer symposium in Atlanta, including challenging her journalistic integrity, she quickly dispatched letters to them. While sticking to her arguments, she joked about now being on the public record as a liar. Realizing that one of the doctors was Jewish, she used a Yiddish term in asking him, "Nu, what can I do?"[43] Kushner would develop her most effective partnership with Bernard Fisher, whose work she increasingly grew to admire. Although her relentless publicity efforts were self-serving to a degree, Kushner's true commitment was to informing women and doctors about the backward state of breast cancer management.

The more conciliatory aspects of Kushner's message were mirrored in a growing number of breast cancer accounts that appeared in the mid- to late 1970s. These works, which included books and magazine articles, were written either by or about women with the disease. Once again, many of the women were either professional writers or well-known personalities. Although some took a stand on the radical mastectomy controversy, most of the authors focused on how the diagnosis and treatment of breast cancer had affected their lives, both positively and negatively. For these women, the war on breast cancer was a personal struggle that took its toll on patients, family, and friends.

Upon learning of her diagnosis in February 1974, Helga Sandburg Crile immersed herself in the poetry and prose that had always surrounded her life. A particularly poignant piece that she recalled was a poem that her father, Carl Sandburg, had written:

> Let a joy keep you.
> Reach out your hands
> And take it when it runs by . . .
> Joy always,
> Joy everywhere—
> Let joy kill you!
> Keep away from the little deaths.

Crile used the first line of this poem as the title of an article she wrote for the November 1974 issue of McCall's.[44] In the piece, she described the experience of being diagnosed with breast cancer as the wife of the country's leading advocate of conservative surgery. Having chosen a lumpectomy, Sandburg downplayed her decision, terming it only a "surface" operation. "I had faced death before," she wrote, mentioning a delayed Cesarean section, two automobile accidents, and uterine cancer.[45]

Ultimately, Sandburg found herself less interested in the treatment debates than in the importance of early detection. With her willing consent, Barney Crile displayed slides of Sandburg's mammogram at the Cleveland Clinic and other hospitals across the country, flimsily disguising her as "a wife of a member of the Clinic staff."[46] The image of Sandburg's breast eventually wound up in an article on breast cancer in the November 19, 1974, issue of *Time* magazine and on the cover of two European magazines. Ending her article on an upbeat note, Sandburg "thanked my lucky stars that all had gone well in my Adventure."[47]

Another woman who emphasized the positive aspects of her breast cancer experience was Marvella Bayh. Bayh was born Marvella Hern in Enid, Oklahoma, in 1933. In 1951, she traveled to Chicago to participate in an oratorical contest sponsored by the National Farm Bureau. Not only did she win the contest, but she met her future husband, Birch Bayh, who was also a contestant. After their marriage, the couple moved to Indiana, where Birch Bayh began a political career. By 1971, he was the junior senator from Indiana and contemplating a run for the presidency of the United States.

Marvella Bayh had first experienced a vague discomfort in her right breast in February 1971. After a negative mammogram and physical examination, her physician gave her a clean bill of health. In September 1971, her breast began to hurt. Although the mammogram was again negative, her physician now recommended a biopsy and possible breast removal. In October 1971, Bayh underwent a modified radical mastectomy. Her surgeon had found a highly invasive cancer that had spread throughout the breast and into the skin. Five axillary lymph nodes showed cancer, but Bayh's doctors told her that only two were positive. Given the extent of the cancer, she underwent radiotherapy and chemotherapy with Thiotepa. Birch Bayh gave up his bid for the Democratic presidential nomination to spend time with his recuperating wife.[48]

After her operation, Bayh was visited by a Reach to Recovery volunteer and was quite impressed. "I just stared at this woman who looked like a model," she later wrote, "and I thought to myself: If she can do it, I can too!"[49] Bayh became very active as a volunteer for the American Cancer Society, serving as cochair of its annual National Cancer Crusade in 1974. Attractive, poised, and energetic, she was a natural "messenger of hope" for the ACS, spreading the gospel of early detection across the United States. "I truly wanted to rush up to every woman on the street," she later wrote, "and say . . . 'Have you examined your own breasts this month for a possible lump?'"[50]

Bayh ultimately published an autobiography, entitled *Marvella: A Personal Journey*, which extensively detailed her diagnosis, treatment, and work with the ACS. As did other authors of breast cancer narratives, Bayh wove her encounter with breast cancer into the daily events of her life, such as marriage, raising a son, and being a political spouse. Bayh, as had Ford and Rockefeller, also noted the ways in which her cancer diagnosis had changed her life for the better. She and her husband "rediscovered the kind of day-to-day marriage we hadn't had since those young days[51] and paid even closer attention to raising their only child, Evan. As of October 1977, Bayh was "sitting on top of the world." Her health and energy, she stated, had never been better.[52]

Weighing Life versus Breast

Among the first books to challenge the typical optimistic breast cancer narrative was Betty Rollin's *First, You Cry*. Rollin was another journalist, in this case a television correspondent for NBC. She first discovered a lump in her left breast in the spring of 1974, but, like Bayh, had received a clean bill of health from both her physician and a mammographer. One year later, radiologists found a suspicious lesion on another mammogram, and Rollin found herself at the office of a Manhattan breast surgeon. Having agreed to a one-step procedure, Rollin underwent a modified radical mastectomy after the frozen section was positive. Rollin told her story in the September 1976 issue of *Family Circle* and then in *First, You Cry*. Poking fun at the "Pollyanna" approach to illness, she had avoided writing a "ladies' how-to-cope-book." Rather, as she wrote in a book proposal, "it is a story—my story—about what the whole experience feels like, what it does to you. And what it doesn't do."[53]

What Rollin's breast cancer did to her was affect every aspect of her life. And she told her readers everything. The book's title referred to her honest admission of how she cried—"the bad, loud, gasping kind"—after learning her diagnosis.[54] Rollin also openly discussed how breast removal would affect her appearance, self-esteem and sex life. "I am vain," she told her surgeon before her operation. "I would like to not be very hideous if that's possible."[55] In confessing concern about her looks in the face of potentially deadly breast cancer, Rollin rejected the approach of other women who stated that only life mattered.

Nor did Rollin downplay her horror at how her body looked after the operation. After her bandages were removed, she wrote, "I felt ugly and freaky; that anybody who saw me would be repelled and revolted the way I had been."[56] Rollin also admitted that she now dreaded sex with her husband. "He found me attractive; he wanted me," she admitted. "The crazy thing was, I didn't want him. . . . I no longer found me attractive. I was damaged goods and I knew it."[57] Rollin went on to describe how she eventually separated from her husband and started dating—and sleeping with—another man.

Like both Rosmond and Kushner, Rollin relied heavily on humor. Other prospective titles for her book had included "What's Left," "Left Out," "A Clean Breast," and "I Dreamt I Was Empty in My Maidenform Bra." "[W]ho needs a breast anyway?" she asked at one point. "[Y]ou can't do anything with a breast, you can't type with it or walk on it or play *Melancholy Baby* with it."[58] Rollin also provided an amusing account of her efforts to buy a suitable prosthesis at a "tit shop" and to construct a homemade nipple.

Rollin's article and book elicited a diverse assortment of letters. Whereas Rosmond's correspondents responded most passionately to the issue of women's choice, those writing to Rollin were most interested in her discussions of physical appearance and sexual relations. One critical letter came from a Massachusetts woman who termed Rollin both "sophomoric" and "narcissistic."[59] First, You Cry, wrote another woman, was "a self-centered, self-abasing and whining account of the mastectomy of your tit."[60]

But other writers identified intensely with Rollin's story. "Thank you again for being so open about your surgery," wrote an Oregon woman.

Referring to Rollin's crusty, bow-tied NBC colleague, she added, "You're so much prettier than Irving R. Levine."[61] A fifty-four-year-old California woman who had undergone mastectomy fifteen years earlier was more serious. She told Rollin that for the first time, she had read about a woman "who had the same crazys I had." Rollin had ably "expressed the anger and fear and the possibility of dying" that she had also experienced.[62] Another California woman, writing her "first fan letter," admitted that she, too, had stood in front of her mirror and said, "[Y]ou ugly thing."[63] Other letter writers found Rollin's account to be much more honest than the "press agent bullshit" about Ford or Rockefeller "smiling bravely through" their surgery.[64] "Happy Rockefeller's story was too glossed over and 'happy,'" wrote a woman whose physicians had originally misdiagnosed her breast cancer as scar tissue.[65]

What most resonated with Rollin's readers, however, was her contention that women approaching and recovering from breast cancer surgery should be allowed to think about issues of appearance. "I still want to walk into a room and have someone think 'attractive dame,'" admitted a forty-four-year-old Kentucky woman.[66] Nor was age necessarily a criterion. "You would think (being 77) that I wouldn't be so vain!" a Massachusetts woman wrote. "But that's the way it is."[67]

Concerns about looks were most evident among women who chose a lumpectomy. Although seen as unacceptably risky by many physicians and other breast cancer patients, certain women, like Babette Rosmond, announced that they preferred breast preservation to operations more likely to remove all of the cancer cells. "Although physicians are trained to save lives," wrote Massachusetts health educator Marie Gately, "I feel the quality of life that is saved must be a factor and the feelings of the individual should carry much more weight than they presently do."[68] Women concerned with the disfigurement caused by radical breast surgery, Rose Kushner stated, might legitimately "choose to live a few years less of such a damaged life."[69] Indeed, nearly half of the women surveyed in the 1973 Gallup poll responded that mastectomy would be more "disturbing" to them than lumpectomy, despite the supposedly greater risks of the smaller procedure.[70]

Yet even those women who ultimately opted for a simple, modified radical or even radical mastectomy carefully considered the physical and emotional ramifications of surgery. "To me," one woman who had undergone a radical mastectomy told Betty Ford, "the psychological effects of enduring the mutilation of my body is worse than the awareness that I have cancer."[71] Realizing preoperatively that "my whole body is aching and grieving for the member that is going to die," a San Diego woman planned to hold a "private funeral" for her left breast.[72]

Faced with the loss of a cherished body part, how did these women come to the decision to have a mastectomy? As letters to Rollin, Ford, and Oliver Cope reveal, women characterized their decision to have a mastectomy in terms of a life versus breast calculus. That is, by deciding to sacrifice their breast, they were choosing to save their lives. At first glance, this strategy appears to have mirrored the traditional attitude of many physicians, who remained "dedicated to the primary concept of longevity, not femininity."[73] But these women were not downplaying the issue of postoperative appearance so much as weighing it against what they believed was another, more important consideration.

"A breast is a small price to have to pay for the rest of your life," a Massachusetts housewife wrote to Rollin. "I thank God I loss [sic] only a breast and still have a long, healed life."[74] A Texas woman told Ford, "I have never cried over losing the breast, because God spared my life, and as long as there is life there is hope."[75] "I dread another mastectomy," a New York woman with a history of breast cancer told Cope, "but if it is a life-saving measure—I must accept it."[76] Marvella Bayh reported a similar reaction upon learning that she might have breast cancer. "I wanted to live," she recalled. "Only later did I think about losing a breast."[77] These thoughts were echoed by a breast cancer survivor appearing on the *Phil Donahue Show* on April 16, 1974. "I personally would not want to gamble with what they call lumpectomy," she informed the audience, "when they're talking about your life."[78]

Women were concerned with both their own lives and those of their families. "I don't care a bit about disfigurement," a thirty-three-year-old mother of three told Rollin, "when I think I may lose my life and my children need me so badly."[79] A mother of two, upon hearing she needed a breast biopsy, wrote to Rollin that "My mind immediately flashed to my children ages 6 and 8, my husband, my parents. . . . Could they survive with me gone, who would really understand my children, could another woman eventually replace me?"[80] The guest on *Phil Donahue* concurred: "I think I was most concerned about—did the doctor get all the cancer? Because I had five children and they ranged from 6 to 15 at the time and I felt that they had to have their mother."[81]

In addition to highlighting the traditional role of women as guardians of the family's health, the tendency to frame breast cancer treatment as one of two stark options spoke to several other familiar American traits. For one, compared with lumpectomy followed by several weeks of radiotherapy, choosing a larger operation was seen as more definitive and thus less risky. "I'm no watcher," a Georgia woman told Rollin. "As soon as possible, I had the biopsy and not to my surprise was minus a 36C left breast."[82] Having chosen a modified radical mastectomy, feminist writer Audre Lorde "was empowered from having made a decision, done a strike for [herself], moved."[83] Marvella Bayh concurred, stating that she would "rather err in doing a little too much than not enough" because she wanted to live a long time.[84] The strength and comfort that women drew from "attacking" their breast cancer at times manifested itself through the same military metaphors that physicians and the American Cancer Society favored. "Remember that your attitude is most of the battle," a New Jersey breast cancer patient entreated Ford, "so never even think about defeat, only about winning and you will win!"[85]

Saving one's life from breast cancer entailed not only aggressive treatment but aggressive early detection. Woman after woman thanked Betty Ford and other celebrity cancer patients for encouraging them to have the checkups that they believed had saved their lives. "I thank God and you that I found it in time," one woman told Ford. "Without you, I may have been too late."[86] Another woman wrote that her sister had discovered a treatable cancer due to Ford's efforts. "This letter," she stated, "is to thank you for having a part in saving my sister's life."[87] What is notable about these statements is less their accuracy than their retrospective assumption that health-seeking behaviors necessarily led to a good outcome. In constructing these teleologic narratives, cancer survivor Jackie Stacey has argued, patients validate the idea that heroic behavior leads to triumph over cancer.[88]

Characterizing the treatment decision as the choice of life over breast also spoke to cultural beliefs about whether women should value "purely" sexual organs. Woman after woman writing to Betty Ford stressed how loss of a breast could never compare to loss of a more important body part. "I've always been thankful," wrote a Michigan woman, "it was a breast I lost instead of an arm, leg or eye."[89] A Nebraska woman asked herself whether she would rather sacrifice an eye, an ear, a leg, or a breast. "I would take 1 breast," she decided.[90] Ford herself agreed with this philosophy, noting that losing a breast was preferable to losing her right arm. The Gallup data also supported this notion that women faced with breast cancer came to view the breast as relatively expendable. Only 18 percent of women surveyed believed that it would be harder to adjust to losing a breast as opposed to an arm or leg.[91]

Although the sentiments of patients who chose life over breast were sincere, such a framing device may also have reflected their unwillingness to admit that concerns about appearance and sexuality were legitimate reasons for desiring breast preservation. The idea that a woman, with her life on the line, would opt for a riskier, breast-sparing lumpectomy remained largely unacceptable. "Isn't it sad," a Missouri woman asked Rollin, "that our society is so oriented toward the body that it causes women to worry more about losing a breast than dying?"[92] In criticizing Rollin's emphasis on appearance, a Chicago woman stated that she could not comprehend "how a bright lady's life can be centered in her tits." If wearing a strapless dress or a bikini was the biggest deal in Rollin's life, she continued, "it's going to take more than highly respected friends to tell me you have a brain in your head."[93] Even Rose Kushner admitted she was "always surprised and appalled at the women whose first thought is loss of a breast."[94]

During their appearance on the *David Susskind Show* in 1973, Jerry Urban had asked Babette Rosmond: "Would you rather keep your breast or die of the cancer?" "There is no such choice," Rosmond astutely replied. "No one knows what the choice is."[95] As usual, Rosmond's voice was in the minority. Most women were perfectly willing to conceptualize breast cancer treatment options in terms of a life versus breast calculus in which losing a breast became a type of *quid pro quo* for getting to live. Such a framework fit well with American cultural norms regarding vanity, sexuality, risk-aversion, and personal responsibility for disease. At the same time, it provided a reassuring strategy for women to order their priorities at a time of tremendous chaos and uncertainty.

Rebuilding the Breast

The concerns about physical appearance identified by Rollin assumed importance for women immediately after their surgery was completed. Because women undergoing the one-step procedure did not know whether they would awaken with one or two breasts, their first knowledge of their mastectomy was often the sensation of pain or heavy bandages at the operative site. As with Betty Rollin, the initial removal of the bandages generated anxiety and often horror as women viewed their newly configured chest wall for the first time.

It was these feelings of discomfort that Terese Lasser had sought to quell when she introduced the Reach to Recovery program in 1954. Central to Lasser's philosophy was the attempt to return women to a "normal" existence despite their history of breast cancer. As we have seen, Lasser's interventions included arm exercises to restore function and advice regarding prostheses that could simulate a woman's preoperative anatomy.

Twenty years later, breast cancer patients treated by mastectomy continued to pursue a normal life and often believed they had achieved this goal. On the David Susskind Show, Susan Schack, who had undergone a radical mastectomy, stated, "I don't let it bother me. . . . I don't have any problems. My problem was taken care of six years ago."[96] A guest on the 1974 Phil Donahue Show agreed. "I'm the same as I ever was," she remarked. "In fact, I may even be better."[97] Patients also conveyed this message to their physicians. "I have never felt anything but a completely whole person," a grateful patient told Cushman Haagensen. "You made it possible for me to have a very rich and rewarding life."[98] As Lasser had hoped, women reported that they could successfully conceal evidence of their radical mastectomies from friends and even family. An accepting husband helped the return to normalcy. Birch Bayh liked to compare his wife's mastectomy to an appendectomy.

Among the women who ultimately decided that a return to normal life was both possible and desirable was Betty Rollin. Although she had criticized other accounts of breast cancer that had ignored the negative consequences of surgery, Rollin believed that a full physical and emotional recovery was realistic. In a memorable line, Rollin analogized herself to a car with a "dent in my fender." The actual car, she implied, was not seriously damaged. Rollin reiterated this point at the end of First, You Cry, stating that if her cancer did not recur, "all I've lost is a breast, and that's not so bad."[99] Five years later, in a follow-up article in the *New York Times Magazine*, she made this point emphatically, chiding her earlier concerns about whether or not she could wear a strapless dress.[100]

As passionately as Rollin and other women celebrated their success at overcoming breast cancer, others reported a persistent inability to do so. "I still can't bear to look at myself," a Massachusetts woman wrote to Rollin in 1976. "I feel like one of those lop-sided Picasso paintings." She included a poem:

> I am lop-sided
> Flatter than a boy.
> S-shaped stitchery
> frames washboard ribs.
> After seven years
> why should I remember
> the way a hand
> curved my breast?
> Old griefs sift through
> this excavation.[101]

Being single and looking for a relationship did not help. "I will never be the person I was before the operation," another woman, who had undergone a radical mastectomy with a skin graft, radiation treatment, and chemotherapy, told Rollin. "[W]hat man would want me the way I am now?" she asked.[102]

The most eloquent discussion of these issues was in *The Cancer Journals*, a 1980 book by Audre Lorde. Lorde, an African American woman born to Grenadian immigrants in New York City in 1934, had begun writing poetry in junior high school. She graduated from Hunter College in 1959, then got married and had two children. Ultimately, however, Lorde realized that she was gay and developed a long-term relationship with Frances Louise Clayton. Having won numerous awards for her prose and poetry, Lorde became a professor of English at John Jay College in New York in 1978.

That same year she was diagnosed with breast cancer. As an African American lesbian feminist poet, Lorde later wrote, she had no role models as a breast cancer patient. Celebrities such as Betty Ford and Betty Rollin, she believed, had little to teach her. Yet, like these women, Lorde agreed that a woman responded to breast cancer based on "who she is and how her life has been lived."[103] Throughout Lorde's treatment and its aftermath, she experienced feelings of pain and loss. "And yet if I cried for a hundred years," she wrote the night before her mastectomy, "I couldn't possibly express the sorrow I feel right now, the sadness and the loss."[104] After the operation, she wrote that "[t]he absence of my breast is a recurrent sadness."[105]

As Lorde began the process of recovery, her physician and other hospital staff offered her advice about rehabilitation and a breast prosthesis. A Reach to Recovery volunteer visited her. But Lorde felt insulted by what both this woman and the medical profession had to offer. As a lesbian, she was not interested in making herself look appealing to men. The lambswool breast form given to her looked "grotesquely pale" compared with her black skin. Most important, Lorde found herself diametrically opposed to what Reach stood for: "the path of prosthesis, of silence and invisibility, the woman who wishes to be 'the same as before.'"[106]

By emphasizing the importance of concealing one's mastectomy, Lorde argued, Reach to Recovery and the cancer establishment was characterizing breast cancer as a "cosmetic problem" that could be "solved by a prosthetic pretense."[107] She believed that such a focus oppressed women by reinforcing societal stereotypes that equated a woman's value with how she looked. Moreover, the notion that a woman could (or should) return to normal after breast cancer was a myth. "Any woman who has had a breast removed because of cancer," Lorde wrote, "knows she does not feel the same."[108] Indeed, the experience of breast cancer enabled women to live more considered, self-scrutinized lives. Ignoring what had occurred was not only unrealistic, therefore, but a lost opportunity. Losing a breast, Lorde concluded, had made her "a more whole person."[109]

As would be expected, Lorde strongly opposed the new technology of breast reconstruction that had emerged in the mid-1970s. For decades, most surgeons had been both unwilling and unable to reconstruct breasts. Because such a high percentage of breast cancers in the Halsted era were rapidly fatal, physicians did not view reconstruction as a priority. Even when such operations were attempted, using tissue from other parts of the body or synthetic sponge material, they generally were unsuccessful.[110] Such efforts failed in part because the extensive Halsted radical mastectomy removed the chest wall muscles needed to support an artificial breast. By the 1970s, however, several factors had changed: women were living longer after surgery because their breast cancers were smaller when discovered; surgeons increasingly spared the pectoralis major and minor muscles; and scientists had introduced silicone gel implants. As a result, plastic surgeons developed successful reconstruction operations, most of which involved inserting the implant under the pectoralis muscles. The surgeons were generally able to preserve the nipple as well. They then sought to publicize their new procedures to other physicians and to women.

In promoting reconstruction, plastic surgeons cited the growing literature on the psychological effects of mastectomy. In what would eventually come to be known as psycho-oncology, researchers were increasingly documenting and characterizing the common emotional side effects that accompanied breast cancer surgery. For those women unable to recover from breast loss, plastic surgeons argued, reconstruction potentially offered both physical and emotional relief. Moreover, the potential for postoperative reconstruction might induce women to pursue early detection more avidly.[111]

To Lorde, reconstruction was an "atrocity" that compounded the sins of a prosthesis. Noting that surgeons had emphasized how implants enabled breast cancer patients "to wear a normal bra or bikini," Lorde ridiculed such a concern. Plastic surgeons, she wrote, were "sexist pigs" who exploited breast cancer patients and remade their bodies into a configuration pleasing to the male eye.[112] Lorde's opposition to breast reconstruction produced some unexpected allies. Many breast surgeons, concerned that desire for an implant might compromise the choice of operation, found the desire for reconstruction to be frivolous or "madness."[113] "Go home and thank God you're alive," they told patients.[114] In addition, Lorde's viewpoint was oddly echoed by a percentage of Reach to Recovery volunteers, who stated that the mastectomy scar should be "preserved and worn as a sort of badge of courage."[115]

Other women with breast cancer agreed strongly with Lorde. These included Paula Armel, a thirty-two-year-old Los Angeles woman who wrote in *Ms.* about "choosing to look different" rather than conforming to the two-breast norm.[116] Lorde's position subsequently won favor among many feminist authors, such as Iris Marion Young, who examined the meanings of reconstruction within a patriarchal culture that most prizes "how breasts look and measure, their conformity with a norm, the impossible aesthetic of round, large and high on the chest."[117] In submitting to or even demanding an implant, Young has argued, a breast cancer patient "is not allowed to be public and honest in her fear and grief."[118] Enthusiasm for reconstruction, according to this argument, is an excellent example of Naomi Wolf's "beauty myth," in which women mistakenly associate improvements in their physical appearance with true autonomy. "Rather than aspiring to self-determined and woman-centered ideals of health or integrity," feminist author Kathryn Pauly Morgan has written in an article on breast reconstruction, "women's attractiveness is defined as attractive-to-men."[119]

But such arguments proved to be of limited appeal to the majority of women with breast cancer. By 1981, 20,000 breast reconstructions were being performed annually; meanwhile, women's magazines and newspapers touted the new procedure. Plastic surgeon Reuven K. Snyderman estimated that three out of five eligible women desired an implant. Among the staunchest early advocates of reconstruction were those women who hoped to put their experiences with breast cancer behind them. According to one such woman, a South Dakota housewife named Patricia Koppmann, reconstruction was far superior to a prosthesis, which was "a constant reminder that you had cancer."[120]

The woman who made this argument most fervently was Jean Zalon, who underwent a modified radical mastectomy in 1970 while working as a researcher on a mammography study being conducted at the Health Insurance Plan of Greater New York. Zalon had very definite opinions about the impact of her mastectomy. "I hated the way I looked," she wrote in a 1978 book. "In addition, the absence of the breast served as a constant reminder of the cancer that had once invaded my body and left me with a sense of dread and foreboding."[121]

In 1973, a friend gave Zalon the name of Saul Hoffman, a breast surgeon who had begun to perform reconstruction. Despite being criticized
by family and friends for being vain and somehow risking a recurrence
of her cancer, Zalon went ahead with the surgery in February 1974. She
was thrilled with the results, describing herself as being freed from
bondage. "The whole cancer experience was behind me," she rejoiced,
"shelved at last, pushed out of daily consciousness."[122] The title of Zalon's book, I Am Whole Again, unabashedly conveyed these sentiments.[123]

But the growing interest in reconstruction was not simply a rejection
of the feminist arguments of Lorde and others. By the mid-1970s, feminism's focus was shifting from social issues to "individual self-realiza-
tion."[124] That is, more than one feminism existed. Some feminists
emphasized the attainment of equal rights with men while others focused on personal empowerment. By helping women achieve an appearance they found more acceptable, and possibly improving romance, sex,
and self-esteem, breast reconstruction fit well with this latter goal. Concern about one's appearance was no longer something that needed to
cause shame for a breast cancer patient.

Zalon herself exemplified how a feminist approach to breast cancer
was not monolithic. Although she was traditional in her allegiance to a
two-breast norm, arguing that every woman had a "right" to reconstruction,[125] Zalon had refused a one-step procedure at the time of her mastectomy. Koppmann, the South Dakota housewife who had undergone
reconstruction, also had her feminist side, suing her insurance company
after it refused to cover what it deemed to be "cosmetic surgery."[126] Plastic surgeons such as Snyderman picked up on this idea that mastectomy
patients were entitled to an implant. "Reconstruction," he stated, "puts a
woman's destiny in her own hands."[127] Although financially and profes-
sionally self-serving, Snyderman's message was exactly what many
women with breast cancer wanted to hear.

The new ability to reconstruct breasts complicated the gender dynam-
ics between doctor and patient. As we have seen, male (and female)
physicians recognized the sexual and cosmetic importance of the breast,
but justified its removal for cancer either because a woman was
menopausal or as the price she had to pay for saving her life. Once reconstruction was available, the situation became more complicated. Not only

were plastic surgeons replacing breasts and nipples, they were at times providing women with firmer and more shapely breasts than those that had been removed. And in order to make both breasts symmetrical, they were also offering women cosmetic work on the second breast. Feminist writers decried this situation, warning patients that treatment of a disease had become hopelessly blurred with a strategy for generating new breasts that were pleasing to the male eye. But other women, such as Zalon, did not find these developments to be so worrisome. "[F]ew of us can detach ourselves from the stereotypes of our time," she wrote. "Take away a breast, and suddenly even the best adjusted of us is likely to feel deprived, diminished, bereft in her essential femaleness."[128]

Although the silence that had previously surrounded breast cancer has probably been overstated, after 1974 the disease unquestionably became a public topic. In addition to books and magazines, television tackled the topic of breast cancer on shows such as *All in the Family* and in made-for-television movies such as *First, You Cry*, in which Mary Tyler Moore portrayed Betty Rollin.[129] Some breast cancer stories publicized the debates over treatment, while others detailed personal experiences with the disease. But the most consistent message of these narratives was the importance of early detection. Finding cancers early, writers reiterated, improved both a woman's chance of survival and her treatment options. But as the 1970s progressed, such claims once again came under scrutiny. Did the fact that mammography could help doctors identify smaller, more curable cancers in some women mean that all women should have the test?

nine

Seek and Ye Shall Find

Mammography Praised and Scorned

A California woman informed Betty Rollin that her breast surgeon had a theory. "If at a certain age, all women would have their breasts removed," the surgeon told the woman in 1976, "there would not be all this anxiety and carelessness and cancer caused deaths." He added that he would "get a large supply of sandpaper and get right down to the ribs."[1] While the surgeon's crude scenario was presumably an exaggeration, physicians in the 1960s and 1970s actually began to implement a more limited version of this strategy. Increasingly able to identify possible precursors of cancer, such as carcinoma in situ, some surgeons encouraged prophylactic breast removal as a way to treat such conditions and prevent the development of actual cancer. Although many women acceded to and even sought out such surgery, the indeterminate nature of such lesions raised legitimate questions about what disease, if any, such operations were actually "curing."

One way these noninvasive precancers and small invasive cancers were identified was through mammography, which was disseminated widely across the United States in the 1970s. In 1972, the American Cancer Society and the National Cancer Institute initiated the Breast Cancer Detection Demonstration Project (BCDDP), which used mammography to screen hundreds of thousands of women for small, presumably curable breast cancers. While the project began with much fanfare, by 1976 it was embroiled in controversy, as critics charged that mammograms in younger women might be producing as much cancer as they were helping to cure. As with breast cancer treatment, the debates over mammography involved not only physicians, the American Cancer Society and women, but also statisticians and epidemiologists. Once again, the more sophisticated mathematical models used by these last two groups threatened the traditional clinical encounter, in which experienced physicians made recommendations to individual patients. Two questions were on the table: Was it riskier to have a screening mammogram or to decline one? And who should make this decision: physician, patient, or researcher?

Understanding Precancers

One of the first physicians to describe "precancerous" or "borderline" lesions of the breast was William Halsted's longtime resident and associate, Joseph Colt Bloodgood. In a series of papers published in the 1910s and 1920s, Bloodgood argued that a pathologist studying a biopsy specimen was likely to find "a pre-existing local defect which is benign and in which later there may be a cancerous development."[2] Although several types of cellular patterns suggested precancerous growth to Bloodgood, Arthur Purdy Stout, and other surgical pathologists, the lesion that drew the most attention after 1930 was carcinoma in situ.

In 1932, Mayo Clinic pathologist Albert C. Broders identified collections of cancer-like cells that had not invaded the underlying tissue. Hypothesizing that these noninvasive lesions were precursors to cancer, Broders termed them "carcinoma in situ," which literally meant "cancer in place."[3] This cellular configuration was identical to the apparent precancers that George Papanicolaou was identifying on vaginal smears.

In the 1940s, Memorial Hospital pathologists Frank W. Foote, Jr., and Fred W. Stewart described such lesions in the breast, distinguishing between lobular carcinoma in situ (LCIS) and ductal carcinoma in situ (DCIS), based on where in the breast the cells were found. As had Bloodgood and Broders before them, Foote and Stewart noted the perils of equating LCIS and DCIS with actual cancer, but they nevertheless urged treatment of such lesions as if they were cancerous.[4]

With the increasing use of mammography in the late 1970s and 1980s, DCIS, which could be detected by x-ray, came to dominate discussions of carcinoma in situ. But between 1950 and 1980, it was the definition and treatment of LCIS that engendered intense debates. LCIS could neither be seen on mammogram nor palpated on physical examination. Indeed, pathologists most commonly discovered it incidentally, often in lumps that were otherwise benign. From the study of mastectomy specimens, pathologists also learned that LCIS, like its invasive variant, lobular carcinoma, was frequently multicentric. That is, in as many as 70 percent of cases, it appeared in multiple places throughout the breast.[5] Because physicians suspected that unremoved foci of LCIS would lead to cancer, patients found to have one area of LCIS generally received some type of a mastectomy. In up to 30 percent of cases, these operations were modified or Halsted radicals, even though no invasive cancer existed.[6]

The most prominent critics of this interpretation of LCIS as a dangerous precancerous lesion were the physicians at Columbia-Presbyterian Medical Center. Haagensen and his pathology colleagues, using their extensive collection of patient records, preferred to characterize LCIS as a "benign pathological-clinical entity." As such, they provocatively argued, it should not be described as carcinoma. "Lobular carcinoma in situ is a misleading and unfortunate name," they wrote, because it implied that the lesion was cancerous and thus warranted breast amputation.[7] Columbia pathologist Raffaele Lattes proposed using an alternative term, "lobular neoplasia," which suggested only that cellular abnormalities were present. The proper "treatment" of lobular neoplasia, Haagensen and Lattes argued, was to examine the patient's breasts every four months.

In downplaying the significance of LCIS, Columbia-Presbyterian was in the minority. Most physicians, confronted with an apparent precancerous lesion of the breast, enthusiastically advocated early aggressive treatment. Simple mastectomy was recommended, surgeons argued, "to cure today what tomorrow may be incurable."[8] Others argued that "what will be, is" and that "boldest counsels are the safest,"[9] in essence attempting to eliminate risk and uncertainty through the surgical removal of ambiguous lesions. Once again, the use of military metaphors to describe LCIS and its treatment indicate the degree to which surgical interventions drew on American beliefs favoring initiative and action. In a 1964 article, appropriately published in *Military Medicine*, Johns Hopkins surgeon Edward F. Lewison, who was actually quite moderate in his opinions, queried: "Does [LCIS] represent merely a benign but intensified localized area of epithelial activity or is it the 'cold-war' precursor of a malign and monstrously destructive disease?" Regarding therapy, Lewison went on to ask: "Does the treatment of this deceptive disease demand the broadsword or will the rapier suffice?"[10] Having framed the choices in this manner, surgeons understandably went on to recommend extensive operations to treat a presumed precancer.

Although the decision to characterize LCIS as precancerous drew on cultural approval of aggressive surgery, it was also supported by data. For example, pathologist Robert W. McDivitt and his colleagues at Memorial Sloan-Kettering had prospectively followed forty-two patients with lobular carcinoma in situ treated only by local excision. In 1967, they reported that 15 percent of these women had developed an invasive cancer after ten years; after twenty years, the figure increased to 35 percent.[11] A follow-up study conducted by Sloan-Kettering pathologist Paul Peter Rosen reported that women with LCIS who did not receive mastectomy were nine times more likely to develop invasive breast cancer than the average woman.[12]

The pathological studies of LCIS revealed another important fact. The condition was not only multicentric within a given breast but was often found in both breasts. McDivitt had thus also followed the incidence of invasive cancer in the second breast among women diagnosed with LCIS. He found that 10 percent of such women developed cancer in the second, or contralateral, breast after ten years and 25 percent after twenty years.[13] As they had in the case of the first breast, physicians assumed that these contralateral cancers also emanated from unremoved areas of LCIS.

Given these findings, physicians in the early 1970s increasingly viewed removal of only one breast in a woman with LCIS as illogical and even a "hazard."[14] When performing a mastectomy on the first breast, therefore, some physicians began to perform a random biopsy of the second breast, excising a small piece of tissue to look for evidence of LCIS or invasive cancer. Although these biopsies never became routine practice across the United States, the procedure received favorable coverage in major medical journals. Not surprisingly, one of the major advocates of random second breast biopsy was Sloan-Kettering's Jerry Urban, who also performed it for actual breast cancer, as in the case of Happy Rockefeller. Such biopsies were of high yield in women with LCIS, revealing contralateral lesions in as high as 59 percent of cases.[15] Physicians recommended a second mastectomy to those women whose biopsies were positive.

Arguing that such random biopsies likely missed LCIS located in other portions of the second breast, a few surgeons were even more aggressive: they recommended prophylactic (preventive) removal of both breasts in women found to have LCIS in one breast. Among the most vocal advocates of this strategy were plastic surgeons, who offered such women reconstruction after their bilateral mastectomies. Prophylactic removal of both breasts in women with LCIS, wrote Simon Fredricks of the University of Texas in 1975, had "great merit in the discovery of occult carcinoma" because it was "almost total breast biopsy."[16]

The phrase "almost total breast biopsy" suggests an additional reason why such dramatic procedures for noncancerous (although potentially precancerous) lesions gained acceptance. In essence, physicians characterized random biopsies and the mastectomies that often followed as cancer screening tests that could save lives. As Urban noted, "[y]ou have to use all methods of diagnosis to maximize detection, and contralateral biopsy is one of these methods."[17] With mortality from breast cancer remaining at an annoyingly stable rate and with high-quality mammography still in its infancy, physicians saw the aggressive pursuit and removal of LCIS-containing breasts as an opportunity they could not bypass. Patients often agreed with such reasoning, consenting to preventive mastectomies when presented with the option.[18] One woman told Betty Ford that her physician had recommended a simple mastectomy of her second breast "due to the finding of tiny tumors that can spread." She added that she was "now waiting to go back and have this done."[19]

Although physicians characterized the removal of LCIS as the preventive elimination of a precancerous lesion, much of the impetus to be aggressive resulted from the conflation of LCIS with actual cancer. LCIS, wrote California surgeon John R. Benfield and his colleagues in 1969, was a "true cancer,"[20] while New York surgeon Charles W. Hayden termed it an "at risk cancer."[21] Identifying LCIS, noted another doctor, was "catching breast cancer as early as possible."[22] This type of reasoning led physicians to inaccurately characterize mastectomies performed for LCIS as "curative" procedures. "The cure rate for lobular carcinoma in situ treated by mastectomy," wrote Memorial Sloan-Kettering pathologist Robert V. P. Hutter and colleagues in 1969, "remains at 100%."[23] By finding early in situ cancers, noted the American Cancer Society's Arthur Holleb, "cure can be assured in almost all instances."[24]

Yet as critics began to argue in the middle 1970s, discovering that a procedure was 100 percent curative called into question what was being treated in the first place. Echoing Neil McKinnon in the 1950s, Massachusetts Institute of Technology biologist Maurice S. Fox claimed that "[r]andom biopsy specimens . . . detect morphological entities that will not be manifested as clinical disease in a normal lifetime."[25] Meanwhile, pathologists had noted that most breast cancers later diagnosed in women with a history of LCIS were of the ductal variety and thus did not arise from unremoved foci of LCIS. Eventually, most physicians began to characterize LCIS as only a marker of future cancer, generally treating it as Haagensen had recommended: with watchful waiting.

But prophylactic second or bilateral mastectomies did not disappear, as women in the 1970s continued to receive them for other supposedly precancerous conditions such as chronic cystic mastitis, sclerosing adenosis, and ductal hyperplasia. Several factors encouraged breast removal for these findings. For one thing, physicians pathologized the healthy breast, going so far as to term it "precancerous"[26] or a "premalignant target organ."[27] One physician, noting the high rates of breast cancer in Western countries, even went so far as saying that "[i]t is a premalignant condition for a female to live in North America or northern Europe."[28] Doctors also stressed the value of prophylactic mastectomies in women, usually with a strong family history of breast cancer, who had developed an inordinate cancerphobia. Stressing its preventive value, San Francisco plastic surgeon Vincent R. Pennisi even argued that "[p]rophylactic surgery is our only hope for breast cancer."[29]

Finally, women themselves, usually those who had already undergone multiple negative biopsies, often requested the procedure. One woman even analogized prophylactic mastectomy to receiving a polio vaccine.[30] By the early 1980s, roughly 14,000 women were undergoing preventive breast removal every year.[31] It might reasonably be argued that America's war on breast cancer reached its pinnacle with the annual removal of thousands of healthy breasts—even in women without significant risk factors for breast cancer. The situation had begun to resemble the hypothetical preventive strategy that the California surgeon had proposed to Betty Rollin's correspondent in 1976.

Among the earliest critics of prophylactic mastectomy was Terri Anne Herman, then a medical student at Mount Sinai School of Medicine in

New York. In 1977, Herman wrote a letter to the *New England Journal of Medicine* objecting to an article it had recently published on the subject. In possibly the first accusation of sexism leveled against breast surgeons in a major medical journal, Herman asked why men's testicles weren't routinely replaced with kumquats to lower the incidence of testicular cancer.[32] Opposition to preventive mastectomies accelerated considerably in 1982, when breast surgeon Susan M. Love and colleagues published an article in the *New England Journal of Medicine* arguing that an aggressive surgical approach to so-called fibrocystic "disease" of the breast was inappropriate.[33] Other commentators argued against aggressive interventions for noncancerous breast conditions by noting that women with actual breast cancer were increasingly undergoing smaller operations that conserved breasts.[34]

As physicians in the 1970s debated which breast lesions warranted prophylactic mastectomies, even more controversy arose over how such biologically indeterminate lesions were being discovered. With the spread of mammography, radiologists could now routinely identify both nonpalpable cancers and areas of DCIS. But was early identification of such tumors necessarily the right thing to do?

Launching a Screening Program

By 1970, despite a quarter-century of accelerated efforts to control breast cancer in the United States, the disease had become the leading cause of death for women aged forty to forty-four. Age-adjusted mortality from the disease, 26.7 per 100,000 women, was basically unchanged from what it had been in 1930. Some commentators put a positive spin on this stable death rate. Based on data from Connecticut and California, statisticians Sidney J. Cutler and Roger R. Connelly of the National Cancer Institute calculated that American women with breast cancer were actually surviving for longer periods of time. Factoring out the type of treatment administered, which had not yet appreciably changed, the authors attributed this improved survival to detection of breast cancers at earlier, more curable stages. The only reason there had been no concurrent decline in mortality, they explained, was that the incidence of the disease was also on the rise—especially among younger women.[35]

Others interpreted the data more pessimistically. Increased incidence and survival in the face of a stable death rate, they argued, indicated only that breast cancers were being detected earlier in their course. That is, women were living longer with the diagnosis of cancer but dying at the same time. This phenomenon, termed "lead-time bias," would become particularly important when statisticians attempted to assess the ability of mammography to lower mortality from breast cancer.

Whether one viewed the cup as half full or half empty, everyone agreed that half a cup was insufficient when it came to fighting breast cancer. Physicians, patients, and politicians openly bemoaned the fact that the perfervid efforts of the ACS and other groups had not budged mortality rates. Although major advances had occurred in the prevention of lung cancer and in the treatment of childhood leukemia, little positive news existed for breast or other cancers.

This dissatisfaction with anticancer efforts to date culminated in passage of the National Cancer Act of 1971.[36] The rhetoric surrounding the new program sounded quite familiar. Mary Lasker and the ACS, working with their allies in business and Congress, argued that the lack of breakthroughs in cancer research was directly attributable to insufficent federal funding. They cited defense spending for the Vietnam War as having diverted support away from the cancer cause. These cancer activists also appealed to patriotism, arguing that a country that had put a man on the moon should also be first in the fight against cancer. Ultimately, President Richard M. Nixon threw his support behind the act, signing it into law on December 23, 1971. As befitted Lasker's wishes, Nixon's "Cure Cancer Program" channeled $334 million annually to the National Cancer Institute to carry out and sponsor research.[37]

The most successful breast cancer research project prior to this legislation was the screening trial conducted at the Health Insurance Plan (HIP) of Greater New York. HIP was a prepaid medical insurance program that had been founded in 1947. The impetus to conduct a breast cancer sceening trial at HIP had come from Philip Strax (see figure). Strax was born in Brooklyn in 1909, the exceedingly bright son of a poor garment worker and his wife. In a remarkably prescient letter, Strax's high school principal had helped his student obtain a scholarship to New York University by asking, "Suppose by his unusual talents and skill this young

Philip Strax in undated photo.

Courtesy of Richard Strax.

man someday in the future succeeds in conquering the dreaded cancer scourge?"[38] Strax ultimately completed medical school and became a radiologist. In the late 1950s, in part due to his first wife's death from breast cancer, he grew interested in mammography. Impressed with the work of pioneering mammographers Jacob Gershon-Cohen and Robert Egan, Strax proposed conducting a clinical trial that would determine whether breast cancer screening in healthy women lowered mortality from the disease.

Despite Strax's enthusiasm, funding for the study was contingent on its scientific merit. Fortunately for Strax, HIP's Director of Research and Statistics was another native New Yorker, Sam Shapiro. Shapiro, a well-respected mathematician and statistician who had previously worked for the United States Public Health Service, carefully designed a study that would become the only randomized trial of mammography ever carried out in the United States. Beginning in 1963, with funding from the NCI,

Strax and Shapiro randomized 62,000 women aged forty to sixty-four into one of two groups. The intervention group received a breast examination and mammogram annually for four years; the control group received its usual care, which at times included some breast cancer screening. By 1966, the authors reported that screening, particularly mammography, had led to earlier detection of breast cancers. Sixteen (70%) of the twenty-three cancers in the intervention group did not involve the axillary nodes and thus had a very good prognosis. Five years later, the news was even better.[39] Writing in the *Journal of the American Medical Association*, Shapiro, Strax, and the surgeon Louis Venet reported that the death rate for the intervention arm was 40 percent lower than that in the control group. (Later data analysis would place this figure closer to 30 percent.) Among the enrolled women aged forty to forty-nine, however, inadequate data existed to draw any conclusions.[40]

The American Cancer Society gratefully welcomed the HIP results as having vindicated its perennial claims regarding the value of early detection. But what remained unclear was the degree to which the HIP data would induce American women to actively pursue breast cancer screening, especially mammography. The ACS had helped sponsor cancer detection centers throughout the United States in the 1940s and 1950s, but the response to such programs had remained disappointing.

With the impending passage of the National Cancer Act and its promise of funding, the cancer society sensed a golden opportunity to spread the gospel of mammography. The man behind this effort was the Senior Vice-President for Medical Affairs and Research, Arthur I. Holleb. Holleb, who had trained as a surgeon at Memorial Hospital, had begun work at the ACS in 1948 helping to promote cervical cancer screening. He had great respect for his predecessor as chief medical officer, Charles S. Cameron, whose aggressive salesmanship had led to the widescale adoption of Pap testing by women and their physicians.

By the fall of 1971, Holleb had decided that "the time has come for the American Cancer Society to mount a massive program on mammography just as we did with the Pap test."[41] Pointing to the 50 percent drop in mortality from cervical cancer, he predicted, "[W]e will undoubtedly do the same for breast cancer that we did for uterine cancer."[42] The type of screening program that Holleb and his ACS colleagues envisioned was one that American voluntary agencies had long sponsored: a demonstration project. In contrast to clinical trials, which formally tested diagnostic or therapeutic strategies, demonstration projects took as a given the value of the interventions to be showcased. These projects sought to show how the technologies in question could be successfully introduced to the public. In this case, the American Cancer Society sought to "demonstrate the feasibility of periodic screening of large numbers of women for breast cancer, using clinical history, physical examination, mammography, and thermography."[43] (Thermography was a technology that used heat sensors to identify areas of high blood flow within breast cancers. It did not prove to be a useful screening device.) In other words, the ACS wished to determine whether these new techniques could "be brought to huge numbers of women in their home communities at reasonable cost."[44]

Originally, the ACS had planned to implement its project at between eight and twelve clinics around the country. But given the momentum and the funding supplied by the National Cancer Act, Holleb reconsidered. In September 1972, he approached Nathaniel I. Berlin, who was then Director of the National Cancer Institute's Division of Cancer Biology and Diagnosis, and asked whether the NCI would participate. After obtaining approval from NCI director Frank J. Rauscher, Jr., Berlin agreed, ultimately contributing over $6 million annually and enabling the establishment of twenty-seven detection centers.[45] The new goal for the Breast Cancer Detection Demonstration Project was to enroll 270,000 women, aged thirty-five to seventy-four, who would undergo free annual testing for five years. To attract poor and minority women, who had been underrepresented among women screened in the HIP study, there was to be no charge for the services provided. The project began enrolling patients in 1973.[46]

The decision to initiate a demonstration project was not the ACS's only choice. One alternative would have been a randomized trial that, in contrast to the HIP study, focused specifically on screening younger women for breast cancer. At the front lines of the invigorated war on breast cancer, however, Holleb and his colleagues rejected this more conservative approach, firmly believing that the HIP study had already "demonstrated the value of periodic screening in a well designed and controlled study in reducing the case fatality rates."[47] The NCI's Nathaniel Berlin conceded that the HIP data had not conclusively shown that mammography lowered mortality for women in their forties, but he believed that this finding had occurred only because the study had enrolled too few younger patients. Recent improvements in mammographic technique, moreover, suggested that x-rays would be an even more valuable screening tool in the BCDDP than they had been in the HIP study. "As of 1970, the whole HIP study showed a benefit," Berlin recently recalled. "I did not think that the small numbers in the 40-49 subset should prevent overall implementation of the BCDDP. We set out to demonstrate what the HIP study had shown."[48]

Holleb, as was customary, was more effusive in issuing his marching orders in October 1971. Using rhetoric that his mentor Cameron might have chosen, he declared: "No longer can we ask the people of this country to tolerate a loss of life from breast cancer each year equal to the loss of life in the past ten years in Viet Nam. The time has come for greater national effort. I firmly believe that time is now."[49]

Although lowering breast cancer mortality was the prime motivating force for the ACS, the organization itself also benefited from a hard sell of mammography. Having a "Pap test for the breast" reinforced the cancer society's optimistic message about cancer which, in turn, could not but help fund-raising efforts.[50] The BCDDP also enabled the ACS to push its larger program of early detection. Thus, the organization had enrolled women as young as thirty-five in order to inculcate them with "good health habits" for when their risk of breast cancer increased.[51] Achieving success in screening, wrote cancer society epidemiologist Herbert Seidman, "also serves to stimulate further interest in developing still better screening procedures."[52] "One of our major efforts," Philip Strax concurred, "must be to make our screenee want to . . . act as a missionary to bring other women into the screening process."[53] Through this self-fulfilling reasoning, the cancer society's ardent promotion of its breast cancer detection program helped to validate its larger philosophy of aggressive screening.

So, too, radiologists viewed mammography as a way to both help individual patients and solidify their professional role as breast cancer diagnosticians. Having demonstrated their ability to detect tiny cancers hidden from the examiner's hand, early mammographers such as Strax and New York's Herman C. Zuckerman received hundreds of grateful letters from patients and surgeons. Indeed, as the 1970s and 1980s progressed, fewer and fewer breast cancers were diagnosed by physical examination alone. The mammogram was becoming an obligatory passage point in the diagnosis of breast cancer.[54]

Mammography's great power stemmed from the fact that it allowed previously hidden breast cancers to be visualized. To be sure, mammograms did not simply reveal cancer. Through an extensive and often arduous process of education, radiologists learned to identify mammographic findings and then assigned them names and meanings. Nevertheless, the public perception of the mammogram was that it transformed the invisible to the visible, thereby providing objective information about breast cancer that saved lives. As one newspaper headline read, "X-Ray Found Able to 'See' Early Breast Cancer."[55] Mammography had a "certain magic appeal," wrote pioneer Robert Egan. The patient "feels [that] something special is being done for her."[56]

Manufacturers of x-ray machines and film actively promoted the growing interest in mammography. Advertisements in medical journals, such as one for Kodak, offered "a hopeful message from industry on a sober topic." Its new x-ray film, Kodak hoped, would increase the benefit-to-risk ratio for women receiving mammography.[57] In marketing its new machine, the Picker company played on the familiar notion that mammographic images themselves revealed cancer. "Mammorex II," the advertisement read, "can see it before she can feel it."[58]

Given the availability of improved early detection technologies, women who chose not to participate were once again seen as culpable if they developed breast cancer. For example, Strax analogized a woman who ignored mammography to someone who walked into traffic without looking and was killed. Strax hoped to send a "clarion call to women to abandon such a fatalistic and passive attitude."[59]

Early news from the BCDDP appeared promising. Based on data from 42,000 women screened at the twenty-seven clinics, the NCI's William Pomerance reported in October 1974 that 77 percent of detected breast cancers—an even higher percentage than in the HIP study—had negative axillary nodes, suggesting early disease.[60] But it was other events the same month that transformed the detection project. When Betty Ford and Happy Rockefeller announced that they had breast cancer, among the clinics eagerly attended by women were those of the BCDDP. The message of the project—that a woman's health depended on frequent medical surveillance of her breasts—was exactly what these women wanted to hear. "Breast project is saving lives," announced the *San Antonio Evening News*.[61] "Mammography makes the difference," reported an article on New York's Guttman Institute, one of the BCDDP sites. "It is truly a life saver."[62] "Breast Cancer Project Called Success," stated the *New York Times*.[63] Yet as the detection project reached its peak in popularity, critics began to question the evidence being used to make such claims. Fittingly, the man who ignited the BCDDP controversy was a nonpracticing physician who had pursued a career in biostatistics and epidemiology.

An Insider Blows the Whistle

On October 1, 1975, the widely syndicated Washington columnist Jack Anderson published excerpts from an unpublished medical article alleging that mammograms in the BCDDP might be causing more breast cancer than the project was helping to cure. Anderson had received a tip from an acquaintance of the article's author, NCI Deputy Associate Director for Cancer Control John C. Bailar III. The piece, eventually published in the "Perspective" section of the *Annals of Internal Medicine* in January 1976, was entitled "Mammography: A Contrary View."[64] Growing up in Urbana, Illinois, Bailar had developed an early interest in mathematics and statistics. Nevertheless, he completed premedical studies and matriculated at the Yale University School of Medicine in 1951. At Yale, to his surprise and delight, he collaborated on a research project with Colin White, who was both a physician and a statistician.

After completing an internship in 1956, Bailar put down his stethoscope permanently to become a field investigator at the National Cancer Institute. Shortly thereafter, Bailar moved to Connecticut where he conducted research using the Connecticut State Cancer Registry. Bailar returned to the NCI in 1962, becoming chief of the demography section. From 1961 to 1973, he obtained his doctoral degree in statistics from American University in Washington, D.C. At the time the BCDDP was be-

John C. Bailar III in undated photo.

Courtesy of John Bailar.

ing conceived, Bailar had become one of the most prominent cancer statisticians and epidemiologists at the NCI and in the United States. As
Deputy Associate Director for Cancer Control, Bailar disbursed funding
for the BCDDP and other cancer projects. In practice, however, Nathaniel
Berlin was in charge of such programs.[65]

Bailar's *Annals* article made two major points. The overall benefits of
screening mammography, he wrote, "have not been determined" and its
risks "may be greater than are commonly understood."[66] In support of
his first point, Bailar revisited the HIP data and suggested that the observed lowering of mortality might have stemmed more from physical
examination than mammography. He also cautioned that a series of biases existed in screening programs that potentially exaggerated the effects
of interventions such as mammography. Lead-time bias referred to the
ability to detect breast cancers earlier but not actually improve the survival of patients. Length-time bias reminded researchers that screening
tests were more likely to identify slow-growing cancers for which early
detection mattered less. In cautioning that "[n]ot every lesion discovered
by screening should be counted as a success of the program," Bailar hear-
kened back to the earlier warnings of the biological predeterminists
about "non-killing cancers."[67]

With respect to the hazards of mammography, Bailar cited several
types of "experimental and clinical evidence . . . that ionizing radiation
can cause breast cancer."[68] He pointed out that this effect appeared to be
dose-dependent: the more radiation a woman received in the breast re-

gion, the higher likelihood that she would develop cancer there in ten to fifteen years. Although Bailar noted that radiation doses used in mammography appeared to be declining, he asked "why questions about the effects of radiation used in mammography have not been investigated more actively."[69] The risks of radiation, he added, were of particular concern in women under fifty, for whom the benefits of mammography had not conclusively been demonstrated. Indeed, it was these younger women who would subsequently receive intense scrutiny as the debates over Bailar's accusations accelerated.

Bailar's challenge to the BCDDP was especially devastating because he was an employee of one of the cosponsoring agencies. Yet Bailar had not blindsided his NCI colleagues. For nearly three years before the publication of Jack Anderson's column, Bailar had raised objections to numerous aspects of the project's protocol. Meticulous by nature, he had created an extensive paper trail documenting his concerns. In addition to his misgivings about radiation exposure, Bailar had pointed out apparent inconsistencies in the BCDDP's goals. Even though "designed as community service programs [and] not research projects,"[70] various lists of the project's objectives indicated that it sought to "determine yield of breast cancer in population screened and evaluate effectiveness in increasing survival rate"[71] and "determine or confirm the observation that non-palpable breast cancer properly treated will provide more years free of known disease than waiting for palpable evidence of disease."[72] In addition, the original consent form for the project indicated that data obtained would be used for "scientific research." In a March 1, 1973, memorandum, Bailar had told Berlin that he doubted that the design of the BCDDP could answer any research questions.[73] Despite Bailar's concerns, however, the NCI formally began to analyze data in January 1974, studying, among other things, the results of treatment.[74]

In his role as Deputy Associate Director for Cancer Control, Bailar had sent preliminary outlines of the BCDDP to outside statisticians. Many registered extensive reservations. For example, John A. H. Lee of the University of Washington, noting the absence of a control group, expressed his skepticism about generating "any satisfactory comparison between the experience of these women in five years' time and the comparison data derivable from other sources."[75] Marvin Zelen, Professor of Statistics at the State University of New York at Buffalo, was more blunt. "The Project is ill-conceived," he wrote to Bailar and Rauscher, "and is not likely to result in significant patient benefit."[76] Others who learned about the BCDDP expressed concern about radiation exposure. "We wonder," wrote Saul Harris of the New York City Office of Radiation Control to Rauscher on January 10, 1973, "if mass screening involving mammography is consistent with good radiation protection theory."[77] Harris urged the NCI to convene an expert panel to make "an independent judgement of the efficacy of screening mammography."[78]

The National Cancer Institute had not ignored the concerns of Bailar and other critics. For example, at a December 21, 1972, research meeting chaired by Berlin, NCI staff discussed the fact that the mammography equipment to be used in the BCDDP had not been standardized.[79] On January 18, 1973, an ad hoc clinical research committee expressed concerns about the possible hazards of ionizing radiation and the ability of an uncontrolled study to generate any meaningful conclusions about the value of screening mammography. On August 7, 1973, Sidney Cutler of the NCI's biometry branch told Berlin, "I too have questioned the scientific validity of the project as a 'research endeavor.'"[80] These issues continued to receive scrutiny as the BCDDP progressed. In December 1974, Malcolm C. Pike, a cancer researcher at the University of Southern California, told the NCI's William Pomerance that a group of statisticians asked to comment on the BCDDP were "all basically in agreement that giving a woman under the age of 50 a mammogram on a routine basis is close to unethical."[81]

Thus, the information contained in the articles by Anderson and Bailar hardly came as a surprise to the NCI or to the American Cancer Society, which had been informed of the various internal objections to the BCDDP. Nor could BCDDP officials claim to be completely surprised at the intense reaction that these articles generated among the medical profession and the public. As Bailar was drafting his *Annals* article, he had strongly encouraged NCI Director Frank J. Rauscher, Jr., to prepare for the intensive media scrutiny that he believed would ensue.[82]

But even Bailar could not have anticipated the media's tenacious response to the BCDDP story. Journalists first challenged ACS officials at the seminar for science writers held in conjunction with the March 1976

American Cancer Society annual meeting. These reporters persistently questioned Holleb and Benjamin F. Byrd, Jr., a surgeon and president of the cancer society, about the validity of Bailar's charges. In response, Holleb and Byrd conceded that the 245,000 women enrolled in the BCDDP had not been told of any possible risks.[83]

In July 1976, members of the media began to do their own investigative work. *Washington Star* science reporter Christine Russell obtained through a Freedom of Information Act (FOIA) request a draft of the first of three internal reports commissioned by the NCI in 1975 in the wake of Bailar's accusations. In reviewing the HIP study, University of California at Los Angeles Public Health School Dean Lester Breslow and colleagues had concluded that it had not proven the value of mammography in women in their forties. As a result, Breslow's group had recommended that the BCDDP stop performing mammograms on women under age fifty.

Soon after, a committee chaired by Arthur C. Upton, dean of the School of Basic Health Sciences at the State University of New York at Stony Brook, completed the second NCI report, which looked at the risks of radiation from mammography. Upton's group had estimated that each low-dose mammogram (one rad) increased the 0.07 (7%) lifetime risk of younger women developing breast cancer by $1/100$ to 0.0707. Even though this increase posed a "very, very small risk to the individual,"[84] Upton had expressed reluctance to continue routine screening of women under fifty, especially given Breslow's findings. But the actual situation was worse than Upton's hypothetical scenario. In November 1976, through another FOIA request, Sidney Wolfe of Ralph Nader's Health Research Group had learned that sixteen of fifty-seven BCDDP mammography machines tested for radiation exposed women to more than the acceptable level of one to two rads per x-ray. One machine even generated 6.5 rads for each mammogram.[85]

Although these committee reports put the American Cancer Society and the National Cancer Institute on the defensive, most damning was an article written by Daniel S. Greenberg in the September 23, 1976, issue of the prestigious *New England Journal of Medicine*. Greenberg was a former writer for the *Washington Post* and *Science* who had become a freelance journalist reporting on science and government. Greenberg's often controversial work had caught the eye of *New England Journal* editor Franz

Inglefinger, who had asked him to become the journal's Washington correspondent. Greenberg's piece on the BCDDP built on a career of questioning the actions of powerful institutions such as the ACS and NCI.

What made Greenberg's article so explosive was its use of internal memoranda and correspondence regarding the BCDDP that he had obtained through another FOIA request. To Greenberg, these documents, which included the concerns of Bailar, Pomerance, the ad hoc clinical research committee, and others, were smoking guns indicating how project supporters had bulldozed the program through the ACS and NCI. "[T]here is more than a bit to be appalled about," wrote Greenberg, "in the archives of the Breast Cancer Demonstration Project."[86]

Criticizing the BCDDP gradually became a cottage industry among Washington journalists, not only Greenberg but also Judith E. Randal and William Hines. For example, in a full-page article in the May 1, 1977, *Washington Post*, Greenberg and Randal reviewed the BCDDP in a piece entitled "The Questionable Breast X-Ray Program." Among other charges, they reported that an eighteen-year-old girl had received three BCDDP mammograms without a physical examination, while a thirty-two-year-old woman had received twenty-seven mammograms over seven years.[87] Increasingly, journalists cited the detection project as exemplifying the larger flaws in American cancer control efforts. In focusing on individual cures as opposed to the environmental causes of the disease, Greenberg and Randal charged, the ACS was "waging the wrong war on cancer."[88] Others who made similar arguments included the syndicated columnists Nicholas von Hoffman and Shana Alexander. "But a human body is not a battlefield," Alexander wrote, "and war on cancer is a faulty concept in every way."[89]

Feminists and other critics of the medical profession praised the efforts of both Bailar and the journalists who had publicized his cause. Rose Kushner, for example, wrote that Bailar had "performed a magnificent service for women—and their men."[90] The behavior of BCDDP officials, wrote Maryann Napoli of New York's Center for Medical Consumers, "has served to deepen the distrust between the people and health professionals."[91] Perhaps Bailar's most avid supporter among fellow statisticians was Irwin D. J. Bross of Buffalo's Roswell Park Cancer Institute, who went so far as to predict in younger women "the worst iatrogenic [physician-caused] breast cancer epidemic in history."[92]

As a result of the public criticisms of the project, the BCDDP was clearly in crisis by mid-1976. Demand for mammography, which had peaked in the wake of Betty Ford's and Happy Rockefeller's illnesses, had declined by 10 to 40 percent. On the CBS Morning News on August 27, 1976, Holleb admitted that women were staying away from mammography "in droves."[93]

The ACS Mounts a Defense

Criticisms of the BCDDP proved especially frustrating for its organizers because of what they believed the project had already accomplished. At least until the scandal broke, women—especially those aged thirty-five to fifty—had eagerly pursued breast cancer screening. Moreover, the BCDDP was detecting extremely small cancers. Of the 308 cases of breast cancer the project had diagnosed in women under fifty as of mid-1976, 100 had been discovered by mammography alone. Some 76 percent of all cancers detected had no axillary node involvement and thus had a high potential for cure; this figure increased to 84 percent for mammographically detected cancers. Indeed, as of early 1977, only one BCDDP enrollee with a cancer diagnosed by mammography had died.[94]

Nevertheless, confronted with both the Breslow and Upton reports and growing criticism in the press, BCDDP organizers decided to make changes in the project. For one thing, they rewrote the consent form to indicate the possible risks of mammography. They also accelerated efforts to standardize radiation dosages at the various BCDDP sites, a process that was under way but progressing slowly. Most notable, in August 1976, the ACS and NCI agreed to stop "routine" mammography on women under fifty, performing it instead only on those who were "high risk."[95]

In adopting this new policy, BCDDP officials had taken a rather remarkable step. On July 29, 1976, National Cancer Institute director Frank Rauscher had assembled all female employees of the NCI to ask their advice about mammographic screening. In telling the 400 women in attendance, "I need your help," the leader of the country's most powerful governmental cancer organization explicitly acknowledged the growing role that patients would come to play in the establishment of cancer policy in the United States. When polled, 45 percent of the women present indicated that, despite the risks, they favored screening mammography in women under fifty, compared with 32 percent who opposed it and 23 percent who were undecided. Based in part of these findings, Rauscher concluded that testing should continue. The decision to have a mammogram, however, needed to be made by each individual "high risk" woman with the input of her physician.[96]

But the manner in which "high risk" came to be defined strongly implied that screening mammography was still indicated for nearly all women under fifty. Holleb and the ACS, with a somewhat more reluctant NCI in agreement, broadly defined as high-risk those women aged thirty-five to fifty who had chronic cystic disease of the breast, lumps or thickenings, nipple discharges or abnormalities, personal breast cancer histories or past diagnostic breast surgery, family breast cancer histories, early menstrual histories, no pregnancies, or a first full-term pregnancy at age thirty or older. Women with an unusual dread of breast cancer (cancerphobia) were also included as high-risk, even though fear alone did not cause an increased likelihood of the disease. Noting that about 80 percent of thirty-five- to fifty-year-old women fell into one of these high-risk categories, Holleb advised them to have at least one baseline mammogram during this period.[97]

Critics responded to such risk estimates with either skepticism or ridicule. Bailar termed as "mathematically absurd" the notion that 80 percent of these women were at high risk for breast cancer: "We simply cannot have everybody, or even a majority, at risks that are significantly above average."[98] In pushing NCI director Rauscher to advocate more restrictive guidelines, Bailar urged him to reject the "[e]motional pleas from mammographers and shrieks of outrage from the American Cancer Society."[99] Similar criticism came from Greenberg and Randal, who asked how four out of five women under fifty could be at high risk for breast cancer if only 8 percent of all women were likely to develop the disease in their lifetimes.[100]

The answer to this paradox again demonstrates Mary Douglas's argument that assessments of risk are not objective but are influenced by the cultural setting in which they are made. Given the success of the BCDDP in detecting tiny cancers, project organizers were sincerely dumbfounded by the notion that a more relaxed approach to the identification of such lesions could be viewed as safe behavior. Every woman, Philip Strax warned, "carries within her body a built-in hazard—the risk of breast cancer."[101] Women who declined to be screened were thus "playing Russian roulette with their lives."[102] This reaction drew directly on the professional status of BCDDP officials: most of them were physicians, whose training had emphasized the need to cure individual patients. Despite the growing role of statistics in medicine, using population-based figures to deprive even one patient of a cure remained entirely unacceptable. "I don't see how you can say there is no benefit [to mammography]," NCI director Rauscher stated. "To those individual women whose cancer is detected, there certainly is a benefit."[103]

It was Arthur Holleb who spoke most powerfully for physicians who had seen far too many women die from breast cancer and were appalled at how statisticians and epidemiologists had interfered with the BCDDP. "As a clinician," he wrote, "I shudder to think of all the undiagnosed and unsuspected women with breast cancer who could be treated promptly and offered an excellent chance for cure." Approvingly quoting Harvard surgeon Francis D. Moore, Holleb added that "one woman in the prime of life, found to have an unsuspected cancer that's removed when it's very favorable surgically, is a triumph." Epidemiology, Holleb vividly concluded, was "the practice of medicine without the tears."[104]

Yet just as surgeons were losing the authority to decide that radical breast cancer operations were the only safe alternative, physicians such as Holleb could no longer unilaterally decide that the benefits of screening mammography outweighed the risks. The BCDDP conflict had arisen because the project was enmeshed in the paternalism of an earlier era, before statisticians and patients played a significant role in determining what was or was not good medicine. Holleb was correct in claiming that the American Cancer Society and the National Cancer Institute had not ignored warnings from Bailar and others about radiation and study design. But they had ultimately made decisions based on what the physicians in the two organizations had thought best. Nathaniel Berlin, for example, had personally believed that the incomplete HIP data for women aged forty to forty-nine should not prevent the overall implementation of the BCDDP. The Hippocratic Oath, Holleb stated, instructed

physicians to make decisions that they believed would benefit their patients. "In practice," he wrote in defending the detection project, "the art
of medicine often lies not only in deciding what is beneficial for the patient and what is harmful, but in evaluating which regimen carries the
greatest benefit and the least risk."[105] Unfortunately for Holleb and others
who had foreseen unmitigated success for the BCDDP, it was exactly this
type of physician behavior that had come under fierce attack in the 1970s.

By 1977, this tension between the old paternalism and new autonomy
enmeshed the BCDDP in yet another controversy. This dispute concerned
the questionable nature of the pathological findings of certain BCDDP
enrollees who had subsequently undergone mastectomy. The issue of
ambiguous pathology was not a new one, stemming back to Bailar's early
concern that screening mammography was apt to detect many slow-
growing lesions unlikely to ever become clinically significant. Indeed, in
April 1974, the NCI had convened a meeting of eminent pathologists to
discuss the issue. The incidence of carcinoma in situ among lesions being discovered at BCDDP sites, the NCI's William Pomerance informed
the attendees, ranged from 25 to almost 50 percent. Pomerance asked
whether the BCDDP was on "safe ground" terming such lesions "cancer"
and if the pathology of such cases needed formal review from a control
lab. Ultimately, the group decided that such a move was unnecessary, although the third internal report that the NCI would commission in 1975
in response to Bailar's accusations did revisit these concerns.[106]

In January 1977, the NCI asked University of Utah pathologist Robert
W. McDivitt to review the pathology of 506 so-called minimal breast lesions (cancer and carcinoma in situ) discovered during the BCDDP that
were under one centimeter in diameter. McDivitt's pathology working
group was part of a larger group, headed by Mayo Clinic surgeon Oliver
Beahrs, that was evaluating the overall results of the detection project to
date. McDivitt presented his panel's preliminary findings at a consensus
conference on breast cancer screening organized by the National Institutes of Health (NIH) in September 1977. This gathering was the first of
many NIH consensus conferences convened in order to help the NCI resolve contentious issues pertaining to breast and other cancers.

The BCDDP organizers believed that the project's ability to find minimal cancers was its greatest achievement. But McDivitt's report created an

outcry. It revealed that pathological specimens obtained from sixty-six of the 506 women had not contained evidence of cancer or even carcinoma in situ. Fifty-three of the women had undergone mastectomies, twenty-seven of which had been radical procedures.[107] These apparent errors in reading the pathology had not been made by BCDDP personnel, but rather by the doctors at the women's individual hospitals. When project physicians identified potential cancers on either physical examination or mammography, they referred patients to their regular practitioners to obtain a diagnostic biopsy and, if necessary, treatment for breast cancer. McDivitt's working group had based its findings on the pathologic specimens subsequently requested from these clinicians.

To those already skeptical about the BCDDP, this latest piece of information confirmed their beliefs about the arrogance of ACS and NCI officials. Journalists covering the so-called "66 cases" were especially scathing. "Mammography—A Vicious Circle of Mistakes," blared one Judith Randal article.[108] William Hines compared the "surgical mutilation" suffered by the BCDDP enrollees to the previous year's swine flu vaccine debacle. He wrote that "the official 'body count' of breast surgery known to have been done on healthy women after program screening is, at a minimum, 58."[109] The American Cancer Society, opined Daniel Greenberg, "feasts on terrorizing the public about a dread disease."[110]

These accusations infuriated supporters of the BCDDP, leading some of them to accuse Bailar, Randal, and other critics of mammography of murdering women. The most frustrated individual was the ACS's Arthur Holleb, who had conceived of and implemented the detection project. With the possibility of lower breast cancer mortality seemingly within reach, he simply could not understand how these small missteps could generate such hostility. Pathology was an "interpretative science," he explained, and thus disagreement over a small number of specimens was inevitable. While Holleb regretted that some unnecessary mastectomies may have occurred, he was more upset that everyone seemed to have forgotten that the BCDDP had found more than 2500 unsuspected cancers between 1973 and 1977.[111] When the New York Times editorial page criticized the detection project as "ill-conceived and even dangerous," Holleb replied in a letter, "Surely you are not opposed to a method which for the first time in the long tragic history of breast cancer facilitates such early diagnosis that more than 90 percent of breast cancers can become curable."[112]

Interestingly, the editors of the *Times*, whose own health and science reporter, Jane Brody, had been accused of being too sympathetic to the ACS,[113] responded to Holleb's letter. No, they wrote, they were not opposed to a method that enabled the earlier diagnosis of breast cancer. What the editors did question was "the indiscriminate use of that method on younger women before research has determined whether it causes more harm than good."[114] Once again, therefore, the BCDDP's problems had resulted from its organizers' characteristic combination of paternalism and zeal. Despite internal concerns about the indeterminate nature of the breast lesions that the project was bound to unearth, BCDDP officials had sacrificed full disclosure in pursuit of what they were certain was the greater good.

Disclosure remained an issue as the debate over the sixty-six cases continued into 1978. Following McDivitt's report, the NCI had asked Beahrs, as part of his overall assessment of the BCDDP, to review the sixty-six specimens with the pathology working group. Using additional clinical information and pathological material obtained from the patients' physicians, Beahrs concluded that only three women, at most, had undergone improper mastectomies. McDivitt, however, continued to disagree, arguing that the pathology working group still had not confirmed the diagnosis of cancer in forty-eight of the sixty-six cases.[115]

Given Beahrs's findings, new National Cancer Institute director Arthur Upton, who had initially favored informing the forty-eight women that errors had possibly occurred, changed his mind. Instead, the NCI informed only the patients' physicians of this possibility, asking them to tell their patients. Upton and his colleagues justified this decision by arguing that they did not want to interfere with the physician-patient relationship, especially since BCDDP staff had only detected the suspicious lesions, not diagnosed or treated them.[116]

But women activists found this arrangement to be unacceptable. Rose Kushner noted the irony that these women possibly still believed that their BCDDP mammograms had led to the "cure" of their breast cancers. "I wonder," she wrote, "if anyone has told these lucky women that they no longer have to worry about recurrences and metastases."[117] In a series of letters to Upton's successor, Vincent T. DeVita, Jr., and to Florida Senator Paula Hawkins, consumer advocate Maryann Napoli argued that, in the interest of humanity and ethics, the National Cancer Institute was obligated to inform the forty-eight women that their cases were still generating disagreement within the BCDDP.[118] DeVita declined, however, and the women never received formal notification from either the ACS or the NCI.

To perceptive observers of the breast cancer screening debates of the 1970s, the fact that the 1977 NIH consensus conference had generated enormous controversy over the unnecessary "mutilation" of women came as no surprise. Given the political, economic, and cultural stakes in the war on breast cancer, many participants had not really been looking for consensus at all. Yet, as usual, voices of moderation could be heard. "At risk of having a contract put out on me by the A[merican] C[ollege] of Radiology," New York City radiologist Floyd Ruesch stated at the 1976 White House Conference on Breast Cancer, John Bailar was owed a "tremendous debt."[119] In 1977, Diane Fink, who had succeeded Nathaniel Berlin in running the BCDDP, admitted that a similar project could no longer be started "without better evidence about the possible dangers of mammography."[120]

And aside from the controversy over the fifty-three unnecessary mastectomies, agreement had been reached by the consensus panel and Beahrs's committee on a number of the controversial aspects of the BCDDP. For example, both groups recommended that routine mammography for women aged forty to forty-nine be limited to those with a personal history of breast cancer or family history of the disease. Women aged thirty-five to thirty-nine needed screening only if they themselves had had breast cancer. The final revision of the BCDDP consent form contained information not only regarding the risks and benefits of mammography, but also about the indeterminate meanings of borderline or noninfiltrating cancers. Both the consensus panel and Beahrs's committee encouraged women to obtain multiple opinions if the diagnosis of breast cancer was uncertain. Finally, both groups acknowledged that the uncontrolled data from the BCDDP would never resolve the issue of whether mammography in women under age fifty reduced mortality. Although Beahrs's panel favored a randomized controlled trial to resolve this question, the consensus committee did not recommend such a study.[121]

And another point of agreement existed as well. Regardless of mammography's ultimate value in lowering breast cancer mortality in younger women, its ability to help identify smaller cancers made less extensive surgery a more reasonable option. By the late 1970s, the radical mastectomy and the one-step procedure were becoming obsolete. But their advocates would stage one last fight.

"The World Has Passed Us By"

Science, Activism, and the Fall of the Radical Mastectomy

B y the late 1970s, the United States was finally coming into line with Canada and Europe: the Halsted radical mastectomy was on its way to obsolescence. Whereas American surgeons performed 46,000 such operations in 1974, by 1979 this number had declined to only 17,000. Within a few years, less than 5 percent of breast cancer operations would be radical mastectomies.[1] A new theory of how breast cancer spread, first proposed by the biological predeterminists in the 1950s and then explicated by Bernard Fisher, had replaced the venerable Halsted paradigm. Despite enormous resistance from his surgical colleagues, Fisher had been able to carry out a series of randomized controlled trials showing that the radical mastectomy provided no survival advantage. But why had surgeons finally stopped performing Halsted's operation? Had Fisher's scientific data really changed their minds? Or had they finally relinquished Halsted's precepts because their women patients had left them no choice?

Despite the apparent triumph of Fisher's biological model, vestiges of the past persisted. A small number of surgeons continued to claim that radical surgery was better and that physicians should make clinical decisions for patients. These surgeons actively opposed a series of informed consent laws that state legislatures drafted in order to ensure that women with breast cancer learned about all possible treatment options. And even those surgeons who had rejected Halsted's radical mastectomy did not immediately embrace the limited operations validated by Fisher's trials. Rather, they settled upon a compromise operation, modified radical mastectomy, that kept vestiges of Halsted—and surgical authority—very much alive.

Halsted Is Dethroned

The year 1979 began with tragic news regarding Marvella Bayh. Interestingly, almost all of the "celebrity" breast cancer patients of the 1970s—regardless of the treatment they had chosen—were doing well. Betty Ford, Happy Rockefeller, Rose Kushner, and Betty Rollin, who had undergone either radical or modified radical mastectomies, were approaching the magical five-year "cure" mark. Babette Rosmond, Shirley Temple Black, and Helga Sandburg Crile, who had chosen less extensive surgery, also remained free from recurrence. Indeed, all of these women would survive over twenty-five years except for Kushner, who died of metastatic breast cancer in 1990 at the age of sixty. Rosmond would die at age eighty in 1997, most likely from a new breast cancer that she refused to have diagnosed or treated. Lumpectomy, in retrospect, had been the correct choice for her.

Bayh was not so lucky, becoming an unfortunate example of the argument that biology—as opposed to type of surgery—determined one's outcome from breast cancer. Bayh's physicians had diagnosed her cancer as highly aggressive and had treated her with a modified radical mastectomy, radiotherapy, and chemotherapy. In her countless appearances for the American Cancer Society, Bayh was routinely characterized as having triumphed over the disease. In 1974, only three years after her operation, *Newsweek* stated that she "seems to have beaten breast cancer."[2] The *Macon (Ga.) Telegram* announced in 1977 that "Mrs. Bayh is cured of cancer."[3] Although the article noted that this designation simply meant that she had survived five years, even better news was implied. Bayh's earnest entreaties regarding the value of early detection gained strength from her apparent recovery.

Thus the diagnosis of metastatic, incurable cancer in February 1978 came as a great shock to Bayh, her family, and the American Cancer Society, which was left with a dying spokesperson. Although the ACS had effectively used other dying celebrities, such as the actor William Talman of *Perry Mason* fame, in an educational role, Bayh's relentlessly upbeat message had been integral to her great appeal. The impending death from cancer of a woman who had so dutifully sought attention for a breast abnormality could not but undermine the ACS's optimistic claims about early detection. The media, too, had difficulty confronting Bayh's mortality. *Good Housekeeping* came under fire when its November 1978 issue stated that "Marvella Bayh is dying."[4] For her part, Bayh demonstrated tremendous dedication, continuing to make appearances across the country. She did not characterize herself as dying but rather as "living with the knowledge that I have cancer."[5] When Bayh died on April 24, 1979, all of the combatants in the breast cancer wars could agree that her contribution, in life and death, had been remarkable. "As for me," wrote ACS Vice-President for Public Information Irving Rimer, "I miss her deeply and will never, never forget her." Bayh's death was a call to arms for the cancer society. "Here I have the promise," Rimer vowed, "to work that much harder to put out this damn disease."[6]

But even the American Cancer Society had come to the realization that such a goal could not be accomplished through aggressive surgery. As the 1970s progressed, the ACS, which had been a bastion of both radical operations and paternalism, quietly began to modify its views. As early as 1973, the organization no longer cautioned women about being *stampeded* into accepting less proven surgery but rather about being *misled* into such surgery.[7] By 1979, ACS chief medical officer Arthur I. Holleb admitted that local tumor excision plus radiotherapy was a viable therapeutic option and that patients should make treatment decisions based on as much information as possible. The cancer society had even contributed funding to Bernard Fisher, who had long been anathema among its leadership.[8]

The shift away from radical breast surgery was formalized at a June 1979 NIH consensus conference, entitled "The Treatment of Primary Breast Cancer: Management of Local Disease." By the time of the conference, preliminary data from the randomized controlled trials of Bernard Fisher and Umberto Veronesi, showing no survival advantage to radical mastectomy, were available. The ten-person NIH panel, chaired by University of California oncologist John Moxley III and including Fisher, Veronesi, Rose Kushner, Jerome Urban, and Harvard Medical School radiation oncologist Samuel Hellman, concluded that "total (simple) mastectomy with axillary dissection should be recognized as the current standard treatment" for stage I and II disease. For early stage breast cancer, therefore, the pectoralis muscles never needed to be removed. The panel deferred recommendations on both the need for postoperative radiotherapy in such patients and the possible use of lumpectomy as primary therapy.[9]

In an editorial accompanying publication of the consensus panel's conclusions in the August 9, 1979, *New England Journal of Medicine*, Bernard Fisher explained how the statement, "wittingly, or unwittingly, also rejects the principles that had provided the scientific basis for the [radical mastectomy]."[10] That is, Fisher believed that his alternative explanation of breast cancer biology, which he had developed in the laboratory and then tested in clinical trials, had replaced the old Halsted hypothesis. Halsted had advocated an *en bloc* dissection of the breast, lymph nodes, and pectoralis muscles to obtain as much local control as possible. But the fact that smaller operations produced equal survival rates in RCTs had proven that local control was relatively unimportant. Breast cancer, Fisher believed, was basically systemic from the outset. Long-term survival depended not on the extent of local surgery but on the ability of the immune system and adjuvant chemotherapy to eliminate disease throughout the body. Most important, positive axillary lymph nodes, which Halsted had seen as the source of future metastases, were in actuality an "indicator of host-tumor relations." If a woman had positive nodes, especially five or more, she almost certainly already had distant disease that aggressive local surgery and radiotherapy alone could not cure.[11]

These conclusions would receive further support in the 1980s with the publication of more definitive survival data by Veronesi and Fisher. In 1981, Veronesi reported that removing a quarter of the breast, when accompanied by radiotherapy, provided equivalent overall survival to the Halsted radical mastectomy for breast cancers two centimeters or less in diameter.[12] In 1985, Fisher published ten-year survival data for women in randomized controlled trial NSABP-04, finding identical rates for those receiving radical mastectomy alone, total mastectomy with radiotherapy, or total mastectomy alone. Moreover, in that same year, Fisher reported five-year survival results from another randomized trial, NSABP-06, which compared total mastectomy with segmental mastectomy alone or with radiation for women with stage I or II breast cancers less than four centimeters in diameter.[13] (Fisher preferred the term "segmental mastectomy" to partial mastectomy or lumpectomy.) Although the women undergoing only segmental mastectomy had a 28 percent rate of local recurrence, all three groups demonstrated identical survival. Based on B-04 and B-06, Fisher argued, radical mastectomy equaled total (simple) mastectomy, which equaled segmental mastectomy (lumpectomy.)

Other than Jerry Urban, there had been remarkable agreement among the nine members of the 1979 consensus panel. Physicians in the United States had held onto the radical mastectomy much longer than those in other Western countries, who had switched to less extensive operations. Indeed, the international community had countenanced Fisher's new biological model of breast cancer at the World Cancer Congress in Florence, Italy, in 1975.[14] But even as it rejected the radical mastectomy, the 1979 NIH panel had been reluctant to overturn one of Halsted's other tenets: the one-step procedure. Although all of the panel members, except for Urban, basically supported separation of biopsy and operation, it took the persistent pleas of Kushner to get them to include a statement promoting the use of a two-step operation. That Kushner, the only woman and nonphysician on the committee, effected this recommendation was vivid testimony to her unique skills of persuasion. It is quite fitting that it was America's first breast cancer activist who convinced the medical community to formally abandon the one-step procedure. Originally introduced for purposes of efficiency and as a way to avoid anesthetizing patients twice, the one-step had come to serve little purpose except to keep women silent.[15]

Yet Kushner by this time had become more insider than outsider. "A maverick no more," she would joke after President Jimmy Carter appointed her to the National Cancer Advisory Board in May 1980. "I'm a full-fledged member of the Establishment."[16] To be sure, someone as iconoclastic and strong-willed as Kushner could never really stop fighting for change. But by the early 1980s, Kushner had made peace with many of her early foes. She and Bernard Fisher spent much less energy arguing about breast cancer treatment and more time strategizing about getting physicians and women to participate in randomized trials and then to accept their results. The "Rose and Bernie show" benefited both of their agendas. "Bernie wanted these doctors to hear an articulate patient," Harvey Kushner, Rose Kushner's widower, recently recalled.[17]

The American Cancer Society also came to applaud Kushner's efforts, presenting her with its highest award, the Gold Medal of Honor, in 1987.

Praising Kushner, the ACS's Arthur Holleb wrote, "You presented data, cajoled, wheedled, needled, smiled, brought information to the forefront, developed programs, spearheaded, wrote and wrote and wrote and never lost sight of your goals."[18] Kushner never apologized for her decision to effect change from within the system, and her judgment has been validated by the subsequent adoption of this strategy by most major breast cancer advocacy groups. Yet a few breast cancer activists, such as Maryann Napoli of the Center for Medical Consumers, believed that Kushner's close association with groups such as the NCI made her less willing to criticize their missteps, such as the BCDDP.[19]

The partnership between Kushner and Fisher highlighted the complex mixture of medical and social factors that eventually led to significant changes in the treatment of breast cancer in the United States. Retrospective assessments of this issue have tended to cite either scientific progress or women's activism as having led to the abandonment of radical surgery. Kushner, for example, once stated that it was the work of scientists such as Fisher—"not the 'women's lib' movement and female pressure"—that had caused the "lessening in the extent of surgery."[20] Conversely, breast surgeon Susan M. Love attributed the spread of lumpectomy to women who told their physicians, "'I refuse mastectomy. You better find another way to treat me.'"[21]

Yet such descriptions minimize how developments in science and activism combined to produce acceptance of less extensive operations.[22] To understand this point, Fisher's own attempts to address how change took place are instructive. Approvingly citing the work of the historian Thomas S. Kuhn, Fisher argued in 1992 that advances in science occurred when discontent among members of the scientific community led to the reevaluation of accepted explanatory paradigms. In the case of breast cancer, discrepancies within the mechanistic Halsted model had led Fisher and other researchers to hypothesize and then establish an alternative biological paradigm.[23]

In agreeing with Kuhn, Fisher acknowledged how activists within and later outside the medical profession induced physicians to perform better studies and then revise long-held assumptions and beliefs. But in claiming that randomized controlled trials—and only randomized controlled trials—generated true facts, Fisher also subtly used rhetoric to convince physicians and the public that the new information was superior. To be sure, RCTs produced more reliable data than other statistical methods. Yet by so successfully contrasting his own "scientific" findings with the "nonscientific," "emotional"[24] arguments of his predecessors, Fisher helped to ensure that randomized trials would henceforth be viewed as the only valid mechanism for obtaining definitive evidence.

Among those who came to embrace randomized trials were women activists, such as Rose Kushner, whose fundamental goal was to democratize medical decision-making. Just as Fisher saw the value of activists in propelling science forward, these activists saw RCTs as a way to ensure that women with breast cancer learned about and then received the best treatment. In this manner, the roles of activism and science intertwined in spelling the end of the Halsted radical mastectomy.

Physicians themselves appreciated how a combination of factors— Fisher's data, the growing availability of effective radiotherapy and chemotherapy, and the expectations of women with breast cancer—had induced them to change their ways. "I was dragged into it," admitted New York City surgeon David W. Kinne. "I thought: I have a long career still ahead of me, and if this works and patients want this . . . I'd better learn how to do it, and we'd better offer it to patients."[25] Edward F. Lewison of Johns Hopkins University recalled how he initially resented having to read both the *Reader's Digest* and the recommendations of the American College of Surgeons in order to arrive at treatment decisions with his patients. But eventually, he noted, there was a "meeting of the minds."[26]

The fact that physicians abandoned radical breast surgery well before the publication of Fisher's definitive B-04 data also raises the issue of what the randomized testing of radical mastectomy actually "proved." Early in their careers, lawyers learn the admonition: "Never ask a question to which you do not know the answer." Such a statement has applicability to RCTs as well. While it would be wrong to imply that the results of most randomized trials can reliably be predicted before they are performed, quite suggestive evidence may exist.

Because Veronesi and Fisher essentially demonstrated what dozens of uncontrolled studies performed over several decades had suggested— that more extensive local treatment of breast cancer did not improve survival—it is reasonable to ask whether their randomized trials mostly corroborated existing knowledge. That is, did they successfully perform RCTs whose outcomes were essentially predictable? Fisher clearly did not think so. Although he constantly praised both Barney Crile and Oliver Cope for their courage in pioneering less radical breast surgery,[27] Fisher believed that they had not proven anything. In his view, before his randomized trials were performed, a true state of uncertainty had existed.

But this perspective downplayed the knowledge generated earlier in the century. In the 1950s, the biological predeterminists, such as Maurice Black, Neil McKinnon, and Reginald Murley, had posited the basic tenets of what would become Fisher's biological paradigm of breast cancer: the disease was systemic from the outset; its spread reflected the biological variability of the disease; and radical surgery did not appreciably improve survival.[28] Meanwhile, Barney Crile, Vera Peters, and others had conducted retrospective trials that appeared to corroborate the predeterminists' claim that radical mastectomies were unnecessary. Yet did this evidence constitute "proof"? The unwillingness of Crile and other critics of radical mastectomy to participate in randomized controlled trials, despite their support of such studies in principle, suggests that they believed that enough proof already existed. But the way that Fisher and other supporters of RCTs have described the defeat of the radical mastectomy has eliminated this possible reading. In order for Fisher to get his colleagues to participate in B-04 and B-06, he needed to minimize what was already known. As a result, once these trials were completed, they appeared to constitute the first proof that less extensive operations were as effective as radical mastectomy. It would be more accurate, however, to state that the improved methodology of randomized controlled trials had provided better proof, as well as the type of proof that the medical profession increasingly agreed was necessary to demonstrate the value of given therapeutic interventions.

This discussion should in no way be taken to minimize the importance of Bernard Fisher's contributions to the evolution of breast cancer treatment. Even if we accept the notion that Crile and other researchers had already demonstrated that radical mastectomies were no longer indicated, most surgeons remained thoroughly unconvinced. As a result, debates about breast cancer treatment had reached a total impasse prior to the NSABP trials. It was Fisher, by organizing and carrying out these randomized studies, who convinced surgeons and other physicians to truly reexamine the basic way they made medical decisions. By the 1980s, thanks to Fisher, one could no longer claim that breast and other cancers could best be treated by courageous surgeons performing heroic operations on stoic patients. Rather, physicians were obligated to learn about the best available data and then communicate this information to their patients. It is little wonder that Fisher's admirers have long argued that his achievements warrant serious consideration for the Nobel Prize.

Haagensen's Last Stand

In taking on the surgeons in the middle 1970s, Rose Kushner and other feminists sought to abolish both the radical mastectomy and the paternalistic model that the medical profession had used to justify this operation. To these critics of medical practice, the two goals went hand in hand. But many surgeons who finally parted ways with the Halsted radical remained unwilling to cede decision-making to their breast cancer patients. Although they acknowledged the growing importance of informed consent, they were too accustomed to making decisions for their patients to relinquish this role so readily. Laying out a series of options hardly seemed to fulfill the Hippocratic legacy of doing the best for one's patients.

Thus, even when surgeons informed their breast cancer patients that numerous choices, including lumpectomy, existed, they continued to make recommendations based on what they believed was best. For example, in justifying his continued use of radical surgery in 1977, Mississippi surgeon Richard J. Field, Jr., remarked that "the Golden Rule is the most effective approach."[29] New York surgeon Charles W. Hayden agreed. After obtaining the biopsy results, he stated, "[W]e can explain what we plan to do and why."[30] Other surgeons characterized smaller operations as "experimental," thereby ensuring that patients would choose more extensive procedures.[31] These physicians often deluded themselves into thinking that such discussions actually constituted some type of informed consent process. New Haven surgeon Sherwin B. Nuland initially took pride in the fact that no patient had ever turned down his recommendation until he realized that his style of presentation left them with no perceived alternatives.[32]

Many patients welcomed this directive approach from their surgeons. For example, one woman writing to Gerald Ford in wake of his wife's operation expressed her frustration at having been told: "[W]e aren't sure what to do, but here are some possibilities we can try—which one shall we try?"[33] But other women resented being pressured into a given choice, a process which one physician aptly characterized as "advised consent."[34] One Long Island, New York, woman told Betty Rollin how her surgeon had convinced her to have a one-step procedure, which she had explicitly sought to avoid. "I don't know why," she wrote, "but somehow I found what he had to say as credible and I agreed."[35] The woman later regretted her acquiescence.

Believing that too many surgeons were subverting their duty to reveal fairly all treatment options, an anonymous Massachusetts woman devised a highly atypical strategy to ensure that breast cancer patients would be able to give truly informed consent. In the late 1970s, when this woman was undergoing evaluation of possible breast cancer, one surgeon had insisted on a one-step procedure and had not discussed treatments other than radical mastectomy. Eventually, she found another surgeon who performed a lumpectomy. Incensed by the behavior of the first physician, the woman induced Massachusetts State Senator Carol C. Amick to introduce legislation mandating that doctors advise "each patient suffering from a form of breast cancer, of all alternatives available for treatment in addition to mastectomies."[36] All physicians in the state needed to indicate compliance with this clause every two years under penalty of perjury. The bill was signed into law on May 23, 1979.

By 1990, sixteen states had passed similar legislation regarding breast cancer treatment. Medical ethicists and other supporters of patients' rights welcomed these laws because they publicized the issue of informed consent not only for breast cancer but for other diseases as well.[37] Still, even advocates admitted that legislative initiatives were a poor strategy for ensuring that physicians respected the autonomy of patients. In addition, as the sociologists Theresa Montini and Sheryl Ruzek have argued, these laws lacked adequate mechanisms for enforcement.[38]

The loudest critics of informed consent were physicians, who objected vehemently to governmental interference with medical decision-making. For decades, organizations such as the American Medical Association had fought attempts by outside parties to influence the physician-patient relationship. The new informed consent laws, doctors argued, destroyed the trust that was basic to encounters between physicians and individual patients. "It's totally inappropriate to practice medicine by legislation," remarked Massachusetts Medical Society President Grant V. Rodkey. "No two patients are alike."[39] Maryland physicians told the state's general assembly that they did a good job of policing themselves.[40]

Surgeons were especially critical, fearing that such legislation would steer patients away from more extensive, potentially curative operations. Objecting to the Kansas law, which was passed in 1984, one physician lamented that "we have 'lib groups,' legislatures with a view to political grist, and those most strident voices which contend that surgeons (mostly male) are sadists whose aim in the treatment of breast cancer is the mutilation of the female body."[41] Surgeons also argued that radiotherapists (now known as radiation oncologists) who advocated lumpectomy and radiation treatment were not necessarily providing better information for their patients; rather, they were presenting the data in their own favor, downplaying the very real side effects of radiotherapy.[42]

The surgeons fighting the passage of informed consent legislation represented the last vestiges of the paternalistic generation of physicians that had dominated American medicine after World War II. And nowhere was this tradition more evident than in New York City, where breast surgeons at Memorial Sloan-Kettering and Columbia-Presbyterian actively contested the dramatic changes occurring in breast cancer treatment. This perspective came across clearly in a minority report that Urban had issued after the 1979 NIH consensus conference. Although Urban now favored a modified radical mastectomy for stage I and even selected stage II cases, he continued to oppose lumpectomy. He also disagreed with Fisher's claim, based on clinical studies of only five years, that breast cancer was a systemic disease from the start. Finally, Urban continued to favor a one-step procedure in most instances.[43]

Urban was especially upset at the consensus process itself, which he believed had been a farce. The prepared consensus statement, he claimed, "was formulated before the meeting took place." Because his own data, which included over fifteen years of follow-up, had not fit the panel's conclusions, they had been "completely disregarded and omitted from

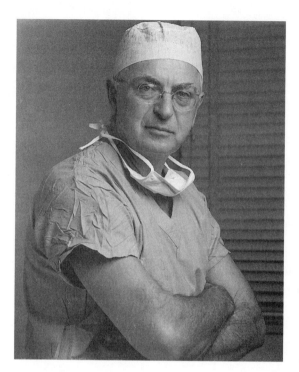

Jerome A. Urban, one of the
last defenders of radical
breast surgery, in 1974.

Courtesy of Neil Selkirk
Photography.

any consideration for inclusion in the Consensus statement."[44] Rose
Kushner, who disagreed with Urban on almost everything, corroborated
his contention that the final recommendation had been prepared in advance. "[T]he unspoken purpose of the Consensus Development Conference," she wrote, "was to hold formal services and bury the Halsted
radical mastectomy once and for all."[45]

Beyond his perceived exclusion from the consensus process, Urban
also opposed the panel's conclusions because they confirmed what critics
of randomized controlled trials had long feared: the era of individual
surgeons unilaterally deciding what was best for their patients was coming to an end. By generating "a sort of cookbook for the surgical treatment of cancer," Urban wrote, Fisher's trials rejected the "art of
medicine."[46] But Urban and his like-minded colleagues at Sloan-Kettering could no longer stave off the new approaches to breast cancer treatment. Michael P. Osborne was a British surgeon who came to
Sloan-Kettering in 1980 as a fellow and joined the surgical staff in 1981.

Although Osborne found Urban to be "an absolutely wonderful man, a delightful individual [and] totally dedicated,"[47] he disagreed with him regarding lumpectomy. Osborne began performing this operation, which he and fellow British physicians termed "tylectomy," in the early 1980s. Osborne's actions generated an accusatory letter from his surgical superiors at Sloan-Kettering, asking him to defend what he was doing.[48]

Fortunately for Osborne, his foray into breast conservation coincided with the naming of the radiation oncologist Samuel Hellman as physician-in-chief of Memorial Sloan-Kettering Cancer Center. In Boston, Hellman had achieved excellent survival rates using a combination of implanted iridium pellets and external megavoltage x-rays that killed breast cancer cells while sparing surrounding healthy tissue. Hellman's 1983 appointment signified the acknowledgment of Sloan-Kettering, the institution that had so extended the frontiers of cancer surgery, that cancer could no longer be considered solely a surgical disease.

At Columbia-Presbyterian, another surgeon was experiencing conflicts similar to those of Osborne. Avram M. Cooperman had spent eight years on the surgical staff of the Cleveland Clinic, where he became an avid supporter of Barney Crile and his theories regarding breast conservation. In 1979, Cooperman left Cleveland for a position at Columbia. Although he knew he was entering a conservative institution, Cooperman was brash and enthusiastic. Upon arriving at Columbia, he quickly invited his mentor Crile to speak at surgical grand rounds. In what was an ominous sign, Cushman Haagensen chose not to attend the talk. As usual, Crile was impolitic, citing the "mutilations inflicted by the Halsted radical mastectomy" at one of the last bastions of that operation.[49] In turn, those in attendance criticized Crile so ardently that Cooperman prematurely truncated the question and answer session. The infighting continued at rounds the next week. The schism over breast surgery was only one of many areas in which Cooperman came into conflict with his new colleagues. Remaining an outsider, he left the institution in 1981.[50]

Despite the negative response of many Columbia surgeons to Cooperman's ideas, others on the breast service had begun to rebel against their mentor Haagensen by the early 1980s. David V. Habif, followed later by Frank E. Gump, Sven J. Kister, and Philip D. Weidel, began to perform modified radical mastectomies and, in some cases, even less extensive operations. Whether due to his advancing age (Haagensen turned eighty in 1980) or an unwillingness to admit that decades of radical surgery had, in hindsight, been unnecessary, Haagensen refused to modify his views. Haagensen's intransigence became clear to breast surgeon Susan Love when she approached him after a talk at Wellesley College in the early 1980s. When Love mentioned alternatives to radical mastectomy, he accused her of killing women. "It was sad," Love recently recalled. "He had lived too long. He just couldn't make that critical jump."[51]

In 1986, Haagensen made one last attempt at proselytizing, remarkably completing the 1,050-page third edition of *Diseases of the Breast* at the age of eighty-six.[52] In a chapter entitled "The Recent Disparagement of Radical Mastectomy," Haagensen repeated his familiar claim that his personal data, which followed over 1000 patients for up to forty-seven years, were superior to those generated in Bernard Fisher's randomized controlled trials. A patient with curable breast cancer who chose lesser surgery, he stated, "is risking her life blindly."[53]

Haagensen's sincere devotion to the Halsted radical mastectomy was never more apparent than in 1984, when Kister, while examining Haagensen's wife, Alice, discovered a mass in the left breast. A subsequent mammogram was strongly suggestive of cancer. Having recently abandoned the Halsted procedure for the modified radical, Kister agreed only reluctantly to perform the more extensive operation, albeit without a skin graft. For her part, Alice Haagensen wanted nothing but the best. "The radical mastectomy takes longer and is more trouble for the surgeon," she had remarked a few years earlier, "but it saves the lives of ten more women out of a hundred."[54] Nor did she fear the operation's side effects, noting that one of her husband's patients had presented him with a tennis trophy won after radical surgery. As of the year 2000, at the age of one hundred, Alice Haagensen remained convinced that the Halsted radical had saved her life.

In addition to maintaining his advocacy of radical mastectomy, Cushman Haagensen also continued to give his patients the same intense, undivided attention that he always had. Although he stopped operating in 1975, he held office hours well into his eighties. Kenneth M. Prager, a young pulmonologist at Columbia in the 1980s, recalls how Haagensen would walk his patients into Prager's office for an unscheduled referral during the middle of a busy afternoon. Haagensen would formally introduce the patient to Prager and then leave, fully expecting that his colleague would see the woman next.[55] Haagensen could also often be seen sitting in the hospital garden, carefully giving a just-discharged patient her follow-up instructions. He also insisted on changing all of his patients' dressings by himself. Haagensen's belief in his patients' trust led him to discontinue his malpractice insurance during the last years of his practice. "My patients won't sue me if they know I've done all that I can for them," he frequently stated.

Nor did Haagensen make distinctions between his poor and wealthy patients. Up through 1986, he continued to charge only $25 per office visit, regardless of the patient's ability to pay. One such patient was Ingrid Bergman, the noted actress of *Casablanca* fame. In October 1973, while appearing in a London play, the fifty-eight-year-old Bergman had felt a breast lump. Ignoring the requests of the noted London breast surgeon Richard S. Handley that she have a biopsy, Bergman scheduled an appointment with Haagensen when she returned to New York in the spring of 1974. Ready to see his next patient, Haagensen appeared in the waiting room and asked the receptionist the patient's name. "Mrs. Bergman," Haagensen was told. Just then, a diminutive woman from the local Washington Heights neighborhood approached the desk, and greeted Dr. Haagensen. Believing the woman to be his next patient, Haagensen bowed in his usual courtly manner and loudly addressed her as "Mrs. Bergman." The patients in the waiting room, well aware that the real Ingrid Bergman was patiently waiting her turn, erupted in laughter.[56]

Once in the office, Haagensen had responded in typical fashion when Bergman offered her latest reason for postponing an operation. "What is more important?" Haagensen had demanded to know. "Your husband's birthday party or your life?"[57] Ultimately, Bergman underwent a modified radical mastectomy and radiotherapy in London. She died from metastatic breast cancer in 1982. While perhaps not to Bergman's taste, Haagensen's benevolent, caring persona continued to reassure hundreds of patients. "I like to leave things in the hands of the man I am seeing, feeling he knows best," explained one of his patients.[58]

Certain surgeons trained by Haagensen continued to perform radical mastectomies at Columbia as late as 1989, when other surgeons and pathologists finally put enough pressure on them to stop.[59] From Barney Crile's initial charge in 1955 that radical mastectomies were never indicated, it had taken thirty-four years for Columbia's breast surgeons to completely reject the teachings of their charismatic but imperious chief. In retrospect, surgeons at Columbia and many other American institutions had persisted far too long in using radical surgery for breast cancer.[60] By the late 1980s, even Haagensen's fiercest allies had to acknowledge that the era of the Halsted radical mastectomy was over. "I guess the world has passed us by," former Haagensen resident Philip I. Partington told his old boss.[61]

Haagensen died in 1990 at the age of ninety. The other famous breast surgeons of his generation died around this time as well. Urban died in 1991, six years after his stroke. Cope died at age ninety-one in 1994, never having experienced a recurrence of his radiation-treated bladder cancer. Crile, age eighty-four, died in 1992 of lung cancer. Crile's last years were happy ones, as he and his wife entertained a steady stream of visitors with an annual film festival, debates over topics ranging from pit bulls to polygamy, and Crile's ukelele playing.

Shortly before his death, Crile received a letter from Reginald Murley, the surgeon who had promoted lesser surgery in Britain while Crile had championed the cause in the United States. Boys until the end, Sir Reginald reminded his longtime friend that "[b]etween us, with Geoffrey Keynes' inspiration, we have certainly saved a lot of tits."[62] They certainly had.

A Quiet Compromise

The most revolutionary aspect of Bernard Fisher's findings was that failure to treat the axillary lymph nodes had no effect on survival from breast cancer. It was the intricate dissection and removal of all accessible lymph nodes, along with the rooting out of as much local cancer as possible, that had been the basis of Halsted's theories. Although at least one third of patients in Fisher's studies had received prophylactic irradiation of the axilla, surgeons had not gone looking for cancer in these nodes. On the basis of B-04 and B-06, therefore, the treatment for presumed stage I or II breast cancer was either total mastectomy or segmental mastectomy (lumpectomy). More surgery, including axillary node dissection, was not necessary, although supplemental radiation could reduce local recurrence rates.

But as radical mastectomy went by the wayside, neither total mastectomy or lumpectomy took its place. Although some surgeons did these two procedures, the vast majority performed the modified radical mastectomy. According to a 1981 American College of Physicians survey that examined the treatment of over 47,000 cases of breast cancer, surgeons used modified radicals 71 percent of the time. Montini and Ruzek reported that nearly 80,000 modified radical mastectomies were performed in the United States in 1984.[63] The definition of a modified radical mastectomy differed from surgeon to surgeon. Some excised one of the two pectoral muscles while others left both in place. Yet all modified radical operations involved removal of the axillary lymph nodes.

There were several medical justifications for the widespread adoption of the modified radical mastectomy in the early 1980s. First, definitive data from Fisher's B-04 and B-06 trials were not published until 1985. Thus, some surgeons remained reluctant to use less extensive procedures. Second, axillary node removal, like radiotherapy, was a way to help prevent local recurrence. Third, and most important, axillary dissection, by revealing whether the nodes contained cancer, helped physicians gauge both prognosis and the need for systemic chemotherapy.[64]

But other factors also promoted the acceptance of the modified radical procedure. For one thing, it represented a mechanism by which radical surgeons could temper but not entirely renounce their allegiance to Halsted. That is, surgeons could still continue to perform a variant of the axillary node dissection that had so long characterized the treatment of breast cancer. And they could continue to rely on data collected in the manner that Halsted had advised: from retrospective case studies performed by individual surgeons. In contrast to total mastectomy and lumpectomy, which were being evaluated in randomized trials, the data supporting modified radicals had largely come from uncontrolled case series.[65]

Thus, as opponents vocally debated the value of the Halsted radical mastectomy versus much less extensive operations, the modified radical mastectomy quietly became a "very reasonable compromise"[66] or a "logical alternative."[67] Feminist writers regretted this development. The triumph of modified radical surgery, they argued, demonstrated how the medical profession had successfully coopted women's attempts to challenge how breast surgeons behaved. In making "as little change as possible,"[68] these physicians had successfully resisted efforts to truly share decision-making power.

The degree to which the treatment of breast cancer had really changed by the 1980s depended on who one asked. Given the new emphasis on less surgery and more adjuvant therapy, Urban, Haagensen, and other radical surgeons believed that the world had been turned upside down. But feminists and other critics of the status quo disagreed. Yes, the radical mastectomy had largely disappeared, but physicians—in particular, surgeons—continued to dominate the clinical encounter. The reality was somewhere in the middle. Many physicians had moderated their views, but many breast cancer patients still looked to their doctors for guidance.

Debates over breast cancer treatment would remain contentious throughout the 1980s and 1990s. So would debates over breast cancer screening, prevention, activism, and, most recently, genetic testing. The final two chapters of this book examine these controversies, emphasizing how social, political, and economic concerns continue to influence the efforts to understand breast cancer as a medical disease.

eleven

The Past as Prologue

What Can the History of Breast Cancer Teach Us?

*S*hould a forty-year-old woman with no family history of breast cancer have an annual screening mammogram? Should a woman with a history of ductal carcinoma in situ think of herself as having had breast cancer? Does the answer to this question change if she elects to have a mastectomy as treatment? Should a woman with a one-centimeter breast cancer and negative axillary nodes undergo chemotherapy to treat invisible disease that may or may not be present throughout her body? Should she elect to have an even stronger chemotherapeutic regimen with greater side effects if there is only a 1 to 3 percent chance that it is better than standard chemotherapy?

As we enter the new millennium, enormously difficult questions such as these confront American women undergoing screening or treatment for breast cancer. With the tremendous growth of breast cancer activism in the 1990s, these issues are discussed not only between health care providers and their patients, but in the media, on the Internet, and in Congress. Indeed, one of the major challenges for the coming decades is reconciling these public discussions, which generally rely on population-based data, to the dilemmas faced by individual women. Some activists have argued that the questions set forth above are the wrong ones to ask. An intensive focus on early detection and aggressive treatment, they believe, has deflected attention from a more important goal: primary prevention of breast cancer through cleaning up the environment and encouraging women to lead healthier lives.

With epidemiologists, oncologists, and other specialists unable to answer many of today's pressing questions regarding breast cancer, a book on the history of the disease certainly cannot. Yet what the historical record can reveal is why these particular questions are being asked and why they remain so difficult to resolve. In an attempt to accomplish these goals, this chapter offers three alternative questions as an approach for understanding the current debates surrounding breast cancer: (1) What can and cannot be achieved through scientific research? (2) What can and cannot be achieved through aggressive medical interventions? (3) What can and cannot be achieved by declaring war on a disease?

Early Detection: The Search Continues

In William Halsted's era, the diagnosis of breast cancer was anything but subtle. Women came to physicians with large, often ulcerating masses whose cause was apparent without biopsy. Based on Halsted's under-standing of the spread of breast cancer, the American Cancer Society and other anticancer organizations entreated women to see their doctors sooner, examine their breasts for lumps, and, eventually, to have screen-ing mammograms. Notwithstanding the arguments of the biological predeterminists, who correctly noted the limitations of early detection, the successes of the strategy also became apparent. On average, an appar-ently localized cancer found on breast self-examination or routine mam-mogram had a better prognosis than a large cancer ignored for months.

But was there a limit to the value of such searches for breast cancer? Did the fact that a woman with a one-centimeter cancer usually did bet-ter than a woman with a two-centimeter cancer indicate that finding half-centimeter cancers would be even more desirable? What about find-ing ductal carcinoma in situ and lobular carcinoma in situ, the so-called precancers? What, if anything, was the discovery and removal of such le-sions curing? And what about the consequences of such search missions? How many mammograms, biopsies, and anxious visits to the doctor was the removal of one tiny cancer or a possible precancer worth?

Following the 1977 consensus conference on mammography, groups such as the American Cancer Society, the National Cancer Institute, and the American College of Radiology have generated guidelines about breast cancer screening. Not surprisingly, the ACS and radiologists have been the staunchest supporters of routine mammography. In 1980, for example, the cancer society resumed its stance of the early BCDDP years, calling for a baseline mammogram between ages thirty-five and forty in addition to annual mammography beginning at age fifty. In 1983, it also advised women aged forty to forty-nine to have a screening mammogram every one or two years. Although the NCI agreed to this latter recommendation in 1987, by 1993 it had broken from the ACS, stating, "Experts do not agree on the value of routine screening mammography for women ages 40 to 49."[1]

Naturally, such guidelines drew on available statistics. Among the data cited in favor of screening younger women were those collected during the BCDDP, even though the project had not been designed to evaluate the utility of mammography. BCDDP statistics published in 1982 revealed that 35 percent of the cancers detected in women under fifty had been discovered through mammography alone. Moreover, the 91 percent five-year survival for younger women found to have breast cancer was even better than the 89 percent figure for women over fifty. As of 1994, 97 percent of younger women diagnosed with breast cancer or carcinoma in situ during the BCDDP had survived fifteen years, obviously an extremely high figure for the treatment of a deadly disease.[2] To screening advocates at the ACS and NCI, such data could be interpreted in only one way: "screening including mammography detects breast cancer at favorable stages and saves lives," both for older women and those in their forties.[3] Although the BCDDP had generated considerable ethical debate by overselling mammography too soon, these advocates believed that the end had justified the means.[4]

But critics of the BCDDP continued to disagree, arguing, for one thing, that self-selection had introduced bias into the data. That is, women with strong risk factors for breast cancer or even symptoms of the disease had preferentially undergone screening.[5] In addition, even though many of the women had been in their forties when they enrolled in the project, their cancers had actually been discovered after they had reached the age of fifty. Thoroughly unconvinced by the BCDDP data, these researchers and clinicians increasingly looked to randomized controlled trials to resolve the issue of screening mammography in younger women. Only one such RCT, the HIP study, had been performed in the United States. Thus, such an analysis would have to rely heavily on data from seven other random-ized trials that were ongoing in Sweden, Scotland, and Canada.

Based on new information that he believed supported screening mam-mography in younger women, NCI director Richard D. Klausner con-vened a two-day National Institutes of Health consensus conference in January 1997. Klausner attempted to obtain as objective an assessment as possible by appointing a thirteen-member panel of physicians, epidemi-ologists, and others whose expertise was not in breast cancer. The com-mittee was chaired by Leon Gordis, a Johns Hopkins University epidemiologist. After reading hundreds of papers and hearing testimony from thirty-two experts, the panel issued its conclusion: there was not enough evidence to support routine screening mammography for women in their forties. Although the panel had initially been unanimous, two members later issued a minority report advocating screening.[6]

When the panel announced its findings on January 23, 1997, a torrent of protest ensued. Critics, especially radiologists, rushed to the micro-phones to assail the decision. Daniel B. Kopans of Harvard Medical School called it "fraudulent."[7] New Mexico mammographer Michael Lin-ver stated that withholding mammography from women in their forties was "tantamount to a death sentence." He added, "I grieve for them."[8] Klausner himself said he was "shocked" by the decision. Many women were equally upset. One was Anne S. Blackwell, a Connecticut woman who had been diagnosed with breast cancer at age forty-five through a screening mammogram. Speculating that mammography might have saved the lives of her two sisters who had died of the disease, Blackwell told the New York Times that she was "appalled" at the panel's verdict.[9]

Also offended by the consensus report were politicians, whose aware-ness of breast cancer had risen with the dramatic expansion of breast cancer activism in the early 1990s. The United States Senate voted 98-0 to endorse a nonbinding resolution encouraging the NCI's National Cancer Advisory Board to reject the panel's conclusions. Senator Arlen Specter urged Klausner to do the same at a special hearing of the Senate Subcom-mittee on Labor, Health and Human Services on February 5, 1997. Thirty-nine women members of Congress sent a letter to the Advisory Board urging it to adopt "definitive guidelines" favoring routine screen-ing. Thoroughly surprised by this backlash to the panel's decision was

Gordis, who had not witnessed such hostility when involved in other controversial medical debates, such as whether "Gulf War Syndrome" was a real entity and whether insufficient scrutiny of the blood supply had promoted the early spread of AIDS.[10]

The efforts of the pro-mammography forces proved persuasive. In March 1997, the American Cancer Society, which already advised that women in their forties have a screening mammogram every one or two years, increased the recommended frequency to every year. Later that month, the National Cancer Advisory Board adopted the ACS's old policy that women aged forty to forty-nine should have a mammogram at least every other year. This decision effectively reversed the earlier conclusion of the NIH consensus conference and brought the NCI in line with the ACS and other proscreening organizations. President Bill Clinton indicated his support for the new guidelines and called on insurers to reimburse women for such testing.[11]

Screening advocates argued that the NCI's revised decision represented a new, more scientific interpretation of the available data. "[Y]ears of confusion," Secretary of Health and Human Services Donna Shalala announced, "have been replaced by a clear, consistent scientific recommendation for women between the ages of 40 and 49."[12] But such a claim was misleading. During and after the consensus conference in January, there had actually been little disagreement about what the statistics showed. With results from eight randomized trials available, there were more good data regarding mammography than any other cancer screening test. Rather, the fighting had resulted from the fact that various interest groups had interpreted the same figures differently. Advocates of mammography for women aged forty to forty-nine, including many politicians and radiologists, defended screening by arguing that it reduced mortality from breast cancer by 16 to 18 percent, at least half as much as did screening older women. Opponents did not so much dispute this figure as interpret it from a different perspective. Given the low rate of breast cancer in younger women, they argued, about 2500 such women would have to be screened regularly in order to extend one life. Such an intervention would not only cost $108,000 for each year of life saved but also lead to many negative consequences—such as extra doctor visits, unnecessary biopsies, and needless anxiety—among healthy women.[13]

According to this reasoning, the proscreening forces triumphed not because the science conclusively supported them, but because they were able to make arguments that the public found more appealing. As we have seen, early detection is consistent with American notions of risk aversion and individual responsibility for preventing disease. As the physician and epidemiologist Harold C. Sox has noted, "[i]n the United States, we accept false positive results [possible 'cancers' that turn out to be benign] in order to avoid missing cases of disease."[14] The positive twist that mammography advocates placed on the data spoke directly to these cultural traits.

A major reason that opponents have questioned routine mammograms in younger women is the uncertain significance of the lesions such tests unearth. As mammographic technique improved in the 1970s, it became more sensitive, able to detect smaller and smaller abnormalities in the breast. These included small invasive breast cancers less than two centimeters in diameter but also more cases of ductal carcinoma in situ, which can be identified by finding small amounts of calcium (microcalcifications) on mammograms. Thus, one out of every three cases of cancer discovered in the BCDDP was either less than one centimeter in diameter or ductal carcinoma in situ. Currently, 18 percent of "cancers" found by mammography are DCIS.[15]

In contrast to lobular carcinoma in situ, which is now thought to be a marker indicating a higher than average risk of future breast cancer, most experts believe that DCIS represents an actual "precancer." Some percentage of these lesions, if not excised, will expand into the breast tissue and become invasive cancers. Nevertheless, many of the same questions that arose with LCIS in the 1970s are relevant to the current management of DCIS.[16] How can one tell which cases of DCIS will progress to cancer? How aggressively should DCIS be treated: with local excision only, local excision plus preventive radiotherapy to the breast, or simple mastectomy? And is "ductal carcinoma in situ" the best name for this entity, given that use of the word "carcinoma" may imply to patients that cancer is already present?

Mirroring the conflict over mammography in younger women, two camps have emerged in the debates over DCIS. Advocates of screening argue that the identification and removal of these lesions prevent breast cancer and thus lower mortality. Detractors contend that between 30 and 75 percent of cases of DCIS, if ignored, would never become cancer. Moreover, they point out that the treatment of DCIS, which is a mastectomy in as high as 40 percent of cases, is often more thorough than the treatment of actual breast cancer, which may be managed by lumpectomy with or without adjuvant radiotherapy.

Just as more comprehensive screening identifies ambiguous lesions within the breast, so, too, can it reveal confusing findings in the axilla. The search for "early" breast cancer has extended beyond the breast to the axillary lymph nodes. Physicians excising a breast cancer now frequently perform a sentinel node biopsy, which involves the injection of either dye or a radioactive tracer in order to identify the axillary node most likely to contain cancer. The surgeon then removes this node and sends it to the pathologist. If cancer is discovered, a more extensive axillary dissection will be performed in order to determine whether other nodes are involved. But if no cancer is found in the sentinel node, advocates of the procedure argue, there is less than a 2 percent chance that other axillary nodes will be positive.[17] Thus, the test can eliminate the need for a complete axillary node dissection, which can cause permanent pain, arm swelling, and other complications.

Although the sentinel node biopsy holds the potential for eliminating unnecessary interventions, the information it reveals is far from straightforward. For one thing, certain women may not be comfortable with the 2 percent chance that the procedure missed a positive sentinel node and may thus request a complete dissection. An even trickier problem, however, stems from the use of much more sensitive tissue stains during the examination of sentinel node specimens. While lymph nodes labeled as positive by pathologists generally contain anywhere from hundreds to millions of cancer cells, so-called cytokeratin stains permit the discovery of as few as one to three such cells in a node. What is the significance of finding a few cancer cells that are visible only with special staining? Does the presence of these cells connote "cancer"? Most oncologists answer "yes" to this question and treat such women as if the node was packed with cancer cells.[18] But are oncologists in such a situation treating cancer or simply attempting to make themselves and their patients feel more comfortable? Studies to examine this issue are only now commencing.

The situation becomes even more complicated when sentinel node biopsies are performed for women found to have DCIS on their breast biopsies. Although cytokeratin staining can reveal cancer cells in 3 to 10 percent of such patients, the ten-year survival of all women treated for one episode with DCIS is over 98 percent without any chemotherapy.[19] Given this excellent overall survival, can one justify giving toxic chemotherapy to women found to have a few cancerous cells on a sentinel node biopsy? Can this intervention rightfully be construed as "curative" if patients live, given the high likelihood they would have lived anyway?

Physicians have also applied cytokeratin staining to other anatomical regions, such as the bone marrow of women with cancers that are seemingly localized to the breast. A German study in the February 24, 2000, issue of the *New England Journal of Medicine* reported that those patients found to have cancer cells in the bone marrow had considerably higher rates of recurrence than women with negative results.[20] Should all patients with stage I, node-negative breast cancer thus undergo a bone marrow aspirate in search of cancer cells? Should a positive result be regarded like metastatic (stage IV) breast cancer and be treated with high-dose chemotherapy?

Cytokeratin staining is only one example of remarkable technological advances in breast cancer screening. For example, radiologists are using highly sensitive magnetic resonance imaging (MRI) and computerized digital mammography to find minuscule breast lesions that standard mammograms may miss.

Although these increasingly sophisticated tests may indeed someday help to lower breast cancer mortality, the historical record provides some important caveats. Throughout the twentieth century, breast cancer control has been predicated on the notion that early, aggressive treatment is the best strategy. Yet, at times, such an approach has backfired. The use of bilateral prophylactic mastectomy for LCIS or various benign breast conditions was only the most dramatic example of the potentially negative consequences of a "search and destroy" mentality.

As we have seen, the gospel of early detection has often had less to do with scientific data than with the professional aspirations of screening advocates. This connection persists today. Thus, one recent textbook on mammography terms early detection "the prime priority in female medicine." The fate of the patient, the author continues, is in the radiologist's hands.[21] A 1993 newspaper advertisement sponsored by a series of mammography centers, later retracted, made the misleading claim that nine of ten women could be saved from breast cancer by having mammographic screening.[22] Organizations with an economic interest in breast cancer control often fund screening campaigns. For example, the main corporate sponsor of Breast Cancer Awareness Month is AstraZeneca, the manufacturer of tamoxifen, a pill now being heavily advertised as a way to prevent breast cancer.[23]

The point here is not that radiologists or others who strongly promote early detection of breast cancer always oversell their product. Indeed, the clear-cut success of mammography in women over fifty belies this notion. But given the desire of Americans to discover and then act upon risky health conditions, careful scrutiny of early detection programs is warranted. As technology increasingly permits the detection of "breast cancers" of uncertain clinical significance, we are likely to reach a point of diminishing returns. Therefore, the ability to find and treat hidden breast cancer cells should not automatically be equated with the need to do so.[24]

History can also remind women considering mammography or other early detection strategies for breast cancer about the complicated nature of scientific data. In the 1950s, biometricians and epidemiologists performing sophisticated analyses of large data pools posed a challenge to the standard understanding of early detection in individual patients. Just because a woman discovered a small cancer and survived five years after her radical mastectomy, they argued, it did not prove that the early intervention had cured her.

Fifty years later, we more readily acknowledge the limits of what these statistical techniques can accomplish. Although some commentators responded to the 1997 consensus conference imbroglio by calling for pure statistical analysis untainted by economic and political interests, such a goal is not attainable, especially when screening a low-risk population. As the consensus conference revealed, different groups of individuals could examine the same data and interpret it completely differently, based on their professional and personal backgrounds. Thus, uncertainty is likely to persist in the scientific assessment of early detection modalities, such as mammography in younger women.[25] But such uncertainty should not be seen as a failure, merely as a reality.

Moreover, even when population-based screening data do appear to be conclusive, it remains a challenge to apply such information to the care of the individual patient. For one thing, the experimental conditions established to conduct successful randomized controlled trials may differ markedly from the lives of patients expected to heed the results of such trials. And women themselves, based on cultural norms and "individual idiosyncracy,"[26] may choose to disregard what the data suggest is the most or least risky behavior. That is, science can provide the right answers for certain women but not for others. "Statistics," a twenty-four-year-old woman with breast cancer told Betty Rollin in 1978, "are just numbers and mean nothing to me."[27]

Issues of gender also continue to play a central role in breast cancer screening. Ever since the American Society for the Control of Cancer developed its seven danger signals in the first decades of the twentieth century, patients have been blamed for not participating in early detection efforts. Women have received special scrutiny, characterized as betraying both themselves and their families should they develop late-stage, less curable cancers.

But the connection of women's rights to breast cancer screening remains a complicated issue. On the one hand, the National Cancer Institute's ultimate decision in March 1997 to recommend screening mammography for patients in their forties was seen as a victory for women. As advocates noted, such a move forced insurers to cover such testing, thereby ensuring its availability to both wealthy and poor women.[28] On the other hand, the decision to formally endorse mammography had paternalistic overtones, as reflected in the sentiment that women required a "consistent message" regarding testing.[29] To this point, debates over the use of a similarly equivocal test, prostate-specific antigen (PSA), have generated no such authoritative screening recommendations for men. Rather, PSA guidelines have stipulated that screening "should be offered annually" in conjunction with a discussion of the pros and cons of the test.[30] Old habits—such as telling women what to do—die hard.[31]

Treatment: Gilding the Lily

Controversies over breast cancer treatment have remained equally charged, as a 1984 article in the *Wall Street Journal* revealed. The treatment a woman received for breast cancer at Memorial Sloan-Kettering Cancer Center, according to reporter Jerry E. Bishop, depended on which door she used to enter the facility. If her appointment was with Samuel Hellman near the York Avenue entrance, she learned that lumpectomy plus radiotherapy was "applicable for the large majority of patients having breast cancer." If the same woman consulted with Jerome Urban in his 68th Street office, however, he would discourage this option in favor of "a proven cure for breast cancer," mastectomy.[32] Bishop was obviously being provocative. In practice, many women saw a range of physicians before making therapeutic decisions. But the basic point was a valid one: at the same institution, diametrically different opinions about how to treat the same breast cancer coexisted. No wonder physicians across the country could not agree on the best therapy for the disease.

In fact, once the radical mastectomy was dethroned, numerous treatment options in different configurations became possible. Modified radical mastectomy remained the most popular operation, but surgeons increasingly offered the option of simple mastectomy or lumpectomy. Patients choosing among these treatments also needed to decide whether they would have radiotherapy, chemotherapy, both, or neither. This range of choices fit well with the new consumerist model of medicine that had begun to emerge quite visibly in the 1980s. Yet with patient empowerment came confusion. If physicians themselves could not determine the best treatment for breast cancer, how could an individual patient?

Particular controversy surfaced around the growing use of chemotherapy. If one believed Bernard Fisher's hypothesis that breast cancer became systemic early in its course—and most physicians did, to some degree—then chemotherapy became the most important therapeutic intervention for long-term survival. After all, it was the only available treatment that could kill dispersed cancer cells. By the late 1970s, physicians were using several chemotherapeutic agents, often the combination of cyclophosphamide, methotrexate, and 5-fluorouracil, to treat breast cancers that

were metastatic. They were also employing these drugs in the adjuvant setting, for women without obvious metastases but with positive axillary
lymph nodes that indicated likely silent dissemination throughout the
body. Building on the early NSABP chemotherapy trials, Italian researcher
Gianni Bonadonna, with funding from the National Cancer Institute, had
demonstrated in 1976 that adjuvant chemotherapy led to improved disease-
free survival in premenopausal women with one or more positive axillary
nodes.[33] Bonadonna would later report improved overall survival as well.

Given these promising findings, there was also growing discussion
about using such agents in a more preventive manner: for women with
negative axillary nodes, who possibly but not certainly had disseminated
cancers. But there was a catch. At least 80 percent of women treated with
surgery for clinical stage I disease survived without a recurrence for ten to
twenty years, indicating that they were probably cured. Of the remaining
20 percent who might benefit from chemotherapy, only a minority, perhaps one fifth, avoided death or a recurrence as a direct result of receiving
chemotherapy. Thus, the vast majority of women treated with adjuvant
chemotherapy for stage I breast cancer would experience no actual benefit
from this therapy, only the side effects, such as nausea, vomiting, fatigue,
and hair loss.[34] These drugs also led to suppression of the bone marrow,
making patients susceptible to infections, some of which could be life-
threatening. Risk of future leukemias was another potential complication.

Among the first persons to express discomfort with the quick embrace
of chemotherapy was, as expected, Rose Kushner. Criticizing the media
blitz that hailed Bonadonna's work as "nothing short of spectacular,"[35]
Kushner feared a return of the therapeutic overkill mentality that had
prolonged the use of the Halsted radical mastectomy. "The notion still,
somehow, persists," she wrote in 1975, "that cancer of any kind can be
burned or cut out entirely, and this is a medical anachronism."[36] In 1984,
Kushner published an article entitled "Is Aggressive Adjuvant Chemotherapy the Halsted Radical of the '80s?" in which she argued that oncologists were ignoring patients' quality of life in their zeal to administer
chemotherapy.[37]

Kushner was hardly the only person leveling such charges. Another
was Michael B. Shimkin, the epidemiologist who had been an early advocate of randomized trials to evaluate radical mastectomy. "So many are

being poisoned so uselessly," he wrote to Kushner in 1984. "Of course, that keeps medical oncologists busy and wealthy, not to mention pharmaceutical companies. And create[s] a built-in lobby for NCI."[38] Maurice Black, the New York pathologist who had been an early proponent of the biological variability of breast cancers, increasingly rejected both chemotherapy and radiotherapy for tumors he believed had a favorable prognosis.[39] Another outspoken critic of aggressive systemic treatment is the breast surgeon Susan M. Love, who has cautioned against "poisoning everybody in the hopes that it will help a few."[40]

Once again, such criticisms have cut against the grain. When confronting a feared disease for which surgery was no longer a panacea, the familiar strategy of taking action was appealing, especially in a country with such a strong tradition of individualism. The tone for this approach was set by the early cancer specialist David A. Karnofsky, who performed pioneering work in the testing of chemotherapeutic agents. In a 1962 article, Karnofsky had strenuously argued that "an aggressive or extraordinary attack on advanced cancer is worthwhile." The major justification for this approach, he continued, was "to avoid defeatism, which is a major barrier to advances in medical knowledge."[41]

Not only did such a positivistic outlook support research into the new drugs and the fledgling profession of oncology, but it also reverberated strongly with patients. Chemotherapy—with its associated imagery of powerful drugs patrolling the body, destroying wayward cancer cells—appealed strongly to a risk-aversive mindset. American patients, the historian of science Ilana Lowy has written, believed they had a "moral obligation" to participate in "aggressive" chemotherapy or research trials of these new agents.[42] As had been the case with radical surgery, Americans responded much more enthusiastically to chemotherapy than did patients in countries such as Great Britain, France, and Canada.[43]

Not surprisingly, therefore, many women with breast cancer who wrote to Betty Ford asked specifically about the chemotherapy she was receiving. "I recently had the same operation you had with a few positive nodes," wrote one such woman. "[I] feel there must be something more that can be done."[44] A Denver woman told Ford that she was "willing to try about anything I can find to keep this 'dread disease' from breaking out somewhere else in my body."[45] One woman writing to Betty Rollin urged her to "get yourself to a cancer clinic and have them give you chemotherapy for a year or so and then quit worrying."[46]

This positive reaction to chemotherapy appeared to be vindicated by a series of new studies that built on Bonadonna's early work. First, in 1985, an overall review (metaanalysis) of randomized controlled trials of adjuvant chemotherapy in women with positive lymph nodes revealed annual reductions in cancer recurrence and death of 21 and 11 percent, respectively. For women under fifty, the percentages rose to 28 and 17 percent. Meanwhile, women who took tamoxifen, an estrogen-blocking compound, lowered their annual risk of recurrence and death by 25 and 16 percent, respectively. Women over fifty, whose cancers were more likely to have estrogen receptors, did even better than the overall group.[47]

In February 1989, research indicated that chemotherapy and tamoxifen also reduced the recurrence of breast cancer in women with negative axillary nodes. In May 1988, the NCI had actually taken the unusual step of alerting 13,000 cancer specialists in the United States that these results were forthcoming. Once again opting for definitive intervention, women and their oncologists quickly embraced chemotherapy, hormonal therapy, or a combination of the two as standard treatment for breast cancers larger than one centimeter with no positive lymph nodes.[48] Subsequent studies have demonstrated that women with breast cancer are willing to undergo chemotherapy in exchange for "remarkably low degrees of net benefit," such as a 0.5 to 1 percent reduction in risk of recurrence.[49]

Clinicians continue to introduce chemotherapy regimens that may cause more severe side effects. For example, dose-intensive chemotherapy, given at more frequent intervals, and high-dose chemotherapy, given in stronger than conventional doses, have become options. These more aggressive regimens, which cause more adverse reactions, appear to improve relapse-free and overall survival over standard chemotherapy by at most one to three percentage points.[50] Nevertheless, both node-positive and node-negative breast cancer patients continue to opt for such treatments, once again tolerating the possibility of worse complications in order to receive the most powerful agents available. This desire for potent chemotherapy was recently demonstrated when a new combination of drugs — adriamycin, cyclophosphamide, and paclitaxel (Taxol) — became the treatment of choice for breast cancer based largely on one presentation made at an oncology meeting and a marketing campaign by Taxol's manufacturer, Bristol-Myers Squibb. Progress in breast cancer treatment, Columbia University Associate Professor of Surgery Freya Schnabel notes, usually occurs by "gilding the lily"—generating incremental improvements—as opposed to the introduction of dramatic new innovations.[51]

When such dramatic treatments have been attempted, progress has often been minimal. For example, beginning in the 1980s, oncologists began to administer stem cell transplants to women with metastatic breast cancer. Patients undergoing this regimen first received very-high-dose chemotherapy (two to twenty times standard strength) in order to kill all cancer cells remaining in the body. This phase was followed by the infusion of previously removed stem cells from the patient's bone marrow to replace the normal white blood cells that were also destroyed by the chemotherapy.

The appeal of this approach was so great in the United States that investigators at major medical centers had great difficulty enrolling patients into randomized controlled trials to evaluate the procedure. Just as certain women in the 1970s had declined to enter NSABP B-04 or B-06 to avoid being randomized to a procedure they did not want, the promise of higher cure rates from stem cell transplant led women to seek the procedure outside formal RCTs. They viewed randomization into the control arm, in which patients were to receive standard chemotherapy, as an unacceptable alternative.[52] Even though stem cell transplants were of unproven benefit, hospitals were more than happy to provide them, especially after insurance companies agreed to foot the bill. Yet when the early results of randomized trials finally became available in May 1999, four of the five studies found that stem cell transplant conferred no survival advantage over chemotherapy alone. The fifth study, which showed benefit, was later determined to be fraudulent. Even though the more responsible researchers had offered no guarantees, patients still viewed these results as a "betrayal of hope."[53] As with superradical cancer surgery in the 1950s, the actual and presumed value of transplantation had been conflated.

The controversy over stem cell transplants speaks to the larger issue of how patients and physicians choose to employ scientific data when making therapeutic decisions. At what point should one treatment replace another?

How should patients respond to physicians who continue to recommend the "wrong" choice? How should physicians respond to patients who request such a choice? These questions have all arisen in recent discussions over the primary therapy of uncomplicated early-stage breast cancers. Having eliminated the radical mastectomy from the list of acceptable treatments, is it now time to do the same for any mastectomy whatsoever?

As has so often been the case, it was the breast cancer diagnosis of a public figure that brought this issue into the spotlight. On October 17, 1987, Nancy Reagan, wife of President Ronald Reagan, underwent a modified radical mastectomy of her left breast. Twelve days earlier, radiologists had identified a suspicious lesion on a routine mammogram. Reagan's physicians, from the Mayo Clinic and Bethesda Naval Hospital, where the surgery was performed, had presented her with a series of options before surgery, which included a two-step procedure with an initial separate biopsy. Reagan, however, had chosen to have a one-step procedure. After pathologists found ductal carcinoma in situ on a frozen section, the First Lady's surgeons had performed an immediate modified radical mastectomy.[54]

Having long railed against the one-step procedure, Rose Kushner was distraught at Reagan's decision. She also disapproved of Reagan's choice of a modified radical mastectomy for a lesion that was confined to the milk duct and had not spread within the breast or to the axillary nodes. Reagan's decision had set the cause back ten years, Kushner stated. "Women will hear that this is what was recommended for the President's wife and will say, 'This is what I want.'"[55]

Yet it was far from clear that Reagan's physicians had actually recommended this course of action. Rather, it appears to have been the First Lady's own decision. Elaine Crispen, her press secretary, stated that the strategy taken "was the most positive way to get it all over with."[56] Pointing out that Kushner seemed to be contradicting her own longtime advocacy of women's choice, members of the cancer establishment criticized her reaction to Reagan's surgery.[57] Kushner herself admitted that Reagan had the right to make her own decision, but nevertheless regretted how little had seemingly changed since Betty Ford's one-step radical mastectomy in 1974.

In responding to Nancy Reagan's cancer surgery, Kushner again confronted one of the enduring realities of breast cancer: different women responded differently to varying treatment options. Indeed, this situation persisted even when additional studies confirmed that lumpectomy plus radiotherapy was equivalent to mastectomy for both ductal carcinoma in situ and small invasive cancers. In 1990, an NIH consensus panel moved well beyond the 1979 consensus report, stating that lumpectomy and radiation was the treatment of choice for most stage I and II breast cancers.[58] After all, if lumpectomy and mastectomy provided equivalent survival, why wouldn't a woman choose the breast-conserving procedure, especially given the historical overuse of the disfiguring radical mastectomy?

But women did not respond in the expected manner. Thus, in 1994, four years after the NIH consensus conference, only 44 percent of women with early-stage disease received breast-conserving treatment. Other studies published at this time also revealed marked geographic variation in the treatment of breast cancer. For example, women living in the Middle Atlantic states were more than three times as likely to have a breast-conserving operation than those who lived in the South.[59] Obviously, some of the continued support for mastectomy came from surgeons, many of whom still remained uncomfortable with a limited operation that potentially left behind small areas of cancer in the breast or axilla. But once again, an explanation that simply blames male (or female) surgeons ignores the agency of breast cancer patients. Women themselves continued to request mastectomy, either due to fear of radiation, a disinclination to undergo six weeks of radiotherapy, a desire to follow their doctor's recommendation, or the enduring sense that undergoing the more definitive mastectomy was somehow a less risky proposition. "[O]n the deepest level I still feel that more is better," wrote one patient, Kathlyn Conway. "Isn't it better to throw out the whole apple if it's rotten?"[60]

These reports of geographic disparity in breast cancer treatment, which persist today, caused great consternation among many commentators. Arguing that Bernard Fisher's randomized trials and other studies had scientifically proven the equivalence of a less mutilating procedure, commentators argued that the "highest priority" of professional societies should be convincing physicians to follow the NIH consensus guidelines for the treatment of early-stage breast cancer. Fisher himself went so far as to suggest that even giving breast cancer patients the choice of mastectomy was "a reversion to Halstedian thinking," "illogical," and possibly "deleterious."[61] To be sure, all women with early-stage breast cancer need to be informed that lumpectomy provides entirely equivalent survival to mastectomy. Yet the expectation that all women should choose the more scientifically indicated procedure remains problematic. Given that RCTs may have limited applicability for individual women, especially in the case of a biologically heterogeneous disease such as breast cancer, perhaps we should agree to let some women disagree. As with the debates over mammography and early detection, women with breast cancer have always responded more positively to information than to proscriptive advice.[62]

Activism: The Growth of a Movement

For all of Rose Kushner's success in publicizing issues related to breast cancer diagnosis and treatment, she tended to be a solo operator. As the 1980s progressed, both she and other breast cancer activists concluded that a more organized, united front was necessary to ensure that the disease received the publicity it deserved. In 1986, Kushner joined with Ruth Spear, Nancy Brinker, and Diane Blum to form the National Alliance of Breast Cancer Organizations (NABCO), an umbrella agency for groups across the United States involved in breast cancer information and education. Today NABCO consists of over 375 member organizations. Four years earlier, Brinker, a wealthy, well-connected Texan, had begun the Susan G. Komen Foundation, named for her sister, who had died of breast cancer at the age of thirty-six. The Komen Foundation, through events such as the annual "Race for the Cure," has subsequently raised over $200 million for breast cancer research and care for the underserved.

In 1981, Rose Kushner had found a skin metastasis near the site of her 1974 operation. Realizing that her modified radical mastectomy had not been curative, she began tamoxifen to try to suppress whatever other systemic disease existed. Kushner later had local radiotherapy when another metastasis appeared in the same area. In 1988, she was diagnosed with a uterine cancer known as a sarcoma, which was surgically removed. By the end of 1989, her health was declining. Given the likely existence of metastatic breast cancer, some physicians urged her to have chemotherapy. Kushner declined, however, being unwilling to experience the side effects "to buy a few months."[63] When she died in 1990, the autopsy showed widely metastatic breast cancer.

Kushner's death left a gaping hole in the world of breast cancer activism. A week before her death, she had been making phone calls from bed in support of mammography legislation. But Kushner's legacy was preserved in 1991, when NABCO executive director Amy Langer, herself a breast cancer survivor, Susan Love, and other activists formed the National Breast Cancer Coalition (NBCC). The NBCC had three goals: (1) increasing research funding, (2) increasing access to screening and treatment for all women, and (3) increasing the role of women in health policy decisions, something that had long been absent from the war on breast cancer.[64] Kushner had stressed this latter aim, especially as she came to emphasize the importance of working within the system.

Breast cancer, the NBCC argued, was the most common non-skin cancer in women and killed over 40,000 American women each year. Moreover, because it threatened both life and an organ associated with intimacy, sexuality, and motherhood, it remained the disease that women feared most.[65] Nevertheless, advocates claimed, federal funding for research into breast cancer was anemic. The government had allotted only $74.5 million in 1989, less than 5 percent of the amount earmarked for AIDS, which killed 22,000 Americans annually. Using characteristic American interest group politics, NBCC members organized letter-writing campaigns and testified before Congress, rapidly becoming a formidable political force on Capitol Hill. The Coalition, President Fran Visco announced, had alerted Washington legislators that "women had declared war on breast cancer, and they'd better find a way to fund that war."[66] By 1996, funding levels had jumped to over $550 million. This figure included an unexpected annual appropriation of over $100 million from the Department of Defense, only too appropriate for financing a "war" on breast cancer.[67] In its lobbying efforts, the breast cancer movement drew explicitly on the aggressive grass-roots lobbying strategies pioneered by AIDS activists in the mid-1980s. They even borrowed the idea of a looped ribbon as a publicity tool, replacing the red ribbon of AIDS awareness with a pink version.

The formation of NABCO and the NBCC have helped to unify the publicity and fund-raising apparatus for breast cancer in the United States. The early activism of Kushner, Langer believes, has matured into a pragmatic and flexible advocacy movement. The NBCC is willing to use confrontational tactics and hyperbole when necessary. In language reminiscent of old American Cancer Society publicity, a recent statement by Visco termed breast cancer a "national tragedy" and stated that "every woman is at risk."[68] But the organization is also willing to use accommodation. The NBCC, Langer states, is a combination of "in your face" and "take you out to dinner."[69]

Within the breast cancer movement, however, participating organizations still have quite different goals and strategies. Perhaps the largest source of contention is the role that corporate America has played. In addition to their ability to garner federal research funding, breast cancer activists have successfully recruited wealthy business executives with personal ties to the disease. As Lisa Belkin wrote in the New York Times Magazine in 1996, breast cancer has become the "darling of corporate America."[70] Ralph Lauren, Ronald O. Perelman of Revlon, and Evelyn Lauder of Estee Lauder, to name but a few, have devised clever marketing strategies to raise tens of millions of dollars for breast cancer research. As a result, many high-profile breast cancer fund-raising events, such as the Komen Foundation's "Race for the Cure" and the Avon Corporation's sixty-mile walk, known as the "Breast Cancer 3-Day," have an enormous corporate presence. Beauty and fashion products, which many of the funding corporations in question produce, are both sold and given away (see figure).

This corporate largesse is characterized by its emphasis on expanding current diagnostic and therapeutic strategies. Thus, a recent Avon walk raised $5 million for early detection programs, including underwriting mammograms and checkups for poor women. The Komen Foundation's Nancy Brinker, who discovered her own breast cancer in 1984, works to "spread the life-saving message of early detection to millions of women and men throughout the country."[71] Much of the funding from Revlon and Ralph Lauren has been earmarked for research in the basic sciences.

Supermodel Gisele Bundchen, wearing the logo of the Fashion Targets Breast Cancer campaign.

Courtesy of the Council of Fashion Designers of America.

These studies seek to learn more about the molecular and genetic aspects of breast cancer and then use this knowledge to develop treatment strategies. An example of this type of research is the discovery that certain metastatic breast cancers make an excess of a protein known as HER2 and the subsequent development of a successful biological therapy, Herceptin, based on this knowledge.[72]

Some critics argue that the breast cancer movement of the 1990s, with its lavish fundraisers and well-connected lobbyists, is largely dominated by upper-class white women voicing their own concerns about getting access to sophisticated diagnostic and therapeutic modalities.[73] They point to the fact that African American women, whose rates of the disease remain lower than those of whites, nevertheless come to physicians with more advanced breast cancers, receive inferior treatment, and have a higher disease-specific mortality rate. Possible contributing factors to this situation include the lower socioeconomic status of African Americans and the paucity of culturally sensitive breast cancer awareness programs in African American communities.[74] Such criticisms discount the explicit efforts of NABCO, the NBCC, Avon, the Komen Foundation, and the National Breast

and Cervical Cancer Early Detection Program to address cross-cultural issues and to improve access to mammography and other interventions for
poor and minority women. In addition, many organizations that participate in NABCO explicitly perform outreach to African American and
Latina women.

But individuals and groups with a more radical perspective suggest
that attempts to provide all women with access to early diagnosis and aggressive drug therapy miss the point. This biomedical perspective, they
contend, is too narrow an approach to breast and other cancers. According to this argument, breast cancer has become a "growth industry in a
capitalist marketplace."[75] The methodical and careful testing of various
therapies has helped some women, but has benefited clinical researchers,
oncologists, and pharmaceutical companies even more.[76] Most important, this focus on early therapeutic intervention has precluded any
meaningful attention to the primary prevention of breast cancer. "True
breast cancer prevention," Barbara Brenner of San Francisco's Breast Cancer Action has written, "will come from understanding and eradicating
the causes of the disease."[77]

Most broadly, such a campaign would entail providing all women with
good jobs, adequate housing, educational opportunities, healthy food, and
access to health care.[78] But given the enormity of this task, activists have
emphasized the issue of the environment, charging that mainstream anticancer organizations have ignored the role of chemical and environmental
toxins in causing breast and other cancers. "We all live downwind," read
the sign of a woman protesting the history of radiation leaks from the
Hanford Nuclear Weapons Facility in Washington State.[79] In a book reminiscent of Rachel Carson's *Silent Spring*, the ecologist Sandra Steingraber has
argued in *Living Downstream* that society is ignoring how daily exposure to
dioxin, pesticides, and other industrial chemicals leads to the buildup of
carcinogenic toxins in the body's organs and tissues.[80] Moreover, activists
contend, corporations that stand to profit from the treatment of breast cancer may be the same ones involved in poisoning the environment. For example, AstraZeneca, the manufacturer of tamoxifen, also produces
fungicides and other chemicals designed to improve plant growth.

The most vocal group pushing the connection of toxic waste to breast
cancer is 1 in 9, a Long Island–based grass-roots organization founded in

1990 in response to breast cancer clusters and otherwise high rates of the disease in the area. The name "1 in 9" refers to the likelihood that a woman anywhere in the United States who lives to the age of eighty-five will develop breast cancer. 1 in 9 members have been among the loudest and angriest critics of the "cancer establishment," arguing that it has "patronized women and neglected or ignored the facts about breast cancer."[81] Women's groups also argue that investigation of possible dietary interventions that could lower the incidence of breast cancer—most notably a low-fat diet—have been given short shrift by the National Cancer Institute and other funding agencies.[82]

This philosophy poses a direct challenge to other elements of the breast cancer movement for three reasons. First, by stressing the actual prevention of breast cancer, these activists are objecting to the emphasis on early intervention, which only addresses cancers that are already present. Critics of overzealous early detection strategies, such as Maryann Napoli, argue that clever marketing of mammography with celebrities such as Whoopi Goldberg has misled women into believing that all breast cancers can be found in early stages and that early detection is the same as prevention.[83] Second, forming an explicit bond with the multi-faceted environmental movement would potentially dilute the focus on breast cancer as a single issue.[84] Third, calls for the investigation and removal of chemical and other toxins incriminate industry, which is largely responsible for environmental pollution. Challenging corporate America on this issue would represent an attack on the breast cancer movement's new, very wealthy friend.

The dual issues of the meaning of "prevention" and the role of industry arose explicitly in 1992 with the growing use of tamoxifen. In learning that tamoxifen was an effective adjuvant treatment for women with breast cancer, researchers also found that it lowered the incidence of cancer in the second, unaffected breasts of women who received the drug. The question thus arose: was it reasonable to give tamoxifen to high-risk women who had never had breast cancer? Among the researchers pursuing this topic was Bernard Fisher, who saw so-called chemoprevention as the next logical step in controlling breast cancer. In 1992, Fisher's NSABP group began to enroll patients in the Breast Cancer Prevention Trial (NSABP P-01), which randomized to either tamoxifen or placebo three groups of high-risk women: (1) those aged sixty years or older, (2) those aged thirty-five to fifty-nine with a five-year predicted risk for breast cancer of 1.66 percent, and (3) those with a history of lobular carcinoma in situ.[85] By March 1994, 11,000 of the 16,000 projected entrants had been enrolled.

But opposition to the trial was building, spearheaded by the feminist National Women's Health Network, the organization that had earlier criticized the National Cancer Institute's unwillingness to inform BCDDP enrollees that they had possibly undergone unnecessary mastectomies. In this case, network organizers charged that women entering the Breast Cancer Prevention Study had not been fully informed that tamoxifen appeared to quintuple a woman's risk of uterine (endometrial) cancer. Opposition increased in March 1994 when the media reported that four women taking tamoxifen as part of an earlier NSABP treatment study had died of uterine cancer.[86]

Women's groups also argued that giving a potentially toxic drug to healthy women distorted the meaning of "prevention," which they associated with lifestyle changes. Moreover, reliance on tamoxifen for such a purpose reinforced the control of medical professionals and pharmaceutical companies over women's bodies. Indeed, the perception that tamoxifen was a true preventive agent had been fostered by its manufacturer, Zeneca (later AstraZeneca) Pharmaceuticals, which marketed it aggressively. The trial, concluded Network board member Adriane Fugh-Berman, was "premature in its assumptions, weak in its hypotheses, questionable in its ethics and misguided in its public health ramifications."[87] This negative publicity slowed enrollment into the trial. Then, on March 25, 1994, accrual was actually halted due to a concurrent scandal involving the NSABP, described below. Active enrollment to the tamoxifen trial did not resume until March 1995.

The debates over the tamoxifen trial created a major rift between Fisher and certain members of the advocacy community. Although he had established a productive collaboration with Rose Kushner in her last years and was still seen as a hero by women for having sped the elimination of the radical mastectomy, Fisher had no tolerance for what he saw as unwarranted outside interference into the scientific enterprise. Adverse events, he acknowledged, were unfortunate, but inevitable, conse-

quences of controlled trials. Well-constructed randomized trials anticipated these complications and reported them as soon as enough data existed to draw meaningful conclusions. When P-01 began enrolling
patients, Fisher claimed, the role of tamoxifen in contributing to the four
deaths remained unclear. As of that time, "no NSABP patient had a
proven death from endometrial cancer."[88]

Fisher had made an almost identical argument regarding the other
scandal that emerged in 1994. On March 13, 1994, the *Chicago Tribune* had
revealed that a Canadian researcher had falsified the records of ninety-
nine patients in the NSABP-06 study of mastectomy versus lumpectomy.
Although Fisher and his superiors at the National Cancer Institute had
known about these irregularities since 1991, they had not alerted trial
participants, in large part, they said, because eliminating the ninety-nine
cases did not alter the overall results (a claim later proven true).[89] Fisher
would later testify to a House of Representatives subcommittee investi-
gating the scandal that scientifically sophisticated randomized trials routinely took into account the possibility that some submitted data might
be inaccurate. Disclosure of the falsified data thus made no sense because
science had corrected itself. Such an explanation proved to be of little so-
lace for organizations such as the Women's Health Rights Network,
which viewed the silence as evidence that the male physicians who ran
the NCI had not learned the overriding lesson from the earlier con-
tretemps over radical mastectomy and screening mammography: the
merits of scientific inquiry notwithstanding, it was a "shocking breach
of trust" to conceal from women with breast cancer potentially relevant
information about their disease.[90] This point was made most dramatically
by Jill Lea Sigal, who had undergone a lumpectomy based on the original
B-06 data. In a vivid photograph taken during her testimony to the
House subcommittee, Sigal radiated frustration and anger, her head
thrown back and her eyes closed.[91]

As a result of the problems with both B-06 and P-01, Fisher increasingly characterized the interference of advocacy groups and governmental oversight committees in the scientific process as "an antiscience
movement" attempting to "discredit the reliability of science and the
soundness of its methodology."[92] The scientific misconduct in P-01, he
contended, was not the decision to enroll patients despite reports of

uterine cancer in another trial; it was the decision to temporarily suspend accrual to P-01. The notion that scientists needed outside oversight, he later stated, was an "affront."[93]

With the publication of P-01 in September 1998, Fisher believed he had been vindicated. The trial revealed that tamoxifen decreased the incidence of invasive breast cancer by 49 percent and noninvasive breast cancer by 50 percent. Adverse events had occurred. Thirty-six women in the tamoxifen group had developed uterine cancer as opposed to fifteen in the placebo group, although all of the tamoxifen-associated cancers were early stage I cases. Eighteen women in the tamoxifen group developed blood clots to the lung in contrast to only six women in the placebo arm. Three of the eighteen women died. Despite the downsides of tamoxifen, Fisher argued, "its use as a breast cancer preventive agent is appropriate in many women at increased risk for the disease."[94] In 1999, he estimated that 482,650 invasive breast cancers could be prevented in the United States if all high-risk women used tamoxifen as a chemopreventive agent.[95]

Predictably, many women's groups were less sanguine about these results. They again argued that the opportunity for true primary prevention of breast cancer, by combating environmental toxins or by getting women to eat healthier foods and to exercise more, had been supplanted by a "quick fix." These feminist critics also worried that the value of tamoxifen was being oversold: even though patients were ostensibly being told about the benefits and downsides of the drug, did such women realize that it had never actually been shown to increase life expectancy?[96] A series of activist organizations would later accuse the National Cancer Institute of downplaying a November 1999 study that they thought revealed that tamoxifen had "a limited customer base." As a result, they asserted in newspaper advertisements and a letter to NCI Director Richard Klausner, AstraZeneca "is making a fortune selling potentially dangerous drugs—and fear—to healthy women concerned about breast cancer."[97]

The continued frustration of women activists with breast cancer politics in the United States is well conveyed by feminist journalist Ellen Leopold in A Darker Ribbon, her recent history of breast cancer treatment in the twentieth century. "Prevailing biases in the research agenda," she writes, "reflect the influence of powerful interest groups in society."[98] That is, breast cancer activists who run, walk, or scream in an effort to raise awareness and funding are unwittingly supporting the industries, drug companies, and research enterprises that preclude a true evaluation of breast cancer as a political issue. In challenging those active in the breast cancer movement to "re-evaluate their wider views of society," Leopold hopes to reconceptualize the disease from a more progressive feminist outlook.[99]

Yet while many women with breast cancer or at risk for it do feel oppressed by the physical, psychological, and financial burdens they must endure to "fight" the disease, this perspective does not necessarily make them more politically radical.[100] Taking on industry may be the last thing that women with breast cancer want to do, especially when studies have never shown a clear association between environmental toxins and elevated rates of the disease. Nor may high-risk women decide to replace ice cream with salads, vegetables, or other healthy foods, especially given the recent comments by longtime nutrition researcher Walter C. Willett. In contrast to tamoxifen, Willett conceded in December 1999, alterations in diet have never been proven to reduce the incidence of breast cancer.[101]

In this setting, a pill such as tamoxifen, despite its complications and ability to generate extensive profits for AstraZeneca, does not look like a bad alternative to many women. Nor does raloxifene, another estrogen-blocking medication used for osteoporosis that may also lower the incidence of breast cancer without the uterine-cancer risks of tamoxifen. Reluctant to wait for the results of randomized trials, patients are already receiving raloxifene to try to decrease their risk for breast cancer.

Beyond these data, the popularity of tamoxifen in the United States has stemmed from another factor. In a culture that has continually sought "magic bullets" to eliminate medical problems, the notion of a daily preventive pill has proven quite compelling. When advance news about P-01 was released to the public in April 1998, women eagerly called their physicians to learn more about tamoxifen. Headlines termed the study's findings "nothing short of spectacular," a "cancer breakthrough," "historic," and "the biggest cancer story in more than a decade."[102] Similar language has been employed to describe raloxifene. While neither tamoxifen nor raloxifene is likely to be a magic bullet, it is hard to ignore data suggesting that these pills may cut the risk of breast cancer by one half. Yet as critics contend, successful chemical prevention of breast cancer may prove to be a mixed blessing, further deflecting attention from the more basic social and environmental problems that may predispose women to breast cancer in the first place.

Of War and Hope

In her 1978 book, Illness as Metaphor, Susan Sontag criticized the use of military imagery to describe cancer and other diseases. Having recently been diagnosed with breast cancer, she believed that her experience with the disease was all too real to be characterized as some type of metaphorical battle. By elucidating these "lurid" metaphors, she hoped to liberate society from them. "My point is that illness is not a metaphor," she insisted.[103] Sontag's goal has not been realized. If anything, the language of war may be even more pervasive today in the world of medicine. As Sontag herself would later note, the appearance of AIDS in the 1980s spawned a war against that disease. The term "war on cancer" remains ubiquitous. Sometimes the commanders of these wars are actual military figures, such as General Norman Schwartzkopf, who is leading the charge against prostate cancer.

Why is the language of battle so entrenched in the world of cancer? As argued above, the use of war metaphors indicates the economic and ideological investment of anticancer organizations and segments of the medical profession in promoting their efforts both to the public and amongst their own membership. Thus, it not surprising that the 1997 announcement that mortality rates from breast cancer and cancer in general were finally declining on the 25th anniversary of the 1971 National Cancer Act led the American Cancer Society, the National Cancer Institute, and politicians to declare that the decades-old battle was finally reaping unequivocal dividends. "Happy birthday, 'War,'" wrote former NCI director Vincent T. DeVita, Jr., "you deserve a pat on the back."[104] This type of response had more to do with rhetoric than reality. When Richard Nixon declared war on cancer in 1971, a decline in mortality of 5 percent over twenty-five years would hardly have been seen as a triumph.

At the same time, skeptics have taken a dim view of what anticancer efforts have achieved. In 1986, for example, John C. Bailar III, who had brought to public attention the limitations of the BCDDP in the 1970s, wrote a controversial article in the *New England Journal of Medicine* entitled "Progress in Cancer?" Terming efforts to date a "qualified failure," Bailar and Elaine M. Smith concluded that the United States was "losing the war" on cancer.[105] The piece infuriated DeVita, who termed it "the most irresponsible article [he had] ever read."[106] A 1997 follow-up article by Bailar, entitled "Cancer Undefeated," argued that "blind-faith in treatment-based approaches" had achieved little meaningful mortality reduction for most cancers.[107] Although Bailar and his coauthor, Heather L. Gornik, undoubtedly chose such stark language to try to redirect the war on cancer to a focus on primary prevention, their use of hyperbole further polarized debate.

Breast cancer is still the most common non-skin cancer in women and forces patients to confront not only their mortality but uncomfortable topics such as sexuality, body image, and personal responsibility for disease. It is hardly surprising, therefore, that the war on breast cancer shows no signs of abating. Indeed, it has become nearly impossible to discuss any initiative to prevent, detect, or treat breast cancer without using the language of battle. Thus, a recent article described a breast cancer activist as a "modern-day warrior doing battle for women."[108] Senator Olympia Snowe has urged Americans "to wage war against a brutal and merciless enemy: breast cancer."[109] Dennis Slamon, the researcher who developed Herceptin, has predicted that combinations of new "biological weapons" will make a huge impact in the fight against breast cancer.[110] At the Columbia-Presbyterian campus of New York Presbyterian Hospital, where Cushman Haagensen first put breast cancer on the map, a program for women at high-risk for the disease is called "WAR" (Women at Risk).

But what relevance do military metaphors have for individual women confronting breast cancer? Is joining the modern-day equivalent of the Women's Field Army helpful as a woman learns her diagnosis and embarks on treatment? Some women themselves use military language and imagery to describe their encounters with breast cancer. These include feminists such as like Audre Lorde, who regarded women with breast cancer as warriors. "I have been to war," she proclaimed, "and still am."[111] This attitude was directly tied to Lorde's decision not to have reconstruction. Her mastectomy scar, like the empty eye socket of the fa-

Deena Metzger, as she appeared in her "warrior" poster, 1979.

Courtesy of Deena Metzger and the Donnelly/Colt Catalog, Hamden, Conn.

mous Israeli soldier, Moshe Dayan, was an "honorable wound." "Every woman," she concluded, "has a militant responsibility to involve herself actively with her own health."[112]

Taking Lorde's philosophy one step further was Deena Metzger, a writer and spiritual healer diagnosed with breast cancer in 1977. Also declining reconstruction, Metzger chose to be photographed unclothed from her navel upward. The picture was subsequently reproduced in numerous feminist publications, including *Our Bodies, Ourselves* and *Her Soul beneath the Bone*, a 1988 book of poetry on breast cancer. In the photograph, Metzger gazes joyously at the sky with her arms outstretched. Covering the scar at the site of her right mastectomy is a tattoo of a tree. "There was a fine red line across my chest where a knife entered but now a branch winds about the scar and travels from arm to heart," reads a Metzger poem that accompanies the photograph. Metzger also revisits Lorde's theme of the breast cancer survivor as fighter, writing, "I have the body of a warrior who does not kill or wound."[113] The warrior references of both Lorde and Metzger drew on the legend of ancient Greek women who supposedly had a breast removed to improve their ability to hunt with a bow and arrow.

Not all feminists approved of Metzger's photograph. The University of Illinois Press, which published *Her Soul beneath the Bone*, had written to Rose Kushner in 1988 to solicit her opinion about putting Metzger's picture on the book's cover. "Very negative," Kushner had responded, likely reflecting both her upbringing in an earlier generation and a growing appreciation for the rehabilitative potential of breast reconstruction.[114] Yet Metzger's picture, graphically depicting her personal battle with breast cancer, was a powerful visual statement that women with the disease should no longer feel ashamed.

In 1993, with the publication of Matuschka's picture on the cover of the *New York Times Magazine*, the exposed mastectomy scar went mainstream. Matuschka's self-portrait differed dramatically from that of Metzger. Matuschka's body is draped and she appears solemn, as if contemplating her disease and mortality. Yet like Metzger, Matuschka converted a sexual and private body part into a symbol of power. "You can't look away anymore," the *Times* informed a society that had long shunned women with breast cancer.[115] Matuschka's reaction to her breast cancer was tied to her broader fight for women's health rights as a member of Women's Health Action and Mobilization (WHAM). Other groups of women have also attempted to connect their experiences with breast cancer to other aspects of their lives. For example, lesbians have campaigned for additional research into the special barriers they face as breast cancer patients.[116] Other women have turned to complementary medicine or mind-body healing techniques, often in conjunction with more traditional medical interventions, to try to prevent or treat breast cancer.

In addition to using war metaphors or making political statements, another manner in which survivors "fight" breast cancer is by participating in strenuous physical activities. Besides the Avon 3-Day walk and the Komen Foundation's Race for the Cure, breast cancer survivors hike mountains and go on long bicycle treks (see figure). "Since 1995," wrote Jeanne F. Allegra, "I have taken my 'battle scarred' breasts to the [Washington, D.C.] Mall, donned the pink shirt, visor, pink shoelaces, etc. and

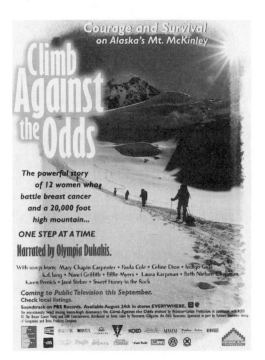

Publicity for the documentary
"Climb Against the Odds," televised
on the Public Broadcasting System
in 1999.

Courtesy of the Breast Cancer Fund.

walked proudly among my fellow veterans of the breast cancer war."[117]
"What does it feel like to be a breast cancer survivor?" asked Avon walk
participant Chris Castro. "I feel like I have really fought for my life."[118] In
September 1999, Komen raised money by sponsoring "Jump for the
Cause," in which 118 women formed a configuration while skydiving.
This total broke the previous record of 100.[119] Corporate sponsors have
promoted such events both as fundraisers and as a way for survivors to
demonstrate their physical and emotional recovery from breast cancer.
Such events also constitute powerful bonding experiences for women
with the disease.

Another essential component of the war on breast cancer is its emphasis on hope. The American Cancer Society and other anticancer organizations have repeatedly sought to counter images of death and disability by
issuing optimistic messages. This climate of hope is important to individual patients as well. First, positive emotions and ideas can help to heal
the body through the powerful placebo effect.[120] Second, the notion that
breast cancer patients deserve to hear an optimistic assessment of their

prognosis—at least initially—has become almost universally accepted. Patients with breast cancer will fight if there is something to fight for.

This theme is continually reiterated in the ever-expanding number of breast cancer narratives now being published with titles such as *Hope Is Contagious: The Breast Cancer Survival Treatment Guide* and *Straight from the Heart: Letters of Hope and Inspiration from Survivors of Breast Cancer*. A 1998 book, *Portraits of Hope: Conquering Breast Cancer*, contains attractive photographs and personal vignettes from famous and ordinary survivors of the disease. By emphasizing the uplifting aspects of their encounters with breast cancer, the authors of these narratives seek to instill in readers both optimism and the courage to continue fighting. Other women battling the disease, through programs such as "Look Good . . . Feel Better," have stressed the psychological value of makeovers and similar beauty regimens. "This is the time to dress your best, even when you're feeling your worst," stated breast cancer survivor Grace Foster.[121]

The degree to which hope has become an expected part of the breast cancer experience can be seen by the moving responses of patients, family members, and the public to publications documenting the less successful aspects of the war on the disease. One woman with breast cancer had believed that "my chances were very good of leading a normal life" until she read a 1974 *Washington Post* article stating that women with positive axillary nodes had a high mortality rate. "That article sounds a death knell for me," she wrote to the editor. "Thanks a lot."[122] A 1981 *Washington Post* piece on the downsides of experimental chemotherapy for breast and other cancers, wrote one woman, "succeeded in terrorizing" patients who might benefit from such treatment.[123] When physician David Plotkin wrote "Good News and Bad News About Breast Cancer" in the June 1996 issue of the *Atlantic Monthly*, Frances Elliott, the mother of a breast cancer patient, criticized "his lack of understanding, his brazen thoughtlessness [and] his disregard for the impact his words might have on those who are already suffering." What was worse, Elliott continued, was that

my daughter read it too, and now she believes that she is absolutely doomed. She has translated Plotkin's examples of premature death to mean her imminent demise, not in ten or twenty years. Now. No chance to live. No hope. No cure.[124]

Over the past decade, growing numbers of women with breast cancer have begun to write accounts of their illnesses that depart from the more traditional narrative structure.[125] Books such as Christina Middlebrook's *Seeing the Crab: A Memoir of Dying Before I Do* and Kathlyn Conway's *Ordinary Life: A Memoir of Illness* might best be termed realist narratives. These books describe in unflinching prose the chaos that a diagnosis of breast cancer brought to the authors' lives. The treatments are often worse than the disease. Isolated in a hospital room while undergoing a bone marrow transplant, Middlebrook graphically details how the high-dose chemotherapy produces painful ulcers in her mouth and stomach, and causes her to vomit black, smelly "inhuman slop."[126] Having made it through the experience, she analogizes herself to a concentration camp survivor.[127]

Moreover, these narratives explicitly reject the claim that an optimistic outlook makes one's experience with cancer more bearable. "I hate hearing that cancer has made someone a better person," Conway, a psychotherapist, writes in a chapter entitled "Despair." "It's only making me a worse person."[128] Nor, claims Middlebrook, does an association between hope and successful treatment exist. "The mere assumption that good thoughts will affect the outcome of my life," she states, "turns me ugly as Medusa."[129]

This repudiation of breast cancer as a transformative experience has led Conway, in subsequent work, to criticize the association of the disease with beauty and athleticism. Why, Conway asks, should publicity regarding early detection or breast cancer research feature attractive supermodels who have not even had the disease? Why is such emphasis given to making women who have had breast cancer appear more attractive? Why does breast cancer fund-raising so often draw women to superhuman athletic tasks they might never have considered before their diagnosis? Conway worries that these culturally sanctioned activities for breast cancer survivors exclude women who either choose not to participate or are too sick to participate. And women who opt out of these more traditional wars on breast cancer, she fears, risk being blamed for any bad medical outcomes that may ensue.[130] As breast cancer patient Dian Marino wrote in 1991, characterizing the disease as a fight implies that "a person like myself who has 'terminal' cancer has lost."[131]

· · ·

Long-term survival from breast cancer cannot help but validate the diagnostic and treatment strategies that a woman has pursued. Thus, having had a screening mammogram or undergone high-dose chemotherapy becomes regarded as the reason one's life was saved. Similarly, surviving breast cancer may also validate the chosen psychological approach, such as maintaining optimism in the face of death or engaging in active battle with the disease. Although the actual effects of such attitudes are difficult to prove or disprove, they form an important belief system for patients and should not be dismissed as unscientific.

Yet, as Conway emphasizes, such assumptions, however compelling and powerful, should not be imposed on others. During her own encounter with breast cancer and two bouts of lymphoma, Conway's major goal was simply restoring the "ordinary life" she had once known. Just as walking sixty miles over three days is a valid goal for women with breast cancer, so, too, should be Conway's option of simply returning to one's previous existence.

twelve

Risky Business

Breast Cancer and Genetics

Amy is a 38-year-old woman whose mother died of breast cancer when Amy was 7. Amy's 42-year-old sister, Louise, who had survived breast cancer five years earlier, is now dying of metastatic ovarian cancer. After months of indecision, Amy decides to consult a genetic counselor. She has chosen to undergo genetic cancer testing, she informs the counselor, and will have her breasts and ovaries prophylactically removed if she tests positive for a genetic mutation. Amy, who is happily married with two children, is relieved to have finally made this decision. She feels as if an enormous weight has been lifted off her.

Janet is 15 years old. Both her grandmother and her mother's sister died from breast cancer in their forties. Janet's mother knows about genetic testing but is entirely opposed. Janet, who has been reading up on the topic, knows that some experts believe that eating a low-fat diet or exercising more—even when a teenager—may help stave off breast cancer later in life.[1] Janet plans to call a genetic counselor to inquire about testing for herself.

These accounts, drawn from actual cases, typify the challenging questions that have arisen since the identification of a gene linked to inherited breast cancer. This gene, located on chromosome 17, was discovered in 1990 by University of Washington researcher Mary-Claire King. For centuries, physicians had known that breast cancer ran in families, but there were limited scientific and technological tools to examine this phenomenon. Although King's gene likely caused less than 10 percent of all breast cancers, her discovery provided important information about the possible role of genetic factors in all cases of the disease.

By 1994, Mark Skolnick and his colleagues at Myriad Genetics, a Utah biotechology company, had succeeded in cloning, or determining the exact DNA sequence of, King's gene, which had been given the name BRCA1. BRCA1, researchers had learned, produced a protein that helped to control the division of cells. If a genetic error, or mutation, existed within BRCA1, this protein might be defective. In such a case, cells in the breast could grow unchecked and be transformed into a cancer. It was these mutations in their BRCA1 genes that Amy and Janet might discover if they underwent testing. They could also be tested for mutations in a second gene involved in regulating cell growth, BRCA2, which was cloned in 1995.[2]

For women with devastating family histories of breast cancer, the news that genetic predisposition could be proven or disproven was potentially empowering. For the first time, such women could learn if they, too, were at high risk. But genetic breast cancer testing also raised a series of challenging questions. Which at-risk women should be tested? What interventions existed for women who tested positive? Who should pay for such testing? And what were the possible social and cultural ramifications of being a carrier of what some commentators were ominously terming the "breast cancer gene"? Although the genetic nature of the information raised new issues for women, these questions also spoke to controversies in breast cancer screening and treatment that had existed for decades.

A Genetic "Time Bomb"

The debate over "nature" versus "nurture" has been ongoing in medicine for centuries. Do diseases develop because they are programmed in the genes or because of events and behaviors that occur during life? In some instances, the genetic contribution to disease is obvious. For example, Huntington's disease, a severe and fatal neurologic disorder that begins in middle age, is transmitted between generations if the child receives the mutated gene from a parent. Huntington's is known as an autosomal dominant disorder, because transmission of the gene invariably results in the disease, regardless of the genetic information received from the other parent. Autosomal recessive diseases, such as cystic fibrosis or sickle cell anemia, occur only if both parents transmit a mutated gene. Both BRCA1 and BRCA2 are inherited in an autosomal dominant fashion. That is, it takes only one BRCA1- or BRCA2-positive parent to transmit a mutation to a child. There is a 50 percent chance that this will occur for each child born.

But even when scientists are able to identify hereditary disorders that contribute to disease, environmental factors usually continue to play a role. Because each individual inherits two of the same gene (one from each parent), children born with one defective gene may have a second copy that works normally and compensates for the first. If someone has a BRCA1 or BRCA2 mutation, therefore, the second gene may produce enough normal protein to inhibit the growth of breast cancer cells. However, if the normal gene is somehow damaged during an individual's life, the person no longer generates the protective protein and thus acquires a higher likelihood of developing breast cancer. Scientists do not yet know what damages the normal genes, but possibilities include exposure to radiation or environmental toxins. Because a BRCA1 or BRCA2 mutation thus might or might not ultimately contribute to the development of breast cancer, these mutations are said to have variable penetrance.[3]

Once researchers had identified the genetic errors on BRCA1 and BRCA2, it became possible to perform blood tests to see whether given individuals with breast cancer carried one of the mutations. Based on this testing, these experts concluded that only a small percentage of breast cancer patients carried relevant mutations. In women from very-high-risk families, the development of breast cancer could be explained by the presence of these mutated genes. These families generally showed multiple cases of breast cancer in successive generations, with most cases beginning earlier in life—from age thirty to fifty—than was customary. These cases of the disease, which came to be termed hereditary breast cancer, accounted for 5 to 10 percent of all breast cancers. In studying the family trees of women with the mutations, researchers also realized that other cancers, especially ovarian cancer, were also occurring at a very high frequency. Women with a strong family history of both early breast and ovarian cancer had the highest rates of mutations.

Because of the issue of variable penetrance, the association of mutated gene and the eventual development of breast or another cancer was not 100 percent. Some women with a mutation in BRCA1 or BRCA2—presumably those whose second gene copy remained intact—would never develop a hereditary cancer. But this fact did not mean that such women would never get breast or ovarian cancer. They remained at risk for the random, nonhereditary cancers that affected the entire population.

Although individual women with mutations might thus be spared from getting cancer, it remained clear that these abnormalities conferred an extremely high risk of future disease for the population that possessed them. Examining the pedigrees of families that carried mutations, genetics experts attempted to estimate the likelihood that a mutation carrier would ultimately develop breast cancer. In 1995, British epidemiologists predicted that a woman with a mutation in BRCA1 had roughly an 85 percent chance of developing breast cancer if she lived into her seventies. Early estimates of ovarian cancer risk in such women were 40 to 60 percent.[4]

Not only did this 85 percent figure generate considerable attention, but so did the fact that these breast cancers were "in the genes." Despite the growing knowledge that hereditary diseases were modulated by environmental factors, the notion that one's genetic makeup irrevocably determined one's destiny had great cultural sanction.[5] For example, a *Time* magazine article referred to BRCA1 and BRCA2 as "lethal genes."[6] This simultaneous belief in and fear of determinism helps to explain why the term "biological predeterminism" had so rankled supporters of early detection in the 1950s. The notion of a "gene test" also appealed to the tendency of Americans, discussed throughout this book, to obtain—and then trust—any available data regarding their present and future health.

Although no evidence yet existed that genetic breast cancer testing could prolong survival or generate other medical benefits, early statements promoting the new technology played on the theme of taking action. "If someone offers you a crystal ball," asked a forty-nine-year-old breast cancer survivor who ultimately chose testing, "wouldn't you want to take a peek?"[7] "The lack of knowledge means you're living blindly," stated another woman seeking the test.[8] If not explicitly recommending

testing, headlines from newspaper and magazine articles at least implied
the dangers of ignorance. "A Cancer Survivor's Genetic Time Bomb,"
read one *Wall Street Journal* headline.[9] "Your Breasts or Your Life?" asked
American Health magazine, noting that a woman who tested positive for a
BRCA mutation and chose to have a prophylactic mastectomy might be
saving her life.[10]

Not surprisingly, the strongest advocates were biotechnology companies that began to offer commercial testing in 1996. Prior to this time,
gene sequencing had been available only through research protocols at
academic medical centers. Typical were advertisements by Myriad Genetics. In one, a woman told her physician: "Doctor, I need to know."[11] A
second advertisement announced that "Knowledge is power. And
hope."[12] Myriad's Mark Skolnick bluntly conveyed the urgency of genetic
testing, remarking, "First, you save lives."[13] As had plastic surgeons promoting breast reconstruction in the 1970s, those who stood to profit
from BRCA testing stressed the right of women to participate. "What's
indefensible to me is not to give people a choice," argued Joseph D.
Schulman of the Genetics and I.V.F. Institute in Fairfax, Virginia.[14]

Despite these enthusiastic claims, others raised cautions about genetic
breast cancer testing. Geneticists, ethicists, and clinicians—as well as organizations such as the American Cancer Society—carefully pointed out
the difficulty of "fortune-telling" based on genetic errors and urged
gradual adoption of testing.[15] Both BRCA1 and BRCA2, critics cautioned,
contained hundreds of known mutations, only some of which seemed to
promote breast cancer. Moreover, even when one of the cancer-causing
mutations was unearthed, physicians could recommend no proven interventions for women who tested positive.[16] Women could examine their
breasts more, have more frequent mammograms or even take the drastic
step of prophylactic mastectomy, but no data existed to suggest that any
of these prolonged survival. In the case of mammography, some commentators even speculated that the extra radiation might actually promote cancerous growth in BRCA1 and BRCA2 mutation carriers. The
notion that genetic susceptibility testing was somehow therapeutic,
therefore, was an "illusion."[17]

Given the unclear value of testing, advertising campaigns for BRCA1
and BRCA2 sequencing seemed to confirm the worst suspicions of crit-

ics. Like the provocative early detection messages issued by the American Cancer Society in the 1950s, commercial test manufacturers were exaggerating the value of their product and thus playing on the anxieties and fears of women at risk for breast cancer.[18] Although Schulman spoke about giving women the right to make choices, University of California at San Diego geneticist Michael M. Kaback stated in 1996, Schulman was first and foremost an entrepreneur.[19]

Critics of testing also strongly highlighted the potential negative ramifications of gathering genetic data. For one thing, history was rife with examples of the misuse of genetic information. For example, during the early decades of the twentieth century, the American eugenics movement had spuriously argued that so-called undesirable traits—such as insanity, mental retardation, and criminality—were inherited conditions. Physicians in this era sterilized tens of thousands of "unfit" individuals with these conditions as a way to prevent the propagation of such traits. In the 1960s and 1970s, entirely asymptomatic African Americans discovered to be carriers of one sickle cell anemia gene were inappropriately characterized as diseased.

As critics pointed out, the most heinous misuse of genetic information had occurred during the Holocaust. The Nazis not only exterminated mentally retarded people and other individuals they believed to be genetically inferior, but they also attempted to eliminate the entire Jewish population of Europe based on pseudogenetic theories. Falsely equating race with biology, the Nazis argued that all Jews possessed defective genes and passed them to subsequent generations. Germany, Hitler argued, needed to be cleansed of this Jewish menace.

Invocation of the Holocaust by critics of genetic testing was not coincidental. Although the Nazis' extermination of the Jews clearly carried genetic discrimination to its maximum level, BRCA1 and BRCA2 testing also raised questions regarding the connection of Judaism and genetic disease. "There is a historical context to this that I don't think you can ignore," stated Michael A. Grodin, a professor of Jewish law and medicine.[21] Many of the highly cancer-prone families that had participated in early breast cancer genetics research were of Ashkenazi Jewish descent. Because the relatively small population of Ashkenazim had inbred for centuries, in both their native Eastern Europe and later throughout the world, they turned out to have an extremely high rate of three specific mutations, two in BRCA1 and one in BRCA2. Recent estimates suggest that as many as one out of every forty (2.5%) Ashkenazi Jewish women carries one of these three mutations.

Given newspaper headlines such as "Bad Genes: A Cancer-Causing Mutation Is Found in European Jews,"[22] commentators feared that the high mutation rates among Ashkenazim would lead to the characterization of breast cancer as a Jewish disease. All the worrisome genes being talked about, said New York rabbi and medical ethicist David Tendler, were "Jewish genes."[23] Connecting BRCA mutations to Judaism was inappropriate for two reasons, Tendler and others argued. First, such an assumption was simply inaccurate. Despite these mutations, Ashkenazi Jewish women did not have higher rates of breast cancer than other groups of women. Second, the association of Judaism with breast cancer had the potential to cause harm. For example, Jewish women who developed breast cancer might be falsely labeled as mutation carriers. Alternatively, those women with a personal or family history of the disease might be assumed to have a duty to be tested.[24] This last issue has caused particular turmoil within the Orthodox Jewish community, given that women from families with a known mutation might be seen as less suitable for arranged marriages.[25]

Of course, the potential negative consequences of genetic breast cancer testing were not limited to Jewish families. The decision of a single individual to undergo testing had immediate ramifications for other relatives. For example, the sisters of a woman who tested positive for a BRCA mutation had a 50 percent chance of having the same genetic error. So did the woman's daughters. In addition, women without a personal history of breast cancer interested in testing often needed to request blood samples from family members who had developed the disease. By ascertaining what mutation, if any, was present in those relatives with cancer, the companies performing the tests would know which of the various genetic errors to try to identify. Otherwise, the entire BRCA1 and BRCA2 genomes would need to be scrutinized, a process costing over $2000 and having a much higher likelihood of generating unhelpful information.

Thus, in the case above, Amy would likely need to ask her sister Louise for a blood specimen, a request she might be reluctant to make given

Louise's terminal illness. To what degree are family members, especially those who have cancer, obligated to participate in genetic testing for the benefit of their relatives? Janet, on the other hand, would need to obtain tissue saved from her grandmother's or aunt's cancers. Of course, Janet's interest in counseling raises even more complicated issues about the right of a minor to undergo genetic testing. Although most commentators have agreed about limiting testing until subjects are age eighteen or older, the questions do not end there. If an eighteen-year-old woman chose to be tested and received a positive result, how should her physicians—and society—respond to a request for a prophylactic mastectomy or ovariectomy?

Testing within families also raised the complicated issue of confidentiality. Was it appropriate—or possible—to test someone and then conceal potentially relevant medical knowledge from her family members? Even if information was successfully hidden from relatives, could those outside the family find out the results? For example, if a woman tested positive for a BRCA1 or BRCA2 mutation, could her daughter's doctor learn the results? Even more distressing, could the daughter's insurance company find out and then raise her premiums or deny her coverage altogether? In a world of computerized data bases, managed care, and suboptimal legal protections, such an event appeared increasingly possible.[26] The same issues arose for the person who had chosen testing. Should she tell her physician? If so, should the physician enter the result into the woman's medical record? Having incomplete information in a medical chart is unfortunate, but may seem preferable in the face of potential job or insurance discrimination.

Beyond these issues of stigmatization and discrimination, critics identifed another important concern. Even though BRCA testing provided information about someone's permanent biological makeup, such data were probabilistic: they addressed the potential risk of disease as opposed to actual disease. Fever, chills, phlegm, and an area of opacity on a chest x-ray indicate that someone has the disease of pneumonia, but a BRCA1 or BRCA2 mutation in a healthy woman only indicates a higher than average probability of future disease. Genetic testing for breast and other cancers, ethicist Albert R. Jonsen and colleagues warned in 1996, would create a class of "unpatients," not diseased but also not free of a "medically relevant" condition. "We will struggle," they wrote, "to find the right words for the status conferred by the presence of these genes."[27]

Critics thus argued that the results of BRCA testing, like other genetic information, were "exceptional," basically different from other types of medical data. Although it might ultimately lead to dramatic advances in the diagnosis and treatment of breast cancer, genetic testing was fraught with hazard. To what extent was this conclusion accurate? What lessons did the historical record reveal regarding BRCA1 and BRCA2 testing?

New Questions, Familiar Issues

Genetic breast cancer testing has raised new controversies, but history suggests that many aspects of these debates (beyond the connection of genetics to eugenics) are quite old. For example, modern BRCA1 and BRCA2 carriers are not the first "unpatients" in the world of breast cancer. As far back as the 1910s, when Joseph Colt Bloodgood began to note "pre-cancers" and "borderline" cancers during the examination of otherwise benign breast biopsies, physicians had struggled to determine the meaning of lesions of unclear biological risk.[28] By the second half of the century, with the adoption of the term "carcinoma in situ," this notion of a potential cancer became codified. As with BRCA1 and BRCA2 mutations, diagnosing LCIS or DCIS was to inform a woman that she had a high—but not certain—likelihood of future invasive breast cancer.

But these were only the most obvious unpatients. It might also be argued that many women with locally treated stage I breast cancer were, in a sense, unpatients. The vast majority of such women needed no further treatment for their breast cancer and were thus no longer "diseased." But because a small percentage would develop metastatic breast cancer, most women with stage I tumors decided to undergo prophylactic chemotherapy to eliminate the foci of cancer that were possibly present throughout the body. Even though the breast cancer was a real disease, what was actually being treated in most of these women was future risk.

In attempting to understand and address these biologically indeterminate conditions, clinicians have relied on scientific data. What percentage of women with these risky lesions ultimately develop breast cancer? Can such women be subdivided into prognostic categories? Which of the available interventions provides the best survival rates? Patients and clinicians can now gain access to such information with computer technologies that generate actual numerical risk estimates. For example, the National Cancer Institute and AstraZeneca have produced a "Breast Cancer Risk Assessment Tool" (known as the "Risk Disk") that calculates a patient's risk of future breast cancer using her personal and family histories. Advertisements for the disk in *People* and other magazines urge women to care more about their "risk assessment number" than their brassiere size.[29] A software program called BRCAPRO estimates the probability that a woman will test positive for a BRCA mutation.

But it is essential to recall that these data are interpreted and acted upon in a specific social setting. Although aggressive efforts to pursue and then eliminate future breast cancer risk have taken place in other countries, they have occurred most forcefully and consistently in the United States. Factors that have encouraged this phenomenon have included the professional ambitions of medical subspecialists, the development and maintenance of organizations seeking to defeat cancer, the introduction and marketing of sophisticated diagnostic and therapeutic technologies, and a culture that prizes risk aversion and individual action while potentially blaming those who do not ascribe to these philosophies.[30]

One possibility suggested by the historical record, therefore, is that American women may also eagerly pursue both genetic testing and subsequent therapeutic interventions as a way to reduce their risk of breast cancer. Indeed, one "treatment" for women with BRCA mutations that has received considerable publicity is preventive removal of both breasts. By eliminating as much breast tissue as possible (although not all of it), such surgery theoretically decreases the risk of breast cancer by a considerable degree. Based on this reasoning, a BRCA-positive woman diagnosed with a new breast cancer might opt for mastectomy over lumpectomy and simultaneously undergo removal of her healthy breast; a woman without any history of breast cancer might choose a prophylactic mastectomy before developing the disease. Once the connection between BRCA mutations and ovarian cancer became apparent, prophylactic removal of the ovaries also became an option. As might be expected, patients and physicians in the United States have responded more positively to the option of preventive surgery than have those in countries with less of an individualist ethos, such as France.[31]

Mathematical models estimating the value of prophylactic mastectomy for BRCA-positive women have made such a strategy seem more appealing. For example, Columbia University researcher Victor R. Grann estimated that such an operation could add an average of three years to the lives of women with a BRCA1 mutation. Similarly, Deborah Schrag, then of Boston's Dana-Farber Cancer Institute, found up to two years of life expectancy gain for gene-positive women with breast cancer who underwent preventive removal of their second breast.[32]

Authors have also compiled retrospective data regarding prophylactic mastectomies performed in the era prior to genetic testing. In the January 14, 1999, issue of the *New England Journal of Medicine*, researchers from the Mayo Clinic estimated that 639 high- and moderate-risk women who had chosen this operation between 1960 and 1993 had lowered their risk of developing breast cancer by at least 90 percent. Mortality also declined, according to the statistical assumptions made by the authors. The twenty anticipated deaths from breast cancer among these women had been lowered to two, thereby saving eighteen lives.[33]

Many media outlets reported these data in a highly favorable light. For example, the headline of one article on prophylactic surgery read: "Breast Cancer: A Radical Solution."[34] "Healthy breast removal is backed," reported *USA Today*. "Study affirms reduced cancer risk."[35] In *U.S. News and World Report*, a woman who had opted for the surgery was described as having made a "pre-emptive strike."[36]

Such a positive interpretation was to be expected. Bilateral prophylactic mastectomy was a decisive action taken against a dreaded disease. "How can you learn you're sitting on a time bomb . . . and do nothing?" asked Californian Helene Jaffe, who had tested positive for a mutation.[37] Such women, once again, were choosing life over breast, doing everything possible to preserve their health. The decision to undergo surgery also helped to shield them from potential guilt or blame if they subsequently developed cancer. Given that BRCA-positive women had the highest risk for future breast cancer, prophylactic mastectomy appeared particularly appropriate for them. "Take 'em both," one such woman, Cindy Valerius, told her surgeon. "Just let me live."[38]

But it was possible to interpret the *New England Journal of Medicine* findings from a very different angle. Although eighteen lives had theoretically been saved by the mastectomies, 619 other women who had agreed to removal of both breasts would have survived without the surgery. Therefore, prophylactic breast removal had actually saved the lives of less than 3 percent of women who had chosen this dramatic intervention. The appeal of almost definitive surgery understandably held great appeal for certain women who had tested positive for a BRCA mutation. But as with the use of prophylactic surgery for LCIS in the 1970s, an "all or nothing" mentality toward eliminating risk was not necessarily better.

Although history thus warns us that overuse of genetic testing may lead to excessive prophylactic mastectomies, it also suggests the downside of this type of cautionary tale. Those who attempt to discourage women from obtaining and acting upon genetic data may be emulating earlier generations of physicians and cancer officials who felt comfortable simply telling women what to do. Thus, when several prominent groups initially sought to put restraints on the dissemination of BRCA testing, advocates of these tests argued that such opposition was yet another example of the medical profession's paternalistic attitude toward women. "I think [they] need to realize that women have brains," stated Joy Simha, a twenty-eight-year-old woman with a history of breast cancer. "Who are they to tell me that knowing the results would do me more harm than good?"[39] Women also pointed out that no similar restrictions were being suggested for men seeking PSA testing, which provided similarly ambiguous information about the risk of prostate cancer.

Clinicians may also be tempted to discourage genetic testing among newly diagnosed breast cancer patients deciding among therapeutic options. Although some women with very strong family histories may themselves request BRCA testing at the time of their diagnosis, to what extent should physicians raise this option with other patients? Some early data suggest that BRCA-positive women might wish to pursue more aggressive treatment if diagnosed with breast cancer.[40] But certain clinicians worry that addressing genetic concerns in women with only a small chance of a mutation may cloud more urgent treatment discussions. Does withholding information about the availability of genetic breast cancer testing violate the principle of informed consent?

Clinicians have also cautioned women who test positive for BRCA mutations about the choice of prophylactic breast removal. Prophylactic mastectomy, Denver surgical oncologist R. Lee Jennings stated, is "a very drastic method of prevention."[41] Chicago breast specialist Melody Cobleigh concurred, terming healthy breast removal "an extremely radical option and not one we recommend."[42] Given such misgivings, some surgeons now require that women requesting such surgery consult a psychiatrist. With the promising new data regarding chemoprevention, prophylactic mastectomy may increasingly become seen as inappropriate and drastic for BRCA-positive women.

Ironically, some breast surgeons, strongly wary of their predecessors' overuse of the knife, may be tempted to err too far in the other direction. Although thorough informed consent discussions should precede any such prophylactic surgery, we should not reflexively characterize the decision to have such an operation as misguided. Different women value their breasts in different ways; thus, individual women remain the most appropriate arbiters of what should happen to their breasts in light of a positive BRCA1 or BRCA2 test. For a woman like Amy, removal of both breasts and ovaries may indeed be the right choice.[43]

No Rush to Testing

Given that women repeatedly exaggerate their likelihood of developing breast cancer,[44] and that genetic testing provides information about risk of the disease, most commentators predicted that BRCA testing would be overused. Wall Street analysts originally forecasted a market of $100 million annually in the United States alone.[45] Early survey data suggested this prediction would come true. For example, in one 1994 study, 75 percent of first-degree relatives of ovarian cancer patients, the vast majority of whom were unlikely to have a relevant BRCA mutation, expressed interest in testing. A 1995 study of women and men from high-risk breast and ovarian cancer families found that 79 percent "definitely" wanted testing while another 16 percent would "probably" pursue it.[46]

But despite these predictions and aggressive marketing by manufacturers, a relatively small number of women have been tested. BRCA screening, the *New York Times* reported on March 27, 1998, had "fall[en] short of public embrace."[47] Companies offering the testing were performing roughly 1000 tests annually, perhaps one-tenth of what had been expected. "It's not exactly a roaring market," noted an executive at Oncormed, a Maryland biotechnology company.[48] This lack of enthusiasm typified not only BRCA testing, but also tests that identified a predisposition to hereditary colon cancer.

There seemed to be many reasons for this development. For one thing, testing was expensive. Because many women preferred to keep their test results secret, they were unwilling to ask their health insurance companies to cover the costs. Issues of payment aside, other women took quite seriously the possibility that positive test results might hinder their own or family members' attempts to obtain reasonably priced health and life insurance. Job discrimination was another concern.[49]

But another important reason for the slow rate of genetic testing appeared to be public awareness that the information thereby generated was of limited value. For example, a 1998 study of 211 patients diagnosed with invasive breast cancer in central and eastern North Carolina found that only three of the women carried a BRCA1 mutation. In the general United States population, the authors concluded, "widespread screening of BRCA1 is not warranted."[50] By this time, moreover, researchers had lowered the earlier estimate that women with a BRCA mutation had an 85 percent chance of developing breast cancer during their lifetime. The actual percentage, according to Jeffrey P. Struewing and colleagues, might be as low as 56 percent.[51] The original figure had been generated from studies of very-high-risk families in which the mutations had proven highly penetrant. Researchers also lowered the possible risk of future ovarian cancer from 40 to 60 percent to 20 to 30 percent. Even when these powerful new genetic markers were present, it was clear that environmental or other exposures still played a major role in determining which women would actually develop breast cancer.[52]

What is perhaps most encouraging about this situation is that the slow but steady testing rates appear to be related to the dissemination of balanced information. Commercial enterprises have determinedly marketed BRCA testing, and advisory panels have opined on the pluses and minuses of being tested. Without having their options limited in any paternalistic manner, women have apparently examined the situation and used—but not overused—such testing. Some of this success may have stemmed from the type of advice that women have received from genetic counselors. More so than other health care providers, those working in genetics favor a nondirective approach that encourages individual women to make choices based on their own life situations.

Is the seemingly reasoned use of BRCA testing to date likely to persist? It is impossible to know. What is clear is that the technological ability to test for genetic breast cancer risk will increase as scientists continue to study the recently decoded human genome. If, as some predict, "genetic profiling" becomes more accessible and affordable and can be protected by confidentiality statutes, it may become harder to resist looking into one's personal crystal ball.

Epilogue

A t first glance, the story of William S. Halsted and the radical mastectomy seems to be one of gender and authority. Male surgeons, doing what they believed was best, developed a highly disfiguring operation because they viewed the female breast and the surrounding muscles as expendable. In turn, the radical mastectomy persisted because imperious physicians did not listen to their critics or their women patients.

There is a good deal of truth to this viewpoint, but it is incomplete. Halsted and his disciples had a much more profound effect on the management of breast cancer and, indeed, disease in general. By urging women to come to the doctor promptly and then promising them a dramatic curative operation, breast surgeons were reconfiguring the way in which medicine approached severe diseases such as cancer. In essence, Halsted was telling his patients, "Get here soon enough and we can cure you."

Was Halsted telling the truth? The answer to this question is complicated. On average, women who showed breast lumps to their physicians sooner had less extensive cancers and a better prognosis after radical surgery. But Halsted's quid pro quo did not apply to all women. Many patients who came immediately to the doctor ultimately died of breast cancer, while others who delayed survived. And Halsted's extensive radical mastectomy, as would later be learned, was not necessary to cure all of the women that could be cured.

What was most influential, however, was the perception of what Halsted was saying. Confronted with a disease that caused great mortality and directly threatened a woman's sexuality, people wanted to believe that what he said was true. The medical profession, increasingly relying on laboratory-based research to establish its authority, saw the radical mastectomy as embodying what scientific medicine could offer to patients. Surgeons, in particular, viewed radical cancer surgery as a way to solidify their professional status. The American Cancer Society embraced early detection and radical surgery because these concepts enabled the organization to present its "war" against breast and other cancers in an optimistic light. Patients, either stricken with or fearing breast cancer, were all too happy to hold up their end of Halsted's bargain. If physicians would do whatever they could to combat breast cancer, following the directions of the medical profession and public health officials seemed the least that women should do. After all, taking responsibility for preserving one's health fit well with American notions of individualism and personal initiative.

An often unstated but crucial component of this arrangement between doctor and breast cancer patient was the notion that many would be treated to benefit the few. Despite the fact that early, radical surgery saved some lives, many patients undergoing such treatment died anyway; at the same time, many who survived would have done so with a less extensive procedure. Because it was difficult to predict which patients would truly benefit from the operation, they all underwent it. This arrangement was driven in large part by the tendency of physicians to present radical surgery as the least risky and thus the most advisable option, a concept that patients either readily or reluctantly embraced.

As the twentieth century progressed, the ante was raised. By the 1950s, patients received the message, "Examine your breasts for lumps and we can cure you." After 1970, the equation became, "Have a screening mammogram and we can cure you." Once again, these understandings fit with the interests and beliefs of groups both within and outside medicine. For example, radiologists and manufacturers of mammographic equipment supported the presumption that regular breast x-rays could save lives. Pathologists also benefited from these early detection strategies, as they assumed a growing role in judging whether the complicated tissue specimens obtained did, in fact, contain cancer. Researchers, supplemented by the growing budget of the National Cancer Institute, built careers on studying the effectiveness of early detection and treatment of breast cancer.

Yet while both medical and social forces promoted earlier intervention for breast cancer, what physicians were searching for and then treating had changed markedly. Halsted's strategy of early and radical therapy had derived from the fact that the cancers he was evaluating were so far advanced. Indeed, diagnostic biopsies were hardly even necessary when lesions occupied such a large proportion of the breast. But cancers discovered by women on breast self-examination or found by a radiologist on a mammogram were tiny, often one centimeter in diameter or smaller. Others were not cancers at all but precancers, which doctors thought might eventually themselves become cancers, or markers, believed to indicate higher future risk of cancer somewhere else in the breast.

What had not changed, however, was the basic "search and destroy" approach that had originated with Halsted. Confronted with biologically indeterminate findings, medicine, and the society of which medicine was a part, chose to view these smaller tumors as being as dangerous as the large cancers that Halsted had seen. Such a choice was not inevitable. Rather, ardent pursuit of such lesions had become too ingrained in the practice of American medicine to allow for an alternative approach.

To be sure, the way physicians attempted to cure such cancers did change over time. Once Bernard Fisher had demonstrated that extensive local control of breast cancer was less important than eradicating possible metastatic disease, the Halsted radical mastectomy was finally laid to rest. But equally aggressive treatments, including radiotherapy and chemotherapy, came to replace a strictly surgical approach to these small, often localized cancers. As with surgery, much of this treatment was preventive in the sense that a majority of patients, in retrospect, would not require it in order to survive. This was also true for the radical surgery that did persist, namely, the prophylactic mastectomies that resulted from Jerome Urban's mirror-image breast biopsies and other efforts to unearth seemingly risky lesions.

Skeptics have questioned the strategy of early intervention since Halsted first popularized it. This challenge became most evident in the 1950s, when the biological predeterminists introduced more sophisticated statistical analysis to the evaluation of breast cancer interventions. Based on these findings, the predeterminists concluded that what most affected the fate of patients was the inherent aggressiveness of individual breast cancers and how successfully women's bodies could combat these cancers. In making this claim, these critics argued that the proponents of early detection and radical mastectomy were using terms such as "early" and "cure" in ways that exaggerated what such strategies were accomplishing.

The predeterminists and their modern disciples have, at times, painted with a broad brushstroke, minimizing what breast cancer control efforts have achieved. After all, probably due to mammographic screening and chemotherapy, breast cancer mortality has finally begun to show a steady decline.[1] The total number of deaths from breast cancer in the United States dropped from 43,844 in 1995 to 41,943 in 1997, a decline of 4.3 percent. Yet the basic point made by the more reasonable critics remains true: at some point screening and treatment themselves may become more aggressive than the cancer, precancer, or marker that one is likely to find. Put another way, the chase assumes as much importance as its outcome. This is especially true when after several appointments, mammography, ultrasound, biopsy, and much anxiety, all that has been unearthed are lesions of unclear biological significance.

This conclusion remains as unpopular today as it was in the 1950s, for several reasons. For one thing, physicians caring for individual patients still have a tendency to "do more," even if population-based data do not support such a decision. Evidence of this process, screening advocates in the 1970s often claimed, was that doctors who opposed mammography for women under fifty made exceptions in the case of their wives. For their part, patients, facing a seeming life-and-death situation, are likely to agree with the decision to act. Moreover, once such women undergo a screening test or cancer treatment, they are apt to attribute any good results to that choice. Thus, when researchers in the 1970s proudly reported that mastectomy cured 100 percent of cases of lobular carcinoma in situ, women who had chosen this treatment, and their physicians, welcomed the news rather than questioning what the surgery had actually "cured." A recent article on prophylactic breast removal in high-risk women makes this same point. Although the intervention prevented death in less than 3 percent of cases,[2] 70 percent of the women expressed satisfaction with their choice of surgery. Only 19 percent regretted the decision.[3]

But beyond this propensity to interpret statistics in a self-validating way, the continued popularity of early action speaks to an ongoing faith in the cancer-fighting mission. Physicians, patients, and family members continue to believe that fighting harder against breast cancer has led—and will continue to lead—to progress. It is telling that the biological predeterminists were critically labeled "fatalists" or "pessimists," as if they had no right to present data that did not support the cause.

This ongoing tension over the "search and destroy" mindset provides an essential framework for understanding the promises and pitfalls of the heralded new genetic technologies. No longer asked to simply avoid delay, examine their breasts, and have mammograms, women are now offered the possibility of discovering mutations on the "breast cancer genes." But the information obtained through such tests has only a theoretical relationship to the actual cancers that Halsted hoped to discover at an earlier stage. All a woman can learn from genetic testing is her statistical likelihood of developing future breast cancer; she learns nothing about whether she personally will or will not become diseased.

Despite the inherent ambiguity of such information, the desire to obtain it remains alluring, as does the expectation that acting on such information will reduce or eliminate a woman's chance of dying of breast cancer. Halsted's original strategy has now become: "Determine your risk and we will cure you." But proposed interventions based on such data—such as preventive breast removal or chemical prevention—are just that: preventive. They are not treatment. What is discovered through genetic testing, by definition, cannot be cured because it is not disease. This search for genetic predisposition to disease is hardly limited to breast or other cancers. With the recent decoding of the human genome, genes are being identified that increase future risk of diabetes mellitus, heart disease, Alzheimer's disease, and numerous other conditions. Here, too, Halsted's quid pro quo is at play, promising some type of benefit from the discovery of relevant mutations.

Is the pursuit of genetic information thus misguided? Hardly. Information itself, even if it cannot predict the future with certitude, can be of value. For example, testing can relieve the anxiety associated with the uncertainty of not knowing one's genetic status. Physicians have also begun to employ genetic data in tailoring therapeutic interventions, such as using a patient's genetic makeup to choose a particular medication. Such use of the latest and most advanced technologies—here, genetics—to fight disease resonates strongly within American culture.

But as the genetic war on breast cancer proceeds, we should recall the basic tension that has characterized previous breast cancer wars. Although we may intuitively associate more aggressive action with better outcomes, this occurs only in some instances. A woman with breast cancer may be able to influence her fate. But in other cases, as with radical surgery or stem cell transplantation, "extra" treatment may provide minimal or no advantages. As much as we want it to be true, there is no guaranteed quid pro quo. This inconsistent association between action and outcome will become even more evident as women make clinical decisions based not on actual disease but on risk estimates.

So how should women with breast cancer or those at high risk for the disease make decisions? Patients and their providers should continue to use the best data available to guide screening and treatment, while acknowledging the limitations of such statistics and the medical profession's frequent inability to provide definitive answers. Rather than feeling compelled to reach decisions that are objectively "right," women should choose what is right for themselves.

Glossary of Breast Cancer Operations

Superradical mastectomy   Removal of the affected breast, underarm lymph nodes, both chest wall muscles, a portion of the rib cage, and the underlying internal mammary lymph nodes. The lymph nodes above the clavicle may also be removed. Other names: *extended radical mastectomy, ultraradical mastectomy*.

Radical mastectomy (Halsted)   Removal of the affected breast, underarm lymph nodes, and both chest wall muscles.

Modified radical mastectomy   Removal of the affected breast and underarm lymph nodes, leaving one or both chest wall muscles in place.

Total/simple mastectomy   Removal of the affected breast only.

Partial mastectomy/lumpectomy   Removal of only the cancer with a small surrounding piece of breast tissue. Other names: *segmental mastectomy, tylectomy*.

Quadrentectomy   Removal of the quarter of the breast containing the cancer.

Bilateral mastectomy   Removal of both breasts, at times accompanied by additional tissue.

Prophylactic mastectomy   Removal of both breasts as a preventive measure. Other name: *preventive mastectomy*.

Sources

Manuscript Collections

American Cancer Society, Atlanta, Ga.
American Cancer Society, Media Office, New York, N.Y.
Betty Ford Papers, Gerald R. Ford Presidential Library, Ann Arbor, Mich.
Betty Rollin Papers, State Historical Society of Wisconsin, Madison, Wisc.
Boston Women's Health Book Collective, Somerville, Mass.
Breast Cancer Task Force, National Cancer Institute, Bethesda, Md.
Cushman D. Haagensen Papers, Haagensen Research Foundation, Columbia University, New York, N.Y.
Ernest M. Daland Papers, National Library of Medicine, Bethesda, Md.
Isidor S. Ravdin Papers, University of Pennsylvania Archives, Philadelphia, Pa.
George Crile, Jr., Papers, Cleveland Clinic Foundation Archives, Cleveland, Ohio
John W. Roberts Papers, Gerald R. Ford Presidential Library, Ann Arbor, Mich.
M. Vera Peters Papers, Princess Margaret Hospital Archives and University of Toronto Archives, Toronto, Canada.
Michael B. Shimkin Papers, University of California at San Diego Library, San Diego, Calif.
Oliver Cope Papers, Countway Library, Harvard Medical School, Boston, Mass.
Rose Kushner Papers, Schlesinger Library, Radcliffe College, Cambridge, Mass.
Sheila Weidenfeld Papers, Gerald R. Ford Presidential Library, Ann Arbor, Mich.
William S. Halsted Papers, Alan Mason Chesney Archives, Johns Hopkins University, Baltimore, Md.

Personal Papers

Babette Rosmond
George E. Moore
George T. Pack
Guy M. Robbins
Herman C. Zuckerman
Jerome A. Urban
John C. Bailar III

Maurice M. Black
Philip Strax

Interviews

John Anlyan, January 13, 1999
Katherine Auchincloss, July 17, 1998
John C. Bailar III, April 22, 1998
Joel W. Baker, December 10, 1998
Michael Baum, August 12, 1998
Nathaniel I. Berlin, November 3, 1998
Beatrice Black and George Black, March 28, 1997
Blake Cady, January 6, 1998
Charles S. Cameron, November 27 and December 26, 1996
Paul Carbone, October 26, 1998
Ranes Chakravorty, May 21, 1999
Seymour Cohen, May 12, 1999
Avram E. Cooperman, February 13, 1998
Mary E. Costanza, January 9, 1998
Helga Sandburg Crile, October 11, 1996
Caldwell B. Esselstyn, Jr., March 10, 1997
Harmon J. Eyre, May 21, 1997
Alvan R. Feinstein, August 20, 1998
Donald J. Ferguson, April 25, 1998
Diane Fink, December 9, 1998
Kenneth A. Forde, July 20, 2000
Roger S. Foster, Jr., March 11, 1997
Maurice S. Fox, June 16, 1998
Albert Fracchia, September 16, 1997
Daniel S. Greenberg, November 24, 1998
Ezra S. Greenspan, February 10, 1999
Frank E. Gump, June 23, 1998
Alice M. Haagensen, September 18, 1996
Samuel Hellman, October 31, 1997, and April 22, 1998
Robert Hermann, October 3, 1998
Jimmie C. Holland, February 25, 1999
Benjamin Kerr, May 16, 1997
David W. Kinne, September 23, 1997

Harvey Kushner, March 18, 1998

Amy Langer, March 24, 1999

Raffaele Lattes, June 22, 1998

Margaret Lazarus, January 14, 1998

Henry P. Leis, Jr., June 26, 1997

Hamblin Letton, October 9, 1998

Edward F. Lewison, May 1, 1997

Maryel F. Locke, January 8, 1998

William P. Longmire, Jr., December 14, 1998

Susan M. Love, July 15, 1998

Eleanor Montague, June 17, 1998

Francis D. Moore, June 19, 1997

George E. Moore, November 20, 1997, and November 21, 1998

Myron Moskowitz, July 27, 1999

C. Barber Mueller, December 30, 1998

Maryann Napoli, June 9, 1998

Sherwin B. Nuland, September 7, 1999

Michael P. Osborne, February 5, 1999

Philip Partington, November 27, 1998

Cynthia Pearson, May 18, 2000

Kenneth A. Prager, November 5, 1999

Judith E. Randal, March 17, 1998

Guy S. Robbins, May 6, 1997

Beall Rodgers, January 15, 1999

Betty Rollin, August 20, 1997

Gordon F. Schwartz, January 13, 1998

Sam Shapiro, January 15, 1997

Charles R. Smart, October 9, 1998

Robert E. Smith, May 21, 1997

Ruth Spear, September 3, 1997

Philip Strax, March 3, 1997

Norma Swenson, January 7, 1998

Agnes Turnback, November 19, 1998

Sadie Unter, June 16, 1998

Xenia N. Urban, March 10, 1997

Umberto Veronesi, July 16, 1999

Philip Wiedel, December 9, 1997

Leslie Wise, December 11, 1997

Herman C. Zuckerman, August 12, 1997

Notes

Chapter 1. Introduction

1. William Bennett, "In Search of the Third Opinion," *Harvard Magazine*, January-February 1978, pp. 13–14.

2. Ibid., 13.

3. Susan Ferraro, "You Can't Look Away Anymore: The Anguished Politics of Breast Cancer," *New York Times Magazine*, August 15, 1993, pp. 24–27, 58, 61–62.

4. Historical literature on cancer, while sparse, is beginning to increase. The best review of cancer historiography is David Cantor, "Cancer," in W. F. Bynum and Roy Porter, eds., *Companion Encyclopedia of the History of Medicine*, Vol. 1 (London: Routledge, 1993), 537–561. The most comprehensive social history of cancer in the United States remains James T. Patterson, *The Dread Disease: Cancer and Modern American Culture* (Cambridge, Mass.: Harvard Univ. Press, 1987). Robert N. Proctor, *Cancer Wars: How Politics Shapes What We Know and Don't Know About Cancer* (New York: Basic Books, 1995), does an excellent job of analyzing the political aspects of anticancer efforts but does not extensively address issues in diagnosis and therapeutics. Ilana Lowy, *Between Bench and Bedside: Science, Healing, and Interleukin-2 in a Cancer Ward* (Cambridge, Mass.: Harvard Univ. Press, 1996), looks mostly at modern cancer research but contains a useful discussion of the history of cancer immunotherapy. Lowy also brings an important cross–cultural focus to her work.

Some histories have focused on breast cancer. Ellen Leopold, *A Darker Ribbon: Breast Cancer, Women, and Their Doctors in the Twentieth Century* (Boston: Beacon Press, 1999) is a cultural history that examines how physicians and breast cancer patients have arrived at treatment decisions. Although Leopold's book is a straight historical account, she is a breast cancer survivor. Another excellent book by a survivor, weaving personal experience with history, is Sharon Batt's *Patient No More: The Politics of Breast Cancer* (Charlotteville, Canada: Gynergy Books, 1994). Nora Jacobson, *Cleavage: Technology, Controversy, and the Ironies of the Man-Made Breast* (New Brunswick, N.J.: Rutgers Univ. Press, 2000), contains several useful chapters on the history of breast reconstruction. Daniel de Moulin, *A Short History of Breast Cancer* (Boston: Martinus Nijoff, 1983), provides a helpful chronology but not much interpretation. Finally, a significant discussion of breast cancer screening may be found in Kirsten Gardner, "By Women, for Women, and with Women: A History of Female Cancer Awareness Programs in the United States, 1913–1970s," Ph.D. diss., Univ. of Cincinnati, 1999.

Several excellent articles on the history of breast cancer have been written and are cited throughout the book. Worth noting, however, is Theresa Montini and Sheryl Ruzek, "Overturning Orthodoxy: The Emergence of Breast Cancer Treatment Policy," *Research in the Sociology of Health Care* 8 (1989): 3–32.

5. See, for example, Roy Porter, "The Patient's View: Doing History from Below," *Theory and Society* 14 (1985): 175–198.

6. Ann Douglas Wood, "'The Fashionable Diseases': Women's Complaints and Their Treatment in Nineteenth-Century America," *Journal of Interdisciplinary History* 4 (1973): 25–52; Barbara Ehrenreich and Deidre English, *For Her Own Good: 150 Years of the Experts' Advice to Women* (New York: Anchor Books, 1989).

7. Charles E. Rosenberg, "Disease in History: Frames and Framers," *Milbank Quarterly* 67 (Suppl. 1) (1989): 1–15.

8. Sherwin B. Nuland, *Doctors* (New York: Alfred A. Knopf, 1988), 421.

9. George Crile, Jr., "Do Ultraradical Operations for Cancer Do More Harm Than Good?," *Surgery, Gynecology & Obstetrics* 100 (1955): 755.

10. Letter to Betty Ford, December 5, 1974, Betty Ford Papers, box 25, correspondence folder, 1/8/75–1/15/75, Gerald R. Ford Presidential Library, Ann Arbor, Mich. The names and addresses of individuals who wrote to Betty Ford have mostly been expunged by the library staff.

11. Quoted in Edward F. Lewison, "The Surgical Treatment of Breast Cancer: An Historical and Collective Review," *Surgery* 34 (1953): 904–953.

12. "Surgery: The Best Hope of All," *Time*, May 3, 1963, pp. 44–60.

13. Howard F. Stein, *American Medicine as Culture* (Boulder, Colo.: Westview Press, 1990), 62.

14. Susan Sontag, *Illness as Metaphor* (New York: Farrar, Straus & Giroux, 1978).

15. Marilyn Yalom, *A History of the Breast* (New York: Alfred A. Knopf, 1998).

16. Sheryl B. Ruzek, *The Women's Health Movement: Feminist Alternatives to Medical Control* (New York: Praeger, 1978), 32, 34.

17. Ellen Frankfort, *Vaginal Politics* (New York: Quadrangle Books, 1972), 7.

18. Dorothy Shinder, *Mayhem on Women* (San Rafael, Calif.: Ombudswomen, 1972), 20.

19. Regina Morantz, "The Perils of Feminist History," *Journal of Interdisciplinary History* 4 (1974): 649–660; Rima D. Apple, "Introduction," in Rima D. Apple, ed., *Women, Health, and Medicine in America* (New York: Garland, 1990), xiii–xxii. See also Rose Weitz, "Preface," in Rose Weitz, ed., *The Politics of Women's Bodies: Sexuality, Appearance, and Behavior* (New York: Oxford Univ. Press, 1998), ix–xii, and Regina Morantz-Sanchez's excellent new book, *Conduct Unbecoming a Woman: Medicine on Trial in Turn-of-the-Century Brooklyn* (New York: Oxford Univ. Press, 1999).

20. Betty Rollin, *First, You Cry* (New York: J. B. Lippincott, 1976).

21. For a complementary analysis of the use of the word "cure," see C. Barber Mueller, "Is Breast Cancer 'Curable'?," in Leslie Wise and Houston Johnson, Jr., eds., *Breast Cancer: Controversies in Management* (Armonk, N.Y.: Futura, 1994), 53–60.

22. Ian MacDonald, "Biological Predeterminism in Human Cancer," *Surgery, Gynecology & Obstetrics* 92 (1951): 443–452.

23. Rose Kushner, *Breast Cancer: A Personal and an Investigative Report* (New York: Harcourt Brace Jovanovich, 1975).

24. Jane E. Brody, "Choosing to Test for Cancer's Genetic Link," *New York Times*, August 17, 1999, pp. F1, F9.

25. S. Vendantam, "Scientists Plan to Use $30 Million in Search of New Cancer Genes," *Houston Chronicle*, November 2, 1996, p. A6; Michael Waldholz, "A Cancer Survivor's Genetic Time Bomb," *Wall Street Journal*, November 10, 1997, pp. B1, B13.

26. Jack D. Pressman, *Last Resort: Psychosurgery and the Limits of Medicine* (Cambridge: Cambridge Univ. Press, 1998).

27. Susan Sachs, "Artist Sees Hope in Mastectomy Ruling," *New York Times*, March 27, 1999, p. B5.

Chapter 2. William Halsted and the Radical Mastectomy

1. Quoted in Edward F. Lewison, *Breast Cancer and Its Diagnosis and Treatment* (Baltimore: Williams & Wilkins, 1955), 18.

2. Ibid., 5.

3. Daniel de Moulin, *A Short History of Breast Cancer* (Boston: Martinus Nijhoff, 1983), 9. See also Robert L. Martensen, "Cancer: Medical History and the Framing of a Disease," *Journal of the American Medical Association* 271 (1994): 1901.

4. Frances Burney, "A Mastectomy," in David J. Rothman, Steven Marcus, and Stephanie A. Kiceluk, eds., *Medicine and Western Civilization* (New Brunswick, N.J.: Rutgers Univ. Press, 1995), 384–389.

5. Quoted in Maarten Ultee, "The Paradox of Early Modern Breast Cancer, 1500–1850," paper presented at the annual meeting of the American Association for the History of Medicine, New Brunswick, N.J., May 8, 1999.

6. Ibid.

7. Lewison, *Breast Cancer*, 18–19; Cornelia S. Bland, "The Halsted Mastectomy: Present Illness and Past History," *Western Journal of Medicine* 134 (1981): 549–555.

8. Lewison, *Breast Cancer*, 16.

9. George Rosen, *A History of Public Health*, expanded ed. (Baltimore: Johns Hopkins Univ. Press, 1993), 293.

10. Emile Holman, "Sir William Osler, William Stewart Halsted, Harvey Cushing: Some Personal Reminiscences," *Surgery* 57 (1965): 589–601; Sherwin B. Nuland, *Doctors* (New York: Alfred A. Knopf, 1988), 414.

11. Ibid., 412; Christopher Lawrence, "Democratic, Divine and Heroic: The History and Historiography of Surgery," in Christopher Lawrence, ed., *Medical Theory, Surgical Practice: Studies in the History of Surgery* (London: Routledge, 1992), 1–47; Gert H. Brieger, "From Conservative to Radical Surgery in Late Nineteenth-Century America," in Lawrence, ed., *Medical Theory, Surgical Practice*, 216–231. On the education of American physicians in Germany, see Thomas N. Bonner, *Becoming a Physician: Medical Education in Britain, France, Germany, and the United States, 1750–1945* (New York: Oxford Univ. Press, 1995).

12. Holman, "Sir William Osler," 596.

13. Nuland, *Doctors*, 417.

14. Quoted in Ellen Leopold, *A Darker Ribbon: Breast Cancer, Women, and Their Doctors in the Twentieth Century* (Boston, Mass.: Beacon Press, 1999), 59.

15. Michael Bliss, *William Osler: A Life in Medicine* (New York: Oxford Univ. Press, 1999), 213.

16. Nuland, *Doctors*, 415.

17. William S. Halsted, "The Treatment of Wounds with Especial Reference to the Value of the Blood Clot in the Management of Dead Spaces," *Johns Hopkins Hospital Reports* 2 (1890–91): 255–314.

18. William Sampson Handley, *Cancer of the Breast and Its Operative Treatment* (London: Murray, 1906).

19. William S. Halsted, "Developments in the Skin-Grafting Operation for Cancer of the Breast," *Journal of the American Medical Association* 60 (1913): 416–418.

20. William S. Halsted, "The Training of the Surgeon," *Bulletin of the Johns Hopkins Hospital* 15 (1904): 267–275. See also Brieger, "From Conservative to Radical," 229.

21. William S. Halsted, "The Results of Operations for the Cure of Cancer of the Breast Performed at the Johns Hopkins Hospital from June 1889 to January 1894," *Johns Hopkins Hospital Reports* 4 (1894–1895): 1–60.

22. Ibid., 32–33.

23. William S. Halsted, "A Clinical and Histological Study of Certain Adenocarcinomata of the Breast," *Transactions of the American Surgical Association* 16 (1898): 144–181.

24. William S. Halsted, "The Results of Radical Operations for the Cure of Carcinoma of the Breast," *Annals of Surgery* 46 (1907): 1–19.

25. Ibid., 4.

26. Quoted in Halsted, "A Clinical and Histological Study," 163.

27. Quoted in ibid., 174.

28. Lewison, Breast Surgery, 13.

29. Quoted in Halsted, "A Clinical and Histological Study," 165.

30. M.A. to William S. Halsted, February 27, 1914. William S. Halsted Papers, box 1, folder 8, Alan Mason Chesney Archives, Johns Hopkins University, Baltimore, Md.

31. Leopold, A Darker Ribbon, 96.

32. H.L. to William S. Halsted, September 10, 1916, Halsted Papers, box 16, folder 7.

33. Kenneth M. Ludmerer, Learning to Heal: The Development of American Medical Education (New York: Basic Books, 1985), 57.

34. Nuland, Doctors, 401. For more on Osler, see Bliss, William Osler.

35. Ludmerer, Learning to Heal, 173–184.

36. On the rise of the scientific hospital, see Charles E. Rosenberg, The Care of Strangers: The Rise of America's Hospital System (New York: Basic Books, 1987).

37. John L. Cameron, "William Stewart Halsted: Our Surgical Heritage," Annals of Surgery 225 (1997): 445–458. See also Joseph C. Bloodgood, "Halsted Thirty-Six Years Ago," American Journal of Surgery 14 (1931): 89–148; Samuel J. Crowe, Halsted of Johns Hopkins: The Man and His Men (Springfield, Ill.: Charles C. Thomas, 1957); Peter D. Olch, "William Stewart Halsted: Legendary Figure of American Surgery," Review of Surgery 20 (1963): 83–90.

38. Quoted in Bland, "The Halsted Mastectomy," 551. For another historian's view on Halsted's legacy, see Robert L. Martensen, "When the 'Truly Conservative' Went 'Radical': The Genesis, Development, and Persistence of the Radical Mastectomy as a Curative Treatment for Breast Cancer," paper presented at the New York Academy of Medicine, New York, N.Y., June 1, 1998.

39. Quoted in Nuland, Doctors, 397–398. See also Wilder Penfield, "Halsted of Johns Hopkins," Journal of the American Medical Association 210 (1969): 2214–2218; Edward F. X. Hughes, "Halsted and American Surgery," Surgery 75 (1974): 169–177.

40. Nuland, Doctors, p. 417.

41. Rudolph Matas, "In Memoriam—William Stewart Halsted: An Appreciation," Bulletin of the Johns Hopkins Hospital 36 (1925): 2–27.

42. Interview with Donald J. Ferguson, M.D., April 25, 1998.

43. Dale C. Smith, "Surgery: It's Not a Random Therapy," Caduceus 12 (1996): 19–38.

44. Halsted, "The Training of the Surgeon," Bulletin of the Johns Hopkins Hospital 15 (1904): 267–275.

45. Quoted in C. C. Simmons and Ernest M. Daland, "Cancer: Factors Entering into the Delay in Its Surgical Treatment," Boston Medical and Surgical Journal 183

(1920): 298–306. On the connection of radical mastectomy and surgical authority, see also Smith, "Surgery," 29; Theresa Montini and Sheryl Ruzek, "Overturning Orthodoxy: The Emergence of Breast Cancer Treatment Policy," *Research in the
Sociology of Health Care* 8 (1989): 3–32.

46. Juan Rosai, "Pathology: A Historical Opportunity," *American Journal of Pathology* 151 (1997): 3–6. See also Regina Morantz-Sanchez, *Conduct Unbecoming a Woman:
Medicine on Trial in Turn-of-the-Century Brooklyn* (New York: Oxford Univ. Press, 1999),
130–133.

47. Robert E. Fechner, "One Century of Mammary Carcinoma in Situ: What
Have We Learned?," *American Journal of Clinical Pathology* 100 (1993): 654–661. On
frozen sections, see Frederick B. Wagner, Jr., Richard G. Martin, Sr., and Kirby I.
Bland, "History of the Therapy of Breast Disease," in Kirby I. Bland and Edward
M. Copeland III, eds., *The Breast: Comprehensive Management of Benign and Malignant Diseases*
(Philadelphia: W. B. Saunders, 1998), 1–18.

48. Joseph C. Bloodgood, "Problems of Cancer," *Journal of the Kansas Medical Society* 31 (1930): 311–316.

49. Bloodgood, "Halsted," 104.

50. Rosai, "Pathology," 5.

51. Barron H. Lerner, *Contagion and Confinement: Controlling Tuberculosis Along the Skid
Road* (Baltimore: Johns Hopkins Univ. Press, 1998).

52. James T. Patterson, *The Dread Disease: Cancer and Modern American Culture* (Cambridge, Mass.: Harvard Univ. Press, 1987), 30.

53. Ibid., 31.

54. Ibid., 26, 40.

55. Charles P. Childe, *The Control of a Scourge* (New York: E. P. Dutton, 1907),
227, 229.

56. Ibid., 111.

57. Patterson, *The Dread Disease*, 38.

58. Victor A. Triolo and Michael B. Shimkin, "The American Cancer Society
and Cancer Research Origins and Organization: 1913–1943," *Cancer Research* 29
(1969): 1615–1640.

59. Walter S. Ross, *Crusade: The Official History of the American Cancer Society* (New
York: Arbor House, 1987), 18–19.

60. Ibid., 23.

61. Patterson, *The Dread Disease*, 83.

62. Bloodgood, "Problems of Cancer," 312.

63. John B. Deaver and Joseph McFarland, *The Breast: Its Anomalies, Its Diseases, and
Their Treatment* (London: William Heinemann, 1918), 578.

64. Janet Lane-Claypon, *Reports on Public Health, Medical Subjects*, no. 51 (London: H.M. Stationery Office, 1924).

65. Quoted in Halsted, "A Clinical and Histological Study," 169.

66. Ibid., 169.

67. Ibid., 157.

68. Ibid.

69. William S. Halsted, "The Swelling of the Arm After Operations for Cancer of the Breast," *Johns Hopkins Hospital Bulletin* 32 (1921): 309–313.

70. Quoted in ibid., 174.

71. Frederick O' Brien, "Irradiation of Primary Cancer of the Breast," *New England Journal of Medicine* 202 (1930): 897–901.

72. Mrs. G.L. to William S. Halsted, June 18, 1914, Halsted Papers, box 32, patient correspondence folder, 1895–1920.

73. J.K. to William S. Halsted, November 5, 1914, Halsted Papers, box 14, folder 3.

74. These letters can be found in the Halsted Papers, box 14, folder 6.

75. Reginald Murley, *Surgical Roots and Branches* (London: British Medical Journal, 1990), 173.

76. Geoffrey Keynes, "The Place of Radium in the Treatment of Cancer of the Breast," *Annals of Surgery* 106 (1937): 619–630. For Keynes's own account of his apostasy, see Keynes, *The Gates of Memory* (Oxford: Clarendon Press, 1981), 211–218.

77. Frank S. Mathews, "Results of Operative Treatment of Cancer of the Breast," *Annals of Surgery* 96 (1932): 871–881. See also R. W. Raven, "An Investigation into the End–Results in the Treatment of Cancer of the Breast," *St. Bartholomew's Hospital Reports* 66 (1933): 45–64.

78. Otto Glasser, "The Discovery of Roentgen Rays and Radium Rays," in George T. Pack and Edward M. Livingston, eds., *Treatment of Cancer and Allied Diseases*, vol. I (New York: Paul B. Hoeber, 1940), 88–97.

79. George T. Pack and Edward M. Livingston, "Introduction: The Treatment of Cancer," in Pack and Livingston, eds., *Treatment of Cancer*, 689–755. See also de Moulin, *A Short History*, 99–100. At times, radiation was given preoperatively.

80. Pack and Livingston, "Introduction," 718; Burton J. Lee, "The Therapeutic Value of Irradiation in the Treatment of Mammary Cancer," *Annals of Surgery* 88 (1928): 26–47.

81. A. W. Erskine, "Cancer of the Breast," *Wisconsin Medical Journal* 34 (1935): 623–624.

82. Jay R. Harris and Monica Morrow, "Treatment of Early-Stage Breast Cancer," in Jay R. Harris, ed., *Diseases of the Breast* (Philadelphia: Lippincott-Raven,

1996), 487–537. See also de Moulin, A Short History, 99–102. On the history of the x-ray, see Bettyann Holtzmann Kevles, Naked to the Bone: Medical Imaging in the Twentieth Century (New Brunswick, N.J.: Rutgers Univ. Press, 1997).

83. P. H. Mitchiner, G. N. Bailey, and A. K. Price, "A Comparison of the Results of Conservative and Radical Surgical Treatment in Carcinoma of the Breast, for the Decade 1924–33," St. Thomas's Hospital Reports 2 (1938): 192–197.

84. Keynes, "The Place of Radium," 624.

85. Lee, "The Therapeutic Value," 35.

86. Edwin J. Grace, "Simple Mastectomy in Cancer of the Breast," American Journal of Surgery 35 (1937): 512–514.

87. Pack and Livingston, "Introduction," 737, 739.

88. Mitchiner et al., "A Comparison of the Results," 197.

89. Keynes, "The Place of Radium," 630.

90. Walter O. Bullock, "Cancer of the Breast: A New Incision with a Review of the Technique," American Journal of Surgery 24 (1934): 396–416.

91. Dean Lewis and William F. Rienhoff, "A Study of the Results of Operations for the Cure of Cancer of the Breast Performed at the Johns Hopkins Hospital from 1889 to 1931," Annals of Surgery 95 (1932): 336–400.

92. Ibid., 338.

93. Halsted, "The Results of Operations," 8.

94. Lewis and Rienhoff, "A Study of the Results," 350, 374.

95. Lawrence, "Democratic, Divine and Heroic." This theme is discussed extensively in Chapter 4. The term "surgical cure" is from Pearl Katz, The Scalpel's Edge: The Culture of Surgeons (Boston: Allyn and Bacon, 1999).

96. Halsted, "The Results of Operations," 6.

97. Childe, The Control of a Scourge, 2.

98. B. Farquhar Curtis, "The Cure of Cancer by Operation," Medical Record 45 (1894): 225–230.

99. Lewis and Rienhoff, "A Study of the Results"; C. A. Kunath, "Problem of Carcinoma of the Breast: Radical Mastectomy in Ninety Cases," Archives of Surgery 41 (1940): 66–78.

100. Montini and Ruzek, "Overturning Orthodoxy," 8.

101. Patterson, The Dread Disease, 97; Lewis and Rienhoff, "A Study of the Results," 337; J. W. Bransfield and S. G. Castigliano, "The Inadequacy of Simple Mastectomy in Operable Cancer of the Breast," American Journal of Roentgenology 47 (1942): 748–763.

102. Mathews, "Results of Operative Treatment," 877.

103. Leopold, A Darker Ribbon, 80.

104. Frank G. Slaughter, *The New Science of Surgery* (New York: J. Messner, 1946); Jurgen Thorwald, *The Century of the Surgeon* (New York: Pantheon, 1956).

105. Carole S. McCauley, *Surviving Breast Cancer* (New York: E. P. Dutton, 1979), 134.

106. Bland, "The Halsted Mastectomy," 554; Jay Katz, *The Silent World of Doctor and Patient* (New York: Free Press, 1984).

Chapter 3. Breast Cancer Control after World War II

1. Claude E. Welch, *A Twentieth-Century Surgeon: My Life in the Massachusetts General Hospital* (Boston: Massachusetts General Hospital, 1992), 142.

2. *Proceedings of the Conference on Cancer Detection, Portsmouth, New Hampshire, September 9–11, 1949* (New York: American Cancer Society, 1949), 2.

3. Ibid., 2.

4. Robert B. Greenough, "Cancer Service in Massachusetts," May 20, 1930. Ernest M. Daland Papers, box 2, Massachusetts Cancer Program folder, National Library of Medicine (NLM), Bethesda, Md.

5. Edward J. Ill, "Cancer of the Breast," *Annals of Surgery* 95 (1932): 401–409. See also Ellen Leopold, *A Darker Ribbon: Breast Cancer, Women, and Their Doctors in the Twentieth Century* (Boston: Beacon Press, 1999), 76–77. The mammary carcinoma summary sheets can be found in the Cushman D. Haagensen Papers, Haagensen Research Foundation, New York, N.Y.

6. "'Cancer Is Curable,'" *Time*, October 31, 1932, pp. 32–33.

7. Herbert L. Lombard, *The Massachusetts Cancer Program* (n.p., 1959), 48–49. In Daland Papers, box 2, NLM. On the role of demonstration in science, see Steven Shapin and Simon Schaffer, *Leviathan and the Air-Pump: Hobbes, Boyle, and the Experimental Life* (Princeton, N.J.: Princeton Univ. Press), 1985.

8. James T. Patterson, *The Dread Disease: Cancer and Modern American Culture* (Cambridge, Mass.: Harvard Univ. Press, 1987), 114–120.

9. Ibid., 72.

10. Quoted in Margaret E. A. Black, "What Did Popular Women's Magazines from 1929 to 1949 Say About Breast Cancer?," *Cancer Nursing* 18 (1995): 270–277.

11. Patterson, *The Dread Disease*, 171; Donald F. Shaughnessy, "The Story of the American Cancer Society," Ph.D. diss., Columbia Univ., 1957, p. 184.

12. Patterson, *The Dread Disease*, 112. On the war on tuberculosis, see Susan Sontag, *Illness as Metaphor* (New York: Farrar, Straus & Giroux, 1978); Mark Caldwell, *The Last Crusade: The War on Consumption, 1862–1954* (New York: Atheneum, 1988).

13. Clarence C. Little, "History of the American Society for the Control of Cancer," unpublished manuscript, 1944, box 9–1816, American Cancer Society Archives, Atlanta, Ga.

14. Deborah O. Erwin, "The Militarization of Cancer Treatment in American Society," in Harold A. Baer, ed., *Encounters with Biomedicine: Case Studies in Medical Anthropology* (New York: Gordon and Breach Science Publishers, 1987), 209.

15. Shaughnessy, "History," 154.

16. Ibid., 98.

17. Robert N. Proctor, *The Nazi War on Cancer* (Princeton, N.J.: Princeton Univ. Press, 1999). See also Shaughnessy, "History," 8.

18. Report of the Executive Vice President, Annual Meeting of the ACS, November 4, 1948, ACS Archives.

19. Howard F. Stein, *American Medicine as Culture* (Boulder, Colo.: Westview Press, 1990), 68. See also Paul Fussell, *The Great War and Modern Memory* (New York: Oxford Univ. Press, 1975).

20. Patterson, *The Dread Disease*, 26–27. See also Robert L. Martensen, "Cancer: Medical History and the Framing of a Disease," *Journal of the American Medical Association* 271 (1994): 1901.

21. "On the Cancer Front with the Field Army," 1939, box 9–1833, Women's Field Army Scrapbook, ACS Archives.

22. "The Fight of the Women's Field Army Against Cancer," 1939, box 9–1833, Women's Field Army Scrapbook, ACS Archives.

23. "On the Cancer Front."

24. Ibid. See also Alan Petersen and Deborah Lupton, *The New Public Health: Health and Self in the Age of Risk* (London: Sage Publications, 1996).

25. Leslie J. Reagan, "Engendering *The Dread Disease*: Women, Men, and Cancer," *American Journal of Public Health* 87 (1997): 1779–1787. Reagan's article is an excellent overview of cancer and gender. See also Shaughnessy, "History," 190–191.

26. For more on this topic, see Kirsten Gardner, "By Women, for Woman and with Women: A History of Female Cancer Awareness Efforts in the United States, 1913–1970s," Ph.D. diss., Univ. of Cincinnati, 1999. The quote from Rogers is on p. 121.

27. Gretta Palmer, "I Had Cancer," *Ladies' Home Journal*, July 1947, pp. 143–148, 150, 152–153. On the role of the AAUW, see chapter 3 of Gardner, "By Women."

28. Harold F. Dorn and Sidney J. Cutler, *Morbidity from Cancer in the United States*, Part I, Public Health Monograph no. 29 (Washington, D.C.: Government Printing Office, 1955), 22, 31; Arthur S. Kraus and Abraham Oppenheim, "Trend of Mortality from Cancer of the Breast," *Journal of the American Medical Association* 194 (1965): 201–202.

29. "Report of Executive Vice President," November 4, 1948; Leopold, *A Darker Ribbon*, 168; Cushman D. Haagensen, *Diseases of the Breast* (Philadelphia: W. B. Saunders, 1956), 367.

30. John W. Emmanuel to Charlotte Payne, February 2, 1950. Records of the National Council of Negro Women, series 6, box 1, folder 1, Mary McLeod Bethune Council House, Washington, D.C. See also Gardner, "By Women," 152–153. Thanks to Vanessa Gamble for this reference.

31. Marlyn W. Miller and Eugene P. Pendergrass, "Some Observations Concerned with Carcinoma of the Breast, Part V," *Pennsylvania Medical Journal* 57 (1954): 421–425.

32. George T. Pack and J. S. Gallo, "The Culpability for Delay in the Treatment of Cancer," *American Journal of Cancer* 33 (1938): 443–462.

33. Walter S. Ross, *Crusade: The Official History of the American Cancer Society* (New York: Arbor House, 1987), 80.

34. Ibid., 80.

35. George Papanicolaou, *Diagnosis of Uterine Cancer by the Vaginal Smear* (New York: Commonwealth Fund, 1943). For a history of Pap testing, see Eftychia Vayena, "The Transformation of a Diagnostic Technique into a Screening Test: ACS, NCI, American Women, and the Pap Test," Ph.D. diss., Univ. of Minnesota, 1999.

36. Arthur I. Holleb in Ross, *Crusade*, 87.

37. Ibid., 35.

38. Ibid., 33.

39. Patterson, *The Dread Disease*, 171–183. For a good discussion of the ACS's growing use of advertising and marketing, see Leopold, *A Darker Ribbon*, 158–162.

40. Patterson, *The Dread Disease*, 142.

41. Ross, *Crusade*, 84.

42. Charles Cameron, "Annual Report of the Medical and Scientific Director, 1950–1951," appended to Minutes of the Annual Meeting of Members of the American Cancer Society, October 25, 1951, ACS Archives.

43. Ibid.

44. Adele E. Clarke and Monica J. Casper, "From Simple Technology to Complex Arena: Classification of Pap Smears," *Medical Anthropology Quarterly* 10 (1996): 601–623.

45. J. D. Ratcliff, "We Could Cure Cancer Now," *Woman's Home Companion* 73 (November 1946): 35, 176.

46. Quoted in the foreward of D. Erskine Carmichael, *The Pap Smear: The Life of George N. Papanicolaou* (Springfield, Ill.: Charles C. Thomas, 1973).

47. Charles S. Cameron, "Cancerphobia [Letter to the Editor]," *Journal of the American Medical Association* 147 (1951): 526. Similar language was used to support

American efforts to eliminate polio in the 1950s. See Allan M. Brandt, "Polio, Politics, Publicity, and Duplicity: Ethical Aspects in the Development of the Salk Vaccine," *Connecticut Medicine* 43 (1979): 581–590.

48. Ellen Herman, *The Romance of American Psychology: Political Culture in the Age of Experts* (Berkeley: Univ. of California Press, 1995), 125.

49. Thanks to Don Reid, Judith Farquhar, and Christopher Lawrence for suggesting this perspective on Cold War era cancer control.

50. Ross, *Crusade*, 89.

51. Hugh Auchincloss, "How More Women Can Be Saved from Dying of Cancer of the Breast," *Medical Journal and Record* 130 (1929): 446–449. See also Ross, *Crusade*, 96.

52. Proctor, *Nazi War*, 31.

53. On technological innovation in medicine, see Joel D. Howell, *Technology in the Hospital: Transforming Patient Care in the Early Twentieth Century* (Baltimore: Johns Hopkins Univ. Press, 1995).

54. Dorn, *Morbidity from Cancer*, 51; United States Public Health Service, *Vital Statistics of the United States, 1947, Part I* (Washington, D.C.: GPO, 1949), 14.

55. Haagensen, *Diseases of the Breast*, 334, 413.

56. Marilyn Yalom, *A History of the Breast* (New York: Alfred A. Knopf, 1998), 138.

57. Ibid., 138, 177.

58. Ellen Leopold has characterized the search for possibly malignant breast lumps somewhat differently, arguing that such efforts created a dilemma between actual survival and social survival. See Leopold, *A Darker Ribbon*, 160–162, 181.

59. "Self-Examination of the Breasts," *Good Housekeeping*, November 1955, p. 32; "Breast Cancer—A Backgrounder," May 1969, unpublished manuscript, Breast Cancer—General folder, American Cancer Society, Media Division, New York, NY.

60. "Is There Something You're Forgetting to Do?," 1955 pamphlet produced by the Philadelphia chapter of the ACS, Isidor S. Ravdin Papers, box 70, folder 3, Univ. of Pennsylvania Archives, Philadelphia.

61. Eileen to George Crile, Jr., 1955. George Crile, Jr., Papers, box 13, Scrapbook on Cancer and Common Sense, Cleveland Clinic Foundation, Cleveland, Ohio.

62. Cushman D. Haagensen, *Carcinoma of the Breast* (New York: American Cancer Society, 1950), 10, 19.

63. Richard Renneker and Max Cutler, "Psychological Problems of Adjustment to Cancer of the Breast," *Journal of the American Medical Association* 148 (1952): 833–838. Renneker and Cutler's work is discussed further in Chapter 7.

64. *Proceedings of the Conference on Cancer Detection*, 45.

65. Minutes of the Meeting of the Board of Directors of the American Cancer Society, May 13, 1966, ACS Archives.

66. Lisa Cartwright, *Screening the Body: Tracing Medicine's Visual Culture* (Minneapolis: MN: University of Minnesota Press, 1995), 169. See also pp. 121–123.

67. Terri Kapsalis, *Public Privates: Performing Gynecology from Both Ends of the Speculum* (Durham, N.C.: Duke Univ. Press, 1997), 103. See also Sue Wilkinson and Celia Kitzinger, "Whose Breast Is It Anyway? A Feminist Consideration of Advice and 'Treatment' for Breast Cancer," *Women's Studies International Forum* 16 (1993): 229–238.

68. "Introducing C.A. Conshus, M.D.," September 1958, pamphlet produced by the Medical Society of the State of Pennsylvania and the Philadelphia chapter of the ACS, Ravdin Papers, box 70, folder 1.

69. Interview with Gordon F. Schwartz, M.D., January 13, 1998.

70. P.A. to George Crile, Jr., February 19, 1956, Crile Papers, box 28, Correspondence on Cancer and Common Sense folder, 1955–8.

71. Cushman D. Haagensen, L. Henry Garland, and Alfred Gellhorn, "A Modern Medicine Interview: Treatment of Breast Cancer," *Modern Medicine* (1957): 110–170.

72. This quotation is from Frank Gump, paraphrasing Haagensen. See interview with Frank E. Gump, June 23, 1998.

73. Reagan, "Engendering the Dread Disease"; Petersen and Lupton, *The New Public Health*; Sylvia N. Tesh, *Hidden Arguments: Political Ideology and Disease Prevention Policy* (New Brunswick, N.J.: Rutgers Univ. Press, 1988); Robert A. Aronowitz, *Making Sense of Illness: Studies in Twentieth Century Medical Thought* (Cambridge, England: Cambridge Univ. Press, 1998).

74. Raymond F. Kaiser, "Why Cancer 'Control?,'" *Public Health Reports* 65 (1950): 1203–1208.

75. "A Frank Film Helps Detect Breast Cancer," *Look*, December 19, 1950, p. 87.

76. Stein, *American Medicine as Culture*, 67.

77. Reagan, "Engendering the Dread Disease"; Leopold, *A Darker Ribbon*, 158–162. The words "guilty" and "negligence" can be found in Miller and Pendergrass, "Some Observations."

78. Ora Marshino, "Breast Cancer," *Hygeia* 23 (March 1945): 176–177, 201–202.

79. Frank S. Slaughter, *The New Science of Surgery* (New York: Julian Messner, 1946), 244.

80. Barron H. Lerner, "Great Expectations: Historical Perspectives on Genetic Breast Cancer Testing," *American Journal of Public Health* 89 (1999): 938–944.

81. Rita E. Watson and Robert C. Wallach, *New Choices, New Chances: A Woman's Guide to Conquering Cancer* (New York: St. Martin's Press, 1981), 104.

82. Quoted in "Report of the Executive Vice President," appended to Minutes of the Annual Meeting of the American Cancer Society, October 27, 1949, ACS Archives.

83. Peter C. English, *Shock, Physiological Surgery, and George Washington Crile: Medical Innovation in the Progressive Era* (Westport, Conn.: Greenwood Press, 1980), 214. See also pp. 20–46.

84. Ibid., 215.

85. "George Crile, Jr. in First Person: An Oral History," 1983, American Hospital Association Oral History Collection, Chicago, Ill., 4–5.

86. George Crile, Jr., "The Life and Times of George Crile, Jr.: A Tale of Fiction, Fact and Fancy," unpublished manuscript, n.d., Crile Papers, box 31.

87. Nathan A. Womack to George Crile, Jr., October 14, 1974, Crile Papers, box 48, Barney's Correspondence folder, 1974.

88. "In First Person: An Oral History," 7.

89. George Crile, Jr., "The Evolution of the Treatment of Breast Cancer," unpublished manuscript, n.d., Crile Papers, box 4, Detroit folder.

90. Ibid.

91. The adrenal operations were so-called denervations, in which the nerves to the adrenal gland were severed in order to treat high blood pressure. This procedure fell out of favor soon thereafter.

92. Crile, "The Evolution of the Treatment."

93. George Crile, Jr., *The Way It Was: Sex, Surgery, Treasure, and Travel, 1907-1987* (Kent, Ohio: Kent State Univ. Press, 1992), 263.

94. Crile, "The Life and Times."

95. George Crile, Jr., to Austin Smith, October 3, 1955, Crile Papers, box 28, Correspondence on Cancer and Common Sense folder, 1955–8.

96. George Crile, Jr., to John Raycroft, December 28, 1955, Crile Papers, box 28, Cancer Article and Cancer and Common Sense, More Correspondence folder, 1956–7.

97. American Medical Association, Judicial Council, *Principles of Medical Ethics: Opinions and Reports of the Judicial Council* (Chicago: American Medical Association, 1958), 55.

98. Don Dunham, "Dr. Crile Praised, Hit for Views on Cancer," *Cleveland Press*, October 27, 1955, p. 16.

99. George Crile, Jr., "A Plea Against Blind Fear of Cancer," *Life*, October 31, 1955, pp. 128–140.

100. George Crile, Jr., *Cancer and Common Sense* (New York: Viking Press, 1955), 7–8.

101. These examples appeared in *Time*, November 15, 1948. See W. B. Russ to George Crile, Jr., October 29, 1955, Crile Papers, box 13, Life Scrapbook.

102. George Crile, Jr., to Charles C. Lund, October 17, 1955, Crile Papers, box 28, Correspondence on Cancer and Common Sense folder, 1955–8.

103. William F. Rienhoff, Jr., "Selected New Books in Review," *Baltimore Sun*, January 16, 1956. In Crile Papers, box 13, Scrapbook on Cancer and Common Sense.

104. J. E. Strode to George Crile, Jr., November 14, 1955, Crile Papers, box 13, Life Scrapbook.

105. Z.S. to George Crile, Jr., November 13, 1955, Crile Papers, box 13, Life Scrapbook.

106. R.A. to George Crile, Jr., October 31, 1955. Crile Papers, box 13, Life Scrapbook.

107. R.W. to George Crile, Jr., June 7, 1956, Crile Papers, box 28, Correspondence on Cancer and Common Sense folder, 1955–8.

108. "A Statement Disagreeing with Dr. Crile," *Life*, October 31, 1955, p. 129.

109. Peter J. Steincrohn, "'Scary' Cancer Warnings," *Washington Evening Star*, May 4, 1956. In Crile Papers, box 13, Scrapbook on Cancer and Common Sense.

110. "Knowledge of Cancer Doesn't Create Hysteria," *Des Moines Tribune*, November 11, 1955. In Crile Papers, box 13, Scrapbook on Cancer and Common Sense.

111. Charles E. Cameron, "Report of the Medical and Scientific Director and Vice President," appended to Minutes of the Annual Meeting of Members of the American Cancer Society, October 27, 1949, ACS Archives.

112. Ibid.

113. Charles E. Cameron, "The Annual Report of the Medical and Scientific Director, 1952–1953," appended to Minutes of the Annual Meeting of the Members of the American Cancer Society, November 5, 1953, ACS Archives.

114. Charles E. Cameron, "The Annual Report of the Medical and Scientific Director, 1951–1952," appended to Minutes of the Annual Meeting of Members of the American Cancer Society, October 23, 1952, ACS Archives.

115. Edmund G. Zimmerer, "Wartime Cancer Education," *Bulletin of the American Cancer Society* 26, no. 2 (1944): 14–16.

116. Cameron, "The Annual Report of the Medical and Scientific Director, 1951–1952."

Chapter 4. Radical Surgery in the 1950s

1. Quoted in Grantley W. Taylor and Richard H. Wallace, "Carcinoma of the Breast: Fifty Years Experience at the Massachusetts General Hospital," *Transactions of the American Surgical Association* 68 (1950): 512–522.

2. History of Cancer Control Project, UCLA School of Public Health, *A History of Cancer Control in the United States, 1946–1971*, book 1 (Washington, D.C.: Department of Health, Education and Welfare, 1978), 373.

3. Quoted in Gert H. Brieger, "From Conservative to Radical Surgery in Late Nineteenth-Century America," in Christopher Lawrence, ed., *Medical Theory, Surgical Practice: Studies in the History of Surgery* (London: Routledge, 1992), 216–231.

4. Quoted in Pearl Katz, *The Scalpel's Edge: The Culture of Surgeons* (Boston: Allyn and Bacon), 1999, 30. Katz's book is a well-researched sociological study of the behavior of surgeons.

5. Christopher Lawrence and Tom Treasure, "Surgeons," in Roger Cooter and John Pickstone, eds., *Medicine in the Twentieth Century* (Amsterdam: Harwood Academic Publishers, 2000).

6. Interview with Donald J. Ferguson, M.D., April 25, 1998.

7. Frank S. Slaughter, *The New Science of Surgery* (New York: Julian Messner, 1946), 7.

8. Ibid., 3.

9. Ibid., 237.

10. Michael B. Shimkin, "Concluding Remarks," unpublished manuscript, July 1, 1977. Michael B. Shimkin Papers, box 40, folder 2, University of California San Diego (UCSD) Library. See also James T. Patterson, *The Dread Disease: Cancer and Modern American Culture* (Cambridge, Mass.: Harvard Univ. Press, 1987), 191–192.

11. Irving M. Ariel, "George T. Pack, M.D. 1898–1969: A Tribute," *American Journal of Roentgenology, Radium Therapy & Nuclear Medicine* 107 (1969): 443–446.

12. George T. Pack and Charles S. Cameron, "Abdominal Cardiectomy or Subtotal Gastric Resection for Cancer of the Proximal Half of the Stomach," *American Journal of Surgery* 59 (1943): 3–8.

13. Gordon McNeer, Walter Lawrence, Jr., Mildred P. Ashley and George T. Pack, "End Results in the Treatment of Gastric Cancer," *Surgery* 43 (1958): 879–896.

14. "Dr. George T. Pack," *MD* 10, no. 1 (1966): 114–115.

15. Roald M. Grant, "Never Say Die: A Personal Tribute to George T. Pack," *Ca* 19 (1969): 199–200.

16. Barron H. Lerner, "The Illness and Death of Eva Peron: Cancer, Politics, and Secrecy," *Lancet* 355 (2000): 1988–1991.

17. W.C. Heinz to George T. Pack, March 5, 1963, courtesy of Helen Pack.

18. Loose paper enclosed in Journal of George T. Pack, courtesy of Helen Pack.

19. Alexander Brunschwig, "Complete Excision of Pelvic Viscera for Advanced Carcinoma," *Cancer* 1 (1948): 177–183.

20. J. W. R. Rennie, "The Early Diagnosis and Treatment of Breast Tumours," *Canadian Medical Association Journal* 68 (1953): 127–130; S. A. Kholdin, "Extended Radical Operations for Mammary Cancer," in Irving M. Ariel, ed., *Progress in Clinical Cancer* (New York: Grune and Stratton, 1965), 438–449.

21. J. Arthur Myers, "Owen H. Wangensteen," *Journal-Lancet* 87 (1967): 216–228.

22. Evan M. Wylie, "24 Hours in the Fight Against Cancer," *Reader's Digest*, June 1956, pp. 107–111.

23. "Cancer—On the Brink of Breakthroughs," *Life*, May 1958, pp. 102–113.

24. "Surgery: The Best Hope of All," *Time*, May 3, 1963, pp. 44–60.

25. George T. Pack, "The Surgeon's Role in the Management of Cancer," *New York State Journal of Medicine* 64 (1964): 376–382.

26. Interview with Robert E. Hermann, M.D., October 3, 1998.

27. Christopher Lawrence, "Democratic, Divine and Heroic: The History and Historiography of Surgery," in Christopher Lawrence, ed., *Medical Theory, Surgical Practice* (London: Routledge, 1992), 1–47.

28. Howard F. Stein, *American Medicine as Culture* (Boulder, Colo.: Westview Press, 1990); Deborah Lupton, *Medicine as Culture: Illness, Disease and the Body in Western Societies* (London: Sage Publications, 1994).

29. Cushman D. Haagensen, "A Technique for Radical Mastectomy," *Surgery* 19 (1946): 100–131.

30. George T. Pack, Commencement Address, University of Alabama Medical School, May 30, 1953, Journal of George T. Pack, 27–28.

31. "Frazell Was Expert in Thyroid Cancer," *San Antonio Express News*, February 10, 1990, in George Crile, Jr., Papers, box 48, Barney's Correspondence folder, 1990, Cleveland Clinic Foundation, Cleveland, Ohio. The connection between the operation and the raids may have resulted from the fact that the initials "C.N.D." (complete neck dissection) resembled the word commando.

32. M. F. A. Woodruff, "New Approaches to the Treatment of Breast Cancer," *Journal of the Royal College of Surgeons of Edinburgh* 6 (1961): 75–92. See also interview with Beall Rodgers, M.D., January 15, 1999.

33. George T. Pack, "Radical Surgery for Malignancy," *Modern Medicine* 19 (1951): 63–64. See also Lawrence and Treasure, "Surgeons."

34. Lupton, *Medicine and Culture*, 67. See also Sheldon M. Retchin, James A. Wells, Alain-Jacques Valleron, and Gary L. Albrecht, "Health Behavior Changes in the United States, the United Kingdom and France," *Journal of General Internal Medicine* 7 (1992): 615–622.

35. Stein, *American Medicine*, 80.

36. Talcott Parsons, *The Social System* (Glencoe, Ill.: Free Press, 1951), 467. See also John P. Bunker, "Surgical Manpower: A Comparison of Operations and Surgeons in the United States and in England and Wales," *New England Journal of Medicine* 282 (1970): 135–144; Keith Wailoo, *Drawing Blood: Technology and Disease Identity in Twentieth-Century America* (Baltimore: Johns Hopkins Univ. Press, 1997), 50–62; Regina Morantz-Sanchez, *Conduct Unbecoming a Woman: Medicine on Trial in Turn-of-the-Century Brooklyn* (New York: Oxford Univ. Press, 1999), 96.

37. I. S. Ravdin, "Conservatism versus Radicalism in Colon and Rectal Cancer," speech given in Atlantic City, New Jersey, November 1955, Isidor S. Ravdin Papers, box 126, folder 1, University of Pennsylvania Archives, Philadelphia.

38. Quoted by Lyle A. French at Wangensteen's Memorial Service, January 23, 1981, Owen H. Wangensteen Papers, Cards, Letters of Condolence box, Memorial Service folder, 1/23/81, University of Minnesota Archives, Minneapolis.

39. Interview with Blake Cady, M.D., January 6, 1998.

40. Quotations are from "Dr. George T. Pack" and the Journal of George T. Pack, 2.

41. Arthur I. Holleb, "Eulogies for Urban," June 27, 1991, courtesy of Hiram S. Cody III and Xenia Urban.

42. I. S. Ravdin, "A Surgeon Takes a Second Look at the Cancer Problem," speech given at Memorial Sloan-Kettering Hospital, October 21, 1959, Ravdin Papers, box 124, folder 53.

43. "Dr. Alexander Brunschwig Dies; A Pioneer in Cancer Operations," *New York Times*, August 8, 1969, p. 33.

44. George T. Pack, "Recent Advances of Present Trends in Cancer Treatment and Research: Surgery," paper presented at Annual Meeting of the American Cancer Society, October 23, 1952, ACS Archives, Atlanta, Ga.

45. Dawson B. Conerly, Jr., "Simple Mastectomy in the Treatment of Carcinoma of the Breast," *Mississippi Doctor* 34 (1957): 207–211.

46. Lawrence, "Democratic, Devine and Heroic." See also Samuel Hellman, "Dogma and Inquisition in Medicine," *Cancer* 71 (1993): 2430–2433.

47. R. S. Handley, "Gordon-Taylor, Breast Cancer and the Middlesex Hospital," *Annals of the Royal College of Surgery of England* 49 (1971): 151–164.

48. Pack, "Recent Advances." The sociologists Renee C. Fox and Judith Swazey have characterized this mindset as the "courage to fail." See Fox and Swazey, *The Courage to Fail: A Social View of Organ Transplantation and Dialysis* (Chicago: Univ. of Chicago Press, 1974).

49. Harold S. Diehl, "Presentation of ACS Special Citation to Dr. Owen Wangensteen," unpublished manuscript, November 14, 1962, Ravdin Papers, box 38, folder 28.

50. Guy F. Robbins, "Changes to Memorial Sloan-Kettering Cancer Center," unpublished manuscript, October 23, 1955, courtesy of Nancy Orr.

51. D.B. to George Crile, Jr., June 25, 1956. George Crile, Jr., Papers, box 28, Correspondence on Cancer and Common Sense folder, 1955–8, Cleveland Clinic Foundation Archives, Cleveland, Ohio.

52. Nathan Hirsch, "They Call Me 'The Cancer Cop,'" *Cancer News*, Fall 1958, pp. 16–17. In Journal of George T. Pack, 127–128.

53. Brunschwig, "Complete Excision of Pelvic Viscera." See also Jackie Stacey, *Teratologies: A Cultural Study of Cancer* (London: Routledge, 1997), 137–141.

54. Brunschwig, "Complete Excision of Pelvic Viscera," 177.

55. Richard S. Handley and A. C. Thackray, "The Internal Mammary Lymph Chain in Carcinoma of the Breast: Study of 50 Cases," *Lancet* 2 (1949): 276–278.

56. Quoted in H. Glenn Bell, "Cancer of the Breast," *Transactions of the American Surgical Association* 67 (1949): 22–29.

57. Everett D. Sugarbaker, "Extended Radical Mastectomy: Its Superiority in the Treatment of Breast Cancer," *Journal of the American Medical Association* 187 (1964): 96–99.

58. "Mastectomy Study: How Relevant?," *Medical World News*, July 7, 1972, pp. 23, 29–30.

59. Bronson S. Ray and Olof H. Pearson, "Treatment of Metastatic Breast Cancer by Hypophysectomy," in George T. Pack and Irving M. Ariel, eds., *Tumors of the Breast, Chest, and Esophagus* (New York: Paul B. Hoeber, 1960), 205–213.

60. Interview with George E. Moore, M.D., November 20, 1997.

61. See, for example, Jerome A. Urban, "Radical Excision of the Chest Wall for Mammary Cancer," *Cancer* 4 (1951): 1263–1285.

62. Jerome A. Urban, "Radical Surgical Therapy of Primary Operable Breast Cancer," *Harlem Hospital Bulletin* 8, no. 2 (1955): 35–45.

63. Jerome A. Urban, "Management of Operable Breast Cancer: The Surgeon's View," *Cancer* 42 (1978): 2066–2077.

64. Jerome A. Urban, "Current Trends in Breast Cancer Treatment, Part II," *New York State Journal of Medicine* 61 (1961): 3289–3301; Umberto Veronesi and P. Valagussa, "Inefficiency of Internal Mammary Node Dissection in Breast Cancer Surgery," *Cancer* 47 (1981): 170–175.

65. George T. Pack and Edward M. Livingston, "Introduction: The Treatment of Cancer," in George T. Pack and Edward M. Livingston, eds., *Treatment of Cancer and Allied Diseases* (New York: Paul B. Hoeber, 1940), 689–755.

66. Cushman D. Haagensen, *Carcinoma of the Breast* (New York: American Cancer Society, 1950), 87, 91.

67. Military metaphors (e.g., "cobalt bomb") also surfaced in the writings of those who advocated the use of radiotherapy for breast and other cancers. See

Keith Wailoo, "Heredity, Pain, and 'Truth': Scientific Models, Clinical Negotia-
tions, and the Making of the Modern Cancer Patient," talk given at the New York
Academy of Medicine, New York, N.Y., April 11, 2000.

68. Curriculum Vitae of C. D. Haagensen, M.D., 1981, Cushman D. Haagensen
Papers, Haagensen Research Foundation, New York, N.Y.

69. Interview with Frank E. Gump, M.D., June 23, 1998.

70. Interview with Gordon F. Schwartz, M.D., January 13, 1998.

71. Raffaele Lattes, "Cushman D. Haagensen," *American Journal of Surgical Pathology*
15 (1991): 813.

72. Quoted during filming of a radical mastectomy at the annual meeting of
the American College of Surgeons, April 1971, Atlantic City, N.J. Tape courtesy of
Gordon F. Schwartz, M.D.

73. Ibid.

74. Gump interview, June 23, 1998; Rodgers interview, January 15, 1999.

75. George Crile, Jr., *The Way It Was: Sex, Surgery, Treasure and Travel, 1907–1987* (Kent,
Ohio: Kent State Univ. Press, 1992), 96.

76. Journal of George T. Pack, 178.

77. Interview with Sherwin B. Nuland, M.D., September 7, 1999.

78. Peter Kourides to Cushman D. Haagensen, June 4, 1985, and Josephine
and Dick Diefendorf to Alice M. Haagensen, n.d., Haagensen Papers. See also
Emil Goetsch and J. D. Ratcliff, "The Most Unforgettable Character I've Met,"
Reader's Digest, June 1958, pp. 126–134.

79. Cushman D. Haagensen, quoted in film of radical mastectomy, April 1971.

80. Nuland interview, September 7, 1999.

81. Nicholas Fox has argued that rituals invest surgery with a power that is
undeserved. See Nicholas J. Fox, *The Social Meaning of Surgery* (Buckingham: Open
Univ. Press, 1992), 127. See also Katz, *Scalpel's Edge*, 194–195, for a defense of
rituals.

82. Rodgers interview, January 15, 1999.

83. Marion W. Flexner, "Cancer—I've Had It," *Ladies' Home Journal*, May 1947,
pp. 57, 150.

84. Journal of George T. Pack, 137.

85. L.E. to Cushman D. Haagensen, July 30, 1959, Haagensen Papers.

86. E.P.R. to Cushman D. Haagensen, May 15, 1961, Haagensen Papers.

87. Henry W. Cave, "A Surgeon's Kindness Comes Through," in Samuel Standard and Helmuth Nathan, eds., *Should the Patient Know the Truth?* (New York:
Springer, 1955), 83–86. For an argument that patients often knew their diagnoses, see Susan E. Lederer, "Medical Ethics and the Media: Oaths, Codes and
Popular Culture," in Robert B. Baker, Linda L. Emanuel, Stephen R. Latham, and

Arthur L. Caplan, eds., *The American Medical Ethics Revolution* (Baltimore: Johns Hopkins Univ. Press, 1999), 91–103.

88. For a similar analysis, see Morantz-Sanchez, *Conduct Unbecoming*, 145–146.

89. Hugh J. Jewett, "Radical Perineal Prostatectomy for Carcinoma: An Analysis of Cases at Johns Hopkins Hospital, 1904–1954," *Journal of the American Medical Association* 156 (1954): 1039–1041.

90. Pack and Livingston, *Control of Cancer*, 689.

91. Joseph H. Farrow, quoted in "Forum: When Primary Cancer of the Breast Is Treated, Should the Second Breast Be Prophylactically Removed?," *Modern Medicine* 34 (1966): 242–260.

92. Roald M. Grant, "Prophylactic Mastectomy for Breast Cancer [Editorial]," *Ca* 16 (1966): 32.

93. T. A. Watson, "Cancer of the Breast: The Janeway Lecture–1965," *American Journal of Roentgenology, Radium Therapy & Nuclear Medicine* 96 (1966): 547–559.

94. Quoted in Gina Corea, *The Hidden Malpractice: How American Medicine Treats Women as Patients and Professionals* (New York: William Morrow, 1977), 236.

95. Richard Renneker and Max Cutler, "Psychological Problems of Adjustment to Cancer of the Breast," *Journal of the American Medical Association* 148 (1952): 833–838.

96. D. L. Weiner, "On Subcutaneous Mastectomy [Editorial]," *Plastic & Reconstructive Surgery* 49 (1972): 654–655; Nora Jacobson, *Cleavage: Technology, Controversy, and the Ironies of the Man-Made Breast* (New Brunswick, N.J.: Rutgers Univ. Press, 2000), 86.

97. George T. Pack, "Argument for Bilateral Mastectomy [Editorial]," *Surgery* 29 (1951): 929–931.

98. Henry P. Leis, Jr., "Prophylactic Removal of the Second Breast," *Hospital Medicine*, January 1968.

99. Rodgers interview, January 15, 1999.

100. Morantz-Sanchez, *Conduct Unbecoming*, 89.

Chapter 5. Biology as Fate

1. Ian MacDonald, "Biological Predeterminism in Human Cancer," *Surgery, Gynecology & Obstetrics* 92 (1951): 443–452.

2. Quoted in Jay Katz, *The Silent World of Doctor and Patient* (New York: Free Press, 1984), 180.

3. Reginald Murley, *Surgical Roots and Branches* (London: British Medical Journal, 1990), 170.

4. Ellen Leopold, *A Darker Ribbon: Breast Cancer, Women, and Their Doctors in the Twentieth Century* (Boston: Beacon Press, 1999), 278.

5. Ernest M. Daland, "Untreated Cases of Breast Cancer," *Surgery, Gynecology & Obstetrics* 44 (1927): 264–268. See also Major Greenwood, *Report on the Natural Duration of Cancer*, Reports on Public Health and Medical Subjects, no. 33 (London: Ministry of Health, 1926).

6. Quoted in Grantley W. Taylor and William P. Rogers, "Cancer of the Breast: End Results of Treatment by Radical Mastectomy at the Massachusetts General Hospital," paper presented at annual meeting of the New England Surgical Society, Portsmouth, N.H., September 23, 1961. Document available in Oliver Cope Papers, box 5AB, New England Surgical '75 folder, Countway Library, Boston, Mass.

7. Daland, "Untreated Cases," 268.

8. Quoted in Taylor and Rogers, "Cancer of the Breast."

9. Robert B. Greenough, "Variable Degrees of Malignancy of Cancer of the Breast," *Journal of Cancer Research* 9 (1925): 453–463.

10. Cushman D. Haagensen, *Diseases of the Breast* (Philadelphia: W. B. Saunders, 1956), 534–535.

11. Ibid., 535.

12. Cushman D. Haagensen, "The Treatment and Results in Cancer of the Breast at the Presbyterian Hospital, New York," *American Journal of Roentgenology and Radium Therapy* 62 (1949): 328–334.

13. My colleague Paul Edelson suggested this notion to me.

14. Cushman Haagensen and Carol Bodian, "A Personal Experience with Halsted's Radical Mastectomy," *Annals of Surgery* 199 (1984): 143–150.

15. Surgeons performing extended radical mastectomies, such as Jerome Urban, disagreed with Haagensen, believing that there was value in removing internal mammary and high axillary nodes.

16. Haagensen, *Diseases of the Breast*, 571, 720.

17. Bernard Fisher, "The Surgical Dilemma in the Primary Therapy of Invasive Breast Cancer: A Critical Appraisal," *Current Problems in Surgery*, October 1970, pp. 3–53.

18. Edward Shorter, *A Century of Radiology in Toronto* (Toronto: Wall & Emerson, 1995), 46.

19. Robert McWhirter, "The Value of Simple Mastectomy and Radiotherapy in the Treatment of Cancer of the Breast," *British Journal of Radiology* 21 (1948): 599–610.

20. Ibid., 608.

21. Ibid., 606.

22. David H. Sprong, Jr., and William F. Pollock, "The Rationale of Radical Mastectomy," *Annals of Surgery* 133 (1951): 330–343.

23. Lauren V. Ackerman, "An Evaluation of the Treatment of Cancer of the Breast at the University of Edinburgh (Scotland), under the Direction of Dr. Robert McWhirter," *Cancer* 8 (1955): 883–887.

24. Reginald Murley, "Earliest Detection and Management of Cancer," speech given to the Royal Society of Medicine, October 11, 1989, George Crile, Jr. Papers, box 4, History of Ca Breast folder, Cleveland Clinic Foundation Archives, Cleveland, Ohio.

25. Quoted in "Beyond the Knife: Pioneers of Surgery," broadcast on NOVA by the Public Broadcasting System, September 27, 1988.

26. Interview with Myron Moskowitz, M.D., July 27, 1999.

27. Quoted in "Panel Discussion on Treatment and Results in Cancer of the Breast," *American Journal of Roentgenology & Radium Therapy* 62 (1949): 349–354.

28. Ian MacDonald, "Biological Predeterminism," 443.

29. MacDonald, "A New Brand of Prohibitionism," *Surgery, Gynecology & Obstetrics* 116 (1963): 239–240.

30. Ibid., 443–452.

31. Ibid., 451.

32. W. Wallace Park and James C. Lees, "The Absolute Curability of Cancer of the Breast," *Surgery, Gynecology & Obstetrics* 93 (1951): 129–152.

33. Ibid., 152.

34. Harry M. Marks, *The Progress of Experiment: Science and Therapeutic Reform in the United States, 1900-1990* (Cambridge, England: Cambridge Univ. Press, 1997). See also John C. Burnham, "American Physicians and Tobacco Use: Two Surgeons General, 1929–1964," *Bulletin of the History of Medicine* 63 (1989): 1–31; Alvan R. Feinstein, "Two Centuries of Conflict-Collaboration Between Medicine and Mathematics," *Journal of Clinical Epidemiology* 49 (1996): 1339–1343.

35. Park and Lees, "The Absolute Curability," 141–142.

36. David Stinson, "Breast Ca Prophecy?," *Medical Post*, January 19, 1993.

37. N. E. McKinnon, "Breast Cancer Mortality, Ontario, 1909–1947: The Lack of Any Decline and Its Significance," *Canadian Journal of Public Health* 40 (1949): 257–269.

38. N. E. McKinnon, "Limitations in Diagnosis and Treatment of Breast and Other Cancers," *Canadian Medical Association Journal* 73 (1955): 614–625.

39. Ibid., 620.

40. N. E. McKinnon, "The Present Status of the Treatment and the Diagnosis of Cancer of the Breast," *Canadian Medical Association Journal* 78 (1958): 781–785. See also McKinnon, "Limitations in Diagnosis," 617.

41. Maurice M. Black and Francis D. Speer, "Biologic Variability of Breast Carcinoma in Relation to Diagnosis and Therapy," *New York State Journal of Medicine* 53 (1953): 1560–1563.

42. Maurice M. Black and Reinhard E. Zachrau, "The Use and Abuse of Therapeutic Modalities in Breast Cancer," *Preventive Medicine* 19 (1990): 723–729.

43. George Crile, Jr., *Cancer and Common Sense* (New York: Viking Press, 1955), 46.

44. George Crile, Jr., "A Plea Against Blind Fear of Cancer," Life, October 31, 1955, pp. 128–140.

45. Harvey B. Stone, "The Limitations of Radical Surgery in the Treatment of Cancer," Surgery, Gynecology & Obstetrics 97 (1953): 129–134.

46. "Some Cancer Surgery Hit," Baltimore Sun [?], March 3, 1953. In Harvey B. Stone biographical file, Alan Mason Chesney Archives, Johns Hopkins University, Baltimore, Md. See also Stone, "The Limitations of Radical Surgery," 131.

47. Bernard Fisher, "Supraradical Cancer Surgery [Editorial]," American Journal of Surgery 87 (1954): 155–159.

48. Danely P. Slaughter, "Wishful Thinking and the Cancer Patient [Editorial]," Surgery, Gynecology & Obstetrics 99 (1954): 770–772.

49. George Crile, Jr., "Breast Cancer in Perspective," unpublished manuscript, n.d., Crile Papers, box 4, Breast Cancer in Perspective folder. See also I. G. Williams, R. S. Murley, and M. P. Curwen, "Carcinoma of the Female Breast: Conservative and Radical Surgery," British Medical Journal 2 (1953): 787–796.

50. George Crile, Jr., The Way It Was: Sex, Surgery, Treasure, and Travel, 1907–1987 (Kent, Ohio: Kent State Univ. Press, 1992), 313–314.

51. Leopold, A Darker Ribbon, 134.

52. M.R. to George Crile, Jr., November 4, 1955, Crile Papers, box 13, Scrapbook on Cancer and Common Sense.

53. W.C. to George Crile, Jr., November 23, 1955, Crile Papers, box 13, Life Scrapbook.

54. John F. Raycroft to George Crile, Jr., December 21, 1955, Crile Papers, box 28, Cancer Article and Cancer and Common Sense, More Correspondence folder, 1956–7.

55. Clara Walter to George Crile, Jr., February 17, 1956, Crile Papers, box 28, Cancer Article and Cancer and Common Sense, More Correspondence folder, 1956–7.

56. D.T. to George Crile, Jr., October 29, 1955, Crile Papers, box 13, Life Scrapbook.

57. Oliver Cope, The Breast: Its Problems, Benign and Malignant, and How to Deal with Them (Boston: Houghton Mifflin, 1977), 24.

58. Ibid., 13–14. The emotional responses of women to radical mastectomy are discussed in detail in Chapter 7.

59. "Significance of Statistical Analysis of End–Results in the Treatment of Breast Cancer," in Proceedings of the Second National Cancer Conference, vol. 1 (New York: American Cancer Society, 1952), 112.

60. Ibid., 114.

61. Ibid., 120.

62. Ibid., 123.

63. Ibid., 117–118.

64. "Significance of Statistical Analysis," 124.

65. Ivan H. Smith, "The Continuing Challenge of Breast Cancer," *Canadian Medical Association Journal* 83 (1960): 1229–1233.

66. Clare G. Peterson and William W. Krippaehne, "The Treatment of Breast Cancer," *American Journal of Surgery* 102 (1961): 321–338.

67. Ian MacDonald, "The Individual Basis of Biologic Variability in Cancer," *Surgery, Gynecology & Obstetrics* 106 (1958): 227–229.

68. Francis D. Moore to George Crile, Jr., January 3, 1956, Crile Papers, box 28, Correspondence on Cancer and Common Sense folder, 1955–8.

69. Raycroft to Crile, December 21, 1955.

70. Allan M. Brandt, "Polio, Politics, Publicity, and Duplicity: Ethical Aspects in the Development of the Salk Vaccine," *Connecticut Medicine* 43 (1979): 581–590.

71. Fred W. Stewart, "Factors Influencing the Curability of Cancer," in *Proceedings of the Third National Cancer Conference* (Philadelphia: J. B. Lippincott, 1957), 62–73.

72. R. C. Harrison, A. A. W. Stanley, D. G. MacGregor, and J. Fahey, "Carcinoma of the Breast: Some Controversial Aspects," *Canadian Medical Association Journal* 77 (1957): 610–614.

73. Joseph Berkson, Stuart W. Harrington, O. Theron Clagett, John W. Kirklin, Malcolm B. Dockerty, and John R. McDonald, "Treatment of Breast Cancer: The Question of Selection," *Lancet* 2 (1958): 516–518.

74. Jerome A. Urban, "Early Diagnosis of Breast Cancer: Salvage Data with Lesions Considered Clinically Benign or Doubtful Prior to Operation," *Cancer* 9 (1956): 1173–1176.

75. Robert C. Hickey, quoted in "Mammary Cancer Trends," *Cancer* 23 (1969):767–774.

76. Black and Speer, "Biologic Variability," 1562.

77. MacDonald, "Individual Basis," 228.

78. Murray M. Copeland to Paul North, January 8, 1962, Michael B. Shimkin Papers, box 8, folder 7, Univ. of California at San Diego Library, San Diego.

79. Ibid.

80. MacDonald, "Individual Basis," 227.

81. David P. Boyd, "Biological Predeterminism," *Lahey Clinic Foundation Bulletin* 18 (1969): 135–136.

82. Isidor S. Ravdin, "The Responsibilities of the Surgeon," speech given to Alabama chapter of the ACS, Point Clear, Alabama, February 2, 1965, Isidor S. Ravdin Papers, box 122, folder 51, Univ. of Pennsylvania Archives, Philadelphia.

83. Edward F. Lewison, "An Appraisal of Long-Term Results in Surgical Treatment of Breast Cancer," *Journal of the American Medical Association* 186 (1963): 975–978.

84. L. Kreyberg, "The Significance of 'Early Diagnosis' in Breast Cancer: A Study of Some Common Usages of the Term," *British Journal of Cancer* 7 (1953): 157–165. See also H. J. B. Atkins, "Carcinoma of the Breast," *British Medical Journal* 1 (1953): 1099–1102.

85. Guy F. Robbins, John W. Berg, Irwin Bross, Caesar De Padua, and Augusto P. Sarmiento, "The Significance of Early Treatment of Breast Cancer: Changes Correlated with the Cancer Education Programs of 1940–1955," *Cancer* 12 (1959): 688–692.

86. Robert L. Egan, "Results of 2,000 Mammograms," *Cancer Bulletin* 14 (1962): 105–107.

87. David H. Patey and W. H. Dyson, "The Prognosis of Carcinoma of the Breast in Relation to the Type of Operation Performed," *British Journal of Cancer* 2 (1948): 7–13.

88. Henry P. Leis, Jr., to the author, May 14, 1997.

89. Ibid.

90. Hugh Auchincloss, "Significance of Location and Number of Axillary Metastases in Carcinoma of the Breast: A Justification for a Conservative Operation," *Annals of Surgery* 158 (1963): 37–46.

91. Ibid., 41.

92. Ibid., 45.

93. Ibid., 45.

94. Interview with Katharine L. Auchincloss, July 17, 1998.

95. Interview with David W. Kinne, M.D., September 23, 1997.

96. Leis to the author, May 14, 1997.

97. "Significance of Statistical Analysis," 140–141.

Chapter 6. Randomized Controlled Trials

1. Roald N. Grant, "Scientific Russian Roulette," *Ca* 13 (1963): 44–45.

2. Sakari Mustakallio, "Treatment of Breast Cancer by Tumor Extirpation and Roentgen Therapy Instead of Radical Operation," *Journal of the Faculty of Radiologists* 6 (1954): 23–26.

3. Reported in Carl M. Mansfield, *Early Breast Cancer: Its History and Results of Treatment* (Basel: S. Karger, 1976), 57.

4. Sigvard Kaae and Helge Johansen, "Breast Cancer. Five Year Results: Two Random Series of Simple Mastectomy with Postoperative Irradiation versus Extended Radical Mastectomy," *American Journal of Roentgenology, Radium Therapy & Nuclear Medicine* 87 (1962): 82–88.

5. See, for example, W. Ralph Deaton, "Simple Mastectomy for Carcinoma of the Breast—Reported Results," *Surgery* 37 (1955): 720–725; Dawson B. Conerly, Jr., "Simple Mastectomy in the Treatment of Carcinoma of the Breast," *Mississippi Doctor* 34 (1957): 207–211.

6. George Crile, Jr., "Simplified Treatment of Cancer of the Breast: Early Results of a Clinical Study," *Annals of Surgery* 153 (1961): 745–761.

7. Quoted in Crile, "Simplified Treatment," 759. Another frequent criticism of Crile's work was that he retrospectively upgraded the stages of cancers that recurred locally in order to conceal the limitations of simple mastectomy. On the pitfalls of staging, see Alvan R. Feinstein and Harlan Spitz, "The Epidemiology of Cancer Therapy: I. Clinical Problems of Statistical Surveys," *Archives of Internal Medicine* 123 (1969): 171–186.

8. Crile, "Simplified Treatment," 757.

9. Interview with Roger S. Foster, Jr., M.D., February 13, 1997.

10. Simmons S. Smith and Alfred C. Meyer, "Cancer of the Breast in Rockford, Illinois," *American Journal of Surgery* 98 (1959): 653–656.

11. For an explanation of this "natural experiment," see M. B. Shimkin, M. Koppel, R. R. Connelly, and S. J. Cutler, "Simple and Radical Mastectomy for Breast Cancer: A Re-analysis of Smith and Meyer's Report from Rockford, Illinois," *Journal of the National Cancer Institute* 27 (1961): 1197–1215.

12. Smith and Meyer, "Cancer of the Breast," 655.

13. "Cover Legend," *Cancer Research* 30 (1970): ii.

14. Shimkin et al., "Simple and Radical Mastectomy," 1214.

15. Ibid., 1214.

16. Paul Meier, "Statistics and Medical Experimentation," *Biometrics* 31 (1975): 511–529; Henry Sacks, Sherman Kupfer, and Thomas C. Chalmers, "Are Uncontrolled Clinical Studies Ever Justified? [Letter to the Editor]," *New England Journal of Medicine* 303 (1980): 1067.

17. On the tension between clinical research and patient care, see David J. Rothman, *Strangers at the Bedside: A History of How Law and Bioethics Transformed Medical Decision Making* (New York: Basic Books, 1991), 101–126.

18. Ilana Lowy, *Between Bench and Bedside: Science, Healing, and Interleukin-2 in a Cancer Ward* (Cambridge, Mass.: Harvard Univ. Press, 1996), 48–50; Harry M. Marks, *The Progress of Experiment: Science and Therapeutic Reform in the United States, 1900–1990* (Cambridge, England: Cambridge Univ. Press, 1997), 133–134.

19. Marks, *The Progress of Experiment*, 128.

20. Abraham M. Lilienfeld, "Ceteris Paribus: The Evolution of the Clinical Trial," *Bulletin of the History of Medicine* 56 (1982): 1–18.

21. J. C. Goligher, "Controlled Trial of Vagotomy and Gastro-enterostomy, Vagotomy and Antrectomy, and Subtotal Gastrectomy in Elective Treatment of Duodenal Ulcer: Interim Report," *British Medical Journal* 1 (1964): 455–460. See also Lowy, *Between Bench and Bedside*, 53; Marks, *The Progress of Experiment*, 121–128, 161.

22. Quoted in "Radical or Simple Mastectomy? [Editorial]," *Journal of the American Medical Association* 178 (1961): 934.

23. George E. Moore, "A Plea for Valid Assessment of Surgical Therapy: The Value of Controlled, Cooperative Clinical Trials," *Surgery* 48 (1960): 481–484.

24. "Radical or Simple Mastectomy?," 934. The original text of this editorial is available in the Michael B. Shimkin Papers, University of California at San Diego Library.

25. J. B. Aust to Owen H. Wangensteen, October 13, 1961, Isidor S. Ravdin Papers, box 35, folder 3, Univ. of Pennsylvania Archives, Philadelphia.

26. Michael B. Shimkin to Isidor S. Ravdin, December 13, 1961, Ravdin Papers, box 35, folder 3.

27. Joseph L. Dennis to Michael B. Shimkin, November 29, 1961, Ravdin Papers, box 35, folder 3.

28. John M. Howard to Michael B. Shimkin, September 8, 1961, Ravdin Papers, box 35, folder 3.

29. Quoted in "A 'Fair Trial' for Simple Mastectomy," *Medical World News*, November 24, 1961, pp. 47–48.

30. Isidor S. Ravdin to Michael B. Shimkin, December 16, 1961, Ravdin Papers, box 35, folder 3.

31. "A 'Fair Trial,' " 47.

32. The terms "clinical expertise" and "clinical science" come from Deborah R. Gordon, "Clinical Science and Clinical Expertise: Changing Boundaries Between Art and Science in Medicine," in Margaret Lock and Deborah R. Gordon, eds., *Biomedicine Examined* (Dordrecht: Kluwer Academic Publishers, 1988), 257–295. See also Theresa Montini and Kathleen Slobin, "Tensions Between Good Science and Good Practice: Lagging Behind and Leapfrogging Ahead Along the Cancer Care Continuum," *Research in the Sociology of Health Care* 9 (1991): 127–140; Theodore M. Porter, *Trust in Numbers: The Pursuit of Objectivity in Science and Public Life* (Princeton, N.J.: Princeton Univ. Press, 1995).

33. Roald N. Grant, "There Are Few Agnostics in Operating Rooms [Editorial]," *Ca* 12 (1962): 81.

34. Ibid., 81.

35. Interview with Gordon F. Schwartz, M.D., January 13, 1998.

36. "Statement Re: Cancer of the Breast," unpublished manuscript, [1970], American Cancer Society, Media Division, New York, N.Y., Breast Cancer Surgery Controversy folder.

37. On the often contradictory uses of the terms "radical" and "conservative," see Gert H. Brieger, "From Conservative to Radical Surgery in Late Nineteenth-Century America," in Christopher Lawrence, ed., *Medical Theory, Surgical Practice: Studies in the History of Surgery* (London: Routledge, 1992), 216–231; Robert L. Martensen, "When the 'Truly Conservative' Went 'Radical': The Genesis, Development, and Persistence of the Radical Mastectomy as a Curative Treatment for Breast Cancer," paper presented at the New York Academy of Medicine, New York, N.Y., June 1, 1998.

38. Cushman D. Haagensen, "Surgical Treatment of Breast Cancer," unpublished manuscript, n.d., Cushman D. Haagensen Papers, Haagensen Research Foundation, New York, N.Y. On the claim that experience constitutes proof, see Joan W. Scott, "The Evidence of Experience," in James Chandler, Arnold I. Davidson, and Harry Harootunian, eds., *Questions of Evidence* (Chicago: Univ. of Chicago Press, 1994), 363–387. See also Christopher Sellers, "Discovering Environmental Cancer: Wilhelm Hueper, Post–World War II Epidemiology, and the Vanishing Clinician's Eye," *American Journal of Public Health* 87 (1997): 1824–1835.

39. Don Marquis has termed this interaction the "therapeutic obligation" of physician to patient. See Don Marquis, "An Ethical Problem Concerning Recent Therapeutic Research on Breast Cancer," *Hypatia* 4, no. 2 (1989): 140–155.

40. Clare G. Peterson and William W. Krippaehne, "The Treatment of Breast Cancer," *American Journal of Surgery* 102 (1961): 321–338. Cushman Haagensen would later condemn studies of lumpectomy and simple mastectomy as "human experimentation" in, of all places, his C.V. See C. D. Haagensen, "Curriculum Vitae," [1980], Haagensen Papers.

41. Interview with Guy F. Robbins, M.D., August 18, 1982, Memorial Sloan-Kettering Cancer Center Oral History Project, courtesy of Nancy Orr.

42. Harry M. Marks, "Notes from the Underground: The Social Organization of Therapeutic Research," in Russell C. Maulitz and Diana E. Long, eds., *Grand Rounds: One Hundred Years of Internal Medicine* (Philadelphia: Univ. of Pennsylvania Press, 1988), 297–336.

43. Interview with Donald J. Ferguson, M.D., April 25, 1998.

44. Guy F. Robbins, "Controversies Concerning Breast Cancer," unpublished manuscript, n.d., courtesy of Nancy Orr.

45. See, for example, Jay Katz, *The Silent World of Doctor and Patient* (New York: Free Press, 1984), 165–206; Paul Atkinson, "Training for Certainty," *Social Science and Medicine* 19 (1984): 949–956.

46. Joan Cassell, *Expected Miracles: Surgeons at Work* (Philadelphia: Temple Univ. Press, 1991), 57.

47. Interview with C. Barber Mueller, M.D., December 30, 1998.

48. William Morris, ed., *The American Heritage Dictionary of the English Language* (Boston: Houghton Mifflin, 1975).

49. Mary Douglas, *Risk and Blame: Essays in Cultural Theory* (London: Routledge, 1992), 11, 13.

50. Ibid., 12.

51. Barbara A. Koenig and Alan S. Stockdale, "The Promise of Molecular Medicine in Preventing Disease: Examining the Burden of Genetic Risk," in Daniel Callahan, ed., *Health Promotion and Disease Prevention: Ethical and Social Dilemmas* (Washington, D.C.: Georgetown Univ. Press, 2000).

52. Alan R. Peterson and Deborah Lupton, *The New Public Health: Health and Self in the Age of Risk* (London: Sage Publications, 1996), xiii.

53. Allan M. Brandt, "Blow Some My Way: Passive Smoking, Risk and American Culture," in S. Lock, L. A. Reynolds, and E. M. Tansey, *Ashes to Ashes: The History of Smoking and Health* (Amsterdam: Rodopi, 1998), 164–191.

54. Ibid., 171. See also Charles E. Rosenberg, "Banishing Risk: Continuity and Change in the Moral Management of Disease," in Allan M. Brandt and Paul Rozin, eds., *Morality and Health* (London: Routledge, 1997). Risk experts Amos Tversky and Daniel Kahneman have described this behavior as "loss aversion." In the case of breast cancer, surgeons believed in doing everything they could to avoid the loss of life. See Peter L. Bernstein, *Against the Gods: The Remarkable Story of Risk* (New York: John Wiley & Sons, 1996), 224.

55. Charlotte George, "I'm Glad I Had My Breast Removed," *Today's Health*, August 1957, pp. 50–51.

56. Quoted in Ira S. Goldenberg, John C. Bailar III, Mark A. Hayes, and Ruth Lowry, "Female Breast Cancer: A Re-Evaluation," *Transactions of the American Surgical Association* 79 (1961): 93–103.

57. Mark M. Ravitch, "Alternatives to Halstedian Radical Mastectomy," *Medical Times* 99 (1971): 119–120, 123. For a fascinating look at how surgeons "excise" risk, see Sandra M. Gifford, "The Meaning of Lumps: A Case Study in the Ambiguities of Risk and Benign Breast Disease," Ph.D. diss., Univ. of California at San Francisco, 1986.

58. Jerome J. DeCosse, "Is the Demise of Radical Mastectomy Premature?," *Surgery* 89 (1981): 398–399.

59. Quoted in L. H. Garland, "The Rationale and Results of Simple Mastectomy Plus Radiotherapy in Primary Cancer of the Breast," *American Journal of Roentgenology, Radium Therapy & Nuclear Medicine* 72 (1954): 923–941.

60. Douglass G. Whitney, Roger F. Smith, and D. Emerick Szilagyi, "Meaning of Five-Year Cure in Cancer of the Breast," *Archives of Surgery* 88 (1964): 637–644.

61. Alvan R. Feinstein has argued that patients have less chagrin in the face of a bad outcome if they have tried all possible alternatives. See Alvan R. Feinstein, "The 'Chagrin Factor' and Qualitative Decision Analysis," *Archives of Internal Medicine* 145 (1985): 1257–1259.

62. "Mastectomy Study: How Relevant?," *Medical World News*, July 7, 1972, pp. 23, 29–30.

63. *The Today Show*, January 24, 1973, film courtesy of Xenia Urban.

64. "Controversies in Managing Breast Cancer," Audio-Digest Foundation. In *Surgery* 18 no. 1, January 13, 1971.

65. Mueller interview, December 30, 1998.

66. Quoted in Allan M. Brandt, "Polio, Politics, Publicity, and Duplicity: Ethical Aspects in the Development of the Salk Vaccine," *Connecticut Medicine* 43 (1979): 581–590.

67. Lawrence G. Crowley, "Is Radical Mastectomy the Best Treatment for Primary Carcinoma of the Breast?,"*California Medicine* 113 (1970): 46–54. See especially Table 5 on p. 50.

68. Quoted in "Mastectomy Study," 23.

69. Cushman D. Haagensen, "A Great Leap Backward in the Treatment of Carcinoma of the Breast," *Journal of the American Medical Association* 224 (1973): 1181–1183.

70. "Controversies in Managing Breast Cancer."

71. Loren J. Humphrey and William G. Hammond, "Treatment of Primary Breast Cancer: Changes Without Improvement [Editorial]," *Archives of Surgery* 104 (1972): 260–261.

72. See, for example, "Controversies in Breast Cancer," Medical Radio Network, n.d., courtesy of the Cleveland Clinic Foundation Archives.

73. See, for example, Herbert W. Meyer, "Modes of Breast–Cancer Spread: They Determine Treatment and Diagnosis," *Ca* 1 (1950): 17–31.

74. Interview with Leslie Wise, M.D., December 11, 1997.

75. George Crile, Jr., *The Way It Was: Sex, Surgery, Treasure, and Travel, 1907–1987* (Kent, Ohio: Kent State Univ. Press, 1992), 323.

76. Ibid., 339.

77. Wyman E. Jacobson, "Cancer of the Breast," *Modern Medicine* 36 (1968): 61–78. Of note, it was not specified whether some of the radical operations in this survey were modified. See also Karen Schachter and Duncan Neuhauser, "Case Study #17: Surgery for Breast Cancer," in *The Implications of Cost-Effectiveness*

Analysis of Medical Technology (Washington, D.C.: Office of Technology Assessment, 1981), 3–29.

78. Edward Shorter, *A Century of Radiology in Toronto* (Toronto: Wall & Emerson, 1995), 49–52.

79. Ibid., 53.

80. M. Vera Peters, "Wedge Resection and Irradiation: An Effective Treatment in Early Breast Cancer," *Journal of the American Medical Association* 200 (1967): 144–145.

81. Interview with Jennifer Ingram, M.D., May 6, 1994, M. Vera Peters Papers, folder 2.2.4, Princess Margaret Hospital Archives, Toronto, Canada.

82. Ingram Interview, May 6, 1994.

83. M. Vera Peters, "The Conservative Management of Breast Cancer," unpublished manuscript, 1974. M. Vera Peters Papers, box 2, folder 1974, University of Toronto Archives, Toronto, Canada.

84. Peters, "Wedge Resection and Irradiation"; Shorter, *A Century of Radiology*, 55.

85. Leslie Wise, Aubrey Y. Mason, and Lauren V. Ackerman, "Local Excision and Irradiation: An Alternative Method for the Treatment of Early Mammary Cancer," *Annals of Surgery* 174 (1971): 392–401.

86. R. E. Qualheim and E. A. Gall, "Breast Carcinoma with Multiple Sites of Origin," *Cancer* 10 (1957): 460–468.

87. "Policy Statement on Mastectomy vs More Conservative Procedures," February 1971, ACS Archives, Media Division, Breast Cancer Surgery Controversy folder.

88. John P. Bunker, "Surgical Manpower: A Comparison of Operations and Surgeons in the United States and in England and Wales," *New England Journal of Medicine* 282 (1970): 135–144; George Crile, Jr., to Babette Rosmond, May 1, 1973, Babette Rosmond Papers, Boston, Mass., courtesy of James Stone.

89. Diana Brinkley and J. L. Haybittle, "Treatment of Stage-II Carcinoma of the Female Breast," *Lancet* 2 (1971): 1086–1087; Hedley Atkins, J. L. Hayward, D. J. Klugman, and A. B. Wayte, "Treatment of Early Breast Cancer: A Report After Ten Years of a Clinical Trial," *British Medical Journal* 2 (1972): 423–429.

90. Umberto Veronesi to the author, July 16, 1999.

91. Bernard Fisher, "The Surgical Dilemma in the Primary Therapy of Invasive Breast Cancer: A Critical Appraisal," *Current Problems in Surgery*, October 1970, pp. 3–53.

92. Carolyn Focht, "Treatment Attacked by Cleveland Doctor," *Columbus Dispatch*, October 15, 1970, p. 17A.

93. "Controversies in Managing Breast Cancer," January 13, 1971, which is an audiotape of the October 14, 1970, program.

94. Ibid.

95. Dennis Connaughton, *Warren Cole, MD and the Ascent of Scientific Surgery* (Chicago: Warren and Clara Cole Foundation, 1991), 149–154.

96. Fisher, "The Surgical Dilemma," 39; Fisher, "The Revolution in Breast Cancer Surgery: Science or Anecdotalism?," *World Journal of Surgery* 9 (1985): 655–666.

97. George E. Moore to the author, October 30, 1997.

98. The group eventually studied chemotherapy in breast and colon cancer, hence the name.

99. Morris, *The American Heritage Dictionary*.

100. "Controversies in Managing Breast Cancer," January 13, 1971.

101. Fisher, "The Surgical Dilemma," 46.

102. Bernard Fisher, "Primary Breast Cancer: Some Considerations Regarding Its Management," *Surgery Annual* 3 (1971): 227–248.

103. Bernard Fisher, "The Biological and Clinical Justification for Relegating Radical Breast Cancer Operations to the Archives of Surgical History," *Debates in Clinical Surgery* 1 (1990): 14–26.

104. Ibid., 14.

105. Edmund A. Gehan and Emil J. Freireich, "Non-Randomized Controls in Cancer Clinical Trials," *New England Journal of Medicine* 290 (1974): 198–203. It should be noted that those doing retrospective studies that favored radical mastectomy were also doing scientific work.

106. Minutes of the Breast Cancer Task Force of the National Cancer Institute, February 17, 1967. Obtained from the NCI through a Freedom of Information Act.

107. Bernard Fisher to Isidor Ravdin, November 2, 1965, Ravdin Papers, box 15, folder 3.

108. "Controversies in Managing Breast Cancer," January 13, 1971.

109. Kathryn M. Taylor, Richard G. Margolese, and Colin L. Soskolne, "Physicians' Reasons for Not Entering Eligible Patients in a Randomized Clinical Trial of Surgery for Breast Cancer," *New England Journal of Medicine* 310 (1984): 1363–1367.

110. Quoted during filming of a radical mastectomy performed at the annual meeting of the American College of Surgeons, April 1971, Atlantic City, N.J., tape courtesy of Gordon F. Schwartz, M.D.

Chapter 7. Patients in Revolt

1. C.C. to Babette Rosmond, February 3, 1972, Babette Rosmond Papers, Boston, Mass. courtesy of James Stone.

2. Leslie Reagan, "Projecting Breast Cancer," paper presented at conference on Gender, Science and Health in Post-War North America, Toronto, Canada, March 5–6, 1999.

3. Peter A. Nelson, Robert L. Schmitz, Eugene Narsete, and Jen H. Chao, "Present Trends in Cancer Surgery," Surgical Clinics of North America 32 (1952): 195–204.

4. Interview with Jimmie C. Holland, M.D., February 25, 1999.

5. G. W. Horsley and J. T. Gianoulis, "Carcinoma of Breast," Virginia Medical Monthly 84 (1957): 12–16.

6. Regina Morantz-Sanchez, Conduct Unbecoming a Woman: Medicine on Trial in Turn-of-the-Century Brooklyn (New York: Oxford Univ. Press, 1999), 144.

7. Barbara Seaman, "Beyond the Halsted Radical," On the Issues, Fall 1997, pp. 48–49, 56–57.

8. Terese Lasser, Reach to Recovery (New York: Simon and Schuster, 1972), 149.

9. Guy S. Robbins, "Controversies in Managing Breast Cancer," Audio-Digest Foundation. In Surgery, 18, no. 1, January 13, 1971.

10. Seaman, "Beyond the Halsted Radical," 48.

11. Letter to Betty Ford, September 29, 1974, Betty Ford Papers, box 26, folder 3, Gerald R. Ford Presidential Library, Ann Arbor, Mich.

12. Audiotape of Phil Donahue Show, April 16, 1974, courtesy of Cleveland Clinic Foundation Archives.

13. Letter to Betty Ford, January 28, 1975, Ford Papers, box 26, Correspondence folder, 2/1/75–2/15/75.

14. Sylvia S. Seaman, Always a Woman: What Every Woman Should Know About Breast Surgery (New York: Argonaut Books, 1965).

15. Richard Renneker and Max Cutler, "Psychological Problems of Adjustment to Cancer of the Breast," Journal of the American Medical Association 148 (1952): 833–838.

16. Walter S. Ross, "Still a Woman," Reader's Digest, March 1969, pp. 165–170.

17. David Schottenfeld and Guy F. Robbins, "Quality of Survival Among Patients Who Have Had Radical Mastectomy," Cancer 26 (1970): 650–655.

18. For example, early investigators assumed that the postoperative psychological problems resulted from the extensive nature of the radical mastectomy. Later research, however, would suggest that a more important factor was having been diagnosed with a life-threatening disease. See Wendy S. Schain, Teresa M. d'Angelo, Marsha E. Dunn, Allen S. Lichter, and Lori J. Pierce, "Mastectomy versus Conservative Surgery and Radiation Therapy," Cancer 73 (1994): 1221–1228.

19. Patrick B. Friel, Glen C. Nicolay, and Ludwig M. Frank, "Adverse Emotional Reactions to Disfigurative Surgery: Detection and Management," Connecticut Medicine 31 (1967): 277–281.

20. Ibid., 279.

21. Ibid., 280.

22. Sue Wilkinson and Celia Kitzinger, "Whose Breast Is It Anyway? A Feminist Consideration of Advice and 'Treatment' for Breast Cancer," *Women's Studies International Forum* 16 (1993): 229–238.

23. Maryel Locke, "An Operation," unpublished manuscript, December 1995, courtesy of Maryel Locke.

24. "A Medical Maverick," *MGH News*, May 1994, p. 2.

25. Oliver Cope, *Man, Mind and Medicine:The Doctor's Education* (Philadelphia: Lippincott, 1968).

26. Oliver Cope, "Unnecessary Surgery and Technical Competence: Irreconcilables in the Graduate Training of the Surgeon," *American Journal of Surgery* 110 (1965): 119–123.

27. Oliver Cope, *The Breast: Its Problems, Benign and Malignant, and How to Deal with Them* (Boston: Houghton Mifflin, 1977).

28. Oliver Cope, "Breast Cancer: Has the Time Come for a Less Mutilating Treatment?," *Radcliffe Quarterly*, June 1970, pp. 6–11.

29. Fredelle Maynard, "Breast Cancer: Is There an Alternative to Surgery?," *Woman's Day*, October 1970, pp. 6, 118–122.

30. James C. Petersen and Gerald E. Markle, "Controversies in Science and Technology," in Daryl E. Chubin and Ellen W. Chu, *Science Off the Pedestal* (Belmont, Calif.: Wadsworth Publishing, 1989), 5–18.

31. Despite his revelations about surgical practice, Nolen was criticized by feminists for sexist remarks. See Ellen Frankfort, *Vaginal Politics* (New York: Quadrangle Books, Inc., 1972), 7.

32. William A. Nolen to William Hines, April 7, 1971, George Crile, Jr. Papers, box 48, Barney Correspondence folder, 1971, Cleveland Clinic Foundation Archives, Cleveland, Ohio.

33. William A. Nolen, "The Operation Women Fear Most," *McCall's*, April 1971, pp. 52–56.

34. George Crile, Jr., to Babette Rosmond, November 29, 1971, Rosmond Papers.

35. Maryel F. Locke to Sidney L. Arje, April 12, 1971, American Cancer Society, Media Division, New York, N.Y., Breast Cancer Surgery Controversy folder.

36. Marilyn Yalom, *A History of the Breast* (New York: Alfred A. Knopf, 1998), 242–243.

37. Elizabeth Wainstock and Kathleen Shortridge, "Woman Doctors and the Male Medical Mystique," *Her Self*, September 1972, p. 12.

38. Camilla Cracchiolo to Rose Kushner, September 9, 1975, Rose Kushner Papers, box 6, Correspondence folder, 1975, Schlesinger Library, Cambridge, Mass.

39. Barbara Seaman, *The Doctors' Case Against the Pill* (New York: Peter H. Wyden, 1969).

40. Eileen Shanahan, "Women Unionists Back Equal Right Plan: Doctor Alleges Unnecessary Surgery by Men," *New York Times*, September 15, 1970, p. 33.

41. Oliver Cope, "Mutilating Surgery: The Need for Women's Perspectives in Medicine," talk given at annual meeting of the American Association for the Advancement of Science, March 1, 1974, San Francisco, Calif., Oliver Cope Papers, box 5AB, Personal AAAS folder, Countway Library, Boston, Mass.

42. Ellen Leopold, book review of *Waking Up, Fighting Back: The Politics of Breast Cancer* by Roberta Altman, *The Nation*, December 9, 1996.

43. "Rosamond Campion: Her Cancerous Times," n.d., Rosmond Papers.

44. Rosamond Campion, *The Invisible Worm: A Woman's Right to Choose an Alternate to Radical Surgery* (New York: Macmillan, 1972), 13. See also M.A. to Babette Rosmond, March 30, 1971, Rosmond Papers.

45. Judy Klemesrud, "New Voice in Debate on Breast Surgery," *New York Times*, December 12, 1972, p. 56.

46. Campion, *Invisible Worm*, 33.

47. Ibid., 45.

48. Ruth R. Faden and Tom L. Beauchamp, *A History and Theory of Informed Consent* (New York: Oxford Univ. Press, 1986), 125.

49. Jay Katz, *The Silent World of Doctor and Patient* (New York: Free Press, 1984).

50. Campion, *Invisible Worm*, 57.

51. Klemesrud, "New Voice," 56.

52. Marie F. Gately to the Editor of *Ca*, January 28, 1974, Cope Papers, box 7AB, accordion folder, letter "C."

53. Rosamond Campion, "Five Years Later: No Regrets," *McCall's*, June 1976, pp. 113, 150.

54. Barbara Abel, "Surgery Only Way?," *Seattle Times*, July 15, 1973; Mary Lou Moser, "'When You've Seen One Breast Surgeon, You Haven't Seen Them All,'" *The Oregonian*, June 27, 1972.

55. Theresa Montini and Sheryl Ruzek, "Overturning Orthodoxy: The Emergence of Breast Cancer Treatment Policy," *Research in the Sociology of Health Care* 8 (1989): 3–32.

56. Frankfort, *Vaginal Politics*, 137.

57. Dorothy Shinder, *Mayhem on Women* (San Rafael, Calif.: Ombudswoman, 1972), preface.

58. Ibid., 80–82, 89. On downtown versus uptown feminism, see Elizabeth S. Watkins, *On the Pill: A Social History of Oral Contraceptives, 1950–1970* (Baltimore: Johns Hopkins Univ. Press, 1998), 130.

59. I.I. to Babette Rosmond, January 23, 1973, Rosmond Papers.

60. Betty Isaac, *A Breast for Life* (Hicksville, N.Y.: Exposition Press, 1974), 25.

61. Win Ann Winkler, *Post Mastectomy: A Personal Guide to Physical and Emotional Recovery* (New York: Hawthorn Books, 1976), 44, 174 (emphasis in original).

62. "Women's Attitudes Regarding Breast Cancer: Summary," Gallup survey, October 1973, p. 10, box 9–1841, American Cancer Society Archives, Atlanta, Ga.

63. Ibid., 9.

64. Era B. Thompson, "I Was a Cancer Coward," *Ebony*, September 1971, pp. 64–71; Bob Lucas, "Minnie Riperton," *Ebony*, December 1976, pp. 33–42.

65. Sis. Cherry, "Wanted: a Choice of Treatment," *Black News*, January 1973, pp. 2–6, Rosmond Papers.

66. Jeanne Campbell, "A Story to be Told," *Borderline Magazine*, February 1987, Kushner Papers, box 8, unlabeled folder.

67. Evryl E. Fisher to Madeleine van Biljon, November 12, 1980, Vera M. Peters Papers, box 2, Breast Cancer Press Clippings folder, Univ. of Toronto Archives, Toronto.

68. George Crile, Jr., "Breast Cancer: A Patient's Bill of Rights," *Ms.*, September 1973, pp. 66–70, 94–97.

69. E.D. to Babette Rosmond, February 9, 1972, Rosmond Papers.

70. A.N. to Babette Rosmond, August 15, 1973, Rosmond Papers. The Lourdes reference is from Philip Nobile, "King Cancer," *Esquire*, June 1974.

71. Interview with Avram E. Cooperman, M.D., February 13, 1998.

72. B.H. to Babette Rosmond, January 19, 1972, Rosmond Papers.

73. V.W. to Babette Rosmond, September 19, 1972, Rosmond Papers.

74. D.M. to Babette Rosmond, March 18, 1972, Rosmond Papers.

75. B.R. to Babette Rosmond, September 19, 1975, Rosmond Papers.

76. M.M. to Babette Rosmond, February 1, 1972, Rosmond Papers.

77. S.S. to Babette Rosmond, March 12, 1972, Rosmond Papers.

78. D.M. to Rosmond, March 18, 1972.

79. The letters from E.P. to Babette Rosmond are dated July 13, 1972, January 20, 1973, June 22, 1974, and February 28, 1975.

80. Isaac, *A Breast for Life*, 28.

81. Letter to Betty Ford, February 9, 1975, Ford Papers, box 26, Correspondence folder, 3/1/75–3/18/75.

82. Jack Star, "How Silastic Transformed Breast Surgery," *Look*, July 27, 1971, p. 12.

83. D.G. to the Macmillan Company, January 15, 1975, Rosmond Papers.

84. B.P. to Babette Rosmond, January 29, 1976, Rosmond Papers.

85. A.C. to Babette Rosmond, 1981, Rosmond Papers.

86. S.M. to Babette Rosmond, 1973, Rosmond Papers.

87. G.M. to *McCall's* magazine, January 26, 1972, Crile Papers, box 48, Barney Correspondence folder, 1971.

88. G.C. Little, "The Gift of Fear," *Good Housekeeping*, March 1973, pp. 26–34.

89. *The Phil Donahue Show*, April 16, 1974.

90. Stanley Edelman, "Is the Radical Mastectomy Operation Obsolete?," *Medical Counterpoint*, September 1973, pp. 15–17, 20, 25, 29, 32.

91. F. Gordon King to Betty Rollin, December 15, 1977, Betty Rollin Papers, box 7, folder 1, State Historical Society of Wisconsin, Madison.

92. Montini and Ruzek, "Overturning Orthodoxy," 15; Dutzu Rosner, Ramez N. Bedwani, Josef Vana, Harvey W. Baker, and Gerald P. Murphy, "Noninvasive Breast Carcinoma: Results of a National Survey by the American College of Surgeons," *Annals of Surgery* 192 (1980): 139–147.

93. *The David Susskind Show*, January 21, 1973, tape courtesy of Xenia Urban.

94. "Breast Cancer Update," Audio–Digest Foundation. In *Obstetrics and Gynecology* 22, no. 7, April 8, 1975.

95. Irving M. Ariel, "The Treatment of Breast Cancer by Radical and Super Radical Mastectomy," *Resident & Staff Physician*, September 1978, pp. 57–62.

96. Interview with William P. Longmire, Jr., M.D., December 14, 1998.

97. Interview with Helga Sandburg Crile, October 11, 1996; interview with Gordon F. Schwartz, M.D., January 13, 1998.

98. "Controversies in Managing Breast Cancer," January 13, 1971.

99. George Crile, Jr., to Julius Wolkin, October 12, 1972, Crile Papers, box 48, Barney Correspondence folder, 1971. See also Montini and Ruzek, "Overturning Orthodoxy," 22; K. McPherson and Maurice S. Fox, "Treatment of Breast Cancer," in John P. Bunker, Benjamin A. Barnes, and Frederick Mosteller, eds., *Costs, Risks, and Benefits of Surgery* (New York: Oxford Univ. Press, 1977), 308–322.

100. Gerald P. Murphy to Rose Kushner, September 3, 1975, Kushner Papers, box 6, Correspondence folder, 1975.

101. Nobile, "King Cancer," 205.

102. M.P. to Babette Rosmond, February 12, 1973, Rosmond Papers.

103. Max R. Gaspar to George Crile, Jr., July 11, 1989, Crile Papers, box 48, Barney's Correspondence folder, 1989.

104. Interview with Cooperman, February 13, 1998.

105. Interview with Sherwin B. Nuland, M.D., September 7, 1999.

106. J.P. Wilson, "Mastectomy, Yes, But Which One?," *Journal of the Medical Association of Georgia* 63 (1974): 407–409.

107. Arthur I. Holleb, "Response to Demands for Patient Participation in the Treatment Selection: A Panel Discussion," in H. Stephen Gallagher, ed., *Early Breast Cancer: Detection and Treatment* (New York: John Wiley & Sons, 1975), 145–150.

108. "How Radical (Must) (Should) Mastectomy Be in Early Breast Cancer?," *Medical World News*, March 3, 1972, pp. 38–49.

109. S.T. to Babette Rosmond, February 17, 1972, Rosmond Papers.

110. William A. Nolen, "How Doctors Are Unfair to Women," *McCall's*, August 1973, pp. 50, 52.

111. Ariel, "The Treatment of Breast Cancer," 62. See also Gately to Editor of *Ca*, January 28, 1974.

112. The following quotations come from *The David Susskind Show*, January 21, 1973.

113. "How Radical (Must) (Should) Mastectomy Be," 49.

114. Arthur I. Holleb to Adele Paroni, December 22, 1978, ACS, Media Division, Breast Cancer Surgery Controversy folder.

115. Nuland interview, September 7, 1999.

116. Interview with Francis D. Moore, M.D., June 19, 1997.

117. Oliver Cope to W. Gerald Austen, July 9, 1972, Cope Papers, box 3AB, Dr. Roy Wirthlin folder.

118. *The Today Show*, January 24, 1973. At other times, Crile was critical of the ACS statement.

119. Theodore Adams to Eleanor Friede, August 31, 1972, Rosmond Papers.

120. Sidney L. Arje, "Conservative or Radical—The American Cancer Society's Viewpoint," talk given at Conference on Breast Cancer—Detection, Management, Rehabilitation, March 10–11, 1971, ACS, Media Division, Breast Cancer Surgery Controversy folder.

121. Nolen to Hines, April 7, 1971.

122. Interview with Frank E. Gump, M.D., June 23, 1998.

123. *The David Susskind Show*, January 21, 1973.

124. Regina Morantz, "The Perils of Feminist History," *Journal of Interdisciplinary History* 4 (1974): 649–660. See also Regina Morantz-Sanchez, *Conduct Unbecoming a Woman: Medicine on Trial in Turn-of-the-Century Brooklyn* (New York: Oxford Univ. Press, 1999), 255.

Chapter 8. Rose Kushner and Breast Cancer Activism

1. Shirley Temple Black, "Don't Sit Home and Be Afraid," *McCall's*, February 1973, pp. 82–83, 114–116.

2. Gerald Caplan, "An Outpouring of Love for Shirley Temple Black," *McCall's*, March 1973, pp. 48–54.

3. Ellen Leopold, *A Darker Ribbon: Breast Cancer, Women, and Their Doctors in the Twentieth Century* (Boston: Beacon Press, 1999), 231.

4. Black, "Don't Sit Home," 114.

5. Sandra Blakeslee, "Shirley Temple Makes Plea Again," *New York Times*, November 9, 1972, p. 52.

6. "Betty Ford's Operation," *Newsweek*, October 7, 1974, pp. 30–33. See also Betty Ford and Isabelle Shelton, "It Feels Like I've Been Reborn," *McCall's*, February 1975, pp. 98–99, 142–143; White House Press Conference, September 28, 1974, John W. Roberts Papers, box 4, Betty Ford Cancer Surgery folder, Gerald R. Ford Presidential Library, Ann Arbor, Mich.

7. Ford and Shelton, "It Feels Like I've Been Reborn," 142.

8. "A Hectic Week for Breast Cancer Researchers," *Medical World News*, October 25, 1974, pp. 19–22.

9. Isabelle Shelton, "Encouragement, Prayers, Hope in Letters to Betty Ford," *Star-News*, October 1974. In Sheila Weidenfeld Papers, box 2, Breast Surgery folder (2), Ford Library.

10. In Betty Ford Papers, box 25, Correspondence folder, 10/22/74–10/31/74, Ford Library.

11. E.R. to Betty Rollin, May 7, 1978, Betty Rollin Papers, box 6, folder 7, State Historical Society of Wisconsin, Madison.

12. "Coping with Cancer," *Time*, October 14, 1974, p. 80.

13. "Happy's Brush with Cancer," *Newsweek*, October 28, 1974, p. 29.

14. The diagnosis and treatment of carcinoma in situ is discussed in Chapter 9.

15. Margaretta Rockefeller and Eleanor Harris, "If It Should Happen to You," *Reader's Digest*, May 1976, pp. 131–134. See also "Urban's Double Check," *Time*, December 9, 1974, pp. 90, 93.

16. White House Press Conference, September 28, 1974.

17. Concerned Buffalo Women to Betty Ford, October 1974, Ford Papers, box 25, Correspondence folder, 11/1/74–11/7/74.

18. Rose Kushner to L.H. Fountain, June 1, 1977, Rose Kushner Papers, box 1, unlabeled manila folder, Schlesinger Library, Cambridge, Mass.

19. Rose Kushner to Bernie, September 25, 1974, Kushner Papers, box 6, Correspondence folder, 1974.

20. Rose Kushner, "Informed Consent," unpublished manuscript, February 22, 1982, Kushner Papers, box 1, unlabeled red folder.

21. Nan Robertson, "A Woman's Crusade Against 'One-Step' Breast Surgery," *New York Times*, October 22, 1979, sec. II, p. 6.

22. Rose Kushner, *Breast Cancer: A Personal and an Investigative Report* (New York: Harcourt Brace Jovanovich, 1975), 27.

23. Rose Kushner to John Cushman, August 11, 1974, Kushner Papers, box 6, Correspondence folder, 1974.

24. Robertson, "A Woman's Crusade," 6.

25. Brenda Stone, "Breast Cancer: A Personal History and an Investigative Report," *Houston Post*, October 26, 1975.

26. Robertson, "A Woman's Crusade," 6.

27. Kushner, *Breast Cancer*.

28. Ibid., 169.

29. Rose Kushner to Dr. Barchilon, December 11, 1975, Kushner Papers, box 6, Correspondence folder, 1975.

30. Ursula Vils, "One Victim with a Mind of her Own," *Los Angeles Times*, October 16, 1975, sec. IV, pp. 1, 4–5.

31. Carol Cancila, "'Mrs. Breast Cancer' Keeps Up the Fight," *American Medical News*, October 11, 1985, pp. 23–24. In 1978, Chicago women founded what would become Y–ME, the largest support group for breast cancer patients.

32. Rose Kushner to Pat Sweeting, October 2, 1974, Kushner Papers, box 6, Correspondence folder, 1974.

33. Rose Kushner to Flora, October 8, 1974, Kushner Papers, box 6, Correspondence folder, 1974.

34. Rose Kushner, "The Breast Cancer Controversy," unpublished manuscript, 1975, Kushner Papers, box 1, In the Works Manuscripts folder.

35. Rose Kushner to Joseph Cullen, September 9, 1975, Kushner Papers, box 1, unlabeled red folder.

36. Rose Kushner to Macmillan Publishing Co., August 1, 1974, and Rose Kushner to Advisory Board on the Pulitzer Prizes, October 26, 1974, Kushner Papers, box 6, Correspondence folder, 1974.

37. Rose Kushner to Dr. Reid, November 17, 1975, Kushner Papers, box 6, Correspondence folder, 1975.

38. Kushner's widower, Harvey Kushner, continues to update this booklet. See Harvey D. Kushner, ed., *Rose Kushner's If You've Thought About Breast Cancer* (Kensington, Md.: Rose Kushner Breast Cancer Advisory Center, 2000).

39. Interview with Harvey Kushner, March 18, 1998.

40. Robertson, "A Woman's Crusade," 6.

41. Quoted in Sharon Batt, *Patient No More: The Politics of Breast Cancer* (Charlottetown, Canada: Gynergy Books, 1994), 300. See also Rose Kushner, "A Patient's-Eye View of Primary Breast Cancer Treatment," unpublished manuscript, April 23, 1979, Kushner Papers, box 8, unlabeled folder.

42. Rose Kushner to Terese Lasser, January 18, 1976, ACS, Media Division, New York, N.Y., Joseph Clark folder.

43. Rose Kushner to Dr. Greenberg, November 8, 1975, Kushner Papers, box 6, Correspondence folder, 1975.

44. Helga Sandburg, "Let A Joy Keep You," *McCall's*, November 1974, pp. 63–68, 148.

45. Ibid., 67.

46. Ibid., 68.

47. Ibid.

48. Marvella Bayh and Mary L. Kotz, *Marvella: A Personal Journey* (New York: Harcourt Brace Jovanovich, 1979), 260; Lester David, "A Brave Family Faces up to Breast Cancer," *Today's Health*, June 1972, pp. 16–21, 71; "Marvelous Marvella," *Cancer News*, Autumn 1979, pp. 4–6.

49. David, "A Brave Family," 20.

50. Bayh and Kotz, *Marvella*, 232; Lynn Lilliston, "A Message of Hope on Mastectomy," *Los Angeles Times*, February 26, 1974, sec. IV, pp. 1, 4.

51. Bayh and Kotz, *Marvella*, 228.

52. Ibid., 258.

53. Betty Rollin, "Outline," unpublished manuscript, n.d., Rollin Papers, box 5, folder 8.

54. Betty Rollin, *First, You Cry* (New York: J. B. Lippincott, 1976), 36.

55. Ibid., 58.

56. "How Two Women Are Coping with Breast Cancer," *Harper's Bazaar*, September 1976, pp. 149, 177, 186.

57. Rollin, *First, You Cry*, 123.

58. Betty Rollin, "First, You Cry," *Family Circle*, September 1976, pp. 118–122. See also "Title Suggestions," Rollin Papers, box 5, folder 7.

59. S.K. to Betty Rollin, January 4, 1977, Rollin Papers, box 7, folder 2.

60. E.D. to Betty Rollin, February 20, 1978, Rollin Papers, box 7, folder 2.

61. C.C. to Betty Rollin, October 20, 1977, Rollin Papers, box 7, folder 3.

62. M.F. to Betty Rollin, n.d., Rollin Papers, box 6, folder 8.

63. F.F. to Betty Rollin, October 1, 1976, Rollin Papers, box 6, folder 8.

64. R.H. to Betty Rollin, September 19, 1976, Rollin Papers, box 6, folder 8.

65. B.B. to Betty Rollin, August 12, 1976, Rollin Papers, box 6, folder 7.

66. G.S. to Betty Rollin, November 23, 1976, Rollin Papers, box 6, folder 4.

67. M.L. to Betty Rollin, January 11, 1977, Rollin Papers, box 6, folder 6.

68. Marie F. Gately to the Editor of *Ca*, January 28, 1974, Oliver Cope Papers, box 7AB, accordion folder, letter "C," Countway Library, Boston, Mass.

69. Rose Kushner to O. Schetin, November 14, 1974, Kushner Papers, box 6, Correspondence folder, 1975.

70. "Women's Attitudes Regarding Breast Cancer: Summary," Gallup survey, October 1973, p. 11, box 9–1841, American Cancer Society Archives, Atlanta, Ga.

71. Letter to Betty Ford, May 24, 1975. Ford Papers, box 28, Correspondence folder, 6/1/75–6/30/75.

72. P.I. to Betty Rollin, April 28, 1977, Rollin Papers, box 6, folder 4.

73. Family Practice News, May 1, 1976, courtesy of Nancy Orr.

74. C.P. to Betty Rollin, September 17, 1976, Rollin Papers, box 6, folder 6.

75. Letter to Betty Ford, September 30, 1974, Ford Papers, box 26, folder 2.

76. R.T. to Oliver Cope, October 11, 1977, Cope Papers, box 7AB, accordion folder, letter "A."

77. Marvella Bayh, "One Woman's Experience," World Health, November 1975, pp. 20–21.

78. Audiotape of The Phil Donahue Show, April 16, 1974, courtesy of Cleveland Clinic Foundation Archives.

79. K.A. to Betty Rollin, March 12, 1978, Rollin Papers, box 6, folder 5.

80. L.I. to Betty Rollin, October 4, 1977, Rollin Papers, box 6, folder 4.

81. The Phil Donahue Show, April 16, 1974.

82. R.G. to Betty Rollin, n.d., box 6, folder 4.

83. Audre Lorde, The Cancer Journals (San Francisco: Spinsters, 1980), 33.

84. Transcript of the MacNeil/Lehrer Report, May 31, 1977, Cushman D. Haagensen Papers, Haagensen Research Foundation, New York, N.Y.

85. Letter to Betty Ford, September 30, 1974, Ford Papers, box 29, folder 3.

86. Letter to Betty Ford, December 5, 1974, Ford Papers, box 25, Correspondence folder, 1/8/75–1/15/75.

87. Letter to Betty Ford, January 5, 1975, Ford Papers, box 25, Correspondence folder, 1/8/75–1/15/75.

88. Jackie Stacey, Teratologies: A Cultural Study of Cancer (London: Routledge, 1996).

89. Letter to Betty Ford from Dexter, Mich., n.d., Ford Papers, box 26, folder 2.

90. Telegram to Betty Ford, September 28, 1974, Ford Papers, box 20, Correspondence folder, 10/9/74–10/15/74.

91. "Women's Attitudes Regarding Breast Cancer," 12.

92. K.H. to Betty Rollin, December 14, 1977, Rollin Papers, box 7, folder 3.

93. S.I. to Betty Rollin, December 16, 1977, Rollin Papers, box 7, folder 2.

94. Vils, "One Victim," 5.

95. The David Susskind Show, January 21, 1973, tape courtesy of Xenia Urban.

96. Ibid.

97. The Phil Donahue Show, April 16, 1974.

98. K.L. to Cushman D. Haagensen, May 31, 1977, Haagensen Papers.

99. Rollin, First, You Cry, 230, 231.

100. Betty Rollin, "The Best Years of My Life," *New York Times Magazine*, February 1980, pp. 36–37.

101. A.D. to Betty Rollin, August 29, 1976, Rollin Papers, box 6, folder 6.

102. J.M. to Betty Rollin, December 27, 1977, Rollin Papers, box 6, folder 5.

103. Lorde, *Cancer Journals*, 9.

104. Ibid., 35.

105. Ibid., 16.

106. Ibid., 10, 44.

107. Ibid., 55.

108. Ibid., 57.

109. Ibid., 55.

110. Nora Jacobson, *Cleavage: Technology, Controversy, and the Ironies of the Man-Made Breast* (New Brunswick, N.J.: Rutgers Univ. Press, 2000), 48–72.

111. Kenneth A. Marshall, "Postmastectomy Reconstruction of the Breast," *Surgery, Gynecology & Obstetrics* 144 (1977): 77–78; Guan C. Chong, James K. Masson, and John E. Woods, "Breast Restoration after Mastectomy for Cancer," *Mayo Clinic Proceedings* 50 (1975): 453–458. On psycho-oncology, see Jimmie C. Holland, ed., Psycho–Oncology (New York: Oxford Univ. Press, 1998).

112. Lorde, *Cancer Journals*, 68, 69.

113. Dee Wedemeyer, "After Mastectomy: The Options," *New York Times*, December 9, 1976, p. 56.

114. Jean Zalon and Jean L. Block, *I Am Whole Again: The Case for Breast Reconstruction after Mastectomy* (New York: Random House, 1978), 88.

115. Gilbert Cant and Toby Cohen, "The Operation Women Never Dreamed Would Be Possible," *Good Housekeeping*, September 1975, pp. 56–68.

116. Paula Armel, "After Mastectomy: Choosing to look Different," *Ms.*, July 1981, pp. 22–23. See also Win Ann Winkler, *Post Mastectomy: A Personal Guide to Physical and Emotional Recovery* (New York: Hawthorn Books, 1976), 170–172.

117. Iris M. Young, "Breasted Experience: The Look and the Feeling," in *Throwing like a Girl and Other Essays in Feminist Philosophy and Social Theory* (Bloomington: Indiana Univ. Press, 1990), 189–209.

118. Ibid., 204. See also Delese Wear, "'Your Breasts/Sliced Off': Literary Images of Breast Cancer," *Women & Health* 20 (1993): 81–100; Sue Wilkinson and Celia Kitzinger, "Whose Breast Is it Anyway? A Feminist Consideration of Advice and 'Treatment' for Breast Cancer," *Women's Studies International Forum* 16 (1993): 229–238.

119. Kathryn P. Morgan, "Women and the Knife: Cosmetic Surgery and the Colonization of Women's Bodies," in Rose Weitz, ed., *The Politics of Women's Bodies: Sexuality, Appearance, and Behavior* (New York: Oxford Univ. Press, 1998), 147–166. See

also Naomi Wolf, *The Beauty Myth: How Images of Beauty Are Used Against Women* (New York: William Morrow, 1991), 10.

120. Judy Klemesrud, "Woman Files Suit to Recover Costs of Breast Rebuilding," *New York Times*, August 3, 1979, p. A12. See also Jacobson, *Cleavage*, 98; Nadine Brozan, "2,000 Attend Teach-in on Breast Cancer," *New York Times*, September 6, 1979, sec. III, pp. 1, 13; Wendy S. Schain, David K. Wellisch, Robert O. Pasnau, and John Landsverk, "The Sooner the Better: A Study of Psychological Factors in Women Undergoing Immediate versus Delayed Breast Reconstruction," *American Journal of Psychiatry* 142 (1985): 40–46.

121. Zalon and Block, *I Am Whole Again*, 3.

122. Ibid., 32, 46.

123. Recent studies have revealed that neither lumpectomy or immediate reconstruction is a panacea for women with breast cancer. See Anne Moyer, "Psychosocial Outcomes of Breast-Conserving Surgery versus Mastectomy: A Meta-Analytic Review," *Health Psychology* 16 (1997): 284–298.

124. Elizabeth Haiken, *Venus Envy: A History of Cosmetic Surgery* (Baltimore: Johns Hopkins Univ. Press, 1997), 275.

125. Zalon and Block, *I Am Whole Again*, 41.

126. Klemesrud, "Woman Files Suit," A12.

127. Quoted in Brozan, "2,000 Attend," C13.

128. Zalon and Block, *I Am Whole Again*, 45. The debates about reconstruction would become considerably more heated in the 1990s, when women charged that leakage from silicone breast implants had caused them to develop an autoimmune disease. For a complete discussion of this controversy, see Jacobson, *Cleavage*.

129. Leopold, *A Darker Ribbon*, 238–242.

Chapter 9. Mammography Praised and Scorned

1. W.L. to Betty Rollin, September 14, 1976, Betty Rollin Papers, box 6, folder 6, State Historical Society of Wisconsin, Madison. For a simliar sentiment, see Saul Hoffman and Peter I. Pressman, "Prophylactic Mastectomy," *Mount Sinai Journal of Medicine* 49 (1982): 102–109.

2. Joseph Colt Bloodgood, "Pre-Cancerous Lesions," *Long Island Medical Journal* 8 (1914): 161–170.

3. Albert C. Broders, "Carcinoma in Situ Contrasted with Benign Penetrating Epithelium," *Journal of the American Medical Association* 99 (1932): 1671–1675. See also Robert E. Fechner, "One Century of Mammary Carcinoma in Situ: What Have We Learned?," *American Journal of Clinical Pathology* 100 (1993): 654–661.

4. Frank W. Foote, Jr., and Fred W. Stewart, "Lobular Carcinoma in Situ," *American Journal of Pathology* 17 (1941): 491–495.

5. Nancy E. Warner, "Lobular Carcinoma of the Breast," *Cancer* 23 (1969): 840–846.

6. Dutzu Rosner, Ramez N. Bedwani, Josef Vana, Harvey W. Baker, and Gerald P. Murphy, "Noninvasive Breast Carcinoma: Results of a National Survey by the American College of Surgeons," *Annals of Surgery* 192 (1980): 139–147; Josef Vana, Ramez Bedwani, Curtis Mettlin, and Gerald P. Murphy, "Trends in Diagnosis and Managment of Breast Cancer in the U.S.: From the Surveys of the American College of Surgeons," *Cancer* 48 (1981): 1043–1052.

7. Cushman D. Haagensen, Nathan Lane, Raffaele Lattes, and Carol Bodian, "Lobular Neoplasia (So-Called Lobular Carcinoma in Situ) of the Breast," *Cancer* 42 (1978): 737–769.

8. Quoted in Maurice M. Black, "Human Breast Carcinoma. Part I: Clinical Considerations," *New York State Journal of Medicine* 70 (1970): 863–868.

9. Quoted in Edward F. Lewison, "Lobular Carcinoma in Situ of the Breast: The Feminine Mystique," *Military Medicine* 129 (1964): 115–123.

10. Ibid., 115.

11. Robert W. McDivitt, Robert V. Hutter, Fred W. Foote, Jr., and Fred W. Stewart, "In Situ Lobular Carcinoma: A Prospective Follow-Up Study Indicating Cumulative Patient Risks," *Journal of the American Medical Association* 201 (1967): 82–86.

12. Paul Peter Rosen, "Detailed Analysis of 99 Patients with Average Follow-up of 24 Years," *American Journal of Surgical Pathology* 2 (1978): 225–251.

13. McDivitt, "In Situ Lobular Carcinoma," 99.

14. Roald M. Grant, quoted in "Forum: When Primary Cancer of the Breast Is Treated, Should the Second Breast Be Prophylactically Removed?," *Modern Medicine* 34 (1966): 242–260.

15. Warner, "Lobular Carcinoma of the Breast"; Jerome A. Urban, "Bilaterality of Cancer of the Breast: Biopsy of the Opposite Breast," *Cancer* 20 (1967): 1867–1870.

16. Simon Fredricks, "A 10–Year Experience with Subcutaneous Mastectomy," *Clinics in Plastic Surgery* 2 (1975): 347–357. See also Feliciano M. Perez, "Speculations: Some Suggestions to Control Breast Cancer," *Medical Times* 102 (1974): 147–160.

17. Quoted in "Bilateral Breast Cancer: How Frequent; How to Find It; What to Do About It: A Panel Discussion," in H. Stephen Gallagher, ed., *Early Breast Cancer: Detection and Treatment* (New York: John Wiley & Sons, 1975), 183–192. An early critic of the conflation of diagnosis and therapy was the sociologist Eliot Freid-

son. See Eliot Freidson, *Medical Work in America: Essays on Health Care* (New Haven, Conn.: Yale Univ. Press, 1989).

18. For more on the nature of these physician–patient interactions, see John R. Benfield, Aaron G. Fingerhut, and Nancy E. Warner, "Lobular Carcinoma of the Breast—1969: A Therapeutic Proposal," *Archives of Surgery* 99 (1969): 129–140; Henry P. Leis, Jr., "Prophylactic Removal of the Second Breast," *Hospital Medicine*, January 1968.

19. Letter to Betty Ford, February 4, 1975, Betty Ford Papers, box 26, Correspondence folder, 2/16/75–2/28/75, Gerald R. Ford Presidential Library, Ann Arbor, Mich.

20. Benfield, "Lobular Carcinoma of the Breast," 129.

21. Quoted in "The Management of Premalignant or Histologically Dubious Lesions: A Panel Discussion," in H. Stephen Gallagher, *Early Breast Cancer: Detection and Treatment* (New York: John Wiley & Sons, 1975), 171–175.

22. Rose Kushner, "A Little Bit Pregnant," unpublished manuscript, March 13, 1980, Rose Kushner Papers, box 1, In the Works folder, Schlesinger Library, Cambridge, Mass.

23. Robert V. Hutter, Ruth E. Snyder, J. C. Lucas, Fred W. Foote, Jr., and Joseph H. Farrow, "Clinical and Pathologic Correlation with Mammographic Findings in Lobular Carcinoma in Situ," *Cancer* 23 (1969): 826–839.

24. Arthur I. Holleb, "Mammography Can Find Curable Breast Cancer," unpublished manuscript, May 23, 1977, American Cancer Society, Media Division, New York, N.Y., Mammography Clips folder.

25. Maurice S. Fox, "On the Diagnosis and Treatment of Breast Cancer," *Journal of the American Medical Association* 241 (1979): 489–494. See also Edwin R. Fisher, Bernard Fisher, Richard Sass, et al., "Pathologic Findings from the National Surgical Adjuvant Breast Project (Protocol No. 4)," *Cancer* 54 (1984): 3002–3011.

26. Fred W. Stewart, *Tumors of the Breast: Atlas of Tumor Pathology*, Section IX—Fascicle 34 (Washington, D.C.: Armed Forces Institute of Pathology, 1950).

27. Robert V. Hutter, "What Is a Premalignant Lesion?," in H. Stephen Gallagher, *Early Breast Cancer: Detection and Treatment* (New York: John Wiley & Sons, 1975), 165–169. See also the discussion of the "medical breast" in Marilyn Yalom, *A History of the Breast* (New York: Alfred A. Knopf, 1998), 205–240.

28. Hutter, "What Is a Premalignant Lesion?," 165.

29. Quoted in Loie Sauer, "Before Proof of Cancer, 'High Risk' Women Opt for Breast Surgery," *New York Times*, September, 23 1980, pp. C1, C2. For more on Pennisi, see Nora Jacobson, *Cleavage: Technology, Controversy, and the Ironies of the Man-Made Breast* (New Brunswick, N.J.: Rutgers Univ. Press, 2000).

30. Quoted in Rose Kushner, "Removing Cancer–Free Breasts," *Washington Post*, Health Section, January 23, 1985, p. 6. On women requesting prophylactic

surgery, see Jack Star, "How Silastic Transformed Breast Surgery," Look, July 27, 1971, p. 12; Elizabeth Haiken, Venus Envy: A History of Cosmetic Surgery (Baltimore: Johns Hopkins Univ. Press, 1997), 261–262.

31. Jacobson, Cleavage, 137.

32. Terri A. Herman, "Sexism and Mastectomy: A Debate [Letter to the Editor]," New England Journal of Medicine 297 (1977): 1126–1127.

33. Susan M. Love, Rebecca S. Gelman, and William Silen, "Fibrocystic 'Disease' of the Breast—A Nondisease?," New England Journal of Medicine 307 (1982): 1010–1014.

34. Petr Skrabanek, "False Premises and False Promises of Breast Cancer Screening," Lancet 2 (1985): 316–320.

35. Sidney J. Cutler and Roger R. Connelly, "Mammary Cancer Trends," Cancer 23 (1969): 767–774.

36. James T. Patterson, The Dread Disease: Cancer and Modern American Culture (Cambridge, Mass.: Harvard Univ. Press, 1987), 247–251.

37. Robert Bazell, "Behind the Cancer Campaign," Ramparts, December 1971, pp. 29–34.

38. Interview with Philip Strax, M.D., March 3, 1997.

39. Sam Shapiro, Philip Strax, and Louis Venet, "Evaluation of Periodic Breast Cancer Screening with Mammography: Methodology and Early Observations," Journal of the American Medical Association 195 (1966): 731–738.

40. Sam Shapiro, Philip Strax, and Louis Venet, "Periodic Breast Cancer Screening in Reducing Mortality from Breast Cancer," Journal of the American Medical Association 215 (1971): 1777–1785.

41. Arthur I. Holleb, "Toward Better Control of Breast Cancer," press release, October 4, 1971, ACS, Media Division, Breast Cancer Facts folder.

42. Ibid.

43. "NIH/NCI Development Meeting on Breast Cancer Screening: Issues and Recommendations," October 18, 1977, ACS, Media Division, Breast Cancer Consensus 9/77 folder.

44. Untitled press release, October 21, 1973, ACS, Media Division, Breast Cancer Facts folder.

45. Daniel S. Greenberg, "X-Ray Mammography—Background to a Decision," New England Journal of Medicine 295 (1976): 739–740; interview with Nathaniel I. Berlin, M.D., November 3, 1998. The $6 million represented two thirds of the annual funding for the BCDDP.

46. Walter S. Ross, Crusade: The Official History of the American Cancer Society (New York: Arbor House, 1987).

47. Minutes of Special Meeting for Discussion of Project Protocol, January 9, 1974, Briefing Document on NCI/ACS Breast Cancer Demonstration Project folder, courtesy of John C. Bailar.

48. Berlin interview, November 3, 1998.

49. Holleb, "Toward Better Control of Breast Cancer."

50. This point is acknowledged in Minutes of Special Meeting, January 9, 1974. The quotation is reprinted in Greenberg, "X-Ray Mammography," 739.

51. "Changing Concepts in Managing Cancer of the Breast," Audio-Digest Foundation. In *Surgery* 20, no. 2, January 31, 1973.

52. Herbert Seidman to Arthur I. Holleb, February 12, 1976, Correspondence folder, 8/8/75 through 1976, courtesy of John C. Bailar.

53. Philip Strax, "Radiologist's Role in Screening Mammography," unpublished manuscript, n.d., courtesy of Philip Strax.

54. Barron H. Lerner, "Seeing What Is Not There: Mammography and Images of Breast Cancer," paper given at conference "Imaging Portraits: Body Imaging Technologies in Medicine and Culture," San Francisco, California, April 1998. The term "obligatory passage point" is borrowed from Bruno Latour.

55. John Van Buren, "X-Ray Found Able to 'See' Early Breast Cancer," *Rochester (N.Y.) Democrat and Chronicle*, 1964, courtesy of Herman C. Zuckerman.

56. Robert L. Egan, "Roles of Mammography in the Early Detection of Breast Cancer," *Cancer* 24 (1969): 1197–1200.

57. "About Breast Cancer and X-Rays," *Science* 193 (1976): back cover.

58. *Radiology* 121 (1976): 140A–141A.

59. Philip Strax, *Early Detection: Breast Cancer Is Curable* (New York: Harper & Row, 1974), xiii–xiv.

60. "A Hectic Week for Breast Cancer Researchers," *Medical World News*, October 25, 1974, pp. 19–22.

61. "Breast Project Is Saving Lives," *San Antonio Evening News*, November 7, 1975, p. 12.

62. Paula Bernstein, "Mammography: It's a Tool That Can Save Lives," *New York Daily News*, March 4, 1975, p. 44.

63. Jane E. Brody, "Breast Cancer Project Called Success," *New York Times*, November 7, 1975, p. 34.

64. John C. Bailar III, "Mammography: A Contrary View," *Annals of Internal Medicine* 84 (1976): 77–84.

65. Berlin interview, November 3, 1998.

66. Bailar, "Mammography," 77.

67. Ibid., 78.

68. Ibid., 80.

69. Ibid., 82.

70. Arthur I. Holleb, untitled manuscript, n.d., Michael B. Shimkin Papers, box 25, folder 5, Univ. of California at San Diego Library, San Diego.

71. Minutes of the Meeting of the Board of Directors of the American Cancer Society, January 11, 1973, ACS Archives, Atlanta, Ga.

72. Benjamin F. Byrd, Jr., "Statement of the American Cancer Society," in *Consensus Development Meeting on Breast Cancer Screening, September 14–16, 1977* (Washington, D.C.: Department of Health, Education and Welfare, 1977), 19–24.

73. John C. Bailar III to Nathaniel I. Berlin, March 1, 1973, Very Early Materials folder, courtesy of John Bailar. See also a packet of consent forms, ACS, Media Division, Breast Cancer Demonstration Projects folder.

74. Byrd, "Statement," 20.

75. John A. H. Lee to John C. Bailar III, June 30, 1973, Correspondence folder, 8/8/75 through 1976, courtesy of John Bailar.

76. Marvin Zelen to Frank J. Rauscher, Jr., July 16, 1973, Very Early Materials folder, courtesy of John Bailar.

77. Saul Harris to Frank J. Rauscher, Jr., January 10, 1973, Shimkin Papers, box 25, folder 5.

78. Ibid.

79. Minutes of the Meeting of the Diagnostic Research Advisory Group, December 21, 1972, Briefing Document folder, courtesy of John Bailar.

80. Minutes of the Meeting of the Ad Hoc Committee for the Central Statistical Center, January 18, 1973, and Sidney J. Cutler to Nathaniel I. Berlin, August 7, 1973, Briefing Document folder, courtesy of John Bailar.

81. Malcolm C. Pike to William Pomerance, December 16, 1974, Briefing Document folder, courtesy of John Bailar.

82. John C. Bailar III to Frank J. Rauscher, Jr., August 8, 1975, Correspondence folder, 8/8/75 through 1976, courtesy of John Bailar.

83. Jane E. Brody, "Radiation Benefits, Risks in Breast Cancer Debated," *New York Times*, March 28, 1976, p. 42.

84. Barbara J. Culliton, "Breast Cancer: Second Thoughts About Routine Mammography," *Science* 193 (1976): 555–558.

85. Ibid., 557; "Mammography for Women with No Symptoms," *Health Facts* (of the Center for Medical Consumers), May 15, 1977.

86. Greenberg, "X–Ray Mammography," 739.

87. Daniel S. Greenberg and Judith E. Randal, "The Questionable Breast X-ray Program," *Washington Post*, May 1, 1977, p. C5.

88. Daniel S. Greenberg and Judith E. Randal, "Waging the Wrong War on Cancer," *Washington Post*, May 1, 1977, pp. C1, C4.

89. Shana Alexander, "Breast Cancer and News Overkill," *Newsweek*, December 9, 1974, p. 122.

90. Rose Kushner, "Cancer Detection [Letter to the Editor]," *New York Times*, December 22, 1976, p. 28.

91. Maryann Napoli, "Mammography: The Deepened Distrust [Letter to the Editor]," *New York Times*, June 23, 1977.

92. Irwin D. J. Bross, interview with Gabe Pressman, WNEW–TV, May 15, 1979, ACS, Media Division, Channel 5 folder. See also Irwin D. Bross, "A History of U.S. Science and Medicine in the Cold War" (CD-ROM), available from Biomedical Metatechnology, Inc., Amherst, N.Y.

93. Arthur I. Holleb, interview with Hughes Rudd, CBS Morning News, August 27, 1976, ACS, Media Division, Breast Cancer Mammography folder.

94. Walter S. Ross, "What Every Woman Should Know About Breast X-Ray," *Reader's Digest*, March 1977, pp. 116–120; "Critics, Defenders Express Views about Routine Mammography," *Journal of the American Medical Association* 236 (1976): 541–542.

95. "Cancer Institute Proposes Limits on Breast X-Rays," *New York Times*, August 23, 1976, p. 12.

96. Culliton, "Breast Cancer: Second Thoughts," 555.

97. Victor Cohn, "Women Avoiding Breast Cancer Test," *Washington Post*, November 23, 1976, p. A3.

98. John C. Bailar III, testimony, *Consensus Development Meeting on Breast Cancer Screening*, 49.

99. John C. Bailar III to Frank J. Rauscher, Jr., August 16, 1976, Correspondence folder, 1/76–12/76, courtesy of John Bailar.

100. Greenberg and Randal, "The Questionable Breast X-Ray Program," C5.

101. Strax, *Early Detection*, xiii.

102. Philip Strax to Benjamin Byrd, "Re: ACS Breast Cancer Task Force Meeting—June '77," courtesy of Philip Strax.

103. Culliton, "Breast Cancer: Second Thoughts," 557.

104. "Presumptive Risks Should Not Nullify Benefits of Mammography, Holleb Says," *Cancer Letter*, July 21, 1978, pp. 5–7.

105. Ibid., 6.

106. Minutes of the Meeting of Working Group of Pathologists," April 22, 1974, Briefing Document folder, courtesy of John Bailar.

107. Daniel S. Greenberg, "A Cancer Controversy: Did Doctor Know Best?," *Washington Post*, April 4, 1978, p. A19.

108. Judith Randal, "Mammography—A Vicious Circle of Mistakes," *San Francisco Chronicle*, October 6, 1977, p. 39.

109. William Hines, "Breast Surgery Cases Probed," *Pittsburgh Press*, September 25, 1977, p. 32.

110. Daniel S. Greenberg, "Perils in a Cancer Screening Project," *Washington Post*, October 10, 1978, p. 19.

111. Arthur I. Holleb, untitled manuscript, December 1978, ACS, Media Division, Mammography folder. This figure included invasive cancers and in situ lesions.

112. Arthur I. Holleb, "Mammography Is Not a Mistake," *New York Times*, October 8, 1977, p. 22.

113. Daniel S. Greenberg, "The Politics of Cancer," *Washington Post*, June 12, 1977, pp. E1, E5.

114. "From the Editor," *New York Times*, October 8, 1977, p. 22.

115. Quoted in Greenberg, "A Cancer Controversy."

116. See also Judith E. Randal, "Must Tell 66 of Breast Surgery Error," *New York Daily News*, October 28, 1977.

117. Rose Kushner, "Addendum to Earlier Submission to the Consensus Committee Regarding the BCDDPs," September 13, 1977, Rose Kushner Papers, box 1, unmarked manila folder, Schlesinger Library, Cambridge, Mass.

118. These letters can be found in a folder labeled Breast Cancer—Policy (Politics) at the Boston Women's Health Book Collective, Somerville, Mass.

119. Discussion following John C. Bailar III's presentation at the White House Conference on Breast Cancer, November 1976, My Writings and Speaking on Mammography folder, courtesy of John Bailar.

120. Victor Cohn, "Cancer Experts Debate Value of X-Ray Program," *Washington Post*, September 15, 1977, p. A3.

121. "Statement on the Final Report of the Working Group for the Review of the NCI/ACS Breast Cancer Detection Demonstration Project," NCI Press Release, October 19, 1978, ACS, Media Division, Breast Cancer Demonstration Projects folder.

Chapter 10. The Fall of the Radical Mastectomy

1. Theresa Montini and Sheryl Ruzek, "Overturning Orthodoxy: The Emergence of Breast Cancer Treatment Policy," *Research in the Sociology of Health Care* 8 (1989): 3–32; Michael Unger, "Alternatives Replacing Radical Mastectomies," *Newsday* (New York), October 23, 1982, p. 32.

2. "Betty Ford's Operation," *Newsweek*, October 7, 1974, pp. 30–33.

3. Linda Wilson, "Cancer Victim Feels Lucky," *Macon Telegram*, March 3, 1977, ACS, Media Division, New York, N.Y., Biography—Marvella Bayh folder.

4. See the discussion in Myra MacPherson, "Marvella Bayh: 'I have learned to value life,'" *Washington Post*, October 23, 1978, pp. B1, B9.

5. Ibid., B1.

6. Irving Rimer to Jane Sinnenberg, April 30, 1979, ACS, Media Division, Biography—Marvella Bayh folder.

7. "American Cancer Society Policy Statement on the Surgical Treatment of Breast Cancer," included with Minutes of the Board of Directors of the ACS, June 8, 1973, ACS, Media Division, Board of Directors folder, 1973.

8. Arthur I. Holleb, interview with David Hartman, *Good Morning America*, ABC–TV, September 13, 1979, ACS, Media Division, Breast Cancer General folder.

9. "Treatment of Primary Breast Cancer," *New England Journal of Medicine* 301 (1979): 379.

10. Bernard Fisher, "Breast-Cancer Management: Alternatives to Radical Mastectomy," *New England Journal of Medicine* 301 (1979): 326–328.

11. Ibid., 327.

12. Veronesi termed his procedure "quadrentectomy." See Umberto Veronesi, Roberto Saccozzi, Marcella DelVecchio, et al., "Comparing Radical Mastectomy with Quadrentectomy, Axillary Dissection, and Radiotherapy in Patients with Small Cancers of the Breast," *New England Journal of Medicine* 305 (1981): 6–11.

13. Bernard Fisher, Madeline Bauer, Richard Margolese, et al., "Five-Year Results of a Randomized Clinical Trial Comparing Total Mastectomy and Segmental Mastectomy with or without Radiation in the Treatment of Breast Cancer," *New England Journal of Medicine* 312 (1985): 665–673; Bernard Fisher, Carol Redmond, Edwin R. Fisher, et al., "Ten-Year Results of a Randomized Clinical Trial Comparing Radical Mastectomy and Total Mastectomy with or without Radiation," *New England Journal of Medicine* 312 (1985): 674–681. Patients in B–06 with evidence of metastatic disease received chemotherapy as well.

14. Michael Baum and Anthony Colletta, "Breast Cancer: A Revolutionary Concept," *Breast Cancer* 2 (1995): 9–18.

15. This conclusion draws on a discussion with Allan Brandt.

16. Rose Kushner to T. George Harris, February 15, 1982, Rose Kushner Papers, box 1, In the Works—MSs folder, Schlesinger Library, Cambridge, Mass.

17. Interview with Harvey Kushner, March 18, 1998.

18. Arthur I. Holleb to Rose Kushner, March 3, 1987. Kushner Papers, box 4, ACS Saga folder.

19. Interview with Maryann Napoli, June 9, 1998.

20. Rose Kushner to Dennis Flanagan, February 16, 1982, Kushner Papers, box 1, In the Works—MSs folder. See also Pamela Sanders-Goebel, "Crisis and Controversy: Historical Patterns in Breast Cancer Surgery," *Canadian Bulletin of Medical History* 8 (1991): 77–90.

21. Quoted in Montini and Ruzek, "Overturning Orthodoxy," 14.

22. Ibid., 14. See also Deborah R. Gordon, "Clinical Science and Clinical Expertise: Changing Boundaries Between Art and Science in Medicine," in Margaret Lock and Deborah Gordon, *Biomedicine Examined* (Dordrecht: Kluwer Academic Publishers, 1988), 257–295.

23. Bernard Fisher, "The Evolution of Paradigms for the Management of Breast Cancer: A Personal Perspective," *Cancer Research* 52 (1992): 2371–2383.

24. See, for example, "Mastectomy," *MacNeil/Lehrer Report*, May 31, 1977, Cushman D. Haagensen Papers, Haagensen Research Foundation, New York, N.Y.

25. Interview with David W. Kinne, M.D., September 23, 1997.

26. Interview with Edward F. Lewison, M.D., May 1, 1997.

27. See, for example, Bernard Fisher to George Crile, Jr., October 3, 1989. George Crile, Jr. Papers, box 48, Barney's Correspondence folder, 1989, Cleveland Clinic Foundation Archives, Cleveland, Ohio.

28. Maurice M. Black and Francis D. Speer, "Biologic Variability of Breast Carcinoma in Relation to Diagnosis and Therapy," *New York State Journal of Medicine* 53 (1953): 1560–1563; Reginald Murley, *Surgical Roots and Branches* (London: British Medical Journal, 1990), 173. Black (and other physicians involved in breast cancer research) believed that Fisher did not give adequate credit to this earlier work. See Maurice M. Black to Bernard Fisher, January 18, 1978, courtesy of Beatrice Black.

29. R. Robinson Baker, "Out-Patient Breast Biopsies," *Annals of Surgery* 185 (1977): 543–547.

30. Quoted in "Response to Demands for Patient Participation in Treatment Selection: A Panel Discussion," in H. Stephen Gallagher, ed., *Early Breast Cancer: Detection and Treatment* (New York: John Wiley & Sons, 1975), 145–150.

31. Guy F. Robbins to Gerhart Hilt, December 9, 1986, courtesy of Nancy Orr. See also interview with Leslie Wise, M.D., December 11, 1997. At times, surgeons who had come to favor lumpectomy strongly lobbied their patients to have this procedure.

32. Interview with Sherwin B. Nuland, M.D., September 7, 1999.

33. G.S. to Gerald R. Ford, October 3, 1974, Betty Ford Papers, box 28, folder 4, Gerald R. Ford Presidential Library, Ann Arbor, Mich.

34. "Controversies in Managing Breast Cancer," Audio-Digest Foundation. In *Surgery* 18, No. 1, January 13, 1971.

35. T.N. to Betty Rollin, December 16, 1976, Betty Rollin Papers, box 6, folder 4, State Historical Society of Wisconsin, Madison.

36. George J. Annas, "Breast Cancer: The Treatment of Choice," *Hastings Center Report*, April 1980, pp. 27–29.

37. Ibid., 29.

38. Montini and Ruzek, "Overturning Orthodoxy," 18. See also Theresa Montini, "Resist and Redirect: Physicians Respond to Breast Cancer Informed Consent Legislation," *Woman and Health* 26 (1997): 85–105.

39. Marjorie T. McAneny, "A State Legislature Trips Over Informed Consent," *Medical Economics*, May 12, 1980, pp. 198–199.

40. Rose Kushner, "Informed Consent," unpublished manuscript, February 22, 1982, Kushner Papers, box 1, unmarked red folder.

41. Calvin R. Openshaw to Jerome A. Urban, May 26, 1985, Society of Surgical Oncology Meeting folder, courtesy of Hiram Cody III and Xenia Urban.

42. Interview with Francis D. Moore, M.D., June 19, 1997.

43. Jerome A. Urban, "Treatment of Primary Breast Cancer. Management of Local Disease: Minority Report," *Journal of the American Medical Association* 244 (1980): 800–803.

44. Jerome A. Urban to Franco M. Muggia, November 27, 1979, unlabeled hanging folder, courtesy of Hiram Cody III and Xenia Urban.

45. Rose Kushner, "The Battle for Our Bulge," unpublished manuscript, April 6, 1981, Kushner Papers, box 1, Articles and Chapters, Cancer folder.

46. Jerome A. Urban to Charles D. Sherman, Jr., October 10, 1979, unlabeled hanging folder, courtesy of Hiram Cody III and Xenia Urban.

47. Interview with Michael P. Osborne, M.D., February 5, 1999.

48. Ibid.

49. George Crile, Jr., "The Treatment of Breast Cancer—1979," unpublished talk, 1979, Unpublished Papers Pertaining to Medicine folder, courtesy of Helga Sandburg Crile.

50. Interview with Avram E. Cooperman, M.D., February 13, 1998.

51. Interview with Susan M. Love, M.D., July 15, 1998.

52. Cushman D. Haagensen, *Diseases of the Breast*, 3rd ed. (Philadelphia: W. B. Saunders, 1986).

53. Ibid., 936.

54. Alice Haagensen to John Oakes, August 13, 1981, courtesy of Alice Haagensen.

55. Interview with Kenneth M. Prager, M.D., November 5, 1999.

56. Interview with Kenneth A. Forde, M.D., July 20, 2000.

57. Ingrid Bergman and Alan Burgess, *Ingrid Bergman: My Story* (New York: Delacorte Press, 1980), 449.

58. S.C. to Cushman D. Haagensen, February 1, 1974, Haagensen Papers.

59. Alice Haagensen to Sidney M. Wolfe, May 14, 1989, courtesy of Alice Haagensen.

60. Ellen Leopold has estimated that two million radical mastectomies were performed in the United States during the twentieth century. See Ellen Leopold, *A Darker Ribbon: Breast Cancer,Women, and Their Doctors in the Twentieth Century* (Boston: Beacon Press, 1999), 89.

61. Julie and Philip Partington to Alice and Cushman Haagensen, [1989?], courtesy of Alice Haagensen.

62. Sir Reginald Murley to George Crile, Jr., February 1, 1992, Crile Papers, box 48, Barney's Correspondence folder, 1992.

63. Unger, "Alternatives," 32; Montini and Ruzek, "Overturning Orthodoxy," 16.

64. Norman C. Delarue, W. D. Anderson, and J. Starr, "Modified Radical Mastectomy in the Individualized Treatment of Breast Carcinoma," *Surgery, Gynecology & Obstetrics* 129 (1969): 79–88; R. C. Golinger, "Breast Cancer Controversies: Surgical Decisions," *Seminars in Oncology* 7 (1980): 444–459.

65. Y. H. Pilch, "Breast Cancer Treatment—Current Status," *Postgraduate Medicine* 74, no. 3 (1983): 126–134. The first RCT comparing radical and modified radical mastectomy was William A. Maddox, John T. Carpenter, Jr., Henry L. Laws, et al., "A Randomized Prospective Trial of Radical (Halsted) Mastectomy versus Modified Radical Mastectomy in 311 Breast Cancer Patients," *Annals of Surgery* 198 (1983): 207–212. Thanks to Mary Anna Denman for her insights regarding modified radical surgery.

66. "How Radical (Must) (Should) Mastectomy Be in Early Breast Cancer?," *MedicalWorld News*, March 3, 1972, pp. 38–47.

67. Delarue, "Modified Radical Mastectomy," 82.

68. Montini and Ruzek, "Overturning Orthodoxy," 14.

Chapter 11. What Can History Teach Us?

1. Gina Kolata, "Mammogram Talks Prove Indefinite," *New York Times*, January 24, 1997, pp. A1, A15. See also Gerald D. Dodd, "American Cancer Society Guidelines on Screening for Breast Cancer," *Cancer* 69 (Suppl.) (1992): 1885–1887.

2. Larry H. Baker, "Breast Cancer Detection Demonstration Project: Five-Year Summary Report," *Ca* 32 (1982): 194–225; Charles R. Smart, Celia Byrne, Robert A. Smith, et al., "Twenty-Year Follow-Up of the Breast Cancers Diagnosed During the Breast Cancer Detection Demonstration Project," *Ca* 47 (1997): 134–149.

3. "The Breast Cancer Detection Demonstration Project (BCDDP): End Results," n.d., ACS, Media Division, New York, N.Y., Breast Cancer Demonstration Projects folder.

4. Interviews with Nathaniel I. Berlin, M.D., November 3, 1998, and Charles R. Smart, M.D., September 30, 1998.

5. John C. Bailar III, testimony, *Consensus Development Conference on Breast Cancer Screening, September 14–16, 1977* (Washington, D.C.: Department of Health, Education and Welfare, 1977), 50.

6. "Breast Cancer Screening for Women Ages 40–49," *NIH Consensus Statement* 15:1 (1997): 1–35.

7. Gina Kolata, "Stand on Mammograms Greeted by Outrage," *New York Times*, January 28, 1997, pp. C1, C8.

8. Kolata, "Mammogram Talks," A15.

9. Anne S. Blackwell, "How Many Will Die? [Letter to the Editor]," *New York Times*, January 28, 1997, p. A20.

10. Kolata, "Stand on Mammograms," C1; Virginia L. Ernster, "Mammography Screening for Women Aged 40 through 49—A Guidelines Saga and a Clarion Call for Informed Decision-Making," *American Journal of Public Health* 87 (1997): 1103–1106.

11. Ernster, "Mammography Screening," 1104.

12. Ibid., 1104.

13. Kay Dickersin, "Breast Screening in Women Aged 40–49 Years: What Next?," *Lancet* 353 (1999): 1896–1897. See also David F. Ransohoff and Russell P. Harris, "Lessons from the Mammography Screening Controversy: Can We Improve the Debate?," *Annals of Internal Medicine* 127 (1997): 1029–1034; Joann G. Elmore, Mary B. Barton, Victoria M. Moceri, Sarah Polk, Philip J. Arena, and Suzanne W. Fletcher, "Ten-Year Risk of False Positive Screening Mammograms and Clinical Breast Examinations," *New England Journal of Medicine* 338 (1998): 1089–1096.

14. Harold C. Sox, "Benefit and Harm Associated with Screening for Breast Cancer [Editorial]," *New England Journal of Medicine* 338 (1998): 1145–1146.

15. "BCDDP Final Report: 3,557 Cancers Found, 90 Percent by Mammography," *Cancer Letter* 8:28 (1982), 3–4; Marilyn A. Leitch, "Breast Cancer Screening: Success Amid Conflict," *Surgical Oncology Clinics of North America* 8 (1999): 657–672.

16. Monica Morrow, "Understanding Ductal Carcinoma in Situ [Editorial]," *Cancer* 86 (1999): 375–377.

17. Eddy C. Hsueh, Roderick R. Turner, Edwin C. Glass, R. James Brenner, Meghan B. Brennan, and Armando E. Guiliano, "Sentinel Node Biopsy in Breast Cancer," *Journal of the American College of Surgeons* 189 (1999): 207–213.

18. Solange Pendas, Emilia Dauway, Charles E. Cox, et al., "Sentinel Node Biopsy and Cytokeratin Staining for the Accurate Staging of 478 Breast Cancer Patients," *American Surgeon* 65 (1999): 500–506.

19. David Brenin, Mahmoud El-Tamer, Andrea Troxel, et al., "Are Results from Sentinel Node Biopsy for DCIS Likely to Be Clinically Significant?," presented at the 22nd Annual San Antonio Breast Cancer Symposium, San Antonio, Texas, December 1999.

20. Stephan Braun, Klaus Pantel, Peter Muller, et al., "Cytokeratin-Positive Cells in the Bone Marrow and Survival of Patients with Stage I, II, or III Breast Cancer," New England Journal of Medicine 342 (2000): 525–533.

21. Parvis Gamagami, Atlas of Mammography: New Early Signs in Breast Cancer (Cambridge, Mass.: Blackwell Science, 1996), xi.

22. "Don't Mess with Your Life. Have a Mammogram," New York Times, October 3, 1993. Thanks to Maryann Napoli for pointing out this advertisement.

23. Marcia Angell, "Overdosing on Health Risks," New York Times Magazine, May 4, 1997, pp. 44–45.

24. H. Gilbert Welch, "Questions About the Value of Early Intervention [Editorial]," New England Journal of Medicine 334 (1996): 1472–1473; Keith Wailoo, Drawing Blood: Technology and Disease Identity in Twentieth-Century America (Baltimore: Johns Hopkins Univ. Press, 1997), 198–199.

25. Steven H. Woolf and Robert S. Lawrence, "Preserving Scientific Debate and Patient Choice: Lessons from the Consensus Panel on Mammography Screening," Journal of the American Medical Association 278 (1997): 2105–2108; Robert A. Aronowitz, "Pure or Impure Science?," Annals of Internal Medicine 127 (1997): 250–254. This point remains unappreciated, as witnessed by the latest controversy over the Canadian breast cancer screening study. See Judith Randal, "After 40 years, Mammography Remains as Much Emotion as Science," Journal of the National Cancer Institute 92 (2000): 1630–1632.

26. Robert Aronowitz, "To Screen or Not to Screen: What Is the Question? [Editorial]," Journal of General Internal Medicine 10 (1995): 295–297.

27. J.F. to Betty Rollin, January 31, 1978, Betty Rollin Papers, box 6, folder 5, State Historical Society of Wisconsin, Madison.

28. Medicare did not pay for mammograms until 1991. See Ellen Leopold, A Darker Ribbon: Breast Cancer, Women, and Their Doctors in the Twentieth Century (Boston: Beacon Press, 1999), 246.

29. Linda Frame, quoted in Christine Haran, "Mammography's Hot Button," Mamm, January 2000, pp. 26–31.

30. "American Cancer Society Updates Prostate Cancer Screening Guidelines," June 12, 1997, available at www.cancer.org.

31. Feminist organizations, such as the National Breast Cancer Coalition and the National Women's Health Network, favored the original consensus decision.

32. Jerry E. Bishop, "Controversy Intensifies over the Best Method to Treat Breast Cancer," *Wall Street Journal*, June 13, 1984, p. 1.

33. Gianni Bonadonna, Ercole Brusamolino, Pinuccia Valagussa, et al., "Combination Chemotherapy as an Adjuvant Treatment in Operable Breast Cancer," *New England Journal of Medicine* 294 (1976): 405–410.

34. Newer agents such as zofran and kytril may reduce some of the side effects associated with chemotherapy.

35. Barbara J. Culliton, "Breast Cancer: Reports of New Therapy Are Greatly Exaggerated," *Science*, March 12, 1976, pp. 1029–1031.

36. Rose Kushner to E.M., December 1, 1975, Rose Kushner Papers, box 6, Correspondence folder, 1975, Schlesinger Library, Cambridge, Mass.

37. Rose Kushner, "Is Aggressive Adjuvant Chemotherapy the Halsted Radical of the '80s?," *Ca* 34 (1984): 345–351.

38. Michael B. Shimkin to Rose Kushner, August 24, 1984, Kushner Papers, box 3, folder 48.

39. In later years, Black advocated large doses of vitamin E to help the body's immune response to breast cancer. He also remained opposed to routine radiotherapy, believing that it did more harm than good in favorable cases of the disease. Black died in 1996, having anticipated in the 1950s many of the century's subsequent developments in breast cancer biology.

40. Quoted in Roberta Altman, *Waking Up, Fighting Back: The Politics of Breast Cancer* (Boston: Little, Brown, 1996), 170. For a comprehensive portrait of Susan Love, see Karen Stabiner, *To Dance with the Devil: The New War on Breast Cancer* (New York: Delacourte, 1997).

41. David A. Karnofsky, "Rationale for Aggressive or Extraordinary Means of Treatment for Advanced Cancer," *Ca* 12 (1962): 166–170.

42. Ilana Lowy, *Between Bench and Bedside: Science, Healing, and Interleukin-2 in a Cancer Ward* (Cambridge, Mass.: Harvard Univ. Press, 1996), 64.

43. Ibid., 66–67. See also Kushner, "Is Aggressive Adjuvant Chemotherapy," 348.

44. Letter to Betty Ford, November 18, 1974, Betty Ford Papers, box 25, Correspondence folder, 12/1/74–12/1974, Gerald R. Ford Presidential Library, Ann Arbor, Mich.

45. Letter to Betty Ford, December 29, 1974, Ford Papers, box 26, Correspondence folder, 1/16/75–1/27/75.

46. B.B. to Betty Rollin, August 12, 1976, Rollin Papers, box 6, folder 7.

47. Gabriel N. Hortobagyi and Aman U. Buzdar, "Current Status of Adjuvant Systemic Therapy for Primary Breast Cancer," *Ca* 45 (1995): 199–226. These figures represent relative risk reductions—that is, the percentage improvement in

survival over other therapies. The numbers given do not represent the actual percentages of women whose survival was improved.

48. Gina Kolata, "Cancer Drug Therapy Urged for All After Breast Surgery," *New York Times*, May 21, 1988, pp. 1, 11; Gina Kolata, "Breast Cancer Patients Face Daunting Array of Options on Therapy," *New York Times*, October 27, 1988, p. B17.

49. P. M. Ravdin, I. A. Siminoff, and J. A. Harvey, "Survey of Breast Cancer Patients Concerning Their Knowledge and Expectations of Adjuvant Therapy," *Journal of Clinical Oncology* 16 (1998): 515–521.

50. Hortobagyi and Buzdar, "Current Status," 207.

51. Personal communication with the author, June 8, 1998. An NIH consensus conference held in November 2000 concluded that paclitaxel had not shown value in node-negative patients. Wishful thinking and aggressive promotion—as opposed to data—had once again ruled the day.

52. Kara Smigel, "Women Flock to ABMT for Breast Cancer Without Final Proof," *Journal of the National Cancer Institute* 87 (1995): 952–955.

53. Tim Johnson, Callie, Crossley, Sarah Adler and Sylvia Johnson, "Betrayal of Hope," 20/20, ABC News, April 14, 2000. Available at www.abcnews.go.com; Denise Grady, "Conference Divided over High-Dose Breast Cancer Treatment," *New York Times*, May 18, 1999, p. A19; Gina Kolata and Kurt Eichenwald, "Business Thrives on Unproven Care, Leaving Science Behind," *New York Times*, October 3, 1999, pp. 1, 40.

54. Lawrence K. Altman, "Surgeons Remove Cancerous Breast of Nancy Reagan," *New York Times*, October 18, 1997, pp. 1, 32.

55. Gina Kolata, "Mastectomy Seen as Extreme for Small Tumor," *New York Times*, October 18, 1987, p. 32.

56. Ibid., 32.

57. Victoria Baker to Adele, October 20, 1987. ACS, Media Division, Rose Kushner—not cured folder.

58. "Treatment of Early-Stage Breast Cancer: Consensus Statement," *NIH Consensus Development Conference*, vol. 8, no. 6 (Bethesda, Md.: NIH, 1990).

59. Anne B. Nattinger, Mark S. Gottlieb, Judith Veum, David Yahnke, and James S. Goodwin, "Geographic Variation in the Use of Breast-Conserving Treatment for Breast Cancer," *New England Journal of Medicine* 326 (1992): 1102–1107. See also Lawrence K. Altman, "Mastectomy Alternative Often Ignored," *New York Times*, May 19, 1988, p. A18.

60. Kathlyn Conway, *Ordinary Life: A Memoir of Illness* (New York: W. H. Freeman, 1997), 49.

61. Bernard Fisher, "On the Underutilization of Breast-Conserving Surgery for the Treatment of Breast Cancer [Editorial]," *Annals of Oncology* 4 (1993): 96–98.

See also Anna Lee-Feldstein, Hoda Anton-Culver, and Paul J. Feldstein, "Treatment Differences and Other Prognostic Factors Related to Breast Cancer Survival," *Journal of the American Medical Association* 271 (1994): 1163–1168; Bernard Fisher, "From Halsted to Prevention and Beyond: Advances in the Management of Breast Cancer During the Twentieth Century," *European Journal of Cancer* 35 (1999): 1963–1973.

62. Gail Geller, Barbara A. Bernhardt, Teresa Doksum, Kathy J. Helzlsouer, Patti Wilcox, and Neil A. Holtzman, "Decision-Making About Breast Cancer Susceptibility Testing: How Similar Are the Attitudes of Physicians, Nurse Practitioners, and At-Risk Women?," *Journal of Clinical Oncology* 16 (1998): 2868–2876. On the current biological understanding of breast cancer, see Samuel Hellman, "Natural History of Small Breast Cancers," *Journal of Clinical Oncology* 12 (1994): 2229–2234.

63. E-mail from Harvey Kushner to the author, November 16, 1999.

64. Interview with Amy Langer, March 24, 1999.

65. Women consistently overestimate the mortality caused by breast cancer as compared with other diseases.

66. Quoted in Lisa Belkin, "How Breast Cancer Became This Year's Hot Charity," *New York Times Magazine*, December 22, 1996, pp. 40–57.

67. See the web site of the National Breast Cancer Coalition at www.natlbcc.org/aboutindx.asp.

68. Frances M. Visco to NBCC membership, September 1999.

69. Langer interview, March 24, 1999.

70. Belkin, "How Breast Cancer Became," 46.

71. This quotation appeared on a website for a Komen Foundation event: www.jumpforthecause.com. See also Jami Bernard, "Roughing It," *Mamm*, January 2000, p. 64.

72. See Gina Kolata and Lawrence A. Fisher, "Drugs to Fight Breast Cancer Near Approval," *New York Times*, September 3, 1998, pp. A1, A24. Extensive funding for Herceptin research came from Revlon.

73. Deborah J. Golder, "Exploiting Breast Cancer Won't Cure It," *New York Times*, October 7, 1996, p. A16.

74. Donald R. Lannin, Holly F. Mathews, Jim Mitchell, Melvin S. Swanson, Frances H. Swanson, and Maxine S. Edwards, "Influence of Socioeconomic and Cultural Factors on Racial Differences in Late-Stage Presentation of Breast Cancer," *Journal of the American Medical Association* 279 (1998): 1801–1807.

75. Anne S. Kasper and Susan J. Ferguson, "Eliminating Breast Cancer from Our Future," in Anne S. Kasper and Susan J. Ferguson, eds., *Breast Cancer: Society Shapes an Epidemic* (New York: St. Martin's Press, 2000), 355–373. The foremost

critic of conflict-of-interest in cancer control has been Samuel S. Epstein. See *The Politics of Cancer Revisited* (Fremont, N.Y.: East Ridge Press, 1998).

76. Irwin D. Bross, Ph.D., to the author, November 2, 1999.

77. Barbara A. Brenner, "STARs in Their Eyes," *Newsletter of Breast Cancer Action*, August–September 1999.

78. Kasper and Ferguson, "Eliminating Breast Cancer," 358.

79. Sandra Steingraber, "We All Live Downwind," in Judith Brady, ed., *1 in 3: Women with Cancer Confront an Epidemic* (Pittsburgh, Pa.: Cleis Press, 1991), 36–48.

80. Critics of Steingraber and other environmental activists argue that no data exist that prove the association of toxins and higher breast cancer rates.

81. Susan Ferraro, " 'You Can't Look Away Anymore': The Anguished Politics of Breast Cancer," *New York Times Magazine*, August 15, 1993, pp. 24–27, 58, 61–62.

82. The one long-term exception has been the federally funded Women's Health Initiative.

83. On this conflation of early detection and primary prevention, see Lenn E. Goodman and Madeleine J. Goodman, "Prevention—How Misuse of a Concept Undercuts Its Worth," *Hastings Center Report*, April 1986, p. 26–38.

84. Interview with Cynthia Pearson, May 18, 2000.

85. Bernard Fisher, "Highlights of the NSABP Breast Cancer Prevention Trial," *Cancer Control* 4, no. 1 (1997): 78–86.

86. Altman, *Waking Up, Fighting Back*, 96; Adriane Fugh-Berman, "Tamoxifen on Trial: The High Risks of Prevention," *The Nation*, December 21, 1992; Bernard Fisher, "Commentary on Endometrial Cancer Deaths in Tamoxifen-Treated Breast Cancer Patients," *Journal of Clinical Oncology* 14 (1996): 1027–1039.

87. Quoted in Sharon Batt, *Patient No More: The Politics of Breast Cancer* (Charlottetown, Canada: Gynergy Books, 1994), 194. See also p. 135.

88. Fisher, "Commentary," 1035.

89. John C. Bailar III, "Surgery for Early Breast Cancer—Can Less Be More? [Editorial]," *New England Journal of Medicine* 333 (1995): 1496–1498.

90. Batt, *Patient No More*, 356.

91. Lawrence K. Altman, "Health Officials Apologize for Problems with Falsified Data in Cancer Study," *New York Times*, April 14, 1994, p. A19.

92. Bernard Fisher, "Democracy in Medicine? [Letter to the Editor]," *The Sciences*, November-December 1995, pp. 3–6. Marcia Angell, former editor of the *New England Journal of Medicine*, also charged feminists and other activists as being "antiscience" in her writings on the breast implant controversy. See Sue V. Rosser, "Controversies in Breast Cancer Research," in Anne S. Kasper and Susan J. Ferguson, eds., *Breast Cancer: Society Shapes an Epidemic* (New York: St. Martin's Press, 2000), 245–270.

93. Bernard Fisher, "Shrinking the Gap Between the Treatment and Prevention of Breast Cancer: The Role of Tamoxifen," paper given at Cornell University Medical College, New York, N.Y., April 20, 1999.

94. Bernard Fisher, J. Constantino, Carol Redmond, et al., "Tamoxifen for Prevention of Breast Cancer: Report of the National Surgical Adjuvant Breast and Bowel Project P-1 Study," *Journal of the National Cancer Institute* 90 (1999): 1371–1388.

95. Fisher, "Shrinking the Gap."

96. Maryann Napoli, "Questions Remain on Cancer Test [Letter to the Editor]," *New York Times*, April 13, 1998, A26. See also Altman, *Waking Up, Fighting Back*, 96.

97. Letter to Richard Klausner, November 30, 1999, letter obtained courtesy of Sharon Batt. The signatories were representatives from the Boston Women's Health Book Collective, the Center for Medical Consumers, Breast Cancer Action, Breast Cancer Action Montreal, the National Women's Health Network, and the Women's Community Cancer Project.

98. Leopold, *A Darker Ribbon*, 272.

99. Ibid., 273.

100. On the challenges of viewing breast cancer in both personal and feminist terms, see Barbara Katz Rothman, *Genetic Maps and Human Imaginations: The Limits of Science in Understanding Who We Are* (New York: W. W. Norton, 1998), 160–169. The historian Susan Reverby characterized this issue as a conflict between the body and the body politic in "Gendering Health Policy: Historical Reflections," paper given at the conference "Women, Science and Health in Post-War North America," March 5–6, 1999, Toronto, Canada.

101. "Report from San Antonio," *NABCO News*, January 2000, pp. 1, 5.

102. "Heroes Among Us," *Solutions: Business News and Commentary for Zeneca Pharmaceuticals U.S. Employees*, 2, issue 3, May 1998. See also Kolata and Fisher, "Drugs to Fight Breast Cancer," A24.

103. Susan Sontag, *Illness as Metaphor* (New York: Farrar, Straus & Giroux, 1978), 3.

104. Vincent T. DeVita, "The War on Cancer Has a Birthday, and a Present," *Journal of Clinical Oncology* 15 (1997): 867–869.

105. John C. Bailar III and Elaine M. Smith, "Progress Against Cancer?," *New England Journal of Medicine* 314 (1986): 1226–1232. See also David Plotkin, "Good News and Bad News About Breast Cancer," *Atlantic Monthly*, June 1996, pp. 53–82.

106. Vincent T. DeVita, Jr., "Comments on the Article by Bailar and Smith," unpublished manuscript, June 3, 1986, Kushner Papers, box 13, folder 203.

107. John C. Bailar III and Heather L. Gornik, "Cancer Undefeated," *New England Journal of Medicine* 336 (1997): 1569–1574.

108. M. Rosen, "Mission Possible: A Cancer Survivor Fights Back," *Good Housekeeping*, April 1997, 30.

109. Olympia Snowe, "Snowe: America Must Declare War on Breast Cancer," *Congressional Press Releases*, June 13, 1996.

110. Quoted in Craig Horowitz, "First to Finish," *New York*, May 25, 1998, pp. 66–71.

111. Audre Lorde, *The Cancer Journals* (San Francisco: Spinsters, 1980), 60.

112. Ibid., 73.

113. Deena Metzger, *Tree: Essays and Pieces* (Berkeley, Calif.: North Atlantic Books, 1997).

114. Richard L. Wentworth to Rose Kushner, June 7, 1988, Kushner Papers, box 4, unlabeled folder. See also Langer interview, March 24, 1999.

115. Ferraro, "'You Can't Look Away Anymore.'"

116. Ian Fisher, "Health Care for Lesbians Gets a Sharper Focus," *New York Times*, June 21, 1998, p. 27.

117. Jeanne F. Allegra, "Thanks, but Do Call Me a Survivor [Letter to the Editor]," *Washington Post*, June 6, 2000, p. Z4.

118. Quoted in advertisement for Avon Breast Cancer 3 Day, *New York Times*, January 9, 2000, p. 22.

119. See www.jumpforthecause.com.

120. Howard Brody, "Hope," *Journal of the American Medical Association* 246 (1981): 1411–1412.

121. A. Scott Walton, "New and Improved: A Breast Cancer Survivor Accentuates the Positive with an Upbeat Makeover," *Atlanta Journal and Constitution*, November 5, 2000, p. 8.

122. Anneliese M. Mitchell, "Mrs. Ford's Operation [Letter to the Editor]," *Washington Post*, October 8, 1974, p. 21.

123. Mary T. Meyn, "'The War on Cancer' [Letter to the Editor]," *Washington Post*, October 26, 1981, p. 12.

124. Frances Elliott, "Breast Cancer [Letter to the Editor]," *Atlantic Monthly*, October 1996, p. 8.

125. Hilda Raz, ed., *Living on the Margins: Women Writers on Breast Cancer* (New York: Persea Books, 1999).

126. Christina Middlebrook, *Seeing the Crab: A Memoir of Dying Before I Do* (New York: Basic Books, 1996), 61.

127. Ibid., 72.

128. Conway, *Ordinary Life*, 193.

129. Middlebrook, *Seeing the Crab*, 114.

130. Kathlyn Conway, "Presumed Behaviors and Attitudes for the Contemporary Breast Cancer Patient," paper presented at the annual meeting of the Ameri-

can Public Health Association, Chicago, Il., November 10, 1999. See also Batt, *Patient No More*, 213–238.

131. Dian Marino, "White Flowers and a Grizzly Bear: Finding New Metaphors," in Midge Stocker, ed., *Cancer as a Women's Issue* (Chicago: Third Side Press, 1991), 183–196.

Chapter 12. Breast Cancer and Genetics

1. Jane E. Brody, "Risks for Cancer Can Start in the Womb," *New York Times*, December 21, 1999, pp. F1, F6.

2. Michael Waldholz, *Curing Cancer: Solving One of the Greatest Medical Mysteries of Our Time* (New York: Simon & Schuster, 1997).

3. Jane E. Brody, "Cancer Gene Tests Turn Out to Be Far from Simple," *New York Times*, August 17, 1999, pp. F1, F9.

4. Douglas F. Easton, Deborah Ford, and D. Timothy Bishop, "Breast and Ovarian Cancer Incidence in BRCA-1 Mutation Carriers," *American Journal of Human Genetics* 56 (1995): 265–271.

5. Dorothy Nelkin, "Genetics and Social Policy," *Bulletin of the New York Academy of Medicine* 68 (1992): 135–143.

6. Sam C. Gwynne, "Living with Lethal Genes: Some Advice," *Time*, October 12, 1998.

7. Michael Waldholz, "A Cancer Survivor's Genetic Time Bomb," *Wall Street Journal*, November 10, 1997, pp. B1, B13.

8. Meredith Wadman, "Women Need Not Apply: The DNA Test That Doctors Don't Want to Share," *Washington Post*, May 5, 1996, p. C3.

9. Waldholz, "A Cancer Survivor's Genetic Time Bomb," B1.

10. Patricia Lynden, "Your Breasts or Your Life?," *American Health*, June 1997, pp. 29–31.

11. *Annals of Surgical Oncology* 4 (1997): 10A–11A.

12. See the back cover of *Mamm* magazine, May 2000.

13. Quoted in Patricia Kahn, "Coming to Grips with Genes and Risk," *Science* 274 (1996): 496–498.

14. Gina Kolata, "Breaking Ranks, Lab Offers Test to Assess Risk of Breast Cancer," *New York Times*, April 1, 1996, pp. A1, A15. See also Harvey J. Stern, Anne Maddalena, and Joseph D. Schulman, "Pitfalls of Genetic Testing [Letter to the Editor]," *New England Journal of Medicine* 335 (1996): 1235.

15. See, for example, Bernadine Healy, "BRCA Genes—Bookmaking, Fortunetelling, and Medical Care [Editorial]," *New England Journal of Medicine* 336

(1997): 1448–1449; "Statement of the American Society of Clinical Oncology: Genetic Testing for Cancer Susceptibility," *Journal of Clinical Oncology* 14 (1996): 1730–1736; American Cancer Society, *Cancer and Genetics: Answering Your Patients' Questions* (Huntington, N.Y.: PRR, 1997).

16. Erik Parens, "Glad and Terrified: On the Ethics of BRCA1 and 2 Testing," *Cancer Investigations* 14 (1996): 405–411; Baruch Modan, "The Genetic Passport," *American Journal of Epidemiology* 147 (1998): 513–515.

17. Tovah G. Freedman, "Genetic Susceptibility Testing: A Therapeutic Illusion? [Editorial]" *Cancer* 79 (1997): 2063–2065.

18. H. Gilbert Welch and Wylie Burke, "Uncertainties in Genetic Testing for Chronic Disease," *Journal of the American Medical Association* 280 (1998): 1525–1527; Sally Lehrman, "Should You Get the Breast Cancer Gene Test?," *Health*, November-December 1998, pp. 129–134.

19. Quoted in Kolata, "Breaking Ranks," A15.

20. Keith Wailoo, *Drawing Blood: Technology and Disease Identity in Twentieth-Century America* (Baltimore: Johns Hopkins Univ. Press, 1997), 180–186.

21. Quoted in Sheryl Gay Stolberg, "Concern Among Jews Is Heightened as Scientists Deepen Gene Studies," *New York Times*, April 22, 1998, p. A24.

22. Gina Kolata, "Bad Genes: A Cancer-Causing Mutation Is Found in European Jews," *New York Times*, October 1, 1995, sec. IV, p. 2.

23. Stolberg, "Concern Among Jews," A24.

24. Ibid.; Lisa S. Parker, "Breast Cancer Genetic Screening and Critical Bioethics' Gaze," *Journal of Medicine and Philosophy* 20 (1995): 313–337.

25. E. J. Kessler, "The Secret Shake-Up in the Shiduch," *Forward*, July 26, 1996, pp. 11, 13.

26. E. Virginia Lapham, Chahira Kozma, and Joan O. Weiss, "Genetic Discrimination: Perspectives of Consumers," *Science* 274 (1996): 621–624; Gina Kolata, "Advent of Testing for Breast Cancer Genes Leads to Fears of Disclosure and Discrimination," *New York Times*, February 4, 1997, pp. C1, C3.

27. Albert B. Jonsen, Sharon J. Durfy, Wylie Burke, and Arno G. Motulsky, "The Advent of the 'Unpatients,'" *Nature Medicine* 2 (1996): 622–624.

28. Joseph Colt Bloodgood, "Diagnosis and Treatment of Border-Line Pathological Lesions," *Surgery, Gynecology & Obstetrics* 18 (1914): 19–34.

29. *People*, April 19, 1999, pp. 66–68; Katrina Armstrong, Andrea Eisen, and Barbara Weber, "Assessing the Risk of Breast Cancer," *New England Journal of Medicine* 342 (2000): 564–571.

30. Alan R. Peterson and Deborah Lupton, *The New Public Health: Health and Self in the Age of Risk* (London: Sage Publications, 1996); Jackie Stacey, *Teratologies: A Cultural Study of Cancer* (London: Routledge, 1996); Barbara A. Koenig and Alan Stockdale,

"The Promise of Molecular Medicine in Preventing Disease: Examining the Burden of Genetic Risk," in Daniel Callahan, ed., *Health Promotion and Disease Prevention: Ethical and Social Dilemmas* (Washington, D.C.: Georgetown Univ. Press, 2000).

31. F. Eisinger, G. Geller, W. Burke, and N. A. Holtzman, "Cultural Basis for Differences Between US and French Clinical Recommendations for Women at Increased Risk of Breast and Ovarian Cancer," *Lancet* 353 (1999): 919–920; François Eisinger, Claire Julian-Reynier, Hagay Sobol, Dominique Stoppa-Lyonnet, Christine Lasset, and Catherine Nogues, "Acceptability of Prophylactic Mastectomy in Cancer-Prone Women," *Journal of the American Medical Association* 283 (2000): 202–203. This discussion builds on work by Jean-Paul Gaudilliere on the response to genetic testing across cultures.

32. Victor R. Grann, K. S. Panageas, William Whang, Karen H. Antman, and Alfred I. Neugut, "Decision Analysis of Prophylactic Mastectomy and Oophorectomy in BRCA1- or BRCA2-Positive Patients," *Journal of Clinical Oncology* 16 (1998): 1–7; Deborah Schrag, Karen M. Kuntz, Judy E. Garber, and Jane C. Weeks, "Life Expectancy Gains from Cancer Prevention Strategies for Women with Breast Cancer and BRCA1 or BRCA2 Mutations," *Journal of the American Medical Association* 283 (2000): 617–624.

33. Lynn C. Hartman, Daniel J. Schaid, John E. Woods, et al., "Efficacy of Bilateral Prophylactic Mastectomy in Women with a Family History of Breast Cancer," *New England Journal of Medicine* 340 (1999): 77–84.

34. Marsha Ginsburg, "Breast Cancer: A Radical Solution," *San Francisco Examiner*, April 18, 1999, p. A1.

35. Rita Rubin, "Healthy Breast Removal Is Backed: Study Affirms Reduced Cancer Risk," *USA Today*, January 14, 1999, p. 1D.

36. Linda Kulman and Marissa Melton, "Sacrificing Breasts Before Cancer Strikes," *U.S. News & World Report*, January 25, 1999, p. 70.

37. Ginsburg, "Breast Cancer: A Radical Solution," A10.

38. Josephine Marcotty, "The Decision Was Both Tough and Easy for Three Sisters," *(Minneapolis) Star Tribune*, November 5, 2000, p. 14A. A recent study using the Mayo Clinic data suggests that the 90 percent risk reduction figure also applies to women with BRCA mutations. See Denise Grady, "Removing Healthy Breasts Found Effective in High Cancer-Risk Group," *New York Times*, April 4, 2000, p. F7.

39. Quoted in Wadman, "Women Need Not Apply."

40. Kathryn Senior, "BRCA Mutations Complicate Conservative Cancer Surgery," *Lancet* 354 (1999): 269.

41. Leslie A. Young, "The Trauma of Healthy Breast Removal," *Denver Rocky Mountain News*, January 26, 1999, p. 3D.

42. Jim Ritter, "Mastectomy Cuts Cancer Risk," *Chicago Sun-Times*, January 14, 1999, p. 3.

43. Parker, "Breast Cancer Genetic Screening"; Gail Geller, Barbara A. Bernhardt, Teresa Doksum, Kathy J. Helzlsouer, Patti Wilcox, and Neil A. Holtzman, "Decision-Making About Breast Cancer Susceptibility Testing: How Similar Are the Attitudes of Physicians, Nurse Practitioners, and At-Risk Women?," *Journal of Clinical Oncology* 16 (1998): 2868–2876.

44. Caryn Lerman, Edward Lustbader, Barbara Rimer, et al., "Effects of Individualized Breast Cancer Risk Counseling: A Randomized Trial," *Journal of the National Cancer Institute* 87 (1995): 286–292.

45. Gina Kolata, "Genetic Testing Falls Short of Public Embrace," *New York Times*, March 27, 1998, p. A16.

46. Caryn Lerman, Mary Daly, Agnes Masny, and Andrew Balshem, "Attitudes About Genetic Testing for Breast–Ovarian Cancer Susceptibility," *Journal of Clinical Oncology* 12 (1994): 843–850; J. P. Struewing, C. Lerman, R. G. Kase, T. R. Giambarresi, and M. S. Tucker, "Anticipated Uptake and Impact of Genetic Testing in Hereditary Breast and Ovarian Cancer Families," *Cancer Epidemiology Biomarkers Prevention* 4 (1995): 169–173.

47. Kolata, "Genetic Testing," A16.

48. Ibid.

49. Ibid., A16. Some have also cautioned that the error rate in interpreting genetic testing is unacceptably high. See Rick Weiss, "Genetic Testing's Human Toll," *Washington Post*, July 21, 1999, A1.

50. Beth Newman, Hua Mu, Lesley M. Butler, Robert C. Millikan, Patricia G. Moorman and Mary-Claire King, "Frequency of Breast Cancer Attributable to BRCA1 in a Population-Based Series of American Women," *Journal of the American Medical Association* 279 (1998): 915–921.

51. Jeffrey P. Struewing, Patricia Hartge, Sholom Wacholder, et al., "The Risk of Cancer Associated with Specific Mutations of BRCA1 and BRCA2 Among Ashkenazi Jews," *New England Journal of Medicine* 336 (1997): 1401–1408.

52. Barbara Katz Rothman, *Genetic Maps and Human Imaginations: The Limits of Science in Understanding Who We Are* (New York: W.W. Norton, 1998).

Epilogue

1. Robert T. Greenlee, Taylor Murray, Sherry Bolden, and Phyllis A. Wingo, "Cancer Statistics, 2000," *Ca* 50 (2000): 7–33.

2. Lynn C. Hartman, Daniel J. Schaid, John E. Woods, et al., "Efficacy of Bilateral Prophylactic Mastectomy in Women with a Family History of Breast Cancer," *New England Journal of Medicine* 340 (1999): 77–84.

3. Marlene H. Frost, Daniel J. Schaid, Thomas A. Sellers, et al., "Long-Term Satisfaction and Psychological and Social Functioning Following Bilateral Prophylactic Mastectomy," *Journal of the American Medical Association* 284 (2000): 319–324.

Index

Ackerman, Lauren V., 97, 133–34
activism. *See* patient activism
Adair, Frank E., 50, 82–83, 98, 123, 124, 127
Adams, Samuel Hopkins, 30
adjuvant chemotherapy, 136–37, 226, 252, 254. *See also* chemotherapy
adriamycin, 254
African American women, 47, 157, 261–62. *See also* Lorde, Audre
age, patient: and mammography, 207, 212, 213, 243–45; and threat of cancer, 54, 216
Agnew, D. Hayes, 15
Alexander, Shana, 214
Allegra, Jeanne F., 271
American Association of University Women (AAUW), 47
American Cancer Society (ACS), 7, 108, 169, 171–72, 268; ambivalence of, 168; Bayh's work for, 183, 224; and breast self-exams, 53–57; Crile's criticism of, 64, 65–67; and genetic testing, 280; and Kushner, 180, 227–28; and mammography controversy, 8, 12, 196, 205–7, 216, 245; Pap smear promotion by, 50–53; and RCTs, 123; and rehabilitation programs, 144; simple mastectomy endorsed by, 225–26. *See also* early detection campaigns (ACS)
American College of Surgeons, 8, 42, 109, 149, 180
American Medical Association, 64, 179–80, 233
American Society for the Control of Cancer (ASCC), 7, 30, 43–50; anticancer campaign of, 43–48; Lasker's work with, 49–50. *See also* American Cancer Society
American Surgical Association, 22, 26

Amick, Carol C., 232
Amputee's Alliance, 142
Anderson, Jack, 209
antibiotics, 70
anticancer campaigns, 41, 43–48
anticancer organizations, 8, 45. *See also* specific organization
antisepsis, 18
appearance issues, 165; breast reconstruction, 191–95; and life *versus* breast calculus, 186–88; mutilation, 33, 159, 186, 233. *See also* disfigurement
Apple, Rima, 9
Ariel, Irving M., 162, 165
Armel, Paula, 193
Ashkenazi Jewish women, 14, 281–82
AstraZeneca (drug manufacturer), 249, 262, 266, 267, 285
Atkins, Sir Hedley, 134
Auchincloss, Hugh, 54, 112–13
Aust, J. Bradley, 121
Austen, W. Gerald, 168
authority, of surgeon, 75, 165, 169, 217, 231, 291–92. *See also* decision making; power, of surgeons
Avon Corporation, 260, 271–72
axillary lymph nodes, 22, 32, 99, 131; and chemotherapy, 252; complete dissection of, 17, 112, 238–39; early detection and, 247; positive, 80, 112, 121, 226, 273; and superradical surgery, 69, 80, 82

Baclesse, François, 116
Bailar, John C., III, 209–13, 216, 221, 268–69
Bayh, Marvella, 144, 161, 182–83, 186, 224–25
Beahrs, Oliver, 218, 220, 221
Benfield, John R., 200

Bennett, William, 3
Bergman, Ingrid, 237
Berlin, Nathaniel I., 206–7, 210, 217
Billroth, Theodor, 20
biological predeterminism, 98–109, 136,
    138, 279, 295; challenges to, 106–10;
    and death rate, 101–2; and early detec-
    tion, 242; and Fisher's model, 223, 230;
    and statistical analysis, 12, 100–101,
    108, 293–94. See also genetic testing
biological/systemic model, of breast can-
    cer, 6, 226–27, 230, 233; and Halsted
    model, 33, 223, 226, 228
biometrics/biostatistics, 10, 93, 101,
    113–14. See also statistical analyses
biopsy, 28, 177; contralateral, 199–200;
    delay in, 171; mirror image, 174, 293;
    and one-step procedure, 146, 153, 173;
    sentinel node, 247, 248; triple, 95–96
biotechnology companies, 280
birth control agents, 150
Bishop, Jerry E., 251
Black, Maurice M., 102–3, 136, 253
Black, Shirley Temple, 7, 170–72, 224
Blackwell, Anne S., 244
bladder cancer, 148
Bland, Cornelia Shaw, 39
Bloodgood, Joseph Colt, 26, 28, 284
Blum, Diane, 258
body mutilation, 33
Bonadonna, Gianni, 252, 254
Boyd, David P., 110
Brandt, Allan M., 126
BRCA mutation. See genetic testing
breast, as dispensible part, 88–90
Breast Cancer: A Personal History and Investigative
    Report (Kushner), 178
"Breast Cancer: Has the Time Come for a
    Less Mutilating Treatment?" (Cope),
    148
Breast Cancer Advisory Center, 178
Breast Cancer Detection Demonstration
    Project (BCDDP), 173, 196, 206–15,
    228, 243; criticism of, 209–15, 269;
    defense of, 215–21; goals of, 206–9;
    and media, 209, 212–14, 219–20

Breast Cancer Prevention Trial (NSABP P-
    01), 263–66
Breast Cancer Risk Assessment Tool, 285
breast cancer screening. See early detection;
    mammography
"Breast Cancer Surgery" (Kushner), 177
Breast Cancer Task Force (NCI), 138
breast conservation therapy, 132–34, 257.
    See also chemotherapy;
    lumpectomy/partial mastectomy;
    radiotherapy
Breast for Life, A (Isaac), 156
breast reconstruction, 191–95
breast removal. See mastectomy; radical
    mastectomy
breast self-examination (BSE), 41, 53–60,
    157; American Cancer Society promo-
    tion of, 53–57; and fear of cancer,
    57–59
"Breast Self-Examination" (film), 55, 59
Brenner, Barbara, 262
Breslow, Lester, 213
Brieger, Gert, 21
Brinker, Nancy, 258, 260
Brinkley, Diana, 133, 134
Bristol-Myers Squibb (drug manufac-
    turer), 255
Britain. See England
Broders, Albert C., 197
Brody, Jane, 220
Bross, Irwin D., 129, 214
Brunschwig, Alexander, 73, 76, 77, 79
Bullock, Walter O., 36
Burney, Frances, 16
Byrd, Benjamin F., Jr., 213

Caceres, Eduardo, 73
Cameron, Charles S., 50–53, 61, 66–67,
    205
Campbell, Jeanne, 157
Campion, Rosamond. See Rosmond,
    Babette
Canada, 4, 45, 101, 133
cancer, 11; as local disease, 17, 30, 31, 37;
    ovarian, 276, 278–79, 285, 288, 289;
    Pap test for cervical, 48–53, 54, 205;

prostate, 88–89, 136, 179; recurrence rate in, 21–22, 36, 37–39, 163, 252; stages of, 94–95; stomach, 72, 79; as systemic disease, 6, 223, 226, 228, 233; uterine, 46, 49, 54, 264, 266, 267. See also carcinoma in situ; models, of breast cancer; precancers

Cancer and Common Sense (Crile), 64

Cancer Journals, The (Lorde), 190

cancerphobia, 29, 65–67, 216. See also fear, of cancer

carcinoma in situ, 218; ductal (DCIS), 197, 243, 246–48, 284; lobular (LCIS), 174, 197–201, 246, 284, 294. See also precancers

Carter, B. Noland, 86

case review, 21, 79, 97. See also retrospective studies; statistical analyses

Casper, Monica J., 51

Cassell, Joan, 125

Castro, Chris, 272

Cave, Henry W., 88

celebrity patients, 170–75; Happy Rockefeller, 7, 12, 170, 174–75, 209, 224; Ingrid Bergman, 237; Marvella Bayh, 144, 161, 182–83, 186, 224–25; Nancy Reagan, 256–57; Shirley Temple Black, 170–72. See also Ford, Betty

Center for Medical Consumers, 179

cervical cancer, pap smear for, 48–53, 54, 205

Chamberlain, Max, 73

chemoprevention, 288, 295. See also tamoxifen

chemotherapy, 6, 13, 173, 229, 251–55; adjuvant, 136–37, 226, 252, 254; prophylactic, 284; side effects of, 252, 254, 274

Cherry, Sis., 157

Childe, Charles P., 30, 38

Churchill, Edward D., 70

Clarke, Adele E., 51

Clarke, William C., 28

class, 47, 156–57, 261–62

Cleveland Clinic, 61, 63, 157, 158. See also Crile, George W., Jr.

Cline, John W., 122

clinical expertise, and RCTs, 100, 122, 123–24

clinical staging, 94–95

clinical trials. See randomized controlled trials

Clinton, Bill, 245

Cobleigh, Melody, 288

Cold War, 41, 52. See also military metaphors

Cole, Warren H., 136

Columbia Clinical Classification System, 95

Columbia-Presbyterian Medical Center, 198, 233, 235, 237–38, 269

commando operation, 75. See also military metaphors

Conerly, Dawson B., 78

confidentiality, and testing, 283, 290

Congress, U.S., 43, 203, 259, 265; Senate, 150, 244

consumerist model, 251

contralateral biopsy, 199–200

Control of a Scourge, The (Childe), 30

Conway, Kathlyn, 257, 274, 275

Cooley, Denton, 78

Cooperman, Avram M., 158, 164, 235

Cope, Oliver, 10, 146–49, 151, 167–68, 238

Crile, George, Jr. (Barney), 10, 61–67, 70, 138, 149, 235; on biological predeterminism, 103, 108; case studies of, 116–18, 128; challenge to Halsted procedure, 6, 86, 104–5, 129–30, 135–36; criticism of, 166–67; criticism of ACS by, 64, 65–67; death of, 238; and father, 61–62, 63; and less radical surgery, 6, 230; and patient activism, 153, 154; and wives' cancers, 130–31, 162–63, 181–82

Crile, George Washington, 61–63

Crile, Helen Sandburg, 162–63, 181–82, 224

Crile, Jane Halle, 130–31, 162

Crowe, Samuel, 26

cure, 11, 21–22, 37–39, 92, 292; and biometricians' challenge, 113–14; and precancer removal, 200–201; three-year, 22, 38; vs. palliation, 77–79, 81. See also recurrence; survival rate

Cure Cancer Program, 203

Curie, Pierre and Marie Curie, 35
Curtis, B. Farquhar, 38, 39
Cushing, Harvey, 20, 26, 32, 84
Cutler, Max, 56, 89, 144–45
Cutler, Sidney, 212
cyclophosphamide, 251, 254
cytokeratin staining, 247–48
cytology, cervical, 48–53

Dahl-Iversen, Erling, 73
Daland, Ernest P., 93–94
Dandy, Walter, 26
Dao, Thomas L., 177, 178
Darker Ribbon, A (Leopold), 266
David Susskind Show (TV program), 165–66,
    188, 189
death rate/mortality, 4, 26, 29, 46,
    221–22; and biological predetermin-
    ism, 101–2; from cervical cancer, 54;
    and class, 47, 261; and cure, 113;
    decline in, 268, 286, 294; and lumpec-
    tomy, 160; and mammography, 207,
    210, 245; and positive axillary nodes,
    112, 273; after radical mastectomy, 22,
    36–37; during RCTs, 266; stability in,
    8, 200, 202–3; from superradical
    surgery, 81. See also survival rate
Deaver, John B., 31, 70
decision making: and patient activism,
    140, 150, 161, 231; right to choose,
    156, 158, 296; women's exclusion
    from, 10, 135, 175, 179, 240
delay, in treatment. See early detection
demonstration project. See Breast Cancer
    Detection Demonstration Project
Denmark, 101, 116
Dennis, Joseph L., 121
Department of Defense, 259
depression, postmastectomy, 144. See also
    psychosocial effects
detection programs. See early detection
    programs; mammography; Pap smear
DeVita, Vincent T., Jr., 221, 268, 269
Diehl, Harold S., 79
diet, and cancer, 267
Diseases of the Breast (Haagensen), 84, 236

disfigurement, surgical, 32, 59, 159, 189;
    emotional effects of, 145, 184–86;
    from superradical procedures, 81, 103.
    See also appearance issues
Doctors' Case Against the Pill, The (Seaman), 150
Douglas, Mary, 126, 216
drug addiction, 25–26
ductal carcinoma in situ (DCIS), 197,
    246–48, 284. See also carcinoma in situ;
    precancers
Dyson, W. H., 111

early detection, 242–50; and DCIS precan-
    cer controversy, 246–48; and mam-
    mography controversy, 12, 243–46,
    248–49; and statistical analysis,
    249–50; vs. prevention, 263
early detection campaigns, 182, 183,
    224–25, 292–93; funding of, 260; and
    patient narratives, 187, 195
early detection campaigns (ACS), 11–12,
    41, 173, 292; criticism of, 61, 65,
    67–68; and precancers, 205, 207, 242
Ebony (magazine), 157
Edelman, Stanley, 161
Egan, Robert L., 111, 204, 208
Elliot, Frances, 273
Ellis, Harold, 98
emotional effects, of mastectomy, 144–46,
    186, 191. See also psychosocial effects
en bloc dissection, 21, 72, 85, 97, 226
England, 4, 35, 45, 97–98, 134, 157
English, Peter, 61
environmental toxins, 262–63, 267, 278
epidemiology, 217. See also randomized
    controlled trials
Esselstyn, Caldwell B., Jr., 158, 162
estrogen-blockers, 80–81, 254, 267. See also
    tamoxifen
ethics, medical, 64, 138, 148, 166
eugenics movement, 281
Europe, 45, 116, 133, 134–35. See also specific
    country
Ewing, James, 35
extended radical mastectomy, 6, 7, 81–82.
    See also superradical mastectomy

falsified data, in trials, 265
family, and genetic testing, 276, 278, 282–83
fatalism, 29, 42–43, 295. *See also* biological predeterminism
fear, of cancer, 41, 52; and breast exams, 57–59; cancerphobia, 29, 66–67, 216
feminist movement, 144, 146, 150–51, 156
feminists, 5, 9, 155, 231, 267; as activist patients, 178, 187; Betty Ford as, 172, 175; and breast reconstruction, 191–95; and modified radical mastectomy, 239–40; and tamoxifen trials, 264, 266. *See also* Lorde, Audre
Ferguson, Donald J., 26, 70, 124
Field, Richard J., Jr., 231
Fink, Diane, 221
Firor, Warfield M., 117
First, You Cry (Rollin), xii, 10, 183, 184, 190
Fisher, Bernard, 12, 96, 129, 162; challenge to radical surgery by, 136, 137–40, 293; partnership with Kushner, 180, 181, 227–29; randomized controlled trials of, 172, 225, 226–27, 228–31, 236, 257–58; systemic cancer model of, 6, 223, 226, 228, 233; and tamoxifen trials, 263, 264–65
Fisher, Edwin, 136
Fitzwilliams, Duncan C. L., 35
5-fluorouracil, 251
five-year cure/survival, 93, 97, 100, 103, 116, 224
Flexner, Abraham, 24
Flexner, Marion W., 87
Flint, Austin, 70
Foote, Frank W., Jr., 197
Ford, Betty, 7, 170, 172–73, 175, 178–79, 224; and early detection efforts, 12, 173, 187, 208
Ford, Gerald R., 172, 178–79
Foster, Grace, 273
Foster, Roger S., Jr., 117
Fouty, William, 172–73
Fox, Maurice S., 201
France, 35, 45, 116, 134
Frank, Ludwig M., 145

Frankfort, Ellen, 9, 155, 156
Fredricks, Simon, 200
Freedom of Information Act, 213, 214
Friedan, Betty, 150
Friedman, Milton, 178–79
Friel, Patrick B., 145
frozen section diagnosis, 28, 146, 176–77. *See also* biopsy
Fugh-Berman, Adriane, 264
fundraising, 50, 259, 260, 272

Galen (Greek physician), 16
Gaspar, Max R., 164
gastrectomy, 72, 79
Gately, Marie F., 154, 165, 185
gender, 9, 69–70, 250; and breast reconstruction, 194; and radical mastectomy, 88–91; roles, 59; stereotypes, 164–65. *See also* sexism
genetic testing, 13–14, 261, 276–90, 295–96; and confidentiality, 283, 290; environmental factors in, 278; and family members, 276, 278, 282–83; and future risk, 14, 277, 284–86; and Jewish women, 14, 281–82; lack of enthusiasm for, 288–90; and prophylactic mastectomy, 276, 280, 285–88
George, Charlotte, 126–27
Germany, 17, 18, 21, 45, 281
Gerrish, Frederic H., 22, 23
Gershon-Cohen, Jacob, 111, 204
Gilman, Charlotte Perkins, 93, 142
Goethe, Johann Wolfgang von, 7
Goldberg, Whoopi, 263
Gordis, Leon, 244–45
Gordon-Taylor, Gordon, 78
Gornik, Heather L., 269
government funding, 259
Grace, Edwin J., 35
Graham, Evarts, 62, 125
Grann, Victor R., 286
Grant, Roald N., 72, 89, 115, 122–23
Greenberg, Daniel S., 213–14, 216, 219
Greenough, Robert B., 42, 94
Greenspan, Ezra M., 162, 165
Gump, Frank E., 169, 235

Guttman Institute, 173, 209
gynecological cancers, 73

Haagensen, Alice, 236
Haagensen, Cushman D., 75, 82, 114,
    235–38, 238; on breast exams, 55–56,
    57, 59; challenge to, 113; patient man-
    ner of, 236–37; on precancers, 198,
    201; and radical mastectomy (Halsted),
    83, 84–87, 124, 129, 140, 235–36; and
    randomization, 114; on stages of malig-
    nancy, 94–95; and triple biopsy, 95–96
Habif, David V., 235
Halsted, William Stewart, 3–4, 17–28, 36,
    142; cure and, 37–39, 291; drug addic-
    tion of, 25–26; and early detection,
    293; and German medical technique,
    18–19, 20, 21; scientific surgery of, 4,
    24, 26, 34, 40, 88; and surgical train-
    ing, 26–28. See also radical mastectomy
    (Halsted)
Halsted model, of breast cancer, 31, 37,
    98, 102; challenges to, 33, 223, 226,
    228
Hampton, Caroline, 18
Handley, Richard S., 80
Hansemann, D. P. von, 94
Harken, Dwight E., 70
Harris, Saul, 212
Harvard Medical School, 167
Haybittle, J. L., 134
Hayden, Charles W., 200, 231
Health Insurance Plan (HIP) of Greater
    New York, 203–7, 213
Heidenhain, Lothar, 17
Hellman, Samuel, 225, 235, 251
Herceptin (biological therapy), 269
hereditary risks. See genetic testing
Herman, Terri Anne, 201–2
Hermann, Robert, 74
Her Soul beneath the Bone (poetry collection),
    270–71
Hines, William, 214, 219
Hippocrates, 15–16
History of the Breast, A (Yalom), 54
Hoerr, Stanley O., 131

Holleb, Arthur I., 52–53, 77, 123, 167, 168;
    and mammmography trials, 205–7,
    213, 216–19; and patient activism, 144,
    164, 228; and in situ cancers, 200; on
    therapeutic alternatives, 225
Holocaust, 281
hope, climate of, 31, 272–73. See also cure
hormonal function, 81, 136, 254
House of Representatives, U.S., 265. See also
    Congress, U.S.
Howard, John M., 121
Howell, Mary C., 151
Huggins, Charles B., 136
Humanectomy, 69. See also superradical
    surgery
Huntington's disease, 227–28
Hutter, Robert V. P., 200

I Am Whole Again (Zalon), 194
Ill, Edward J., 42
Illig, Marjorie G., 47
Illness as Metaphor (Sontag), 268
individualism, 59, 76
infectious disease, 29
informed consent laws, 10, 153–54, 223,
    231–33
Inglefinger, Franz, 213–14
insurance, and genetic testing, 289
Invisible Worm, The (Rosmond), 152–54, 158
Isaac, Betty, 156

Jaffe, Helene, 286
Jennings, R. Lee, 288
Jewish women, 14, 281–82
Johansen, Helge, 116, 133
Johns Hopkins Medical School, 23–24
Johnston, Dorothy, 178
Jones, Tom, 62
Jonsen, Albert R., 283
Journal of the American Medical Association, 52,
    82, 121, 132, 205
journalists, 183, 219. See also media; specific
    journalists

Kaae, Sigvard, 116
Kaback, Michael M., 281

Kaiser, Raymond F., 59
Karnofsky, David A., 253
Katz, Jay, 39
Kelly, Howard, 24
Keynes, Geoffrey, 33, 35, 36, 93, 105
Kholdin, S. A., 73
King, F. Gordon, 161
King, Mary-Claire, 276–77
Kinne, David W., 113, 229
Kister, Sven J., 129, 235
Klausner, Richard D., 244, 266
Koch, Robert, 29
Kocher, Theodor, 18–19
Kodak corporation, 208
Komen Foundation, 258, 260, 271
Kopans, Daniel B., 244
Koppman, Patricia, 193, 194
Krippaehne, William W., 124
Kuhn, Thomas S., 228
Kunath, C. A., 38
Kushner, Rose, xii, 12, 169, 175–81, 188, 271;
    ACS praise for, 227–28; as author, 175,
    177–78; as critic of one-step procedure,
    176, 178, 227, 256–57; death of, 224,
    258–59; and mammography trials, 214,
    220; and NIH consensus, 225, 234; oppo-
    sition to chemotherapy, 252; partnership
    with Fisher, 227–29, 264; as patient,
    176–77; physicians' criticism of, 179–81

Laetrile (cancer remedy), 160
Lane-Claypon, Janet, 31
Langer, Amy, 259, 260
Lasker, Albert, 49
Lasker, Mary, 49–50, 203
Lasser, Terese, 143–44, 165, 166, 189
Latina women, 262
Lattes, Raffaele, 85, 198
Lauren, Ralph, 260
Le Cat, Nicolas, 17
Lee, Burton J., 35
Lee, John A. H., 211
Lees, James C., 100–101, 106–7, 113
legislation: informed consent laws, 10,
    153–54, 223, 231–32; National Cancer
    Act (1971), 203, 205, 268

Leis, Henry P., Jr., 90, 111–12, 113
Leopold, Ellen, 39, 266–67
L'Esperance, Elise S., 55
Lewis, Dean, 36, 37
Lewison, Edward F., 70, 110, 198–99, 229
Life (magazine), 64, 65–66
life versus breast calculus, 186–88
Lind, James, 120
Linver, Michael, 244
Lister, Joseph, 18
Little, Clarence Cook, 44
Little, Geraldine Clinton, 161
Living Downstream (Steingraber), 262
Livingston, Edward M., 35–36, 89
lobular carcinoma in situ (LCIS), 174,
    197–201, 246, 284, 294. See also carci-
    noma in situ; precancers
local disease, cancer as, 17, 30, 31, 37
Locke, Maryel F., 146, 148, 149
Longmire, William P., Jr., 162
Lorde, Audre, 187, 190–93, 269–70
Louis, Pierre, 100
Love, Susan M., 202, 228, 236, 253, 259
Lowy, Ilana, 120, 253
L-phenylalanine mustard (L-PAM), 173
Lukash, William, 172
lumpectomy/partial mastectomy, 12,
    132–34, 154, 158, 161, 257–58; ACS
    endorsement of, 226; and appearance
    issues, 185; criticism of, 168; death fol-
    lowing, 159–60; physicians' critique
    of, 162–63; and radiotherapy, 132, 134,
    148, 226, 233
Lupton, Deborah, 76
lymph nodes. See axillary lymph nodes
lymphedema (arm swelling), 33, 117, 132,
    145

MacDonald, Ian, 92, 98–100, 103, 108,
    109–10
MacMahon, Charles E., 108
Madden, John L., 111
magic bullets, 267. See also prevention
magnetic resonance imaging (MRI),
    248
Making of a Surgeon, The (Nolen), 149

mammography, 110–11, 196–222, 280;
   Bailar's critique of, 209–13; and early
   detection controversy, 12, 243–46,
   248–49; industry promotion of, 208,
   249; and patient's age, 207, 212, 213,
   243–45; and precancers, 197–202; and
   prophylactic mastectomy, 196,
   200–202; randomized trials of, 204–7;
   risks of, 210–12, 213, 215–17. See also
   Breast Cancer Detection Demonstration
   Project
"Mammography: A Contrary View"
   (Bailar), 209, 210
manufacturers, marketing by, 208, 249,
   255, 288–89. See also specific manufacturers
Marino, Dian, 274
Marks, Harry M., 100, 119, 124
Marvella: A Personal Journey (Bayh), 183
Mason, Aubrey York, 133
Massachusetts General Hospital (MGH),
   147, 148, 167–68
mastectomy: pre-modern history of,
   16–17; prophylactic, 90, 196, 200–202,
   285–88, 294, 295; superradical, 69,
   80–82. See also lumpectomy/partial
   mastectomy; radical mastectomy; sim-
   ple mastectomy
Matas, Rudolph, 22, 26, 31–32
Mathews, Frank S., 33, 39
Matuschka (model), 4, 14, 271
Mayhem Against Women (Shinder), 155
McCall's (magazine), 141, 149, 158, 170, 181
McCarthy, Joseph, 52
McDivitt, Robert W., 199, 218–20
McFarland, Joseph, 31
Mcfarlane, Catherine, 56
McKinnon, Neil E., 101–2, 106–8, 230
McWhirter, Robert, 96–98, 99, 133, 134
media, 65, 74, 164, 225, 273; and BCDDP,
   209, 212–14, 219–20; and genetic test-
   ing, 280, 286; and patient activism,
   148, 154–57, 164; television, 149,
   165–66, 186, 188, 189, 195; women's
   magazines, 141, 148, 149, 158, 170, 181
medical education: reform of, 23–24; surgical training program, 26–28

Medical Education in the United States and Canada
   (report), 24
medical ethics, 64, 138, 148, 166
Memorial Sloan-Kettering Cancer Center,
   50, 79, 96, 123, 142, 251; lumpectomy
   opposition at, 233–35
metastatic disease, cancer as, 6. See also sys-
   temic/biological model
methotrexate, 251
Metzger, Deena, 270–71
Meyer, Alfred C., 118
Meyer, Willy, 38
Middlebrook, Christina, 274
military metaphors, 8, 14, 187, 274, 295;
   in anticancer campaigns, 41, 43–45,
   59, 66; and patient activists, 268–72;
   for precancers, 198–99; and superradical surgery, 69, 70, 75; and war, 51–52,
   214. See also World War II
minority women, 47, 156–57, 206, 261–62
mirror-image biopsy, 174, 293
Mitchiner, Philip H., 35, 36
models, of breast cancer: biological/sys-
   temic, 6, 223, 226–27, 228, 230, 233;
   Halsted, 31, 33, 37, 98, 102, 223, 226,
   228
modified radical mastectomy, 110–14, 178,
   223, 235, 238–40, 251
Montini, Theresa, 155, 161, 232, 239
Moore, Charles, 17, 20
Moore, Francis D., 168, 217
Moore, George E., Jr., 81, 121, 136
Morantz-Sanchez, Regina, 9
Morgan, Kathryn Pauly, 193
Morgan, Rex (comic-strip doctor), 60
mortality. See death rate/mortality; survival
   rate
Moxley, John III, 225
Moynihan, Lord Berkeley, 32
Mueller, C. Barber, 125, 128
Murley, Reginald, 98, 104–5, 230, 238
Murphy, Gerald P., 163
Mustakallio, Sakari, 116
mutations, genetic. See genetic testing
mutilation, 33, 159, 186, 233. See also dis-
   figurement

Myriad Genetics (biotech company), 277, 280

Napoli, Maryann, 214, 221, 228, 263
National Advisory Cancer Council (US), 120–21
National Alliance of Breast Cancer Organizations (NABCO), 258, 260
National Breast Cancer Coalition (NBCC), 259, 260
National Cancer Act of 1971, 203, 205, 268
National Cancer Institute, 12, 50, 172, 180, 268; and chemotherapy research, 137, 254; and Cure Cancer Program, 203; early detection programs, 173, 292; and mammography screenings, 196, 212, 213, 215, 250; National Cancer Advisory Board, 227, 244, 245; and randomized controlled trials, 172, 264; and self-exam, 55; and tamoxifen trials, 266
National Institutes of Health consensus conferences: 1977, 218, 221; 1979, 225–26, 227, 233–34; 1990, 257; 1997, 244–45, 249
National Surgical Adjuvant Breast and Bowel Project (NSABP), 137, 139, 172, 226–27, 230, 265
Nazi atrocities, 115, 281
New England Journal of Medicine, 202, 213–14, 226, 248, 269, 286
New Science of Surgery, The (Slaughter), 71
New York Times, 14, 209, 219, 244, 289
New York Times Magazine, 4, 190, 260, 271
Nickson, James J., 138
Nicolay, Glen C., 145
Nixon, Richard M., 203
Nolen, William A., 149, 164, 166
Norris, Frances, 150
Nuland, Sherwin B., 86, 164, 231

Oncormed (biotech company), 289
one-step procedure, 28, 173–75, 189, 233; activists' objections to, 146, 153, 156, 176, 178, 227, 256–57. See also Halsted radical mastectomy

Ordinary Life: A Memoir of Illness (Conway), 274
Osborne, Michael P., 234–35
Osler, William, 20, 24
Our Bodies, Ourselves (health manual), 150, 270
ovarian cancer, and genetic testing, 276, 278–79, 285, 288, 289

Pack, George T., 35–36, 75–79, 89; case studies of, 79; on palliation, 77–78; superradical surgery of, 71–73, 75, 76–77
paclitaxel (Taxol), 254
palliation, vs. cure, 77–79, 81
Papanicolaou, George N., 48, 51, 197
Pap smear, 41, 48–53, 54, 197, 205, 206
Park, Edwards, 25
Park, Wallace, 100–101
partial mastectomy. See lumpectomy/partial mastectomy
paternalism, physician, 9, 141, 153, 159, 165, 287; in demonstration project, 217–18, 220
Patey, David H., 111
pathology, 17, 27–28, 102, 199, 218–19
patient activism, 141–69, 227–28, 258–68; and cancer prevention, 262–64; and Cope's advocacy, 146–49; and death of Kushner, 258–59; and decision making, 140, 150, 156, 158, 161, 231; and feminism, 144, 146, 150–51, 156, 178, 187; growth of, 241, 244; and life vs. breast calculus, 186–88; and military metaphors, 268–72; and psychosocial effects of cancer, 144–46; and rehabilitation, 142–44; Rosmond's writings, 141, 151–54, 156, 158–61; and tamoxifen trials, 262, 263–66, 267. See also Reach to Recovery; and specific activists
patients, 8–10; and all-powerful doctor, 87–88; and breast conservation surgery, 257; empowerment of, 251; narratives of, 10, 106, 170, 181, 185–88, 195, 273–75; physicians' wives, 130–31, 162–63, 181–82, 236;

patients (*continued*)
  silence of, 3, 144–45; as victims, 9. *See also* celebrity patients
patriarchy, 150
Patterson, James T., 29, 31
pectoral muscles, removal of, 20, 31, 113, 225
pelvic exenteration, 73, 77, 79
Pennisi, Vincent R., 201
personal choice, 154. *See also* decision making
personal responsibility, 59, 76, 143
Peters, M. Vera, 7, 129, 132–33, 230
Peterson, Clare G., 124
physician-patient relationship, 10, 87–88, 143. *See also* patients
physicians: and breast exams, 55–58; and informed consent laws, 231–33; Kushner's criticism of, 179–81; and patient activism, 141–42, 161–69; and patient's feelings, 145; power of, 87–88, 240; and wives as patients, 130–31, 162–63, 181–82, 236. *See also* paternalism, physician; surgeons
physiology, of breast cancer, 20, 33. *See also* models, of breast cancer
Picker company, 208
Pike, Malcolm C., 212
plastic surgery, 191–95
Plotkin, David, 273
Pollock, William F., 97
Pomerance, William, 208, 212, 218
Pondville Hospital, 42, 43
Poor women, and cancer, 47, 157, 206, 262
power, of surgeons, 87–88, 90. *See also* authority, of surgeons
Prager, Kenneth M., 236–37
precancers, 13, 174, 242, 246; and mammography, 197–202. *See also* carcinoma in situ
predeterminism. *See* biological predeterminism; genetic testing
prevention, 262–64, 269; chemo-, 288, 295
preventive breast removal. *See* prophylactic mastectomy
privacy issues. *See* confidentiality
Proctor, Robert N., 45
Professionalization, of surgery, 26

prophylactic mastectomy, 90, 196, 200–202, 294, 295; and genetic testing, 285–88
prostate cancer treatment, 88–89, 136, 179
prostate-specific antigen (PSA), 250
psychosocial effects, 144–46, 186, 192, 273

"Questionable X-Ray Program, The" (Greenberg and Randal), 214

radiation risks, 210–12, 213, 215–17. *See also* mammography; radiotherapy
radical mastectomy (Halsted), 3, 11, 13, 20–40, 95–105; and Betty Ford, 172–73, 175; and biological predeterminism, 98–103; and biopsy, 95–96, 146; and breast cancer physiology, 20–21; and breast reconstruction, 191–92; chemotherapy alternative to, 136–37; consequences of, 32–33, 159; Crile's challenge to, 6, 86, 104–5, 129–30, 135–36; criticism of, 12, 92, 98, 104; cure rate for, 21–22, 37–39, 92, 292; and *en bloc* dissection, 21, 72, 85, 97, 226; extended, 6, 7, 81–82; fear of, 58–59; Fisher's challenge to, 136, 137–40, 293; and gender, 88–91; as innovation, 5–6; and lumpectomy alternative, 132–34; McWhirter's alternatives to, 96–98; modified, 110–14, 178, 223, 235, 238–40, 251; as outdated procedure, 13, 176, 178, 223; and patient rehabilitation, 142–43; physicians' preference for, 161; popularity of, 15; and radiotherapy, 33–36; and superradical compared, 69, 80–82; and surgeon's authority, 169, 291–92; survival rates for, 31, 36–37, 82, 97, 105, 112, 117; tradition of, 163–64
radical surgery, and shock, 61. *See also* superradical surgery
radiotherapy, 82, 96, 97, 229; as alternative to radical surgery, 35–36, 148, 257; introduction of, 33–36; and lumpectomy, 132, 134, 148, 226, 233; and

RCTs, 116, 117; side effects from, 152.
See also mammography
raloxifene, 267
Randal, Judith E., 214, 216, 219
randomized controlled trials (RCTs), 12,
114, 115–29, 225; for chemotherapy,
254, 255; and clinical expertise, 122,
123–24; and early detection, 250; in
Europe, 134–35; Fisher's promotion of,
6, 137–40, 228–31; and mammography controversy, 204–7, 243–44;
NSABP, 137, 139, 172, 226–27, 230,
265; and retrospective studies compared, 116–18; and risk assessment,
125–29; validity of, 119–20, 124–25,
265. See also statistical analysis
Rauscher, Frank J., Jr., 204, 212, 215–16
Ravdin, Isidor S., 66, 76, 77, 110; and randomized controlled trials, 120, 122
Ravitch, Mark M., 127
Reach to Recovery (program), 154, 180,
182, 190, 192; Lasser and, 143–44, 166,
189
Reagan, Leslie, 46
Reagan, Nancy, 256–57
recovery, 185, 189–90. See also appearance
issues; psychosocial effects; rehabilitation
recurrence, 21–22, 36, 37–39, 163; and
chemotherapy, 252. See also cure
rehabilitation, patient, 142–44
Reid, Mont, 98
Renneker, Richard, 56, 89, 144–45
responsibility, personal, 59, 76, 143
retrospective studies, 21, 112, 116–18, 124,
132, 230, 286. See also case review; statistical analysis
Revlon Corporation, 260
Reynolds, Edward, 27
Richards, Gordon, 132
Riemann, Stanley, 70
Rienhoff, William F., Jr., 36, 37, 162
right to choose, 156, 158, 296. See also decision making; personal choice
"Right to Choose, The" (Rosmond), 141
Rimer, Irving, 225

Rinehart, Mary Roberts, 47
Riperton, Minnie, 157
risk assessment, 11, 115, 125–29, 187; and
genetic testing, 14, 277, 284–86; and
mammography, 210–12, 213, 215–17.
See also radiation risk
Robbins, Guy F., 79, 110, 124–25, 129,
145, 163
Rockefeller, Margaretta (Happy), 7, 12,
170, 174–75, 209, 224
Rockefeller, Nelson, 174
Rodgers, Beall, 87
Rodkey, Grant V., 233
Roentgen, Wilhelm von, 33–34
Rogers, Edith Nourse, 46
Rollin, Betty, xii, 183–88, 189–90; personal
narrative of, 10, 183, 190; readers'
response to, 184–87, 188
Rosen, Paul Peter, 199
Rosenberg, Charles, 5
Rosmond, Babette, 151–54, 156, 158–61,
165, 166, 188; death of, 224; personal
narrative of, 141, 152, 168
Ruesch, Floyd, 221
Russell, Christine, 213
Russian roulette, randomized controlled
trials as, 115
Ruzek, Sheryl, 151, 155, 161, 232, 239

Salgo, Martin, 153
Sampson-Handley, William, 45
Sandburg, Carl, 181
Sandburg, Helga. See Crile, Helga Sandburg
sanocrysin (gold-based compound), 120
Schack, Susan, 165, 166, 189
Schnabel, Freya, 255
Schrag, Deborah, 286
Schulman, Joseph D., 280, 281
Schwartz, Gordon, 163
scientific surgery, 24, 26, 34, 40, 88, 137
screening, for breast cancer. See mammog-
raphy
Seaman, Barbara, 144, 150, 155
search-and-destroy mindset, 295. See also
military metaphors
Secret World of Doctor and Patient, The (Katz), 39

Seeing the Crab: A Memoir of Dying Before I Do
    (Middlebrook), 274
segmental mastectomy, 226–27. *See also*
    lumpectomy/partial mastecomy
Seidman, Herbert, 207
self-examination. *See* breast self- examination
Semken, George, 84
Senate, U.S., 150, 244. *See also* Congress, U.S.
sentinel node biopsy, 247, 248
sexism, 9, 192, 202. *See also* gender
Shalala, Donna, 245
Shapiro, Sam, 204–5
Shimkin, Michael B., 71, 118–19, 121, 122,
    140, 252–53
Shinder, Dorothy, 155
shock, and radical surgery, 61
Shottenfeld, David, 145
Sigal, Jill Lea, 265
Simha, Joy, 287
simple mastectomy, 131, 132, 161, 225–26;
    McWhirter's introduction of, 96–98,
    134; survival rates for, 117–18
Skolnick, Mark, 277, 280
Slamon, Dennis, 269
Slaughter, Frank G., 60, 71
Smith, Elaine M., 269
Smith, Ivan H., 108
Smith, Simmon S., 118
Snowe, Olympia, 269
Snyderman, Reuven K., 191, 194
socioeconomic status. *See* class
Sontag, Susan, 8, 268
Sox, Harold C., 246
Spear, Ruth, 258
Specter, Arlen, 244
Speer, Francis D., 102–3
Sprong, David H., Jr., 97
Stacey, Jackie, 187
staging systems, for cancer, 94–95
statistical analysis, 10–11, 92, 119; and bio-
    logical predeterminism, 12, 100–101,
    108, 293–94; biometrics, 10, 93, 101,
    113–14; early detection and, 249–50;
    methods for, 108, 229. *See also* random-
    ized controlled trials; retrospective
    studies

Stein, Howard F., 76
Steincrohn, Peter J., 66
Steingraber, Sandra, 262
stem cell transplants, 13, 255
Stewart, Fred W., 109, 197
Stinson, David, 101
stomach cancer, 72, 79
Stone, Harvey B., 103
Stout, Arthur Purdy, 84, 94–95, 197
Strax, Philip, 203–5, 207, 208, 217
streptomycin evaluation, 120
Strode, J. E., 65
Struewing, Jeffrey P., 289
Sugarbaker, Everett D., 80
superradical mastectomy, 12, 69, 80–82.
    See also radical mastectomy
superradical surgery, 68, 69–82; critics of,
    103–4; disfigurement from, 81, 103;
    military metaphors for, 69, 70, 75;
    Pack's advocacy of, 71–73, 75, 76–77;
    and palliation, 77–79, 81; technical
    advances for, 70, 74; Wangensteen's
    role in, 69, 74
surgeons: authority of, 75, 165, 169, 217,
    231, 291–92; as pathologists, 17,
    27–28; power of, 87–88, 90; and RCT
    threat, 122, 123–24; as soldiers, 70, 75;
    women as, 132–33. *See also* physicians
Surgery, Gynecology and Obstetrics (journal), 99,
    100, 106
surgery, scientific, 24, 26, 34, 40, 88, 137
surgical training programs, 26–28
survival rate, 82, 93–94, 112, 133, 243;
    five-year, 93, 97, 100, 103, 111, 116,
    224; from radical mastectomy, 31,
    36–37, 82, 97, 105, 117–18; and RCTs,
    226–27; and treatment strategies, 275.
    See also cure; death rate/mortality
Susan G. Komen Foundation, 258, 260, 271
Susann, Jacqueline, 151
Susskind, David, 166
systemic/biological model, of breast can-
    cer, 6, 223, 226, 228, 230, 233, 251

Talman, William, 224
tamoxifen, 249, 254, 262, 263–66, 267

Taylor, Grantley W., 107–8, 127
technology, and superradical surgery, 70, 74
television programs, 149, 165–66, 186, 188, 189, 195
Tendler, David, 282
Thackray, A. C., 80
Thiessen, Norman, 64
Thio-tepa (chemotherapeutic agent), 137, 182
Thistlethwaite, J. Richard, 172–73
Thompson, Eva Bell, 157
three-year cure, 22, 38. See also cure
toxic waste. See environmental toxins
Treatment of Cancer and Allied Diseases (Pack and Livingston), 35
Truth About Cancer, The (Cameron), 67
tuberculosis, 29, 120
tylectomy, 235. See also lumpectomy/partial mastectomy

U.S. Congress. See Congress, U.S.
Upton, Arthur C., 213, 220
Urban, Jerome (Jerry), 77, 84, 130, 165, 166, 169; on contralateral biopsy, 199–200; death of, 238; extended radical mastectomy of, 6, 7, 12, 80–81; on heroic surgery, 78–79; mirror-image biopsy of, 174, 293; and NIH consensus, 225, 227, 233–34; on predeterminism, 109; as radical mastectomy advocate, 129, 162, 251; and randomization, 114
uterine (endometrial) cancer, 46, 49, 54, 264, 266, 267. See also cervical cancer

Vaginal Politics (Frankfort), 155
Valerius, Cindy, 286
Valley of the Dolls (Susann), 151
vanity. See appearance issues
Veronesi, Umberto, 134–35, 162, 225, 226
Virchow, Rudolf, 17, 21
Visco, Fran, 259, 260
Volkmann, Richard von, 17, 20, 21

Walters, Barbara, 149, 174
Wangensteen, Owen H., 69, 74, 76, 77; superradical surgery of, 79, 80, 81
war metaphors, 51–52, 214, 268–72. See also military metaphors
Washington Post, 177, 179, 213, 214, 273
Watson, T. A., 89
Weidel, Philip D., 235
Welch, Claude E., 41, 42, 70, 168
Welch, William, 24
"What Can We Do About Cancer" (Adams), 30
Willett, Walter C., 267
Wilson, John P., 164
Winkler, Win Ann, 156
Wise, Leslie, 133–34
Wolf, Naomi, 193
Wolfe, Sidney, 213
women, activism of. See celebrity patients; feminists; patient activism
Women at Risk (WAR), 269
Women's Field Army (WFA), 43–44, 46–47
Women's Health Action and Mobilization (WHAM), 271
women's health movement, 9, 150
Women's Health Rights Network, 264, 265
women's liberation, 150, 153, 179. See also feminist movement
women's magazines, 148, 154–55, 164; McCall's, 141, 149, 158, 170, 181
World Cancer Congress, 227
World War II, 70, 75, 90, 118. See also military metaphors

x-ray treatment. See mammograms; radiotherapy

Yalom, Marilyn, 9, 54
Young, Iris Marion, 193

Zalon, Jean, 193–94, 195
Zelen, Marvin, 211–12
Zeneca. See AstraZeneca
Zuckerman, Herman C., 208

	DATE DUE		